Lecture Notes in Computer Science

Lecture Notes in Computer Science

Vol. 1: GI-Gesellschaft für Informatik e.V. 3. Jahrestagung, Hamburg, 8.–10. Oktober 1973. Herausgegeben im Auftrag der Gesellschaft für Informatik von W. Brauer. XI, 508 Seiten. 1973. DM 32,–

Vol. 2: GI-Gesellschaft für Informatik e. V. 1. Fachtagung über Automatentheorie und Formale Sprachen, Bonn, 9.–12. Juli 1973. Herausgegeben im Auftrag der Gesellschaft für Informatik von K.-H. Böhling und K. Indermark. VII, 322 Seiten. 1973. DM 26,–

Vol. 3: 5th Conference on Optimization Techniques, Part I. (Series: I.F.I.P. TC7 Optimization Conferences.) Edited by R. Conti and A. Ruberti. XIII, 565 pages. 1973. DM 38,–

Vol. 4: 5th Conference on Optimization Techniques, Part II. (Series: I.F.I.P. TC7 Optimization Conferences.) Edited by R. Conti and A. Ruberti. XIII, 389 pages. 1973. DM 28,–

Vol. 5: International Symposium on Theoretical Programming. Edited by A. Ershov and V. A. Nepomniaschy. VI, 407 pages. 1974. DM 30,–

Lecture Notes in Computer Science

Edited by G. Goos, Karlsruhe and J. Hartmanis, Ithaca

5

International Symposium on Theoretical Programming

Edited by Andrei Ershov and Valery A. Nepomniaschy

Springer-Verlag
Berlin · Heidelberg · New York 1974

Prof. Dr. Andrei Ershov
Dr. Valery A. Nepomniaschy

Computer Center
Informatics Division
Novosibirsk 630090/USSR

AMS Subject Classifications (1970): 68-02, 68A05, 68A10, 68A20, 68A25, 68A30, 68A40, 68A45, 02E10, 02E15, 02F10

ISBN 3-540-06720-5 Springer-Verlag Berlin · Heidelberg · New York
ISBN 0-387-06720-5 Springer-Verlag New York · Heidelberg · Berlin

Table of Contents

INTRODUCTION

1971 and 1972 were the culminating years in the establishment of theoretical programming. During 15 months at least ten scientific meetings have been held in the United Kingdom, Poland, U.S.S.R., U.S.A., Jugoslavija, Japan, and certainly in some other countries, demonstrating an existence of an invisible team of scientists who had produced altogether about three hundred papers relevant to a section of computer science of a certain objective content.

It is no mere chance that the sentence you have just read contains so many indefinite articles: the process of identification of the team of scientists, of the corresponding section of computer science and of its subject matter is still going on.

Theory of computing, mathematical foundations of computer science , theory of programs, theoretical programming - are not a complete list of identifiers used. However, it is more and more recognized that these identifiers are to a certain degree synonyms signifying that a new mathematical discipline has come into being.

The Symposium on Theoretical Programming held in Novosibirsk on August 7 - 11, 1972 whose proceedings we bring forward to the reader in the marked period of establishment seem to play a special role. It was attended by 50 specialists from Moscow, Leningrad, Kiev, Novosibirsk, Riga, Yerevan, Rostov-on-the-Don and Tallin and also by 17 foreign scientists from Austria, United Kingdom, Hungary, U.S.A., France, Switzerland and Japan.

The Novosibirsk symposium received a lucky priviledge: it was the first thematical scientific meeting at which the representatives of practically all presently existing trends of theoretical programming met. This representation made the symposium especially interesting for the participants, and, we hope, for a wider group of specialists through publication of the proceedings.

The symposium itself (if not to consider the general discussion) did not practically deal with the questions of self-determination. In fact there are no review papers. However, the wealth and variety of ideas, concreteness of the results and methods, the authors' scientific influence, many of whom made a basic contribution to theoretical programming - all these make the Proceedings of the Novosibirsk Symposium a book to be read by everyone who wants to master the present-day state and tendencies of the development of theoretical programming.

Corresponding Member of Soviet
Academy of Sciences
A.P. Ershov, Chairman of the
Organizing Committee of the
Symposium

An Axiomatic Definition of the Programming Language PASCAL

C.A.R. Hoare

0 Introduction

The purpose of a formal language definition is to act as a "contract" between the implementor and user of the language. It is not intended to be read straight through, but rather to be used by both parties as a work of reference; it will also be used as the basis of more readable descriptions of the language. Thus the objective of a formal description is to make it easy to identify the chapter and subsection relevant to any query, and to consult it in isolation, without having to follow cross-references to other sections and chapters. The axiomatic definition of PASCAL seems to achieve this objective to a remarkable degree.

The language treated in this paper is a version of PASCAL which has been simplified in several respects.

(1) No variable occuring in the record variable part of a with statement may be changed within its body.

(2) A procedure may not access non-local variables other than those in its parameter list.

(3) All actual parameters corresponding to formals specified as <u>var</u> must be distinct identifiers.

There are other changes to PASCAL which would considerably simplify the axiomatisation, and might also be of benefit to its user.

(1) The alfa type could be regarded as just a packed representation for a character array.

(2) Conditional and case expressions could be allowed.

(3) Explicit constructors and type transfer functions for defined types could be included in the language.

(4) Some simplification of the file type is to be recommended.

(5) The variable parameters of a procedure should be indicated on the call side as well as on declaration.

(6) Exclusion of backward jumps and mutual recursion would simplify the proof rules.

(7) The replacement of classes by partial mappings and permitting recursive data type definitions would make the language into a more high-level tool.

But there are very good reasons for avoiding these "improvements", since their inclusion would undoubtedly detract from the very high quality of the PASCAL implementation. In particular, point (7) would entirely change the nature of the language.

The treatment given in this paper is not wholly formal, and depends on the good will of the reader. In particular

(1) Free variables in axioms are assumed to be universally quantified.

(2) The expression of the "induction" axiom is left informal.

(3) The types of the variables used may be supplied by context.

(4) The name of a type is used as a transfer function constructing a value of the type. Such use of the type name is not available to the programmer.

(5) Axioms for a defined type must be modelled after the definition, and be applied only in the block to which the definition is local.

(6) The context-free and context-dependent aspects of the syntax are defined in [2], and are not repeated here.

(7) Where hypotheses and subsidiary deductions are given in the proof rules, the hypotheses may be accumulated, and the subsidiary deductions may be nested in the usual manner.

(8) The use of a type name in its own definition is not permitted to the PASCAL programmer.

The following abbreviations are standard:

(1) $n < m$ for $\neg m \leq n$
$n \geq m$ for $m \leq n$
$n > m$ for $m < n$

(2) $s_1, s_2, \ldots, s_n : T$ for $s_1 : T; s_2 : T; \ldots ; s_n : T$

(3) P {Q} R, where P and R are propositional formulae and Q is a statement of PASCAL is interpreted as stating that if P is true of the program variables before initiating execution of Q, then R will be true on termination. If Q never terminates, or exits by a jump to a label outside itself, P {Q} R is vacuously true.

(4) X^x_y stands for the result of substituting y for all the free occurrences of x in X. If y contains free variables which would thereby become bound, this unintended collision is avoided by preliminary change in the name of the bound variables of X.

The axioms for data and data structures comprise about half the definition. They are modelled on the constructive definition of integers. Axioms defining the basic operators are modelled on primitive recursive definitions, so that it is easy to check that they define a unique computable result for every desired combination of operands, and leave other cases (e.g. division by zero) undefined. The axioms are formulated to apply to the normal unbounded domains of mathematics. An implementor is free to discontinue execution of any program which invokes operations which would exceed the range of efficient operation of his machine (e.g. integer overflow, or exhaustion of stack space). However, to continue execution with the wrong result would violate this axiomatic definition.

Most of the formal material of this paper is more fully explained in the references. The main extensions made by this paper are:

(1) Definitions of files and classes

(2) Treatment of mutual recursion

(3) Attempted definition of the whole of a large, efficient, and useful language.

1 Standard Scalar Types

1.1 The Integer Type.

1.1.1 0 is an integer.
1.1.2 if n is an integer, so are succ(n) and pred(n)
1.1.3 These are the only integers.
1.1.4 $n = succ(pred(n)) = pred(succ(n))$.
1.1.5 $n \leq n$.
1.1.6 $n < succ(n)$.
1.1.7 $n \leq m \supset n \leq succ(m)$.
1.1.8 $m < n \supset m < succ(n)$.
1.1.9 $n + 0 = n$.
1.1.10 $n + m = pred(n) + succ(m) = succ(n) + pred(m)$.
1.1.11 $n - 0 = n$.
1.1.12 $n - m = succ(n) - succ(m) = pred(n) - pred(m)$.

1.1.13 $n * 0 = 0$
1.1.14 $n * m = n * \mathrm{succ}(m) - n = n * \mathrm{pred}(m) + n$.
1.1.15 $n > 0 \supset m - n < (m \ \underline{\mathrm{div}}\ n) * n \leq m$.
1.1.16 $n < 0 \supset m \leq (m \ \underline{\mathrm{div}}\ n) * m < m - n$.
1.1.17 $m \ \underline{\mathrm{mod}}\ n = m - ((m \ \underline{\mathrm{div}}\ n) * n)$.
1.1.18 $\mathrm{abs}(m) = \underline{\mathrm{if}}\ m < 0 \ \underline{\mathrm{then}}\ -m \ \underline{\mathrm{else}}\ m$.
1.1.19 $\mathrm{sqr}(m) = m * m$.
1.1.20 $\mathrm{odd}(m) \equiv (m \ \underline{\mathrm{mod}}\ 2 = 1)$.
1.1.21 an integer constant consisting of digits

$$d_n d_{n-1} \ldots d_0 \quad \text{means}$$

$$10^n * d_n + 10^{n-1} * d_{n-1} + \ldots + 10^0 * d_0$$

1.1.22 1 means succ(0), 2 means succ(1), ..., 9 means succ(8)

1.2 The Boolean Type.

1.2.1 false and true are distinct Boolean values.
1.2.2 These are the only Boolean values.
1.2.3 true = succ(false) & false = pred(true)
1.2.4 $\mathrm{false} \leq x \leq \mathrm{true}$.
1.2.5 $\neg(\mathrm{true} \leq \mathrm{false})$.
1.2.6 $(\neg \mathrm{false}) = \mathrm{true}$ & $(\neg \mathrm{true}) = \mathrm{false}$.
1.2.7 $\mathrm{true} \wedge \mathrm{true} = \mathrm{true}$
1.2.8 $\mathrm{false} \wedge x = x \wedge \mathrm{false} = \mathrm{false}$
1.2.9 $\mathrm{false} \vee \mathrm{false} = \mathrm{false}$
1.2.10 $\mathrm{true} \vee x = x \vee \mathrm{true} = \mathrm{true}$.

1.3 The Character Type.

1.3.1 "A", "B", ..., are distinct elements of type Char.
1.3.2 These are the only elements of type Char.
1.3.3 if x is a Char, then int(x) is an integer and x = chr(int(x)).
1.3.4 if n is an integer in the range of int, then chr(n) is a character and n = int(chr(n)).
1.3.5 if x and y are Char then

$$x \leq y \equiv \mathrm{int}(x) \leq \mathrm{int}(y).$$

(1) The set of constants denoting values of type Char may be selected by the implementor. They should begin and end with the symbol chosen by the implementor to denote quotation.

1.4 The Alfa Type.

1.4.1 the type name "alfa" is an abbreviation of <u>array</u> [1..alfalength] <u>of</u> Char.

1.4.2 $x < y \equiv$

$$\exists n\ (1 \leq n \leq \text{alfalength}\ \&\ x[n] < y[n]\ \&\ \forall m (1 \leq m < n \supset x[m] = y[m])).$$

1.4.3 unpack(z,a,i) means
<u>for</u> j = 1 <u>to</u> alfalength <u>do</u> a[i + j - 1] : = z[j].

1.4.4 pack(a,i,z) means
<u>for</u> j = 1 <u>to</u> alfalength <u>do</u> z[j] : = a[i + j - 1].

1.4.5 If $c_1, c_2, \ldots, c_n$ are characters and $n \leq$ alfalength and $c = "c_1c_2\ldots c_n"$ then $c[1] = "c_1", c[2] = "c_2", \ldots, c[\text{alfalength}] = "c_{\text{alfalength}}"$. where if n < alfalength, $c_{n+1}, \ldots, c_{\text{alfalength}}$ are all equal to the character blank.

(1) For the properties of array types see 2.3.

(2) The programmer is not permitted to subscript a variable declared as alfa.

(3) The constants alfalength and blank are not available to the programmer.

1.5 The Real Type.

I dont know of any wholly successful axiomatisation of the real type (floating point). The ideal solution would be, as in the case of integers, to give axioms for the real continuum familiar to mathematicians; and certainly this will considerably simplify the task of program proving. Unfortunately, the properties of floating point numbers are very different from those of true reals; and (in contrast to the case of integers), it is not practical merely to permit an implementation to refuse to execute programs which invoke operations involving loss of significance

Thus it appears necessary to construct a separate machine-independent axiomatisation for floating point arithmetic. The axiomatisation must describe the relationship between floating point and true reals; and the use of axioms in practical program proofs is likely to be at least as complicated as the error analysis techniques practised by numerical mathematicians.

2 Defined Types

2.1 Scalar Types.

$T = (k_1, k_2, \ldots, k_n);$

2.1.1 $k_1, k_2, \ldots, k_n$ are distinct elements of T.

2.1.2 These are the only elements of T.

2.1.3 $k_2 = succ(k_1)$ & ... & $k_n = succ(k_{n-1})$.

2.1.4 $k_1 = pred(k_2)$ & ... & $k_{n-1} = pred(k_n)$.

2.1.5 $k_1 \leq x \leq k_n$.

2.1.6 If $y \neq k_n$ then $x \leq y \equiv succ(x) \leq succ(y)$.

2.1.7 <u>case</u> x <u>of</u> $(k_1{:}y_1, k_2{:}y_2, \ldots, k_n{:}y_n)$
= <u>if</u> $x = k_1$ <u>then</u> y_1
<u>else</u> <u>if</u> $x = k_2$ <u>then</u> y_1
....
<u>else</u> <u>if</u> $x = k_{n-1}$ <u>then</u> y_{n-1}
<u>else</u> y_n.

2.1.8 $k_i{:}k_j{:}\ldots k_m{:}y$ (in a case construction) means $k_i{:}y, k_j{:}y, \ldots, k_m{:}y$.

(1) The case expression defined in 2.1.7 is not available to the programmer.

2.2 Subrange Types.

<u>type</u> T = min..max;
where min and max are of type T_0

Let a, b $\in T_0$ and min $\leq$ a $\leq$ b $\leq$ max, and x, y $\in$ T.

2.2.1 If $a \in T_0$ and min $\leq$ a $\leq$ max then T(a) is a T.

2.2.2 These are the only elements of T.

2.2.3 $T^{-1}(T(a)) = a$.

2.2.4 If θ is any monadic operator defined on T_0 then θx means $\theta(T^{-1}(x))$

2.2.5 If $\odot$ is any binary operator defined on type T_0, then
$x \odot y$ means $T^{-1}(x) \odot T^{-1}(y)$
$x \odot a$ means $T^{-1}(x) \odot a$
$a \odot x$ means $a \odot T^{-1}(x)$

2.2.6 x : = a means x : = T(a)
a : = x means a : = $T^{-1}(x)$.

(1) Any operation on subtype operands causes automatic conversion to the base type. This was not made explicit in [2].

2.3 Array Types.

<u>type</u> T = <u>array</u> D <u>of</u> R;

2.3.1 If r is an R then T(r) is a T.

2.3.2 If d is a D and r is an R and a is a T (a,d:r) is a T.

2.3.3 These are the only elements of T.

2.3.4 (T(r))[d] = r.

2.3.5 (a,d:r)[d'] = <u>if</u> d = d' <u>then</u> r <u>else</u> a[d'].

2.3.6 a = a' = ∀d (a[d] = a'[d]).

2.3.7 a[d] := r means a := (a,d:r).

2.3.8 <u>array</u> $[D_1,\ldots,D_n]$ <u>of</u> R means <u>array</u> $[D_1]$ of (<u>array</u> $[D_2,\ldots,D_n]$ <u>of</u> R).

2.3.9 $a[d_1,d_2,\ldots,d_n]$ means $(a[d_1])[d_2,\ldots,d_n]$.

(1) T(r) is the constant array, all of whose component values are equal to r.

(2) (a,d:r) is the result of assigning the value r to element d in the array a.

(3) Neither of these operations is explicitly available in PASCAL.

2.4 Record Types.

<u>type</u> T = <u>record</u> $s_1{:}T_1;\ s_2{:}T_2;\ldots;s_n{:}T_n$ <u>end</u>;

2.4.1 If x_1 is a T_1, x_2 is a T_2, x_n is a T_n then $T(x_1,x_2,\ldots,x_n)$ is a T

2.4.2 These are the only elements of T.

2.4.3 $T(x_1,x_2,\ldots,x_n).s_1 = x_1$.

$T(x_1,x_2,\ldots,x_n).s_2 = x_2$.

....

$T(x_1,x_2,\ldots,x_n).s_n = x_n$.

2.4.4 $x.s_1 := x_1$ means $x := T(x_1,x.s_2,\ldots,x.s_n)$.

$x.s_2 := x_2$ means $x := T(x.s_1,x_2,\ldots,x_n.s_n)$.

....

$x.s_n := x_n$ means $x := T(x.s_1,x.s_2,\ldots,x_n)$.

2.5 Union Types.

$$\underline{\text{type}}\ T = \underline{\text{case}}\ d{:}D\ \underline{\text{of}}\ \begin{array}{l} k_1{:}(s_{11}{:}T_{11};s_{12}{:}T_{12};\ldots;s_{1n_1}{:}T_{1n_1});\\ k_2{:}(s_{21}{:}T_{21};s_{22}{:}T_{22};\ldots;s_{2n_2}{:}T_{2n_2});\\ \ldots\ldots\ldots\ldots\ldots\ldots\ldots\ldots\ldots\ldots\ldots;\\ k_m{:}(s_{m1}{:}T_{m1};s_{m2}{:}T_{m2};\ldots;s_{mn_m}{:}T_{mn_m}); \end{array}$$

Let $x_{ij} \in T_{ij}$ for $i \in 1..m$,
$j \in 1..n$

2.5.1 The following are distinct elements of T:

$T.k_1(x_{11},x_{12},\ldots,x_{1n_1})$
$T.k_2(x_{21},x_{22},\ldots,x_{2n_2})$
$\ldots\ldots\ldots\ldots\ldots\ldots\ldots\ldots$
$T.k_m(x_{m1},x_{m2},\ldots,x_{mn_m})$.

2.5.2 These are the only elements of T.

2.5.3 $(T.k_i(x_{i1},x_{i2},\ldots,x_{in_i})).d = k_i$ for $i \in 1..m$.

2.5.4 $(T.k_i(x_{i1},x_{i2},\ldots,x_{in_i})).s_{ij} = x_{ij}$ for $i \in 1..m$, $j \in 1..n_i$.

(1) In PASCAL, a union type may feature only as the type of the last component in a record type; and this component has no selector.

(2) The use of i and j and indices in these axioms is for purposes of abbreviation only. For any given union type, the relevant axioms may easily be written out in full.

2.6 Powerset Types.

$\underline{\text{type}}\ T = \underline{\text{powerset}}\ T_0;$

Let $x_0, y_0 \in T_0$.

2.6.1 $[\,]$ is a T.

2.6.2 If x is a T and x_0 is a T_0,
then $x \vee [x_0]$ is a T.

2.6.3 These are the only elements of T.

2.6.4 $\neg x_0\ \underline{\text{in}}\ [\,]$.

2.6.5 $x_0\ \underline{\text{in}}\ (x \vee [x_0])$.

2.6.6 $x_0 \neq y_0 \supset (x_0\ \underline{\text{in}}\ (x \vee [y_0]) \equiv x_0\ \underline{\text{in}}\ x)$.

2.6.7 $x = y \equiv \forall x_0(x_0\ \underline{\text{in}}\ x \equiv x_0\ \underline{\text{in}}\ y)$.

2.6.8 $x_0\ \underline{\text{in}}\ (x \vee y) \equiv (x_0\ \underline{\text{in}}\ x)\ (x_0\ \underline{\text{in}}\ y)$.

2.6.9 $x_0\ \underline{\text{in}}\ (x \wedge y) = (x_0\ \underline{\text{in}}\ x) \& (x_0\ \underline{\text{in}}\ y)$.

2.6.10 $x_0\ \underline{\text{in}}\ (x - y) = (x_0\ \underline{\text{in}}\ x)\ \& \neg (x_0\ \underline{\text{in}}\ y)$.

2.6.11 $[x_1,x_2,\ldots,x_n]$ means $(\ldots(([\,] \vee [x_1]) \vee [x_2]) \vee \ldots) \vee [x_n]$.

(1) $[\,]$ is the empty set, $[x_0]$ is the unit set of x_0.

(2) This theory of hierarchically typed finite sets suffers from none of the traditional problems of set theory.

2.7 Sequence Types.

<u>type</u> T = <u>sequence</u> T_0;

Let $x_0, x_0' \in T_0$.

2.7.1 $[\![\,]\!]$ is a T.

2.7.2 If s is a T and x_0 is a T_0 then $s^\frown[\![x_0]\!]$ is a T

2.7.3 These are the only elements of T

2.7.4 $s^\frown[\![x_0]\!] \neq [\![\,]\!]$

2.7.5 $s^\frown[\![x_0]\!] = s'^\frown[\![x_0']\!] \equiv s = s' \;\&\; x_0 = x_0'$

2.7.6 first $([\![\,]\!]^\frown[\![x_0]\!]) = x_0$

$s \neq [\![\,]\!] \supset$ first $(s^\frown[\![x_0]\!])$ = first(s)

2.7.7 tail $([\![\,]\!]^\frown[\![x_0]\!]) = [\![\,]\!]$

tail$(s^\frown[\![x_0]\!])$ = tail$(s)^\frown[\![x_0]\!]$

2.7.8 $[\![x_1, x_2, \ldots, x_n]\!]$ means $(\ldots(([\![\,]\!]^\frown[\![x_1]\!])^\frown[\![x_2]\!])^\frown\ldots)^\frown[\![x_n]\!]$

(1) Sequences are not represented directly in PASCAL; they are required in the definition of files.

(2) $[\![\,]\!]$ is the empty sequence, $[\![x_0]\!]$ the sequence whose only element is x_0, and is the operator for concatenation.

(3) first picks out the first element of a non-empty sequence.

(4) the tail is obtained by striking off from a non-empty sequence its first element.

2.8 File Types.

2.8.1 <u>type</u> T = <u>file</u> <u>of</u> D means:

```
type T' = record all, rest: sequence D;
                 this: D;
                  eof: Boolean;
                 mode: (in, out, neutral)
          end
```

2.8.2 the declaration f:T means

f:T; f:=T'($[\![\,]\!]$, $[\![\,]\!]$, undefined, false, neutral),

where the assignment is considered as moved to the right

of any following declarations.

```
2.8.3  put(f) means:
       with f do
            begin if mode = in then go to error;
                  if mode = neutral then
                     begin mode := out;
                           all := [ ];
                          rest := [ ];
                     end;
                 all := all^[this]
            end
2.8.4  reset(f) means
            with f do
                  begin rest := all;
                        mode := neutral;
                         eof := false;
                        this := undefined
                  end;
2.8.5  get(f) means
            with f do
                  begin if eof ∨ mode = out then go to error;
                        if mode = neutral then mode := in
                        else if rest = empty then eof := true
                        else begin this := first(rest);
                                   rest := tail(rest)
                             end;
                  end;
2.8.6  f ↑ means f.this
```

(1) all contains the value of the whole file; and rest contains that part of the file which remains to be read (empty in the case of an output file). this contains the value of the current item.

2.9 Partial Mapping Types.

type T = D ⇛ R;

2.9.1 omega is a T.

2.9.2 if t is a T, d is a D and r is a R then (t,d:r) is a T.

2.9.3 These are the only elements of T.

2.9.4 (t,d:r) [d'] = if d = d' then r else t[d'].

2.9.5 domain(omega) = [ ].

2.9.6 domain(t,d:r) = domain(t) ∨ [d].

2.9.7 t = t' ≡ (domain(t) = domain(t') &
∀d(d <u>in</u> domain(t) ⊃ t[d] = t[d']))).

(1) Partial mappings do not feature directly in PASCAL; they are required in the definition of classes.

(2) omega is the partial mapping that is everywhere undefined. domain(t) is the set of subscripts d for which t[d] is defined.

2.10 Classes and Pointer Types.

c:<u>class</u> <u>of</u> R means

<u>type</u> C = ((↑c) ⇒ R); <u>var</u> c:C;c := omega;

where C is a new type name exclusive to this purpose and the assignment is considered as moved to the right of any subsequent declarations.

2.10.1 nil is a ↑c.

2.10.2 next(c) is a ↑c.

2.10.3 These are the only elements of c.

2.10.4 ¬nil <u>in</u> domain(c).

2.10.5 ¬next(c) <u>in</u> domain(c).

2.10.6 if p is a ↑c, then p↑ means c[p]

2.10.7 alloc(p) means <u>begin</u> p := next(c);
<u>if</u> p ≠ <u>nil</u> <u>then</u> c := (c,p:arbitrary) <u>end</u>

2.10.8 alloc(p,t) means the same as alloc(p).

(1) next(c) yields the pointer value of the next "free" location in the class; and <u>nil</u> if the class is full.

(2) This axiomatisation deals with only one variable declared as of class type. Where several variables are declared to be of the same class type, this should be regarded merely as an abbreviation for a program containing separate class declarations for each such variable.

(3) The axioms are deliberately incomplete; it is not known whether they are sufficiently complete for proof purposes.

(4) The declaration of a maximum number of elements in a class is not represented in these axioms; it seema to belong more to the implementation strategy than to the language itself.

3 Statements

3.1 Assignement Statements.

$$R^x_e \ \{x:=e\}R$$

3.2 Composition.

$$\frac{P\{Q_1\}S_1,\ S_1\{Q_2\}S_2,\ldots,S_{n-1}\{Q_n\}R}{P\{Q_1;\ Q_2;\ \ldots,\ ;\ Q_n\}R}$$

3.3 Conditional Statements.

3.3.1
$$\frac{P_1\{Q_1\}R,\ P_2\{Q_2\}R}{(\underline{\text{if}}\ B\ \underline{\text{then}}\ P_1\ \underline{\text{else}}\ P_2)\ \{\underline{\text{if}}\ B\ \underline{\text{then}}\ Q_1\ \underline{\text{else}}\ Q_2\}R}$$

$$\frac{P\{Q\}R}{(\underline{\text{if}}\ B\ \underline{\text{then}}\ P\ \underline{\text{else}}\ R)\ \{\underline{\text{if}}\ B\ \underline{\text{then}}\ Q\}R}$$

3.3.2
$$\frac{P_1\{Q_1\}R,\ P_2\{Q_2\}R,\ldots,P_n\{Q_n\}R}{\underline{\text{case}}\ e\ \underline{\text{of}}\ (k_1:P_1,k_2:P_2,\ldots,k_n:P_n)}$$

$$\{\underline{\text{case}}\ e\ \underline{\text{of}}\ k_1:Q_1;\ k_2:Q_2;\ldots;k_n:Q_n\underline{\text{end}}\}R$$

(1) $k_1,k_2,\ldots,k_n$ stand for sequences of one or more constants (separated by :) of the same type as e.

3.4 Repetitive Statements.

3.4.1
$$\frac{S\{Q\}P,\ P\supset \underline{\text{if}}\ B\ \underline{\text{then}}\ S\ \underline{\text{else}}\ R}{P\{\underline{\text{while}}\ B\ \underline{\text{do}}\ Q\}R}$$

3.4.2
$$\frac{S\{Q\}P,\ P\supset \underline{\text{if}}\ B\ \underline{\text{then}}\ R\ \underline{\text{else}}\ S}{S\{\underline{\text{repeat}}\ Q\ \underline{\text{until}}\ B\}R}$$

3.4.3 <u>for</u> v:=el <u>to</u> e2 <u>do</u> Q means

```
exhausted:=(el > e2); if ¬ exhausted then v:=el;
while ¬ exhausted do begin Q; if v < e2 then v:=succ(v)
                                 else exhausted:=true
                    end
```

where exhausted is a Boolean variable specific to this for statement and local to the smallest procedure containing it.

3.4.4 <u>for</u> v:=e1 <u>downto</u> e2 <u>do</u> Q means

exhausted:=(e2 > e1);
<u>if</u> ¬ exhausted <u>then</u> v:=e1;
<u>while</u> ¬ exhausted <u>do</u> <u>begin</u> Q; <u>if</u> v > e2 <u>then</u> v:=pred(v)
<u>else</u> exhausted:=false
<u>end</u>

(1) The body of a for loop may not change the value of the counting variable v, nor the value of the limit e2.

3.5 Procedure Statements.

$$R^{a_1,\, a_2, \ldots, a_m}_{f_1(\underline{a}), f_2(\underline{a}), \ldots, f_m(\underline{a})} \qquad \{f(a)\}R$$

(1) $\underline{a}$ is the list of actual parameters. $a_1, a_2, \ldots, a_m$ are those actual parameters corresponding to formal parameters specified as <u>var</u>. $f_1, f_2, \ldots, f_m$ are specific to and stand for functions yielding the values left in $a_1, a_2, \ldots, a_m$ by an application of the procedure f to a.

3.6 Labels and go to Statements.

3.6.1
$$\frac{S_1\{\underline{\text{go}}\ \underline{\text{to}}\ \ell_1\}\ \underline{\text{false}}, \ldots, S_n\{\underline{\text{go}}\ \underline{\text{to}}\ \ell_n\}\ \underline{\text{false}} \vdash P\{Q_1\}S_1, S_1\{Q_2\}S_2, \ldots, S_{n-1}\{Q_n\}R}{P\{\underline{\text{begin}}\ Q_1;\ \ell_1{:}Q_2; \ldots;\ _n{:}Q_n\ \underline{\text{end}}\}R}$$

3.6.2
$$\frac{S\{Q\}R,\ P \supset S}{P\{Q\}R}$$

3.6.3
$$\frac{P\{Q\}S,\ S \supset P}{P\{Q\}R}$$

(1) In this rule, the Q_i stand for sequences of none or more statements separated by semicolons.

(2) This rule is very similar to the rule of composition (3.2) expect that in the proof of the component statements, certain assumptions

may be made, which specify the properties of any jumps which they contain.

3.7 With Statements.

$$\frac{P\,\{Q\}\,R}{\underline{\text{with}}\ r\ \underline{\text{take}}\ P\quad \underline{\text{with}}\ r\ \underline{\text{do}}\ Q\quad \underline{\text{with}}\ r\ \underline{\text{take}}\ R}$$

(1) Neither r, nor any variable occuring in r, (for example as a subscript) may be changed by Q.

(2) <u>with</u> r <u>take</u> P means the same as the result of replacing in P every free occurrence of a selector s defined for r by r.s (i.e. the result of performing on P the same substitutions as PASCAL specifies for Q).

4 Declarations

4.1 Constant Definitions.

<u>const</u> $x_1 = k_1,\ x_2 = k_2, \ldots, x_n = k_n$;Q means

$$Q^{x_1,x_2,\ldots,x_n}_{k_1,k_2,\ldots,k_n}$$

(1) Q is of the form:
< type definition part > < variable declaration part >
< procedure and functions declaration part > < statement part >

4.2 Variable Declarations.

$$\frac{P\,\{Q^x_y\}\,R}{P\,\{x{:}T;Q\}\,R}$$

(1) y does not occur free in P,Q or R.

(2) Q takes the form:
{ < variable declarations >; }* < procedure and functions declaration part > < statement part >

(3) The first variable declaration in any procedure is preceded by var, which is ignored for proof purposes.

4.3 Procedure and Function Declarations.

4.3.1

$$\frac{P_1\{h_1\}R_1, P_2\{h_2\}R_2, \ldots, P_n\{h_n\}R_n \vdash P_1\{Q_1\}R_1, P_2\{Q_2\}R_2, \ldots, P_n\{Q_n\}R_n, P\{Q\}R}{P\{h_1; Q_1; h_2; Q_2; \ldots; h_n; Q_n; Q\}R}$$

4.3.2 $P\{\underline{\text{functions}}\ f(\underset{\sim}{x})\}R \vdash \forall_{\underset{\sim}{z}}\ (P \supset R^{f}_{f(x)})$

4.3.3 $P\{\underline{\text{procedure}}\ f(\underset{\sim}{x})\}R \vdash \forall_{\underset{\sim}{z}}\ (P \supset R^{x_1, x_2, \ldots, x_m}_{f_1(\underset{\sim}{x}), f_2(\underset{\sim}{x}), \ldots, f_m(\underset{\sim}{x})})$

(1) $h_1, h_2, \ldots, h_n$ are procedure or function headings; $Q_1, Q_2, \ldots, Q_n$ are the corresponding procedure bodies, each consisting of < constant definition part > < type definition part > < variable declaration part > < procedure and function declaration part > < statement part > Q is the statement part of the whole construction.

(2) $\underset{\sim}{x}$ is the list of formal parameters; $x_1, x_2, \ldots, x_m$ is the list of those formal parameters as var. $\underset{\sim}{z}$ is a list of all free identifiers of the formula which follows is, excluding the function names $f, f_1, f_2, \ldots, f_m$, and any other free function names of $Q_1, Q_2, \ldots, Q_n$.

(3) $f_1, f_2, \ldots, f_m$ act as functions yielding the values left by the procedure body in its variable parameters $x_1, x_2, \ldots, x_m$.

(4) The use of the procedure heading in the hypotheses is a formal trick to simplify the combination of proof rules for functions and procedures.

Acknowledgement

The author gratefully acknowledges his indebtedness to N. Wirth for many discussions on PASCAL and the proof rules appropriate for it.

References

[1] Floyd, R.W. - Assigning Meanings to Programs. Proc. Amer. Math. Soc. Symposium in Applied Mathematics. Vol. 19, 19-31.

[2] Wirth, N. - The Programming Language PASCAL. Acta Informatica I 1. (1971), 35-63.

[3] Hoare, C.A.R. - An Axiomatic Approach to Computer Programming. Commun. ACM. 12, 10 (October 1969), 576-580, 583.

[4] Hoare, C.A.R. - Procedures and Parameters; an Axiomatic Approach. Symposium on Semantics of Algorithmic Languages. Ed. E. Engeler, Springer-Verlag, 1970. 102-115.

[5] Clint, M.& Hoare, C.A.R. - Jumps and Functions: an Axiomatic Approach Acta Informatica (to appear).

[6] Hoare, C.A.R. - Notes on Data Structuring (to appear).

The Logic of "can do"

Erwin Engeler
ETH Zürich

The present note presents the first steps in the semantics and proof theory of a basic assertion about programs φ , namely the statement that some available equipment is able to execute φ . Such statements will be called "can-do statements". We shall interpret the program φ , considered as a string of symbols, as the statement asserting the executability of the program named by φ . Observe that the internal structuring of φ by composition, branching, parallelism of subprograms φ_i reflects itself in a structuring of the can-do statement φ as a composite of can-do statements φ_i .

Such structuring of can-do statements is reminiscent of the structuring of the statements of symbolic logic by means of the logical connectives "and", "or",... etc. Indeed, one even uses the same words. Thus, for example, if φ and ψ are can-do statements, then so are $\varphi \vee \psi$ (the equipment can do φ or can do ψ) and $\varphi \wedge \psi$ (the equipment can do ψ and can do ψ). Unlike the logical connectives "and", "or", etc., the can-do connectives "and", "or", etc., have a rather inprecise meaning in everyday discourse[1]). For example: does $\varphi \wedge \psi$ mean that the equipment can perform whichever of φ or ψ one chooses, or that, like in parallel machines, it can do φ and ψ simultaneously? This type of ambiguity, while confusing, may be acceptable to the man in the street, but in the context of exact planning,

[1]) The logical connectives get their precise meaning through a truth-functional interpretation which is adopted in mathematics but only loosely adhered to in everyday discourse.

such as in computer programming, it is not.

In addition to being inprecise, the can-do connectives of everyday discourse are quite restricted in number and complexity. Thus, we can easily find ourselves in a situation where we simply cannot express the executability of a complicated plan of action by common linguistic means in terms of the executability of individual components of the plan,[2]).

What can we gain from a formal analysis of the concept of "can-do"? Assume that we have reached the stage where we can express any can-do statement as a formula φ in an appropriate formal language. Imagine also that we have a class of abstract mathematical models M for the concept of available equipment, for example some abstract computer models. Assume furthermore that we have explained $M \models \varphi$ as the statement that M can do φ. Typically, the computing power of M is known to us as a set Γ of (not very complex) formulas ψ such that $M \models \psi$.

To prove that M can do φ means to give a (formal) proof of the formula φ from the set of formulas Γ. It is reasonable to expect that such a formal proof gives us detailed information, if not an explicit description, of how and in what sequence to employ the capabilities Γ of M in order to verify φ. In other words, the proof furnishes a control mechanism for the execution of the program whose executability is asserted by φ. It is to be hoped that the formal proof processes are sufficiently simple as to be mechanizable and that they result in control mechanisms to which reasonably effective optimization methods can be applied.

[2]) This is again in contrast to the logical connectives, where $\neg, \vee$ for example are sufficient to express all truth-functional connectives.

In the present note we report on the realization of a small segment of the above, rather ambitious, project. We chose to treat only a very limited type of can-do connectives, whose semantics and proof theory are given below. In the concluding remarks we indicate some directions in which further investigations have gone or are planned.

We base the semantics of can-do statements on a computer concept which is given axiomatically as follows:

A <u>Boolean partial computer</u> is a pair $(\mathcal{S},\Sigma)$, where $\mathcal{S} = \{S_i\}_{i\in I}$ is a set of, not necessarily disjoint, Boolean algebras and Σ is a set of countable sequences $s_1s_2s_3\ldots$ of elements $s_j \in \cup\mathcal{S}$, where not all s_j are 0 . Elements S_i of $\mathcal{S}$ are called <u>configurations</u>, elements of S_i are called partial <u>configurations</u>; elements of Σ are called <u>partial computations</u>.

The Boolean operations are denoted by $\cup$, $\cap$ and $-$; the partial ordering by $\leqslant$ and the top and bottom elements by 1 and 0 respectively. The Boolean operations and ordering are extended in the obvious fashion (direct product), to sequences of equal lengths of partial configurations. E.g. $s_1s_2\ldots s_n \leqslant t_1t_2\ldots t_n$ iff $s_i \quad t_i$ for all i . We do not postulate, however, that Σ is closed under $\cup$ or $\cap$, nor do we impose any conditions as to the effectiveness of the structures S_i and the set Σ . We write $u|v$ if $u\ v = 0$ and more generally $u_1|u_2|\ldots|u_n$ if $u_i|u_j$ for all $i \neq j$. If u and v are sequences and u is finite, we denote by $u\cdot v$ the concatenation of u and v in that order.

To motivate the ensuing definitions, the reader best visualizes each partial configuration $s \in S_i$ as the complete description of "state plus memory content" of a collection of individual pieces of equipment (e.g. Turing Machines).

Let $\alpha_1, \alpha_2, \ldots$ be a countable set of <u>atomic</u> can-do formulas. The set L_o of simple can do formulas contains the atomic can-do formulas and is closed under the following binary syntactical operations: $\wedge$, $\&$, $\vee$, $\circ$.

Let $(\mathfrak{S}, \Sigma)$ be a partial computer, L_o the set of simple can-do formulas. An <u>interpretation</u> M of L in $(\mathfrak{S}, \Sigma)$ is a function which assigns to each $\varphi \in L_o$ a subset $M(\varphi)$ of Σ in such a fashion that the following conditions are satisfied:

$$M(\varphi \,\&\, \psi) = \{w \in \Sigma \mid \text{there exists } u \in M(\varphi), v \in M(\psi) \text{ such that } u, v \leq w\};$$

$$M(\varphi \wedge \psi) = \{w \in \Sigma \mid \text{there exists } u \in M(\varphi), v \in M(\psi) \text{ such that } u, v \leq w \text{ and } u \mid v\};$$

$$M(\varphi \vee \psi) = \{w \in \Sigma \mid w \in M(\varphi) \text{ or } w \in M(\psi)\};$$

$$M(\varphi \circ \psi) = \{u \cdot v \in \Sigma \mid u \in M(\varphi) \text{ and } v \in M(\psi)\}$$

Observe that the above conditions allow to uniquely extend an assignment of subsets of Σ to atomic formulas to an interpretation of L_o .

Intuitively, $M(\varphi)$ is the set of all partial computations by which φ can be realized in the partial computer $(\mathfrak{S}, \Sigma)$. In this way $\varphi \,\&\, \psi$ asserts the free choice of doing one of φ and ψ . The formula $\varphi \wedge \psi$ asserts the possibility of doing φ and ψ simultaneously, $\varphi \circ \psi$ asserts that one can do first φ and then ψ , and $\varphi \vee \psi$ asserts that at least one of φ and ψ can be done.

The selection of these particular connectives is not compelling, it is at best historically or linguistically motivated. Indeed, it turns to our advantage if we introduce an infinitude of can-do connectives as follows:

Let n, s be positive integers, and let $k_1,\dots,k_s$ be positive integers $< 2^n$. Then $\wedge^n_{k_1,\dots,k_s}$ is an s-ary syntactical connective. Let L be the extension of the language L_o by these connectives and let M be extended to an interpretation of L in $(\mathfrak{S},\Sigma)$ by setting

$$w \in M(\wedge^n_{k_1,\dots,k_s}(\varphi_1,\dots,\varphi_s)) \quad \text{iff}$$

there exist $u_1,\dots,u_n \leq w$ such that $u_1|u_2|\dots|u_n$ and $\bigvee(u_1,\dots,u_n)_{k_i} \in M(\varphi_i)$ for $i = 1,\dots,s$. Here, $(u_1,\dots,u_n)_k$ denotes the k-th non-empty subset of $\{u_1,\dots,u_n\}$ in some fixed numbering; for definiteness, if $k = 2^{n-1} p_1 + 2^{n-2} p_2 + \dots + 2^0 p_n$, take $(u_1,\dots,u_n)_k = \{u_i | p_i \neq 0\}$.

The basic semantical notions of L are introduced in the spirit of classical model theory as follows.

Let M be an interpretation of L in $(\mathfrak{S},\Sigma)$, let $\varphi,\psi \in L$ and $\Gamma,\Delta \subseteq L$.

$M \models \varphi$ ("M realizes φ"), if $M(\varphi) \neq \emptyset$;

$\varphi \equiv \psi$ iff $M(\varphi) = M(\psi)$ for all M;

$M \models \Gamma$ ("M realizes Γ"), if $M \models \varphi$ for all $\varphi \in \Gamma$;

$\Gamma \models \Delta$ ("the sequent $\Gamma \to \Delta$ is valid") if for each M with $M \models \Gamma$ there exists $\varphi \in \Delta$ with $M \models \varphi$.

We shall first discuss some obvious properties of the equivalence relation $\equiv$ on L. Clearly, both $\&$ and $\wedge$ are definable in terms of $\wedge$ and $\vee$. Namely:

(1) $\varphi \wedge \psi = \wedge^2_{1,2}(\varphi,\psi)$;

(2) $\varphi \mathbin{\&} \psi = \wedge^2_{1,2}(\varphi,\psi) \vee \wedge^3_{3,6}(\varphi,\psi) \vee \wedge^2_{1,3}(\varphi,\psi)$.

We may therefore restrict attention to the connectives $\vee$, $\circ$, and $\wedge$. Apart from the obvious associativity of $\vee$ and $\circ$ we have the following two rules which allow to "move $\vee$ across $\circ$ ":

(3) $\varphi\circ(\varrho\vee\sigma) \equiv (\varphi\circ\varrho) \vee (\varphi\circ\sigma)$;

(4) $(\varrho\vee\sigma)\circ\varphi \equiv (\varrho\circ\varphi) \vee (\sigma\circ\varphi)$.

They are easily verified by consulting the interpretations of the connectives. Actually $\vee$ can be moved across any of the connectives $\wedge^n_{k_1,\ldots,k_s}$:

(5) $\wedge^n_{k_1,\ldots,k_s}(\varphi_1,\ldots,\varphi_r'\vee\varphi_r'',\ldots,\varphi_s)$

$\equiv \wedge^n_{k_1,\ldots,k_s}(\varphi_1,\ldots,\varphi_r',\ldots,\varphi_s) \vee \wedge^n_{k_1,\ldots,k_s}(\varphi_1,\ldots,\varphi_r'',\ldots,\varphi_s)$.

This rule is again verified in the same fashion. Finally we have:

(6) For every expression of the form

$$\wedge^n_{k_1,\ldots,k_s}(\varphi_1,\ldots,\wedge^m_{l_1,\ldots,l_r}(\psi_1,\ldots,\psi_r),\ldots,\varphi_s)$$

we can effectively find a finite disjunction of expressions of the form

$$\wedge^p_{q_1,\ldots,q_{r+s}}(\varphi_1,\ldots,\varphi_s,\psi_1,\ldots,\psi_r)$$

which is equivalent to the given expression.

The proof of (6) is a straightforward observation of the kinds of case distinctions that arise for words $\neq 0$ to combine in the fashion prescribed by the expression. A simple example serves to point out the crux:

$$w \in M(\wedge^3_{5,3,2}(\varphi_1,\wedge^2_{3,2}(\psi_1,\psi_2),\varphi_2))$$

iff $\exists u_1, u_2, u_3 \leq w(u_1|u_2|u_3 \wedge u_1 \cup u_3 \in M(\varphi_1) \wedge u_2 \in M(\varphi_2) \wedge u_2 \cup u_3 \in M(\wedge^2_{3,2}(\psi_1, \psi_2)))$.

iff $\exists u_1, u_2, u_3 \leq w(u_1|u_2|u_3 \wedge u_1 \cup u_3 \in M(\varphi_1) \wedge u_2 \in M(\varphi_2)$

$\wedge \exists v_1, v_2 \leq u_2 \cup u_3 (v_1|v_2 \wedge v_1 \cup v_2 \in M(\psi_1) \wedge v_1 \in M(\psi_2)))$.

One of the finitely many essentially distinct ways to satisfy this last condition is

$$\exists w_o, w_1, w_2, \dots, w_6 \leq w(w_o|w_1|\dots|w_6 \wedge w_o \cup w_3 \cup w_4 \cup w_6 \in M(\varphi_1)$$
$$\wedge w_2 \cup w_3 \cup w_5 \cup w_6 \in M(\psi_1) \wedge w_2 \cup w_3 \in M(\psi_2) \wedge w_1 \cup w_2 \cup w_5 \in M(\varphi_2))\ ,$$

which is $\wedge^7_{k_1,\dots,k_4}(\varphi_1, \varphi_2, \psi_1, \psi_2)$ for appropriate $k_1, \dots, k_4$. This last expression thus is one of the disjuncts mentioned in (6); the others are as easily found.

Observe, then, that as a result of rules (1)-(6) every expression in terms of &, ∧, ∨, ∘ and the ∧'s can be equivalently transformed into a normal form. By an expression in normal form we understand a disjunction of expressions which are themselves only composite of ∧'s and ∘, and where ∧ is only applied to expressions that are either atomic or of the form $\varphi \circ \psi$. We can state the result:

Every formula $\varphi \in L$ is equivalent to a formula in normal form.

Let us call a formula which is in normal form but is not a disjunction a primitive formula. {The plan of action represented by a primitive formula is best visualized as a chart (such as the "bar charts" used e.g. by building contractors)}. We say that a primitive formula φ is an initial part of a primitive formula ψ , in symbols $\varphi \lesssim \psi$, if it is so by virtue of the following explanation:

(a) $\varphi \lesssim \varphi$;

(b) if $\varphi \lesssim \varrho$ then $\varphi \lesssim \varrho \circ \sigma$;

(c) if $\varrho_i \leq \sigma_i$ then $\wedge^{n}_{k_1,\ldots,k_r}(\varrho_1,\ldots,\varrho_r) \leq$

$\leq \wedge^{n+p}_{l_1,\ldots,l_s}(\sigma_1,\ldots,\sigma_r,\sigma_{r+1},\ldots,\sigma_s)$

whenever the conjunctive clauses in the definition of $\wedge^{n}_{k_1,\ldots,k_r}(\varrho_1,\ldots,\varrho_r)$ are the same as the conjunctive clauses concerning $\sigma_1,\ldots,\sigma_r$ in the definition of $\wedge^{n+p}_{l_1,\ldots,l_s}(\sigma_1,\ldots,\sigma_r,\ldots)$.

Intuitively, $\varphi \leq \psi$ expresses that the plan of action φ involves doing all the steps of some of the components of the plan of action ψ up to some point. For example:

$$\alpha \circ \gamma \leq (\alpha \wedge \beta) \circ (\gamma \wedge \delta) .$$

Clearly, the relation $\leq$ is decidable in L and

(7) If $M \models \psi$ and $\varphi \leq \psi$ then $M \models \varphi$.

Results (1)-(7) above lead at once to a complete proof system for the language L . I.e. we are now in a position to select axiomatic sequents $\Gamma_o \to \Delta_o$ (for which $\Gamma_o \models \Delta_o$) and formal rules of proof such that, for finite Δ , the sequent $\Gamma \to \Delta$ is formally provable iff $\Gamma \models \Delta$.

Intuitively, the rules of proof are chosen in such a way that some formulas in the hypothesis of a rule are always closer to being primitive than those in the conclusion (the other formulas are left the same). The rules (1)-(7) indicate how this is to be accomplished.

<u>I. Axioms</u> $\Gamma \to \Delta$ where Δ is a finite set of primitive formulas for which at least one, ψ, has the property that $\psi \leq \varphi$ for some primitive formula $\varphi \in \Gamma$.

II. Rules of Proof

IIa $\dfrac{\Gamma,F(\varphi)\to\Delta}{\Gamma,F(\psi)\to\Delta}$ and $\dfrac{\Gamma\to\Delta,F(\varphi)}{\Gamma\to\Delta,F(\psi)}$ if $\varphi \equiv \psi$,

where $F(\varphi)$ denotes a formula which has φ as a subformula, $F(\psi)$ is the result of replacing that subformula by ψ .

IIb $\dfrac{\Gamma,\varphi\to\Delta;\ \Gamma,\psi\to\Delta}{\Gamma,\varphi\vee\psi\to\Delta}$ and $\dfrac{\Gamma\to\Delta,\varphi,\psi}{\Gamma\to\Delta,\varphi\vee\psi}$

{The sequents above the horizontal line are the hypotheses, the sequent below the line is the conclusion of the rule of proof; formal proofs are best visualized as (finite) trees; at the top of each branch is an axiom, the nodes correspond to applications of rules of proof, and at the root of the tree is the sequent proven by the formal proof.}

The above axioms and rules are obviously correct, in the sense that whatever sequent $\Gamma \to \Delta$ can be proven from them is valid, i.e. $\Gamma \models \Delta$. This follows directly from the definition of $\models$, from (1)-(7) and the definition of $M(\varphi\vee\psi)$.

The converse is also true; i.e. if $\Gamma \models \Delta$ and Δ is finite then the sequent $\Gamma \to \Delta$ is provable. Actually, the hypothesis in this theorem can be weakened.

To state the thus strengthened form of the completeness theorem we need the definition of a Boolean automaton. Let $\mathfrak{S} = \{S_i\}_{i\in I}$ be a (finite) set of (finite) Boolean algebras, let A be a non-empty input alphabet, and let

$$\sigma : A\times U\mathfrak{S} \to U\mathfrak{S}$$

be a partial function, the next-partial-state function. Σ is the set of all countable sequences of partial states that correspond to input words: $s_{i_o} s_{i_1} \ldots s_{i_n} \in \Sigma$ iff there exists a word $a_1 \ldots a_n \in A^*$ such that $s_{i_{k+1}} = \sigma(a_{k+1}, s_{i_k})$, for $k = 0,1,\ldots,n-1$. Then $(\mathcal{S},\Sigma)$ is called a (finite) Boolean automaton.

If $\Gamma \to \Delta$ is valid for all Boolean automata then $\Gamma \to \Delta$ is formally provable; if both Γ, Δ are finite, we need consider only finite Boolean automata.

To prove the completeness theorem stated above we follow the usual completeness proofs for Gentzen-type calculi. We sketch the main idea of the proof. Note first the reversibility of the rules of proof, i.e. observe that if the conclusion of a rule of proof is valid then so is the hypothesis (or hypotheses). In other words, all sequents occurring in the proof of a valid sequent are valid. Consider, then, the deduction tree of a valid sequent.

No finite branch can terminate other than with a sequent which is an axiom. For otherwise the top sequent would be of the form $\Gamma_o \to \Delta_o$ where both Γ_o and Δ_o are sets of primitive formulas. In case this is not an axiom it is easy to construct a (finite) Boolean automaton and an interpretation M which realizes Γ_o but does not realize any formula of Δ_o .

If the proof tree is infinite, consider an infinite branch. Let Φ be the set of all primitive formulas that occur on the left of a sequent in this branch, Ψ the set of those formulas on the right of such a sequent. Then construct a Boolean automaton and interpretation which realizes Φ but does not realize any formula in Ψ . This interpretation turns out to contradict the validity of all sequents in the branch, hence that of $\Gamma \to \Delta$.

We conclude with some miscellaneous remarks.

(1) On Boolean automata. It is easy to see that the implications $\varphi \models \psi$ and $\varphi \equiv \psi$ are decidable by checking them for finite Boolean automata of limited size. This is not practical, however, the proof procedure is - proveably - more efficient.

(2) On logical identities. Clearly, not all logical identities of classical logic remain valid for the logic of can do. For example, the idempotent law for $\wedge$ fails:

$$\varphi \wedge \varphi \not\equiv \varphi ,$$

so does one distributive law:

$$\varphi \vee (\sigma \wedge \varrho) \not\equiv (\varphi \vee \sigma) \wedge (\varphi \vee \varrho) ,$$

and the absorption law:

$$\varphi \wedge (\varphi \vee \psi) \not\equiv \varphi .$$

(3) On flow-charts. The language L is adequate to treat questions of equipment organization, e.g. "compiling", "analysis of algorithms", for loop-free programs which may include parallelisms. Much work has to be done here to turn our approach into an effective tool even for that restricted class of programs. - Our method to deal with loops involves the introduction of infinitary rules of proof.

(4) On negation. The connective "not" is missing in the language L . There are various ways to understand negation in the context of "can do". For example, $\neg\varphi$ could mean "the equipment can do something which does not realize φ", or "the equipment can prevent φ from being realized", etc. Both of these concepts are obviously useful (the latter for example in connection with the question of security of computer programs), and deserve further study.

(5) On quantifiers. The notions "the equipment can eventually do φ" and "the equipment can always do φ" also appear to be useful. They can be made precise in different fashions. We have approached this by introducing, more generally, something akin to the existential and universal quantifiers of classical logic. This allows us to write the notion "eventually" as $\exists\xi(\xi\circ\varphi)$, which we interpret by

$$M(\exists\xi(\xi\circ\varphi)) = \{u\cdot v\in\Sigma | u\neq O \wedge v\in M(\varphi) \quad .$$

The analogy to existential quantifiers is underlined by a formal analogy in the proof theory of the language which is obtained by adding $\exists$.

(6) An additional facility may be gained by introducing a sort of first-order variables into the language L (in distinction to the second-order variables of (5) above). Semantically, if $s,t \in \cup\mathcal{S}$, $\varphi \in L$ and M is a interpretation of L in $(\mathcal{S},\Sigma)$ then

$$[s]\varphi[t] = \{w\in M(\varphi) : w \text{ begins with } s \text{ and ends with } t\} .$$

Copying in Commutation - Operator Schemata

M.I. Schwartzman

(Novosibirsk)

Annotation:

In this paper we shall consider the class of program schemata, so-called, commutation-operator schemata (c.o. schemata) developed in connection with the problem of designing an internal language for a universal optimizing translator from input language ALGOL 68, PL/1 and Simula 67.

Here we discuss in detail c.o. schemata constructions expressed by the general term copying. A c.o. scheme which has a means of copying contains certain designated fragments, a part of which can be copied and this c.o. scheme may be supplemented with copies of these fragments. The copies preserve the structure and the fragment object's membership. Special operators in c.o. schemata link fragments with other fragments and connect them to information and control connections of the c.o. scheme.

In particular, copying deals with such program features as the use of procedures and together with constructions describing the branching of the control in the program gives collateral execution of the program.

1. Introduction

In the Computing Centre of the Siberian Branch of the USSR Academy of Sciences a multilanguage optimizing programming system BETA [1] is being developed. The kernel of the system is an internal language (i.l.), with its main external requirements being laid down in [1,2]. From our point of view, while creating the internal language it is necessary to decide first of all which i.l. is to be built-"free" or "conformal".

By a free i.l. we mean a language which due to its well studied theory "dictates" possible and desirable ways of developing algorithmic languages and hardware.

A conformal i.l. in its structure essentially allows features of modern and future algorithmic languages and hardware, extrapolation being done through natural developing of languages and hardware. The effects of the conformal i.l. on this development are considered to be lagging.

T h e f i r s t h y p o t h e s i s while creating the i.l. of system BETA is as follows: the i.l. of the system must be conformal.

Note that the boundary between the conformal and free i.l. is rather vague, and, probably, it is very interesting and important to study the following problems: to what extent is the given conformal i.l. close to the free i.l., how many essentially different conformal i.l.'s may exist, are there several essentially different free i.l.'s, etc.

The creation of the conformal i.l., despite its own ultimate objective - i.l. of the BETA system has also secondary goals: investigation of one of the possible ways of building the free i.l.

The internal language, conformal or free, is not from our point of view, a base or semantic language in the broad sense of these notions. A part of the input language facilities, most of all connected with the memory control, i.e. facilities setting the so-called s p a c e - t i m e r e l a t i o n s [4] in the program, are not described by the internal language.+)

Let us briefly give the external requirements for an i.l.

The internal language

- is a configurator of input languages
- is a medium for formal transformations
- is not intended for use in writing programs by man.

Satisfying the first two requirements, which are, in general, inconsistent turns out to be a rather complicated problem. In the paper we do not touch upon the solution to this problem [6].

T h e s e c o n d h y p o t h e s i s that we have been guided by in our work on i.l. is as follows: the program in i.l. is an interpreted scheme of programs and if necessary, must allow for the possibility of analysis and transformation of only this scheme.

In [4,5] we have suggested commutation-operator schemata (c.o. schemata) as the program schemata of the BETA system internal language. In the present paper we shall discuss in general and informally only a part of the facilities of c.o. schemata, namely:
the means which in terms of copying are described in [5].

+) A so-called "second intermediate language" [4] developed on the basis of the internal language is being created for describing space-temporal relations in BETA system.

2. Principal elements of commutation-operator schemata

A rather simplified description of c.o. schemata is given below.

2.1. Commutation and operator media in c.o. scheme.

C.o. scheme consists of two parts - commutation medium (c. medium) and operator medium (o. medium).

O. medium is a pair of graphs: control flow and information flow where the information flow graph realizes the generalization of the idea by setting information connections between operators by means of the so-called d i s t r i b u t e d m e m o r y [3].

C. medium is a structured memory abstraction and consists of objects of two kinds: selectors and descriptors, some of them being connected by edges of commutation graphs. Figure 1 gives an example of c.o. scheme.

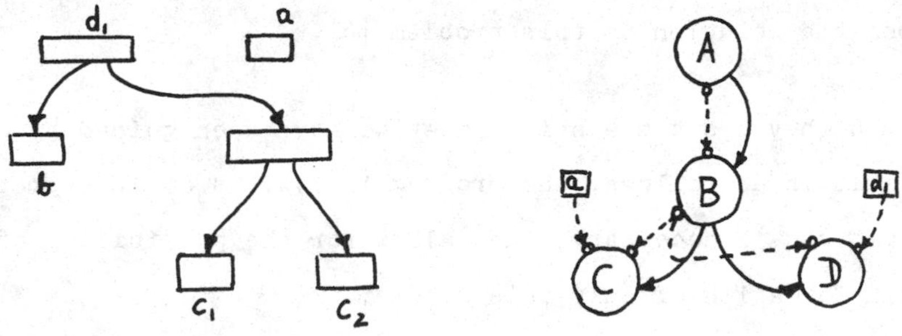

c. medium o. medium

Fig. 1. An example of c.o.scheme

Every object in the c.o. scheme is either an edge or a vertex (of some graph). Each vertex in the scheme has one and only one name, the name being different from all the others in the scheme. Values are sent through information edges and are stored in selectors and operator inputs; every value is either a name, or a terminal value.

Fetching from selector and sending to selector operators together with c. medium objects perform implicit information connections through the

c. medium. These information connections can be performed in a more complicated manner, namely using fetching from descriptor operators. Given a descriptor name, such an operator yields the name of an object, linked to this descriptor by a commutation edge. This object in it's turn will be a selector or a descriptor.

2.2. Breakes in the information flow graph of c.o. scheme.

In the information flow graph of o. medium there can be vertices which are called input breaks and output breaks. Fig. 2 shows a c.o. scheme (with empty c. medium) including both an input break, and an output break.

At any moment of the scheme execution each pair (output break, input break) has either closed status, or broken status.

Fig. 2. A broken pair of breaks in the information flow graph information flow graph.

A pair of breaks closed at a given moment, is "equivalent" to the existence at the same moment of an information edge between the output and the input which are connected by edges involving the closed pair of breaks.

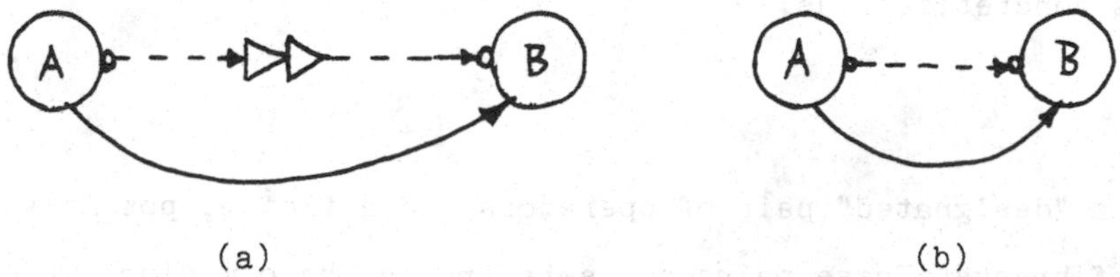

Fig. 3. Scheme (a) including a closed pair of breaks, Scheme (b) is "equivalent" to it at this moment.

Sending a value from the operator output to an output break which does not belong to any closed pair results in the loss of the value. Fig. 4 shows an example of information connections of some operator A at the moment of the end of its execution. The value produced by output W_1 is lost, by output W_2 - arrives at input V_2, by output W_3 - is not lost and arrives at input V_3 "through" the information edge (W_3, V_3).

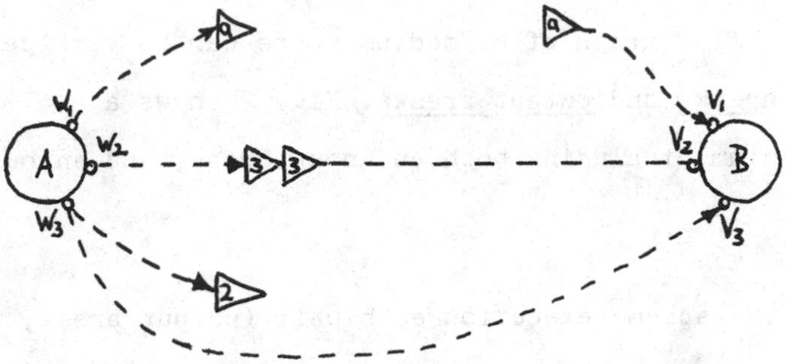

Fig. 4. Breaks in information flow graph.

The break is in some state which is a value. The break state is not related to the values which will probably be sent "through" the rupture, and it is only used when pairs of breaks are brought into a closed status, viz.: in the closed status as a result of execution of some operations there happen to be only breaks with the same states. States of breaks are shown in Fig. 4.

3. Copying

A fragment and generation are central notions in copying. The notion of a fragment per se is rather general, and we shall first consider notions as being its concretizations.

3.1. Bodies

The body is a "designated" pair of operators and a finite, possibly empty, set of breaks. These pairs and sets are in the o.medium. The body operators are the body entry and the body return. It should be clearly understood that a body is not, for example, the set of operators on a path in the control flow graph from the body entry to its return. The body is just the two operators (and the breaks)"designated" in the o. medium. Figures 5a - 5d give examples of bodies where Ent, Ret and Bre mean the entry, return and break of the corresponding body. The body operators and body breaks are shaded in the figures.

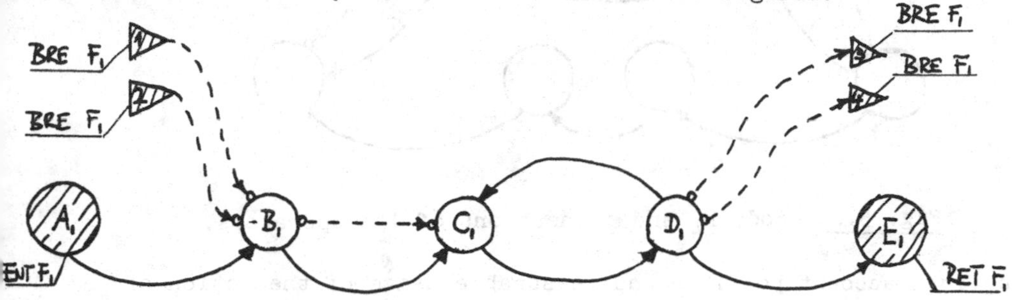

<u>Fig. 5.a.</u> Body F_1.

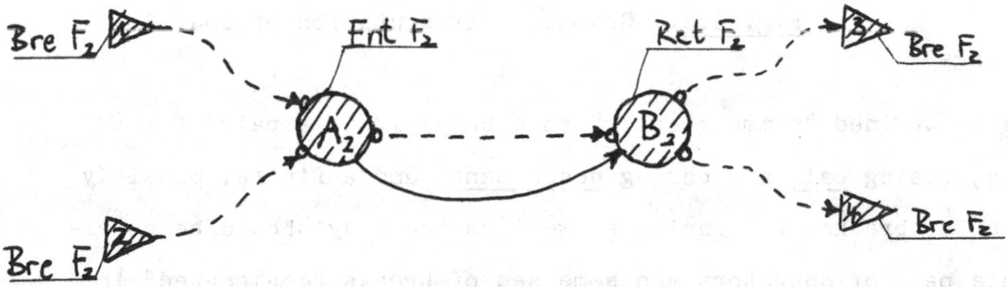

<u>Fig. 5.b.</u> Body F_2.

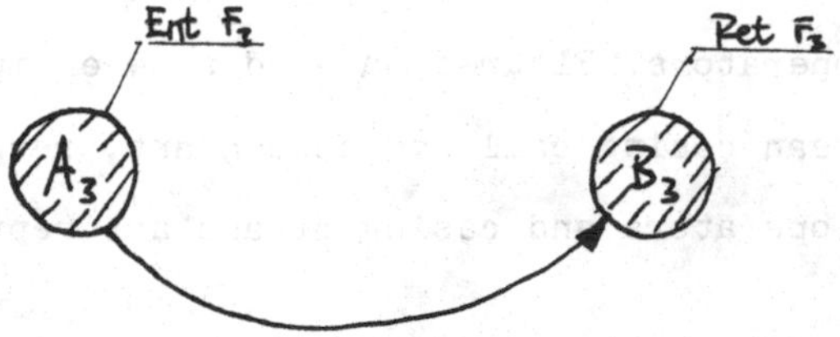

<u>Fig. 5.c.</u> Body F_3.

No restrictions are imposed upon the information and control connections of the body operators. Fig. 5d shows body F_4 whose operators are connected by information and control edges with other scheme operators.

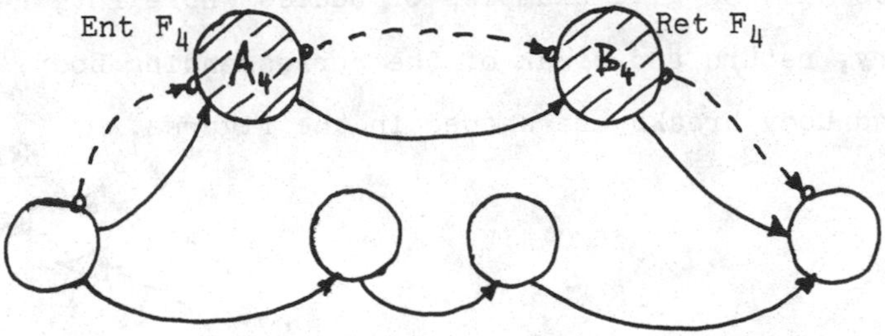

<u>Fig. 5.d.</u> Body F_4 and connections of its operators.

Taking into account possible and reasonable usage of the notion of body we shall draw it as in Fig. 5e.

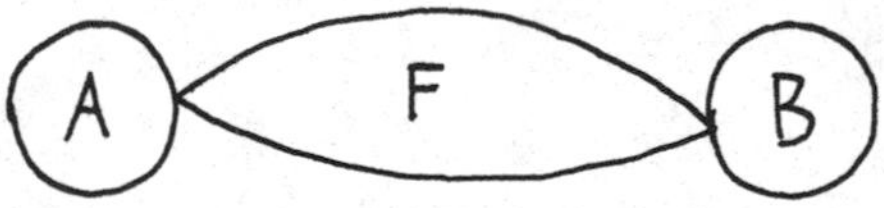

A - body entry

B - body return

<u>Fig. 5.e.</u> Graphic representation of body F.

3.2. Casings

A <u>casing</u> is defined "symmetrically" to a body: it is a pair of operators, casing <u>call</u> and casing <u>descendant</u>, and a finite, possibly empty, set of breaks. The casing as well as the body should be understood as a pair of operators and some set of breaks "designated" in the o. medium and "joined" by their belonging to the same casing. The casings we consider in this paper, the so-called <u>nonautosupplanting</u> casings [5] place no restrictions on the control and information connections of their operators. Figures 6a - 6d show examples of casings call and Des mean casing call and descendant, respectively. In the figures casing operators and casing breaks are represented by double lines.

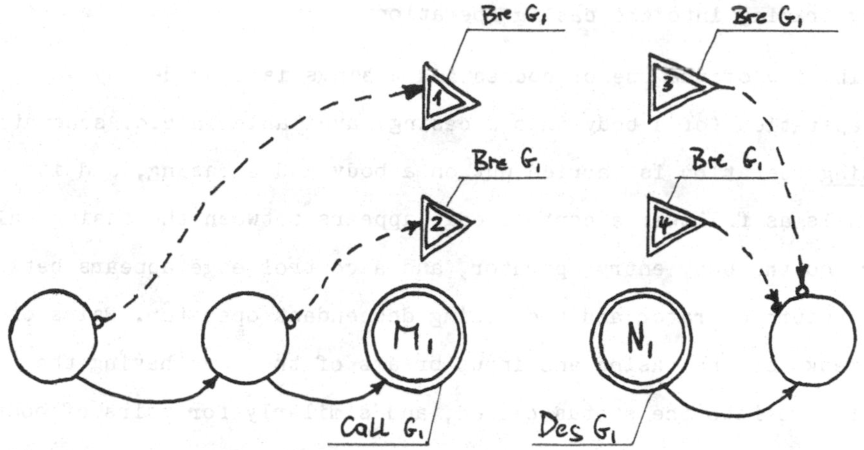

Fig. 6.a. Casing G_1.

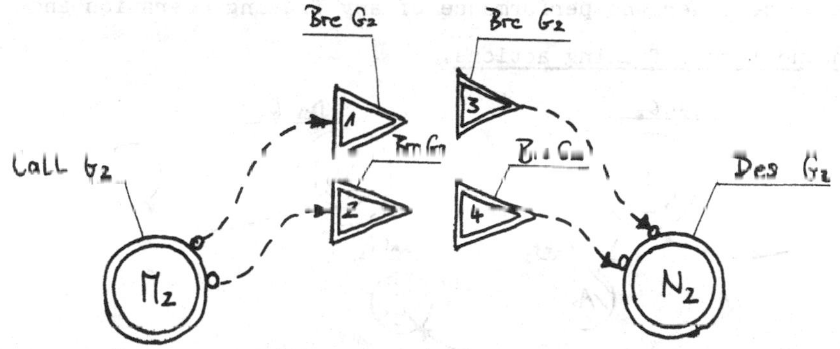

Fig. 6.b. Casing G_2.

Fig. 6.c. Casing G_3.

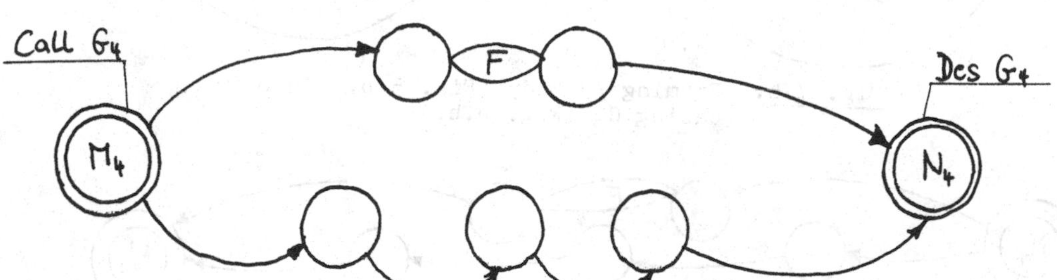

Fig. 6.d. Casing G_4 and connections of its operators.

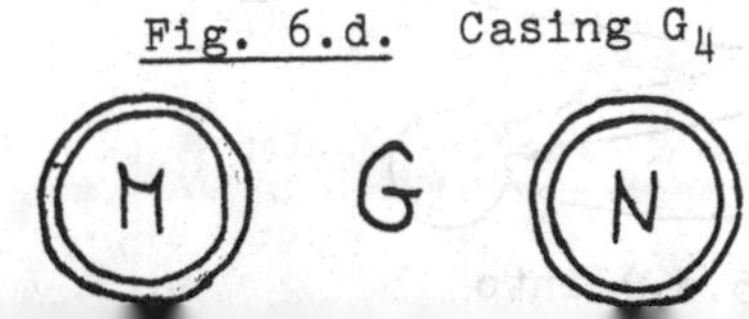

M - casing call

N - casing descendant

3.3. Body framing into the casing operation.

The possibility of the use of bodies and casings is provided by a framing operation (of a body into a casing) available in c.o. schemata. The <u>framing</u> operation is carried out on a body and a casing, and its execution is as follows: a control edge appears between the casing call operator and the body entry operator, and a control edge appears between the body return operator and the casing descendant operator. Pairs of output breaks of the casing and input breaks of the body having the same states go into the status closed, and similarly for pairs of body output breaks and those of casing input breaks. These actions unconditionally take place under the performance of any framing operation and are called <u>unconditional framing actions</u>.

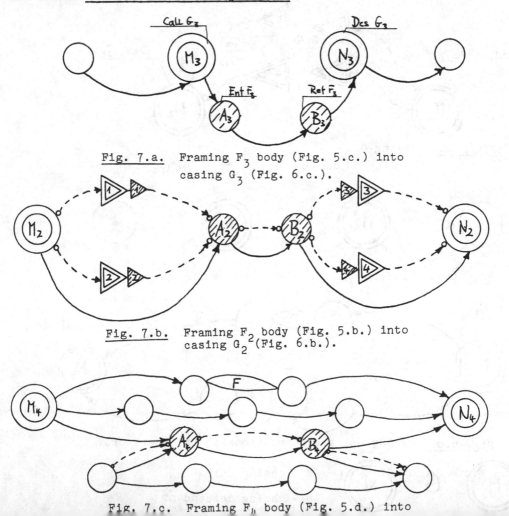

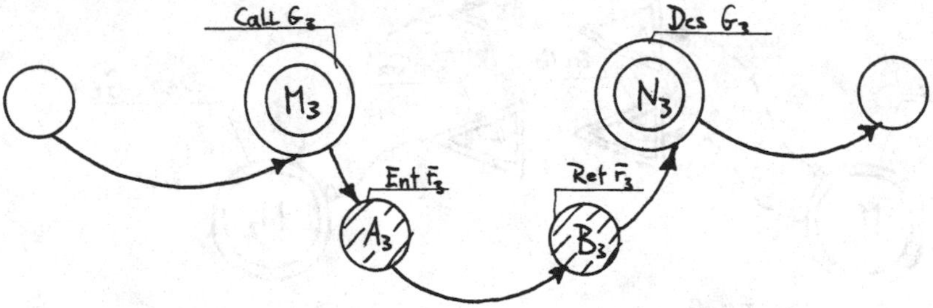

<u>Fig. 7.a.</u> Framing F_3 body (Fig. 5.c.) into casing G_3 (Fig. 6.c.).

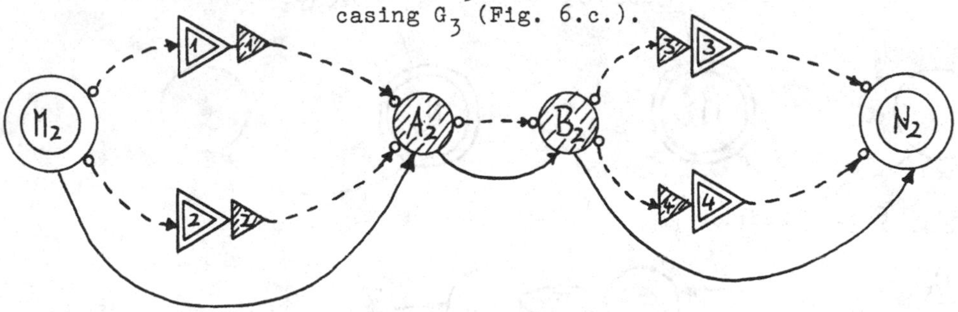

<u>Fig. 7.b.</u> Framing F_2 body (Fig. 5.b.) into casing G_2 (Fig. 6.b.).

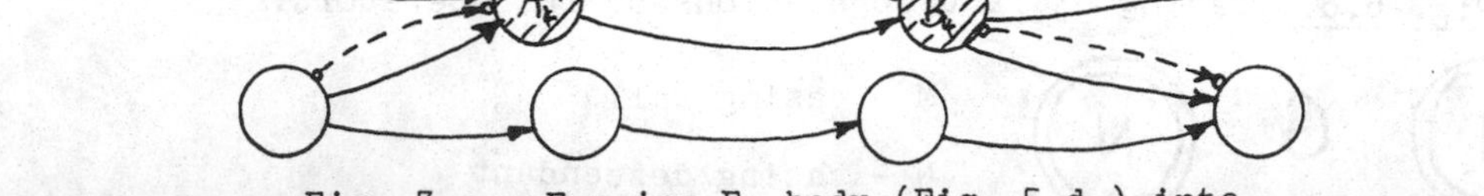

Fig. 7.c. Framing F_4 body (Fig. 5.d.) into

As we have already said in this paper we consider only nonautosupplanting casings. While framing a body into such a casing one can show which body that has already been framed into the casing should be supplanted by the framed body. This being indicated, all the unconditional framing actions are accomplished by framing some body into the casing and then abolishing control edges between casing operators and operators of the supplanted body. Only those breaks which are necessary for performing unconditional actions (every break entering only one closed pair) are broken.

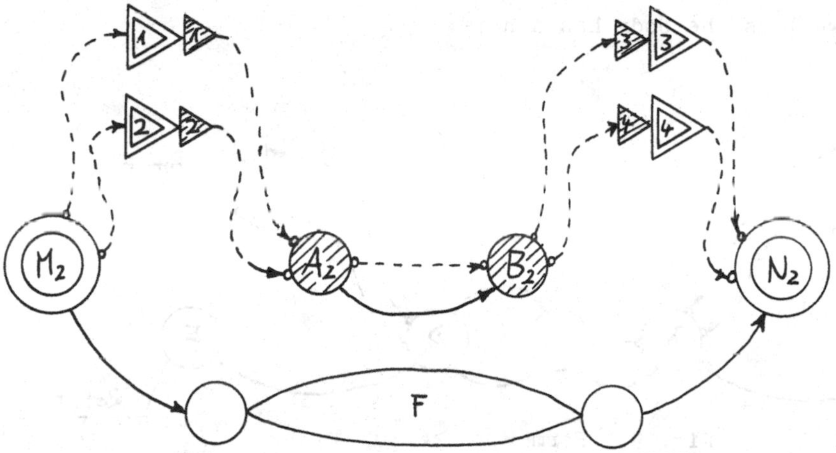

Fig. 8. Framing F body into casing G_2 with the supplanting of the already framed body F_2 (Fig. 7.b.).

Bodies and casings can be introduced into the c.o. scheme by its "a priori" labels. Under framing execution control edges appear and are abolished and pairs of breaks change their status. Below we shall show how the scheme can be reconstructed more profoundly during execution by, for example, introducing new vertices into it.

3.4. Forms

The form is some set of vertices and edges "designated" in the o. medium.

Each form has so-called specialized vertices. They are an operator-form entry, an operator-form return and a finite, possibly empty, set of breaks.

The form differs from the body in the following way: other objects, for example, operator inputs and outputs, information and control edges, other operators, etc. may be members of the form in addition to entry, return and breaks. The form, in contrast to the body, may be copied; the strict form definition has conditions which guarantee that form copying does not move the o. medium out of the operator medium class. The form as well as the body has a name.

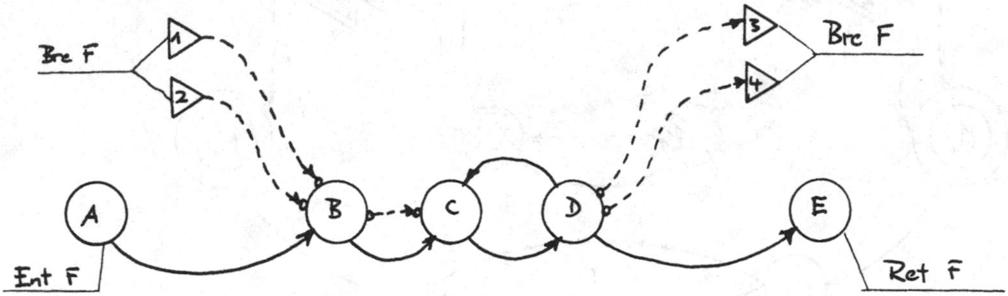

Fig. 9. Form F.

3.5. Copying the forms

Now, let us consider what copying the forms consists of. The result of copying lies in the appearance of new objects in the scheme, being copies of the form objects. The copies of objects are obtained according to the following rules:

- every object of the form is copied and, if the model (i.e. the form object) has a specialization then its copy has the same one;
- the copy of the vertex is a vertex with the same "appellation", i.e. the copy of the operator is an operator, the input copy is an input, and etc.;

- if the model is an edge, then its copy is incident with conservation of orientation to the copies of edge vertices. When one of the edge vertices is not a member of the form, then the copy of the edge is incident to this vertex and to the copy of the other one.

Fig. 10 shows what the o. medium consisting of only form F (Fig. 9) will convert to after copying this form.

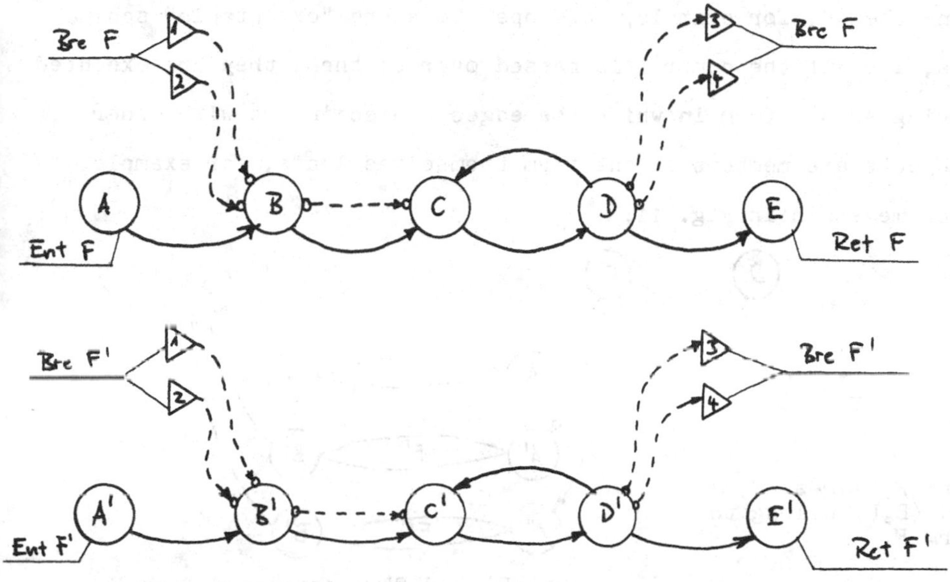

Fig. 10. The result of copying form F.

The form copying may be done in two ways: with conversion into a form or into a body.

In the first case all the appearing copies of the objects of the form are turned out to be joint again into a form and this form, like any other, may be copied.

In the second case only a part of the copies join in a body, i.e. entry operator, return operator and breaks, but the other objects resulting from copying are "assimilated" in the scheme.

The bodies resulting from copying may be used in the operation of framing, for example. Note that the form may be used as a body in this operation, i.e. to frame the form into the casing, and the form object specialization will be taken into account as well as the body object specialization.

In general, both the form objects and body objects "attend to their duties in scheme", for example, form operators are "executable" scheme operators, i.e. if the control is passed over to them, they are executed etc. Copying such a form in which the edges connecting it with other scheme objects are members of the form themselves leads, for example, to the scheme shown in Fig. 11.

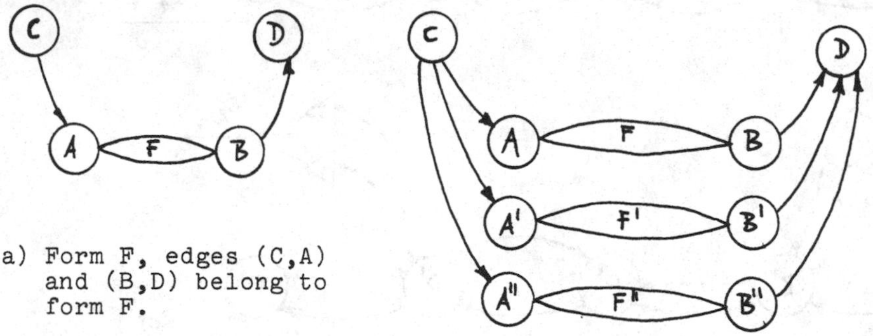

a) Form F, edges (C,A) and (B,D) belong to form F.

b) F' and F" - copies of form F.

Fig. 11. An example of copying the form.

The "recursive" execution of a body may be given by framing some casing into a form and using copying and framing operations, see Fig. 12.

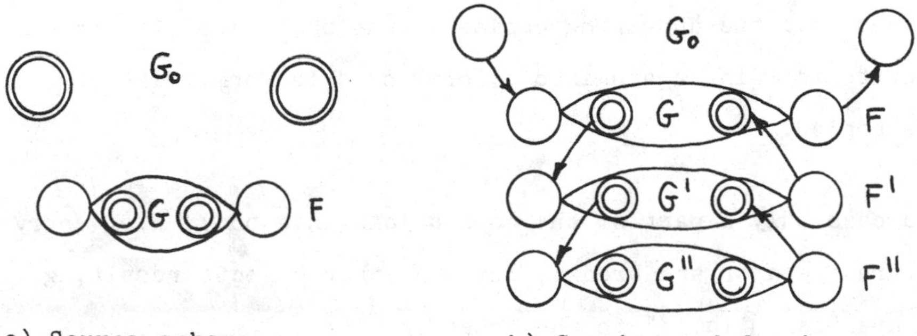

a) Source scheme.

b) Copying and framing operations are applied to the scheme (a).

Fig. 12. "Recursive" execution of a body.

3.6. Markings in the c.o. scheme and fragments

All the above notions of copying are described formally in [4,5] in terms of the marking (of a scheme) and labels (on objects), and in terms of fragments and pseudofragments being derived from them. For example, the form is a scheme fragment, some of the bodies are fragments and the other pseudofragments. We hope that the technique of marking will be useful not only for the formal analysis and description of the c.o. schemata but for efficiency of computers implementation of c.o. schemata.

3.7. The object name and generation

The technique developed below by the concept of generation gives, for instance, the possibility of a flexible access to different copies of the same object. It allows exact "desposition" with respect to surrounding scheme objects of bodies which are copies of forms.

As we have already stated every vertex in the c.o. scheme has one and only one name, and in any scheme vertices of scheme graphs have different names.

In consequence of copying some vertex its copy can either coincide with an already available vertex in the scheme - if the name of the copy is identical to the name of this vertex, or the copy will be different from all other scheme vertices - if the name of the copy differs from all the names in the scheme.

How is the name of the copy "calculated"? Whenever a form is copied it is always indicated in what generation to locate copies of vertices of the form, so various acts of copying this form can naturally locate form copies in different generations. The model-vertex name and that of a generation completely and uniquely determine the copy-vertex name. It occurs in the following way.

3.8. The name generating operation

The component part of the copying operation is called name generating operation; it is a two-argument operation which by the name of a model and that of the generation in which the copy is located "calculates" the copy name. We shall denote this operation by [x,P] where x is the name of a model, P - the name of the generation. Operation [x,P] with different pairs of arguments relates different names and can be executed not only when it is a component of a copying operation, but also as a separate one. Through this operation it is possible to know the future or current name of an object knowing in which generation it will be or is located, and what is its model.

Note, that the form and the body have the name, the name of the form or of the body appearing as a result of copying is also "calculated" by the name generating operation.

It is considered that all the objects which are not copies of any other ones are not located in any generation. Let us try to compare the names of two objects resulting from multiple copying. The first object is obtained in this way:

- to copy object x, to locate in generation P,
- to copy the result, to locate in Q,
- to copy the result, to locate in S.

The second object is obtained in the following manner:

- to copy x, to locate in P,
- to copy the result, to locate in R,
- to copy the result, to locate in S.

The first object name - [[[x,P],Q],S],
the second object name - [[[x,P],R],S].

One can easily see that the names are identical only when such representing these names chains are identical lexicographically: x, P, Q, S and x, P, R, S.

Hence, the results of multiple copying of the same object are not necessarily identical even if they are located in just the same generation. If the model is not located in a generation, then its copy is always different from this model since chains representing them are of different length, the model chain - x, the copy chain - x,P.

3.9. Generations

Thus a generation is a set of objects each of which resulted from copying and were located in the same generation at the moment of copying.

From our point of view, it is important to note the following. Object characteristics, such as for example, "to be a descendant of this casing", "to be a member of this form" are different by their nature from such a characteristic as "to be located in this generation". First characteristics are explicitly given on the object by labels of various types, the property "the object is located in this generation" is, by no means, explicitly marked on the object and is only used for creation of the object name.

3.10. Stabilizers in the information flow graph of c.o. scheme

Before the treatment of other notions relevant to generation we shall consider one more type of information flow graph vertex - the stabilizers.

A stabilizer in the information flow graph may be incident only to the operator input, and this input state is equal to the stabilizer state which is a value. Fig. 13 gives examples of the use of stabilizers, in the figures they are reprensented as squares.

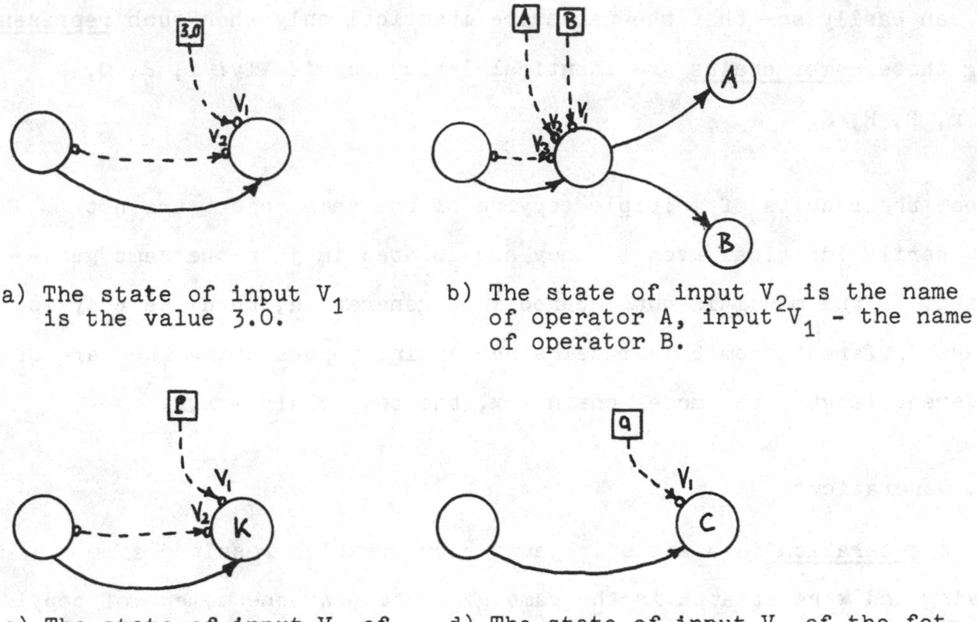

a) The state of input V_1 is the value 3.0.

b) The state of input V_2 is the name of operator A, input V_1 - the name of operator B.

c) The state of input V_1 of the copying operator K is the name of generation P.

d) The state of input V_1 of the fetching operator C is a - the name of some selector.

Fig. 13. The examples of the use of stabilizers.

3.11. Producer of the names for generations

The value of the name of a generation in which it is necessary to locate some copy can like any other value, appear in two ways.

The first - the value is given "a priori" in the scheme by the use of the stabilizer.

The second - the value is calculated. The operator elaborating generations names is called producer of names for generations.

For a given producer the discipline of producing generations names is determined by an operation related to it by interpretation. One operation can, for example, in every execution produce a generation name different from all those produced up to the given set of producing. It is clear that the copying of one and the same form into a loop is reasonable only when the copying operator "is provided" by names of generations from a producer with just that operation.

Through all acts of producing some other operations elaborates one and the same generation name until the values of its arguments do not change, etc.

3.12. Commutation form and commutation body

Similar to forms and bodies in o. medium we define forms and bodies in c. medium (c. forms and c. bodies).

A c. form is a "designated" set of selectors and descriptors possibly connected by edges of commutation graphs; c. form copying involves the appearance in the c. medium of new selectors and descriptors and edges between them.

While copying the c. form, as well as the form of o. medium, a generation is necessarily indicated in which the copy of the c. form should be located.

Fig. 14 shows examples of the c. form, objects which are members of the form being given by the following notation: K = {x,y, (x,y)} means that the form consists of vertices x and y and edge (x,y).

C. medium before copying

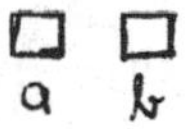

K = {b}

C. medium after one act of copying

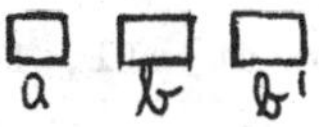

a) An example of the c. form consisting of one selector.

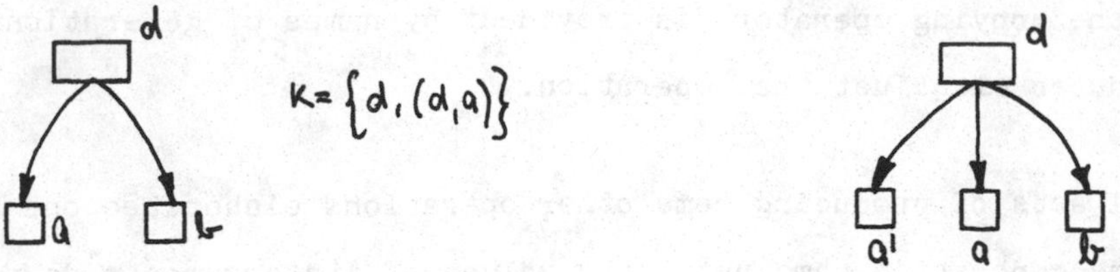

b) An example of the c. form consisting of a selector and an edge.

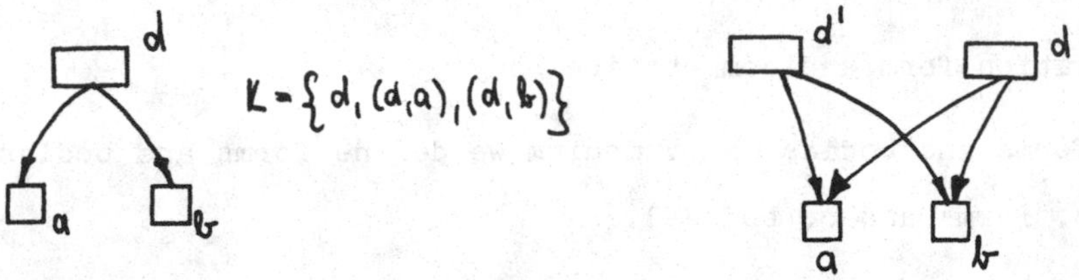

c) An example of the c. form consisting of a descriptor and edges.

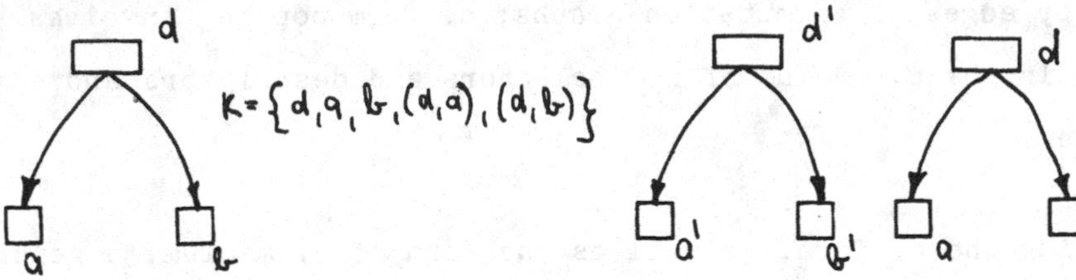

d) An example of the c. form consisting of a commutation graph.

Fig. 14 - Examples of the c. form usage.

3.13. Conforming in c.o. schemata

This section gives a description of the means of altering the c.o. scheme different from those of copying and framing mentioned above. The actions specifying these means are, in a sense, between the actions which do not alter the scheme at all, for example, the execution of arithmetic operations or sending into selectors of the c. medium, and actions which result in "non-predictable" alterations of the scheme, say, "deleting a control edge between two given arbitrary operators", "introducing a given arbitrary operator into the scheme", "altering the state of a given arbitrary stabilizer", etc. "Non-predictability" of the latter actions consists in the fact that any part of the c.o. scheme at any moment of its execution may be subjected to arbitrary alterations.

Conceptually, conforming operation described below consists in the following. Let some form containing stabilizers be copied.

One of the functions which stabilizers perform in the c.o. scheme is as follows: stabilizers organize "transput" between the commutation and operator medium, for example, sending and fetching operators can be connected with stabilizers prescribing arguments of these operators - names of selectors and descriptors.

As a result of copying the form of some bodies will appear. Under their execution stabilizer states prescribing "areas" of the c. medium used for "transput" by the given body will be used.

A natural case will occur often when each body is in correspondence with its own "area" of the c. medium resulted in its turn from copying some c. form. Conforming performs "bringing" the bodies to "areas" of the c. medium varying accordingly the stabilizers states (while copying the stabilizers states "are transferred" to their copies).

While copying the form it may turn out that some information and control edges connect vertices in resulting copies of the form with "stationary vertices", i.e. with those which are not members of this form and, therefore, are not copied. But if these "stationary" vertices are members of some other form themselves, they can be copied independently of this form. In this case conforming allows "to bring" generations of this form (i.e. some bodies) to corresponding generations of "stationary" vertices.

Let us describe conforming more formally. One more specialization is introduced for body objects - <u>conformable</u> objects. Conformable objects can be edges and some stabilizers. A conformable edge, control or information, can be an edge which is a member of the body, with one of its vertices not being a member of the body. The body definition is widened, and a body in addition to entry, return and breaks may contain conformable stabilizers and edges.

<u>Operation of conforming</u> with a given generation is executed at a body and consists in conforming every conformable body object with this generation.

Body <u>object conforming</u> is made in such a way. Let stabilizer x be subjected to conforming with generation P, the state of this stabilizer being a. Then as a result of conforming the value [a,P] will become the state of the stabilizer.

Let edge (c,d) be subjected to conforming with generation P, vertex c not being a member of the conformable body. As a result of conforming edge (c,d) will disappear and edge ([c,P],d) will appear. Similarly, in the case when d is not a member of the conformable body.

Likewise, the form definition is widened, and form conforming is made.

a) C. form K and form F with conformable stabilizers

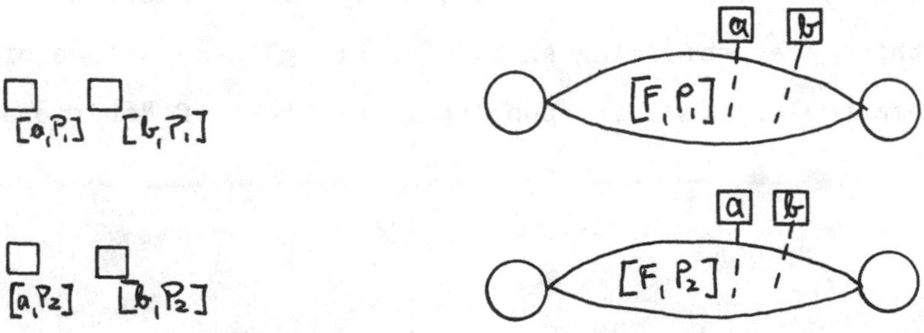

b) Copies of forms K and F in generations P_1 and P_2.

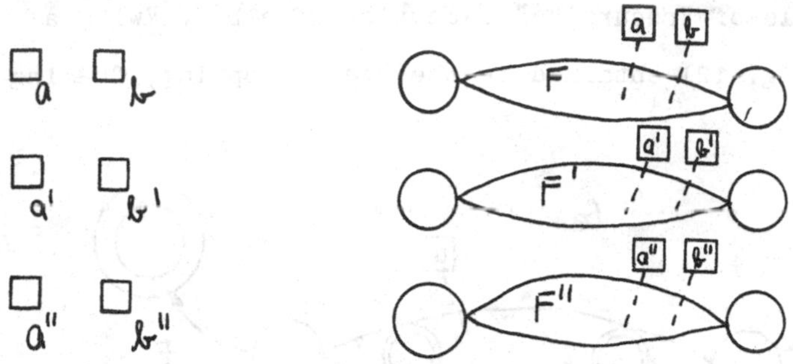

c) Body F' conformed with generation P_1, body F" conformed with generation P_2 (the abbreviations: $[F,P_1]=F'$, $[a,P_1]=a'$, etc. are used in the Fig.).

Fig. 15. Bodies with conformable stabilizers.

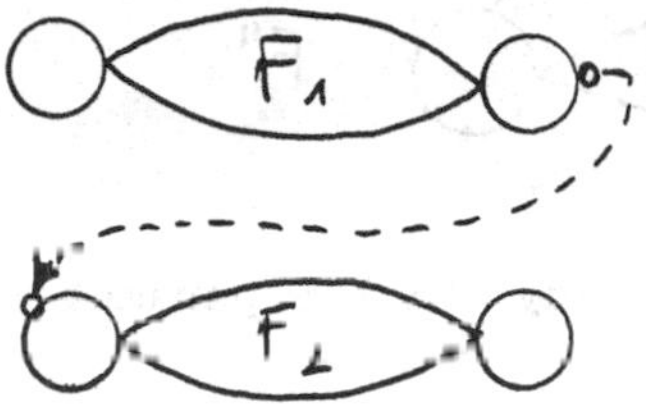

a) Forms F_1 and F_2, the information edge is a member of form F_2.

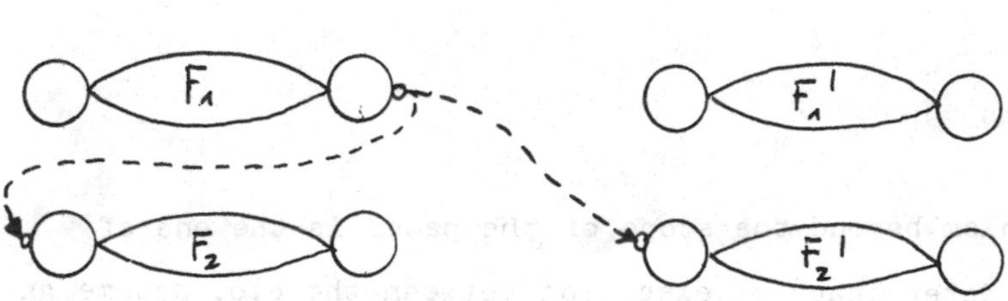

b) First a copy of F_2 is located in generation P_1 - this is F_2' and then a copy of F_1 is created in generation P_1 - this is F_1'.

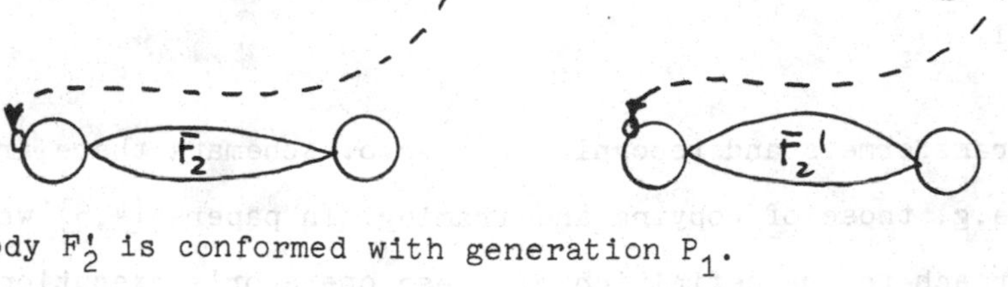

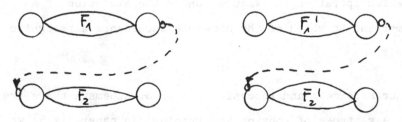

c) Body F_2' is conformed with generation P_1.

Fig. 16. Bodies with conformable edges.

Fig. 17 shows an example of "recursive" execution of a body "with a parameter" (see also Fig. 12) obtained by the use of copying, framing and conforming.

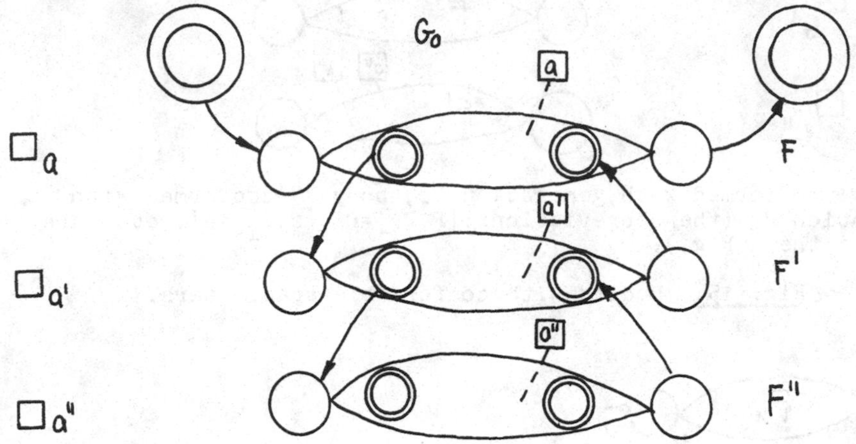

Fig. 17. "Recursive" execution of a body "with a parameter".

4. Conclusion

4.1. Some problems

An important problem beyond the scope of the paper is the one of "distributing" indeterminacy of execution between the c.o. scheme and the program, i.e. the interpreted scheme. Usually the execution of program schemes containing only recognizers and transformers leaves indeterminate which operation is executed under the execution of a given transformer and to which of the possible successors a recognizer gives the control.

In addition to transformers and recognizers in c.o. schemata there are also operators, e.g. those of copying and framing. In papers [4,5] we describe our approach to the definition of these operator's execution in the c.o. scheme, show some possible operations interpreting these operators. Fig. 18 represents indeterminacy under framing execution.

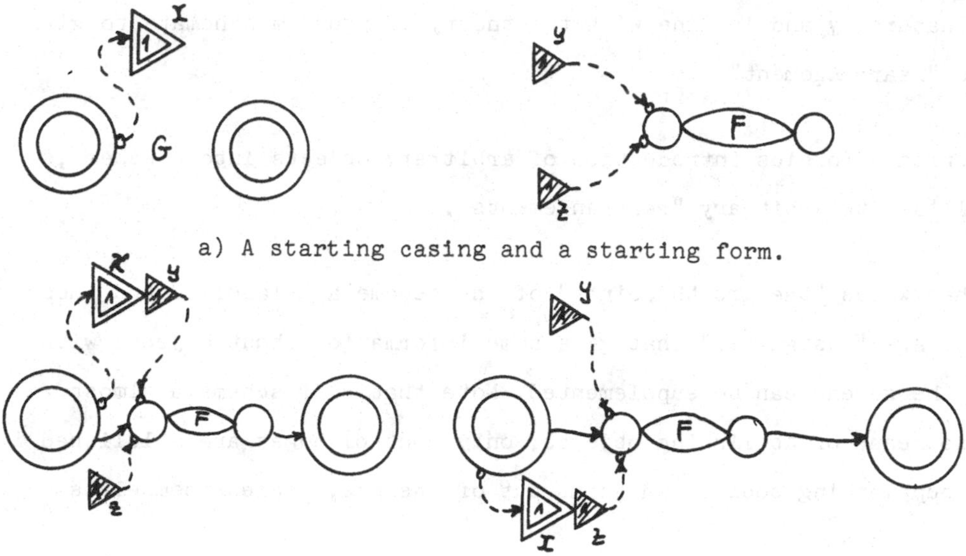

a) A starting casing and a starting form.

b) Framing execution results in any of represented schemes

<u>Fig. 18.</u> Framing a body whose breaks have identical states.

Problems of "distribution" of indeterminacy also arise in the c.o. schemata allowing multigraphs.

4.2. Review of the paper

A c.o. scheme contains some "designated" fragments a part of which (forms) may be copied. The copies of the fragments preserve the structure and the fragment object's membership, and the c.o. scheme is supplemented with the copies.

Each of the scheme fragments obtained as a result of copying is located in some generation, the name of the generation and of the form the fragment is obtained from, determines this fragment name. The name of every object of the fragment is also fully determined by this generation in which the fragment is located and by the model-object name.

Special operations "link" fragments with other fragments (conforming) and "connect" fragments appearing in the c.o. scheme to the objects

The concepts of copying represented in the paper reflect an attempt to introduce into program schemata, a means which, from our point of view, allow naturally and in line with the theory of program schemata to give scheme "rearrangement".

Our approach forbids introduction of arbitrary objects into a scheme, as well as its arbitrary "rearrangements".

In other words "the growth points" of the scheme are labelled and those objects are "designated" that give some information about objects with which the scheme can be supplemented. Note that c.o. schemata almost have no means of abolishing objects, only control edges are ablolished while supplanting bodies and forms out of casings; bodies themselves are not abolished.

We believe "non-abolishment of objects from the inside of a scheme" to be inherent to those schemata, the main requirement to which is subjection to formal, in particular, optimizing transformations.

We hope that the ideology of fragments and generations along with a view on a program as some interpreted scheme will turn out to be useful for designing universal algorithms of transformation of schemata containing fragments.

Partial applications of these algorithms may be the traditional problems of optimization of procedures, including recursive and problems of optimization of programs containing procedures and collaterally executed parts of the program.

Representation of schemata adequately describing operating systems is another important field for applications of notions of copying.

REFERENCES

[1] A.P. Ershov, A multilanguage programming system oriented to languages description and universal optimization algorithms, Proc. IFIP working conf. "ALGOL 68 implementation" (Munich, July 20-24, 1970).

[2] A.P. Ershov, Theory of Program Schemata, IFIP Congress 71, (Ljubljana, August 23-28, 1971).

[3] A.P. Ershov, On program schemata over common and distributed memory, Kibernetika, Kiev, 4 (1968).

[4] M.I. Schwartzman, Commutation-operator schemata - description of the main concepts. Preprint. The Computer Centre of Siberian Branch of the USSR Academy of Sciences, Novosibirsk, 1972.

[5] M.I. Schwartzman, The growing commutation-operator schemata. Preprint. The Computer Centre of Siberian Branch of the USSR Academy of Sciences, Novosibirsk, 1972.

[6] Prospect of System BETA draft. Material BETA/M-07. The Computer Centre of Siberian Branch of the USSR Academy of Sciences, Novosibirsk, 1971.

The author thanks A.P. Ershov for his advices and A.A. Kodatko for her kind help to prepare this paper for printing.

On Synthesizing Programs Given by Examples

J. Barzdin

We shall consider the problem in general without going into details of practical implementation. At first we have to choose a programming language. Since the results of this paper don't depend essentially on the choice of the language (only some constants are to be changed), let us take a language as simple as possible from the theoretical point of view - the language defined by Post machines.

Now let us review briefly the definition of a Post machine. A Post machine just like a Turing machine consists of infinite tape divided into cells and a read-write head moving along it. Each cell can contain only one of the symbols 1 or "blank".

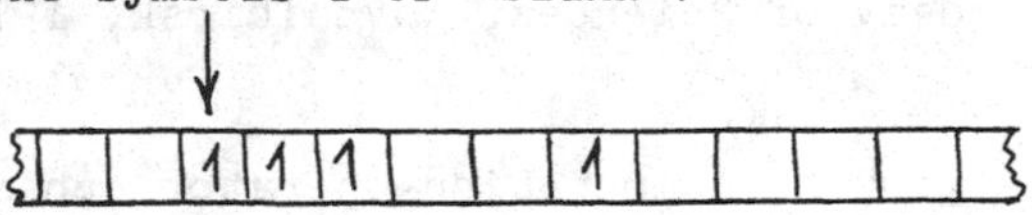

Fig. 1

A machine has the following universal set of instructions:

a. ← b Move to the left: move the read-write head to the left by one cell, then go to the instruction with number b (a is the number of the given instruction).

a. → b Move to the right.

a. ∨ b Print one (in the cell scanned by head).

a. ↕ b Erase the cell.

a. ?$<^{b}_{c}$ Conditional branch: if the cell scanned by the head contains 1 then go to the instruction with number b, otherwise to the instruction with number c.

a.! H a l t .

An Example of a Program

1. ?$<^{2}_{3}$	3. → 4	5. ∨ 6
2. → 1	4. ?$<^{1}_{5}$	6. !

The control flow graph of this program is the following:

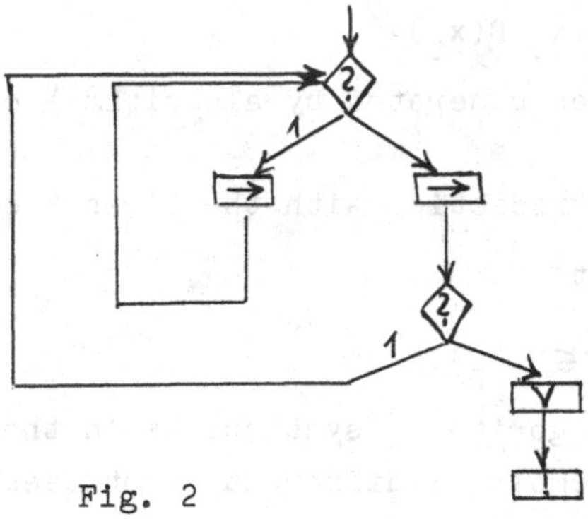

Fig. 2

In what follows by the program we shall understand a program for a Post machine. We shall denote the number of instructions in program P by $|P|$. We associate with every program P a partial recursive function P(x) computed by it. It is clear that in such a way we can get all partial recursive functions. We shall call program P general recursive (g.r.) if the function computed by it is general recursive. In what follows we shall consider only g.r. programs.

Now let us consider the exact statement of our problem.

Let P be a g.r. program and $\Omega = \{x_1, x_2, \ldots, x_t, \ldots\}$ an infinite sequence of natural numbers (list of all possible values of the argument).

Let the first t examples (the first t values of P(x) on inputs from Ω):

$$(x_1, P(x_1)), (x_2, P(x_2)), \ldots, (x_t, P(x_t))$$

be given.

It is required to determine program P' which is identical to P on Ω, i.e. $P'(x) = P(x)$ for all $x \in \Omega$ (the set of all such P' we shall call $\{P_\Omega\}$). The only information available is the first t example.

It is clear that this problem in general cannot be solved without any mistakes. We investigate the solution of this problem in the case $t \to \infty$.

For the solving of this problem we can use any effective rules $\sum$ (called algorithms of synthesis). Formally $\sum$ is a partial recursive function of one argument. Let $<z_1, \ldots, z_s>$ be the number of strings of integers $\{z_1, \ldots, z_s\}$ under a fixed numbering of all such strings. Let also a fixed numbering of all programs be given. By hypothesis generated by algorithm $\sum$ at time t (i.e. after the first t example), we understand the program P_t with number

$$\Sigma(< x_1, P(x_1), x_2, P(x_2), \ldots, x_t, P(x_t) >).$$

Let P_1, P_2,..., P_t,... be hypotheses generated by algorithm Σ on the sequence Ω. Let us assume that

a) for any t P_t is not in contradiction with the first t example , i.e. $P_t(x) = P(x)$ for $x = x_1, \ldots, x_t$;

b) there exists such a τ that

$$P_\tau = P_{\tau+1} = \ldots = P' \qquad \text{and } P' \in \{ P_\Omega \}.$$

In such a case we shall say that algorithm Σ synthesises in the limit the program P on sequence Ω. The number of different hypotheses gene-rated by Σ until the right hypothesis P' is found, is denoted by $\Sigma^A(\Omega,P)$. In other cases let $\Sigma^A(\Omega,P) = \infty$.

We shall say that the set U of programs is synthesizable in the limit if there is such an algorithm Σ that for any $P \in U$ and for any sequence Ω , $\Sigma^A(\Omega,P) < \infty$.

It was shown by Gold [1], that the set of all g.r. functions (programs) is not synthesizable in the limit.

Further we shall consider a case when some additional information is given about program P (and it is usually the case in applications).[x)]

A. Effectively Enumerable Classes of Programs.

A set of programs is said to be effectively enumerable if the set of numbers of these programs is recursively enumerable. It is easy to see (Gold [1]) that any set of programs contained in an effectively enumer-able set of g.r. programs is synthesizable in the limit.

It can be shown [3] that this condition is not necessary (an answer to the question stated by Gold [1]).

It can be also shown (M.Augston, J.Barzdin) that there are such sets of g.r. programs which are synthesizable in the limit, but the union of which is not synthesizable in the limit.

However the case of synthesizing recursively enumerable sets of g.r. programs is general enough in practice. This case has been studied in more detail in [2], [3], [4]. Let us mention some of the results.

Let U be an effectively enumerable set of g.r. programs with fixed ef-

---

x) Some other aspects of this problem regarding synthesis of grammars in the limit are considered in [6] and [7].

fective enumeration u of this set. Let $\sum_u^A(\Omega,n) = \max \sum^A(\Omega,P)$ where the maximum is taken over all programs $P \in U$ with u-numbers not exceeding n. It is easy to see that there exists an algorithm $\sum$ such that $\sum_U^A(\Omega,n) \leq n$. E.g. thus is the algorithm which takes hypotheses from U one after another until the searched program is reached. However, the following more powerful theorem can be proved (R.Freivald, J.Barzdin[4]):

For any U there exists an algorithm $\sum$ such that for any sequence Ω

$$\sum_U^A(\Omega,n) \leq \log_2 n + o(\log_2 n).$$

This estimate shows that number of mistakes occuring in the process of synthesis is very small. But, unfortunately, the given algorithm synthesizes very uneconomical programs. In the first approximation hypothesis can be considered economical if they all are chosen from the same set U. In order to characterize this situation the quantity $\sum^{A'}(\Omega,P)$ (and respectively $\sum_U^{A'}(\Omega,n)$) is introduced which is defined identical to $\sum^A(\Omega,P)$, when all the hypotheses belong to the set U, and equal to ∞ otherwise.

The following theorem holds:
There exists an effectively enumerable set U of g.r. programs such that for any algorithm $\sum$ $\sum_U^{A'}(\Omega_o,n) \geq n$, where $\Omega_o = \{1,2,3,\ldots\}$.

The latter result shows that effective enumerability of a set is a condition too weak to guarantee in general the existence of an economical synthesizing algorithm. Further we shall consider the case when additional information of a different nature is given about the program to be synthesized.

B. Synthesizing a Program when the Number of Instructions is Known.

Now we shall consider the case when there is given $|P|$- the number of instructions in P. In this case the t-th hypothesis is defined as the program with number $\sum(<x_1,P(x_1),\ldots,x_t,P(x_t),|P|>)$
where in addition to the first t examples $|P|$ is also used. $\sum^B(\Omega,P)$ is defined just like $\sum^A(\Omega,P)$ in the previous case.

It is easy to show the following:
There exists an algorithm $\sum$ such that for any g.r. program P and for any sequence Ω

$$\sum^B(\Omega,P) \leq |P|^{3|P|} \quad .$$

At the same time it can be shown that this estimate cannot essentially be lowered:
For any algorithm $\sum$ and for any natural n there exists a program P with

$|P| = n$ such that

$$\sum^{B}(\Omega_o,P) \geq |P|^{c|P|}$$

where c is a positive constant.
The latter estimate shows that additional information used here is insufficient to construct an economical algorithm of synthesis.

C. Synthesizing a Program When Program History Is known.

By the complete history of a program on an argument x, we mean the record of the sequence of all instructions performed during program execution for the given argument.
E.g., the program shown in Fig. 2 while working on arguments in Fig. 1 generates the following complete history:

?→?→?→?→?V!

For the case when some of the branch instructions (?) are omitted we shall call the corresponding history partial. In the previous example, the following history will be partial:

→?→?→→V!

Concepts of complete and partial history as a matter of fact coincide with concepts of operational-logic and operational histories investigated by A.P.Ershov [5].

Partial history on particular examples is apparently the minimum information given to the programmer by any customer, even the most incompetent However, the language more powerful than that of Post programs is used. But programming language is not very essential, when investigating the theoretical possibilities of synthesis.

Let us investigate the case when together with x_t and $P(x_t)$ the partial history of program P on argument x_t (denoted by h_t) is also given.
In this case the t-th hypothesis is defined as the program with the number $\sum(< x_1,P(x_1),h_1,\dots,x_t,P(x_t),h_t>)$.
As in the previous cases we introduce $\sum^{C}(\Omega,P)$ - the number of different hypotheses given by algorithm $\sum$ during the process of synthesis.
It is clear that in this case there exists an algorithm which synthesizes in the limit every g.r.program. However it turns out that in this case it is possible to construct a synthesizing algorithm which surveys a relatively small amount of hypotheses:

There exists an algorithm $\sum$ such that for any g.r. program P and for any sequence Ω

$$\sum^{C}(\Omega,P) \leq 3|P| \log_2|P| + 4 .$$

The order of this estimate cannot be lowered in general. Now let us consider the case when all the histories used are complete. In this case we shall use the notation $\sum^{C'}(\Omega,P)$ instead of $\sum^{C}(\Omega,P)$. An important characteristic of each program P is the number of branch instructions in it. This quantity will be denoted by $||P||$. For most real programs $||P|| << |P|$. It turns out that $\sum^{C'}(\Omega,P)$ depends only on $||P||$. The following theorem holds:

There exists an algorithm $\sum$ such that for any g.r. program P and for any sequence Ω

$$\sum^{C'}(\Omega,P) \leq 3||P|| \log_2||P|| + 4.$$

The program P' synthesized in the limit by the above mentioned algorithm $\sum$ may have, in the general case, histories different from those of program P. It is not clear if it is possible to find an analogical estimate in the case when the histories of program P' must be identical to those of P.

Further investigations are connected with the constructions of synthesizing algorithms which not only survey few hypotheses during the process of synthesis but also are easy to realize and give economical hypotheses as a result. It is possible that in the general case these demands cannot be fulfilled simultaneously. Therefore we restrict the set of programs to be considered. It turns out that the very essential feature of a program is its loop structure. So far we have managed to construct synthesizing algorithms (A.Kalnins, J.Bichevskis) which meet the demands mentioned above for programs with depth of loop structure not exceeding 2 (a loop in the loop). Let us note that the depth of a loop structure in real programs usually is not large. This depth for data processing programs usually does not exceed 2 and for programs of computational mathematics respectively 3.

A different situation is possible when the programmer (synthesizer) interacts with the customer during the process of synthesis. He sets various situations on the tape and asks the customer how the program would proceed from this situation, i.e. which instructions are to be executed (it is assumed, that the situation on the tape can be changed by the programmer at any moment). Apparently this case is the closest to practice.

In the case when complete history of the program is given by the customer during this "conversation", the problem of synthesis can in fact be reduced to the problem of deciphering finite automata by multiple experiment (the upper bound of the number of states of automata not being given). The latter problem is investigated in detail in [8]. There it is shown that under the conditions mentioned before, most automata can be deciphered, even to the extent that no erroneous hypotheses are produced. However, the total length of the experiment is of order of magnitude of K^c where K is the number of states of the automaton and c is a sufficiently large positive constant. We have investigated the case when the depth of loop structure of the program is bounded. In this case it is possible to construct (J.Bichevskis, J.Barzdin) sufficiently economica synthesizing algorithms (using histories with total length of order KlogK , the number of instructions in the program to be synthesized).

Thus the depth of a loop structure is a rather important characteristic when synthesizing programs.

The depth of a loop structure changes when transfering from one concept of algorithm to another. E.g. in this case of recognizing symmetric words the usual informal algorithm has the depth of a loop structure equal to 1, but realization of this algorithm on a Post machine with one head demands loop depth 2. At the same time on a two-head Post machine we can accomplish the same task with loop depth 1. From this point of view, the concept of an algorithm proposed by Kolmogorov and Uspensky [9]and described in a way more convenient for our purposes in [10] .The very interesting, characteristic feature of this concept is that the loop structure of programs for it, is as simple as possible and approximately coincides with the structure resulting from informal treating of the corresponding algorithm. Of course, this concept of algorithm uses "powerful" instructions. But this does not seem very essential when constructing algorithms of synthesis. The fact is that all the previous algorithms (in the case of bounded depth of loop structure) never use the semantics of instructions considered. Therefore all these results remain valid when instructions of any kind are considered instead of those of Post machines.

Hence these results can be carried over to any class of program schemes.

In conclusion let us observe that at least for data processing where the programmer often works in a close contact with the "customer" who is able only to explain the desired algorithm on particular examples, the construction of the above mentioned synthesizer seems to deserve attention.

The author wishes to thank his colleagues A.Kalnins and J.Bischevskis for their participation in preparing this report.

REFERENCES

[1] M. Gold, Limiting Recursion, J. Symb. Logic, 30, 28-48.

[2] J.M. Barzdin, Prognostication of Automata and Functions, IFIP Congress 71, TA-2, Ljubljana, 1971, 180-184.

[3] Я.М.Барздинь, Сложность и частотное решение некоторых алгоритмически неразрешимых массовых проблем, Докторская диссертация, 1971.

[4] Я.М.Барздинь, Р.В.Фрейвалд, О прогнозировании общерекурсивных функций, ДАН СССР, 206, № 3, 1972.

[5] A.P. Ershov, Theory of Program Schemata, IFIP Congress 71, 1, Ljubljana, 1971, 144-163.

[6] M. Gold, Language Identification in the Limit, Informat. and Control, 10, 1967, 447-474.

[7] J. Feldman, Some Decidability Results on Gramatical Inference and Complexity, Informat. and Control, 20, 224-262.

[8] Б.А.Трахтенброт, Я.М.Барздинь, Конечные автоматы (поведение и синтез), "Наука", М., 1970.

[9] А.Н.Колмогоров, В.А.Успенский, К определению алгоритма, УМН, 13, № 4, 1958, 3-28.

[10] Я.М.Барздинь, Я.Я.Калниньш, К общей концепции алгоритма и автомата, Теория языков и методы построения систем программирования, Труды симпозиума, Киев-Алушта, 1972, 43-47.

CENTRAL TECHNICAL ISSUES IN PROGRAMMING LANGUAGE DESIGN

J. Schwartz

New York University

The comments which follow grow out of work concerning languages of very high level (maximum expressivity) which we have been conducting for the last two years at New York University. We have been studying such a language, called SETL, which has sets as its fundamental data type, and which draws for its notations and fundamental semantic concepts on mathematical set theory. The specific language with which we have been working is a full-fledged "user language". That is, we assign it a specific, and fairly elaborate, syntax, and intend it for direct use rather than as a base requiring a good deal of extension before use. Here we may usefully distinguish between "host" and "user" languages. A *host language* is a language providing a full set of semantic facilities, but with a syntax deliberately kept simple. Such languages are intended not for direct use, but rather as a basis and target for language extension. By keeping their syntax simple and modular, one confines the mass of irregularities which an attempted extension must digest. In designing a *user language*, one incorporates a fairly elaborate collection of syntactic facilities, hoping that these will be directly useful in a wide range of applications. SETL as currently specified is a user language; in the present note, however, we envisage the sort of host language which could underlie it, attempting thereby to clarify various basic semantic issues arising in programming language design.

At the most basic level, a procedural programming language merely provides a framework which allows the storage and retrieval of some family of data objects and the sequenced application to these objects of some sufficiently general set of primitive operations. Concerning this, the following remarks can be made.

i. The semantic framework of a language should allow an arbitrary combination of primitives to be disguised as a primitive and to be invoked in the same way as a primitive. This is the essential point of the system of 'calling conventions' which is always part of the semantic core of a programming language. One will wish not only to provide subroutines capable of manipulating and modifying their arguments, but also to provide from the start for the recursive use of subroutines, as recursion is a technique of established power related directly to a language's basic inter-routine linkage conventions.

ii. Computer hardware characteristically look at computations through a 'peephole'. In each cycle of its action hardware can manipulate only those several hundred bits which are contained in some limited set of active registers. Moreover, internal limitations on available data-flow paths will slightly (though not strongly) constrain the transformations possible on a single cycle. To the extent that its primitives directly reflect hardware constraints, a programming language is of low level; to the extent that it provides compound data objects upon which highly 'global' primitives act, a language is of high level.

iii. If compound data objects are to be freely usable in a programming language, and if processes creating such objects are to be usable in the same way as hardware primitives would be, then at the implementation level the language must incorporate some automatically acting space allocation scheme. In this sense, we regard the type of 'garbage collector' first developed in connection with the LISP language as an invention fundamental for programming.

iv. The semantic extensibility of a language will depend to a large extent on the ease with which different abstract compound objects of varied structure can be represented in terms of the specific semantic objects which a language provides. SETL aims to gain advantage from the fact that the objects of most fields of mathematical discourse can be represented rather easily using sets and mappings.

v. The primitive operations most advantageously incorporated into a language are those which combine smoothly into broadly applicable families of transformations, especially if they use simple, heuristically comfortable actions which are nevertheless challenging to program. Some at least of the set-theoretic operations provided by SETL have these advantages; note in particular that efficient implementation of set theoretic operations will probably imply the use of hashing techniques, and that the heuristically innocent notion of set equality is implemented by a fairly complex recursive process.

vi. A programming language built upon a family of primitives can be optimized if enough information concerning the inputs and effect of each primitive is made available to a sufficiently powerful optimizer. Optimization will normally require extensive processing of program text, and one's attitude toward optimization will therefore have important impact on a language design. In general, a decision to optimize extensively will imply a relatively static approach to certain design issues; if optimization, especially global optimization, is abandoned, a considerably more dynamic, incremental language can be provided. This observation bears upon the question of whether some appropriate intermediate-text form of its own code is to be a data type available within a language. If this is done, then highly flexible forms of dynamic compilation become available. In this opposite case, compilation (with the optimization it implies) is a more serious step, and in the place of truly dynamic compilation a language system will probably provide a facility for input text editing plus total recompilation. Dynamic compilation is certainly more than a luxury; on the other hand reasonably flexible and quite useful systems can exist without it. Of course, it is possible to provide both modes of operation, one for the earliest stages of program development, the other to allow more substantial runs of more fully developed programs.

vii. An optimizer will normally require substantial information concerning all the primitives which it can encounter. This information will be used in complex ways during the analyses which constitute the optimization process. For this reason, it will not be easy to allow extension of the semantic primitives of a language which is to be elaborately optimized. On the other hand, extensibility of the primitives of a high level language is quite desirable, as this will allow levels of efficiency to be reached which can probably not be attained in any other way. Note, for example, that SETL provides no SNOBOL-like string-to-pattern matching primitive, a primitive which would be highly desirable if SETL or an extension of it were to be used for extensive string-processing. Similarly, it might be highly desirable to provide, let us say, a set of matrix manipulation primitives in an extension of SETL which was to be used to support large scientific calculations. To keep open the possibility of adding such primitives is certainly not a goal which it is easy to accommodate if, as in SETL, careful optimization is to be undertaken. Nevertheless, it may be hoped that careful organization of an optimizer will lend a rational structure to the information concerning primitives which an optimizer must use. To the extent that the hope is borne out, it may be possible to allow new primitives to be installed within an optimized high level language. This will of course require that certain interface conventions be observed carefully, and that information of significance to the optimizer be supplied in prescribed form whenever a new primitive is established.

viii. The use of high level dictions should, at least to a certain extent, make a language more optimizable. It is probably easier to supply an optimizer with information concerning important special cases of high level operations than to enable it to detect 'gestalts' once these have been expanded into detailed code sequences. Appropriate combination of high level procedural code with declaratory hints to an optimizer may very possibly make possible the production of rather efficient object code from concise and straightforward source text. For this to succeed however, we will have to learn to express essential aspects of a programmer's overall optimization strategy in a suitably devised formal declaratory style.

ix. A facility for the description and control of processes proceeding in parallel is vital for languages intended for certain important areas of application. Such a facility can be provided either in a broad form suitable for use in connection with true multiprocessor-multitasking environments, or in a narrower form sufficient to allow response to semi-autonomous external activities generating 'input data files', 'clock signals', and 'interrupts'. At least the latter facility is necessary for a language which is to be used to describe operating systems. While SETL does not now include any features of the type just described, it is certainly interesting to attempt to extend SETL to provide such features. Errors and error recovery, as well as memory hierarchy management, raise additional significant operating-system related programming issues with which a language intended for the comprehensive description of such systems must come to grips.

x. The provision of a structure which can supply good run-time diagnostics is an issue which ought to be faced during the basic semantic design of a language. Diagnostics of this sort will be issued when the routines interpreting the primitives of a language detect malformed arguments or other illegal circumstances. In such cases, 'traceback' data allowing the situation surrounding an error to be described in user-interpretable terms must be available. One will wish to be able to report on

a) the chain of subroutine calls made up to the error event;

b) the source-code statement, and the particular operation in it being executed at the time of the error event;

c) the values of all variables immediately prior to the error event, and the identity of those variables discovered to be illegal in format.

The importance of providing all this information in an 'external' form typing it to the source text with which a user is directly concerned, rather than in a difficult-to-interpret internal form, deserves to be stressed. Note that many of the necessary 'external-to-internal' connections (such as the association of external names with variables) can be set up at compile time by an adequately conceived translator. Nevertheless, the diagnostic 'hooks and eyes' needed at the basic execution level deserve careful design.

The issues discussed above are strongly semantic in flavor, in that they arise during the design of the base-level interpreter routines and target-code conventions which directly allow the operations of a language to be carried out. Beyond these issues arise others, still fundamental, but of a more nearly syntactic character.

We may regard these latter issues as belonging to the design of those processes which take one from some internal parse-tree form of a host language to the target code which is directly interpreted. Here, the following main points may be noted.

i. In designing a full host language system, one will have to decide whether the system is to include a fairly complete 'front end', or whether only host language mechanisms will be provided. If the former path is taken, one will strive to invent 'syntac extension' tools allowing the external form of a language to be varied within wide limits. If only host language mechanisms are provided within the core system, one will intend to allow any one of a wide variety of parsers to be used to define external language syntax. The first course can provide quite a range of users with languages reasonably well tailored to their requirements, which can be made available without any very great effort on their part. Several arguments can be given in favor of the latter course. Parsing is the best understood, the most manageable of all the elements of a language system. Diagnostic generation is an important part of parsing, and a specially designed parser can generally give much more adequate diagnostics than are available via a less flexible syntax extension scheme. In particular, the use of a syntax extension scheme may make it difficult to avoid the generation of diagnostics at the host language level, which however may involve the user in dictions and circumstances that he would prefer to know nothing of. A pre-defined syntax extension scheme may not readily allow the use of source text forms requiring elaborate, unexpected pretransformations, as for example, forms in which initially segregated fragments of code must be merged to produce required host language forms. Especially if this merging involves elaborate consistency checks, or is guided by specialized declarations peculiar to a given user language, attempts to use a pre-defined extension scheme may lead to difficulties.

ii. Even a host language will generally provide more than the minimally necessary operation, argument, and transfer patterns required to sustain interpretation (a language providing only this much would in effect be an assembly language for an abstract machine). Indeed, since some basic elements of syntactic 'icing' are so easily provided, and so apt to be useful in connection with almost any ultimate external syntax, one will generally wish to provide at least this much syntax as part of a host language. The list of features which one will probably prefer to include is fairly short. Expressions with embedded function calls are a syntactic form used in almost every programming language. They derive their special utility from the fact that the output of one operation is quite likely to be an input to the very next operation performed; when this is true, use of expression syntax allows one to elide the 'temporary variable' names which would otherwise have to be used, yielding condensed dictional forms. The 'on-the-fly' assignment (within an expression) pioneered by APL can be regarded as generalizing this advantage; it exploits the fact that one will often use the value of a subexpression twice in rapid succession, often within the confines of a single compound expression. Certain dictions related to the control of program flow have equally general appeal, and deserve equally to be provided even by a host language. The *if...then...* form popularized by ALGOL exploits the fact that binary tree-like branching is the commonest form of 'forward' conditional transfer. By providing this diction at the host language level, one eliminates the need to generate many of the explicit transfer labels which would otherwise be necessary. The commonest form of control structure involving backward branching is the 'while' loop, which is another form which it is desirable to include even in a host language. One will wish a collection of statements to be usable in any position in which a single statement can be used; for this reason, it is desirable for a host language to include some statement grouping scheme. Finally, one will wish to be able to use any code passage returning some single data object as part of an expression; a facility allowing this is also appropriate for a host language.

iii. Name protection, embodied in a suitably powerful and general namescoping scheme, will appropriately be included in the host language level of an overall language system. We regard a namescoping system as a set of conventions which assign a unique 'resolved name' or 'semantic item' x to each 'source name' y appearing in a mass of text. The particular x to be assigned to each occurrence of y depends on the location of x within what will ordinarily be a nested, tree-like family of *scopes*.

The purpose of a namescoping system is of course to balance the conflicting pressures toward globality and protection of names. Unrestrictedly global use of names is unacceptable, since it creates a situation of 'name crowding' in which names once used become, in effect, reserved words for other program sections. Hard-to-diagnose 'name overlap' bugs will abound in such situations.

'Globalization' of any subcategory of names can recreate this problem; for example, in large families of subroutines it may become difficult to avoid conflicts between subroutine names. In sufficiently large program packages, it will be desirable to give even major scope names a degree of protection.

On the other hand, a system in which names tend very strongly to be local unless explicitly declared global can tend to force one to incorporate large amounts of repetitive declaratory boilerplate into almost every protected bottom-level namescope or subroutine. Particularly in a language like SETL, which aims at the compressed and natural statement of algorithms, this burden would be irritating.

What one therefore requires is a system capable of dividing a potentially very large collection of programs into a rationally organized system of 'sublibraries', between which coherent cross-referencing is possible in a manner not requiring clumsy or elaborate locutions.

The design of such a system is by no means trivial, especially since the problems which namescoping addresses emerge full-blown only in the development of very large systems of programs. Note also that a name-scoping scheme to be used in connection with an extensible host language ought to be general enough to support a variety of user-level name-scoping conventions. The stereotyped subsidiary text necessary to be such a variety of surface effects will of course be supplied by the specialized 'front ends' defining the different user languages supported by a given host language. However, before any of these issues can be faced with confidence, more experience is required.

Having said what we can concerning the basic semantic and semi-semantic issues arising in language design, we now turn to a discussion of some important syntactic issues. Any language syntax will 'fill' a given space of syntactic possibilities to a given level of completeness. Of course, one will never wish to assign a meaning to every possible string of tokens; to do so would completely destroy all possibility of detecting error during translation. On the other hand, it can be advantageous to allow a language to fill the syntactic space available to it rather completely; say, for purposes of discussion, to the 50% level. This will tend to make many very compact dictions available; a possibility especially attractive if an interactive keyboard language is being designed. To attain this level of syntactic packing, one will assign meanings to operator-operand combinations not ordinarily used, and reduce the number and length of keywords appearing in a language. In particular, monadic significance will be assigned to ordinarily dyadic operators, a semantic interpretation will be assigned to sequences of variable names following in succession with no intervening operators, and elision of keywords will be allowed wherever possible. A precedence structure favoring the use of infix operators over parentheses may also be found desirable. All this leads to a very compact language, in which helpful syntactic diagnostics can nevertheless be generated. Syntactic packing to the degree indicated may on the other hand lead to source text forms which, lacking helpful redundancy, become somewhat difficult to read. For this reason, one may prefer in designing a language intended for extensive use in cooperative programming efforts to make use of a higher degree of redundancy. In such case, the syntactic structure chosen ought to promote good programming habits, allowing and even inducing its user to group passages of text in a manner which makes clear the logic of the process which this text describes. Moreover, as a return for the redundant modes of expression imposed upon him, the user can gain the use of a subtler and more complete set of compile-time consistency checks.

It is desirable to include a fairly powerful macropreprocessor in the front end of a language system. This will allow the particular syntax provided by language to be 'perturbed' in ways a user is bound to find convenient. In particular, local abbreviations can be introduced, minor special dictions set up, etc. Macros with parameters, nested and conditional macro-calls, macro iteration, and a certain amount of compile time calculation power are all desirable. More elaborate built-in string transformation schemes, which involve the parsing of an input string into a tree form which is then transformed into an output string, can be used to give a higher degree of syntactic variability to a language.

Of course, the more far-reaching a transformational scheme of this sort, the more delicate is its correct use apt to become.

In the ordinary course of a syntactic design, the most desirable syntactic constructions will be used at once; if they are not reusable, less than optimal dictional forms will have to be employed subsequently. Note, for example, that depending on context one might want a*b to denote the product of numbers, the dot-product of vectors, the product of matrices or of group elements, the intersection or cartesian product of sets, as well as any one of a great number of vaguely 'product like' constructions occurring in other application areas. We see the solution of the dilemma implicit here as lying in the use of a mechanism important in natural language usage. Namely, the interpretation of syntax must depend on context; specifically, the manner in which an operator applies to an object (or collection of objects) should depend on the object's nature. Thus, we find it desirable for a linguistic system to incorporate a formal mechanism allowing the definition of indefinitely many different 'object kinds', which can be used to control the manner in which statements of a fixed external appearance are interpreted. Such an approach has in fact been tried in a number of languages, sometimes on a dynamic (run-time) basis, sometimes on a static (compile-time) basis, occasionally in a manner having both dynamic and static features. In a later section, a static system of object kinds will be proposed for SETL. A static rather than a more flexible dynamic approach may well be adequate, and does not imply any loss of efficiency. The system proposed will probably also be useful in debugging.

SUR QUELQUES SYSTEMES DE PROGRAMMATION POUR LES RECHERCHES SCIENTIFIQUES

A.A. Liapounov

Novosibirsk

Le problème posé est d'élaborer des systèmes spéciaux de programmation (et ultérieurement, peut être, des ordinateurs spéci - lisés) pour les collectifs où les ordinateurs doivent exécuter des tâches très importantes.

Exemples:

1. Centre de calcul pour le problème "L'homme et la biosphère" dont le but est de simuler, en modèles hiérarchiques, des systèmes biologiques complèxes (tels que associations biologiques 'océan et de grands lacs, biogéocénoses, populations, fonction du systèmes endocrinien etc.).

2. Centre de calcul pour la traduction mécanique.

3. Centre de calcul qui doit réaliser la synthèse des doctrines linéenne et darwinienne pour la taxonométrie biologique

Actuellement les systèmes de programmation spécialisés représentent nécessairement une partie importante dans les recherches scientifiques de toutes directions.

On est très souvent obligé de créer des ensembles de modèles mathématiques, par exemple, pour étudier des procéssus d'inter - action de biohydrocénoses d'un grand lac. Notamment il faut pour cela effectuer les travaux suivants:

1. Établir les types essentiels de biohydrocénoses (relativement homogènes et autonomes) pour le lac en question. On distingue des biohydrocénoses abyssaux, latéraux et pélagiques.

2. Décrire des structures de ces biohydrocénoses et les procéssus biogéochimiques et biologiques qui s'y découlent.

3. Déterminer la distribution des biohydrocénoses du lac, le cartographier convenablement pour de différentes saisons et, peut être, pour de différentes années.

4. Construire les modèles mathématiques du bilan matériel pour les biohydrocénoses élémentaires.

5. Décrire le système hiérarchique de biohydrocénoses voisins et des procéssus d'échange à partir des associations élémentaires jusqu'au lac tout entier. On doit tenir compte des courants d'eaux, de la perturbation des associations différentes et, peut être, des diversités saisonnières et annuelles.

Cette hiérarchie de simulation présente plusieurs niveaux différents. D'autre part, beaucoup de modèles possèdent des éléments semblables. Dans le cas où une équipe de chercheurs étudie durant quelque temps le lac en question, on est obligé de créer beaucoup de divers modèles, qui décrivent les variations des procéssus étudiés. Il convient alors d'avoir un système spécialisé de programmation pour construire de tels modèles.

Nous considérons, plus en détails, comment est-ce qu'on doit réaliser le système de programmation pour la simulation des procéssus vitaux qui se découlent dans un lac. On doit partir d'un certain langage de programmation. Outre cela, on a besoin d'un système de procédures différentes, organisées d'une façon hiérarchique, et des procédures standartisées, pour décrire les actes élémentaires qui se découlent dans ce biohydrocénose: la multiplication des êtres vivants, la dévoration d'une forme par d'autre, l'affaissement des cadavres, etc.. On doit aussi avoir des procédures pour décrire les rapports mutuels de biohydrocénoses voisins, ainsi que des procédures décrivant les mouvements des aquatiques dans les courants d'eaux. Certaines de ces procédures doivent être décrites au moyen des programmes de dimensions considérables qui contiennent à leur tour d'autres procédures du même système. La procédure supérieure doit contenir des sous-programmes spéciaux pour effectuer, d'une façon automatique, l'ajustage préliminaire des procédures inférieures, intercalées dans celles supérieures. Il faut savoir s'adresser aux systèmes de procédures considérées au moyen du langage de programmation choisi. Ce langage doit être capable d'utiliser des objets de caractère différent, par exemple, des échelles pour les variables logiques qui désignent la présence ou l'absence de telle ou telle circonstance dans telle ou telle situation. Il faut avoir des moyens spéciaux de la codification des objets utilisés pour pouvoir décrire facilement la structure de biohydrocénoses. Par exemple, une unité géogrphique complèxe doit être parfois composée d'unités géographiques subordonnées. Puis au moyen d'un arbre logique, on doit expliquer comment l'unité initiale est formée de ces sous-unités. La codification de cet arbre est utilisée dans les calculs. Quand il s'agit de la programmation on doit surtout porter attention sur la simplification du procéssus de programmation lui-même, pour la plupart des problèmes qui se présentent dans la programmation. Dans la majorité de ces cas on peut ne pas faire attention aux volumes de la mémoire utilisée ni à la durée du travail de l'ordinateur. Il est beaucoup plus important de pouvoir varier les modèles utilisés, c'est-à-dire, les programmes qui les réalisent d'une façon économe, et de les effectuer en peu de temps. Il s'agit d'une transformation du programme, telle que la variation des données initiales, des valeurs des coefficients et de la structure logique du système à simuler. Les calcules expérimentaux vont parfois prendre plus de temps que les calculs définitifs. Ce qui est important, c'est la possibilité de comparer les résultats de recherches empiriques à ceux fondés sur les considérations théoriques, prédire le sort du biohydrocénose ainsi que les résultats de l'intervention de l'homme dans la vie du biohydrocénose, au moins, pour un temps limité. Ce sont des études de premier ordre d'importance. Elles évoquent des discussions acharnées à partir de l'O.N.U. jusqu'aux révues quotidiennes. Un service de simulation mathématique étant organisé, on pourrait remplacer les tournois verbaux par es calculs bien fondés.

Je veux noter que les problèmes considérés sont très importants de point de vue de la programmation théorique. En effet, on est obligé de réaliser des synthèses des modèles de biohydrocénoses de niveau inférieur qui doivent, à leur tour, être synthésés par l'ordinateur d'une façon automatique. Tout cela doit etre effectué en utilisant une information très laconique.

Le problème d'élaboration d'un système de programmation pour la traduction mécanique se pose de façons différentes. Pendant la mise à point de l'algorithme on est obligé de changer constamment le programme. Les règles de l'algorithme se transforment différemment tandis que la structure totale de cet algorithme reste intacte. On se sert d'habitude des règles de quelques types définis.

Chaque algorithme individuel doit correspondre non seulement à deux langages bien définis, mais aussi à un domaine déterminé des connaissances humaines, car la description des ces domaines différents se fait avec de divers souslangages composant un seul langage bien déterminé. Il s'agit tout d'abord de la diversité structurale d'un texte en question. Puis l'homonymie des paroles différentes dépend du domaine scientifique auquel le texte se rattache. Ces deux circonstances peuvent servir à une simplification considérable de l'algorithme supposant que ce dernier doit être appliqué seulement aux textes appartenant à un souslangage bien déterminé d'avance.

L'algorithme étant donné, on est obligé à lui approprier un de deux régimes: celui de la mise à point et celui de la traduction pratique. Pour le premier régime il est surtout important de simplifier le procéssus de programmation. Pendant la mise à point on n'accourt à chaque variante du programme que pour la traduction d'un petit nombre de phrases. Il est favorable pour cela d'utiliser un régime d'interprétation. Au contraire, quand il s'agit de la traduction pratique l'algorithme peut être utilisé mainte fois. Il est important alors de limiter le temps de travail de l'ordinateur, donc il est favorable de se servir d'un régime de compilation. En somme, il est convenable de créer des systèmes mixtes d'interprétation et de compilation. On doit s'assurer seulement, étant donné un algorithme ajusté en régime d'interprétation, qu'on puisse l'utiliser sans ajustage spécial dans le régime de compilation. Il paraît qu'il est favorable dans ce cas de se servir d'un système de programmation composé d'un langage et d'un ensemble hiérarchique de procédures. Ce système de programmation doit satisfaire à quelques conditions spécifiques. Pour qu'il soit efficace il faut économiser le temps de travail de l'ordinateur et le volume de mémoire utilisée dans le régime de compilation. Cela permettrait d'introduire dans la mémoire de l'ordinateur des morceaux considérables du texte, ce qui est important pour réduire les appels à la mémoire extérieure et, par suite, le temps du travail. Outre cela l'ordinateur va permettre l'utilisation des algorithmes qui font appel aux liens distancés intertextuels. Le langage de programmation, faisant partie de ce système, doit être capable d'utiliser les moyens typiques de la traduction mécanique, tels que l'information grammaticale sur les mots et les structures des phrases.

Des systèmes opérationnels de programmation pour la traduction mécanique ont été créés par M-lles Koulaguina et Korovina. M-lle Korovina a préparé un système hiérarchique de procédures qui permettent de reprogrammer facilement les algorithmes expérimentaux. M-lle Korovina, toute seule, a programmé pendant un hiver plus de 25 variantes d'algorithmes expérimentaux, chaque programme possédant quelques mille de commandes. Et elle a parveuu à faire des expériences avec chacun de ces programmes. Ce travail s'est rendu possible parce que la création de chaque programme du système en question était relativement simple. Malheureusement les résultats des traductions effectuées au moyen d'une classe d'algo - rithmes trop primitifs n'étaient pas satisfaisants.

Un langage type ALGOL, mais adapté au travail avec des objets typiques pour la traduction mécanique a été créé par M.M. D.Y. Levin et G. I.Nekrasov. Il se peut que la synthèse des travaux cités peut servir de base pour un nouveux système de programmation spécialisé.

Je ne veux pas décrire les conditions nécessaires pour le système de programmation servant aux expériences des jeux avec les ordinateurs. Ce système peut inclure des jeux tels que jeux de dames, domino, diverses variantes de croix et de zéro. Les échecs sont trop compliqués pour être inclus dans ce système . Il est possible d'y inclure encore quelques jeux de carte, relativement simples, mais les jeux intellectuels (bridge ou whist) sont trop compliqués de ce point de vue.

Considérons maintenant un système de programmation approprié à un système d'information pour la taxonométrie biologique.

La taxonométrie en biologié poursuit deux buts différents: d'un coté, on cherche à classer les êtres vivants d'après le principe dit "ressemblance-différence" prenant on considération les formes contemporaines, ainsi que les fossiles; d'autre coté, on se force à mettre en lumière la généalogie des diverses formes et à réunir les formes de même origine, c'est-à-dire, construire l'arbre phylogénétique des êtres vivants. Il est naturel d'appeler ces deux principes linnéen et darwinien. Un problème important consiste à réunir ces deux principes pour créer une classification des êtres vivants qui serait simultanément linnéenne et darwinienne. Il paraît qu'il est possible d'établir une base théorique d'une telle classification. Mais sa réalisation paraît être pénible, je crois qu'elle n'est possible que sur la base d'ordinateur et d'un système de programmation très spécial. Tout cela est réalisable seulement dans le cadre d'un centre de calcul spécial. Il faut prendre comme base d'un système simultanément linnéen et darwinien les traits caractéristiques de la nature vivante. A savoir: les êtres vivants sont munis d'un système hiérarchique de système gouvernant leurs fonctions vitales différentes. En ce qui se rattache à ce système gouvernant on peut formuler le principe suivant. Les niveaux supérieurs de l'hiérarchie sont essentiellement plus stables dans le procéssus d'évolution que les niveaux supérieurs. En effet, une mutation qui transforme considérablement la structure d'un des niveaux supérieurs aura comme conséquence un grand nombre de changements très différents dans les niveaux inférieurs qui sont subordonnés au niveau supérieur en question. Etant donné que l'organisme est un produit d'une longue évolution, il est clair qu'il est bien adapté au milieu de son existance, c'est-à-dire qu'une variation considérable d'un grand nombre de ses structures locales doit amener à un désaccord entre le fonctionnement de cet organisme et le milieu de son existance. Donc, il doit périr. D'ici on peut déterminer comme critère de parenté de deux organismes le niveau le plus bas jusqu'auquel leurs systèmes de régulation restent semblables. On doit prendre en considération tous les niveaux à partir du niveau supérieur. Il est entendu que l'application de ces principes se heurtera en réalité à des difficultés dues à la nécessité d'avoir une information précise sur la structure et le fonctionnement des procéssus vitaux dans un organisme. Pour tourner ces difficultés il faudra établir des enquêtes spéciales qui se rattachent aux particularités des organismes vivants différents. Les données de ces enquêtes doivent être traitées par un ordinateur dans un régime automatique. En se basant sur les résultats obtenus des enquêtes on a à construire une hiérarchie de propriétés caractérisant ces êtres vivants. En se servant des ressemblances ou bien des divergences de ces propriétés on doit établir l'appartenance de telles ou telles formes à un rang taxonomique. Il est à noter que l'hiérarchie des propriétés en question doit correspondre à l'hiérarchie des systèmes gouvernants qui sont responsables de ces propriétés. On doit construire de cette façon logique la base d'information de la taxonométrie biologique. Ce système doit être approprié à plusieurs types d'utilisation : 1) Un naturaliste qui veut établir la situation de quelque organisme dans le système proposé doit remplir une enquête qui décrit les propriétés de cet organisme et l'introduire dans l'ordinateur avec une demande corresponadante. L'ordinateur répond si la forme décrite se trouve dans ce catalogue et puis, suivant la demande faite, peut communiquer quelle information sur cette forme il possède. Il peut annoncer, par exemple, son aréal d'habitation, des renseignements sur sa biologie, sa bibliographie etc. Si les êtres considérés ne sont pas dans le catalogue de l'ordinateur, ce dernier peut dire quelle forme plus ou moins semblable s'y trouve et à quel niveau taxonomique elles appartiennent. Dans le dernier cas l'ordinateur introduit la description des êtres considérés dans une mémoire spéciale. 2) Supposons que l'ordinateur possède un grand nombre de descriptions des formes non classées. Dans ce cas l'ordinateur introduit dans la mémoire spéciale des descriptions des êtres considérés. Il doit aussi assurer la reconstruction, d'une façon automatique, de la classification* prenant

* Au cours du Symposium le Professeur Dénnis a attiré mon attention au fait qu'il ne faut pas détruire le système vielli en construisant un nouveau système. L'organisation du nouveau système doit assurer la conservation du système ancien et la création d'un système de correction pour le système ancien. On doit être en état d'utiliser, à volonté, le système ancien et le nouveau. Cela parait être utile parce qu'il y aura toujours beaucoup de publications fondées sur le système ancien. On doit pouvoir utiliser le système d'information de l'ordinateur pour les données qui se rattachent à tous les deux systèmes.

en considération les nouvelles formes. Quand, après une telle reconstruction, on s'adresse à l'ordinateur pour classer une forme quelconque, l'ordinateur doit se référer à la classification dont il se sert.

Considérons maintenant quelques systèmes de programmation caractéristiques qu'on pourrait utiliser pour la solution des problèmes considérés. Il paraît qu'il est nécessaire d'avoir la synthèse mixte de la forme d'un langage et d'un système de procédures spéciales qui doivent être capables de travailler avec des classes d'objets qui se présentent dans le problème considéré. Le système de procédures c'est un système de microprogrammes ainsi que des stockages de sousprogrammes pouvant être regrouppés, d'une façon formelle, en programmes. Il est important que l'utilisation de ces sousprogrammes soit suffisamment simple, même dans le cas où la formation des programmes s'effectue au moyen d'une série d'opérations de différents degrés. Le langage de programmation doit être bien approprié à créer des algorithmes autonomes ainsi qu'à s'adresser aux systèmes de procédures. Pour commencer on peut utiliser le langage type ALGOL, peut être, un peu simplifié. J'ai l'impression que dans le futur le langage proposé par le Professeur Schwarz sera bien adopté au problème en question.

Dans chaque cas spécial il faut construire ce système de programmation d'une façon qui soit suffisamment souple pour être appliqué à la programmation des tâches qui sont les plus communes dans le collectif considéré.

Decision Problems in Computational Models *)

by Michael S. Paterson

Abstract

Some of the assertions about programs which we might be interested in proving are concerned with correctness, equivalence, accessibility of subroutines and guarantees of termination. We should like to develop techniques for determining such properties efficiently and intelligently wherever possible. Though theory tells us that for a realistic programming language almost any interesting property of the behaviour is effectively undecidable, this situation may not be intolerable in practice. An unsolvability result just gives us warning that we may not be able to solve all of the problems we are presented with, and that some of the ones we can solve will be very hard.

In such circumstances it is very reasonable to try and determine necessary or sufficient conditions on programs for our techniques to be assured of success; however, in this paper we shall discuss a more qualitative, indirect, approach. We consider a range of more or less simplified computer models, chosen judiciously to exemplify some particular feature or features of computation. A demonstration of unsolvability in such a model reveals more accurately those sources which can contribute to unsolvability in a more complicated structure. On the other hand a decision procedure may illustrate a technique of practical use. It is our thesis that this kind of strategy of exploration can and will yield insight and practical advances in the theory of computation. Provided that the model retains some practical relevance, the dividends are the greater the nearer the decision problem lies to the frontier between solvability and unsolvability.

---

*) The paper was published in "Proceedings of ACM Symposium on Proving Assertions About Programs", Las Cruces, New Mexico, Jan. 6-7, pp. 74-82, 1972

NON-DETERMINED ALGORITHM SCHEMATA OR R-SCHEMATA

R.I. Podlovchenko (Yerevan)

The starting point of this work is the analysis of results obtained by Yu. I.Yanov in his studies of algorithm schemata [1]. This analysis has been considerably facilitated by the publication of A.P.Ershov [2]. We shall use nomenclature suggested in [2] and the algorithm schema defined by Yu.I.Yanov shall be called Yanov's schema.

Our initial objectives were as follows:

a. Providing interpretation of equivalency relation and partial equivalency relation of Yanov's schemata.

b. Studying reducibility of one of these relations to the other.

c. Constructing a complete system of transformations retaining partial equivalence of Yanov's schemata.

Consideration of these problems resulted in the concept of non-determined algorithm schema or, shortly, R-schema. R-schema is a generalization of Yanov's schemata performed in several directions simultaneously. Let us consider one of them.

It is known that construction of Yanov's schemata is preceded by fixing two finite sets

$$A = \{\mathcal{A}_1, \mathcal{A}_2, \ldots, \mathcal{A}_n\},$$

$$P = \{p_1, p_2, \ldots, p_k\};$$

elements of the first one are called operators, elements of the second one are called logical variables; each variable assumes two values: 0 or 1. Yanov's schema is a pair consisting of a controlling graph and shift relation. The controlling graph is constructed upon two sets: set A of operators and set $U = \{\alpha(p_1,p_2,\ldots,p_k)\}$ consisting of all propositional functions of variables $p_1,p_2,\ldots,p_k$.

The vertices of the graph are operators and identifiers; each identifier is associated with its own function $\alpha \in U$; transitions in a graph are determined.

A shift relation is a correspondence such that each operator is associated with a set of variables from P; this set is called the operator shift. Let $P_{\mathcal{A}_1} \subseteq P$ be the operator shift $\mathcal{A}_1 \in A$; it is interpreted as follows: if $p \in P_{\mathcal{A}_1}$, then realization of operator $\mathcal{A}_1$ may result in variable p changing its value; if, however, $p \not\in P_{\mathcal{A}_1}$, then its value quite definitely shall not be changed.

The set of values of variables $p_1,p_2,\ldots,p_k$ (i.e. the vector on {0,1} of length k) is called an ordered sequence, a multitude of possible sets being designated by X = {x}.

Let us suppose that the set of values assumed by variables from P and functions from U is an arbitrary finite set (which only in a particular case consists of two elements). To avoid considering different cases we suggest the following:

1. Set X is to be considered as an independently given finite set of objects (without connecting with set P);

2. One of the basic elements of the controlling graph, vis.: identifier R with corresponding functions $\alpha_R \in U$ is to be substituted by filters with sets of elements from X associated with them.

The difference between the identifier and filter is as follows: identifier R lets through any ordered sequence $x \in X$; this ordered sequence is going out of R along its marked directed edge if $\alpha_R(x) = 1$ and along an unmarked one in the opposite case; filter τ lets through only such ordered sequences $x \in X$ for which $x \in \alpha_\tau$; here α_τ is a set associated with the filter; all other ordered sequences are not allowed to pass through filter τ at all; the filtered ordered sequence is supplied to each directed edge going out of filter τ.

We shall now give strict definitions of the notions used here. Given the set $\bar{A} = \{\mathcal{A}_{-1}, \mathcal{A}_0, \mathcal{A}_1, \ldots, \mathcal{A}_n, \ldots\}$, whose elements shall be called <u>operators</u>, and also set

$$X = \{x_1, x_2, \ldots, x_m\}, \quad m \geq 1,$$

whose elements shall be called <u>information bits</u> or simply bits.

The name of <u>R-schema</u> shall be used for a triplet consisting of a controlling graph, shift relation and equivalency relation in a set of operators.

An equivalency relation in set A is introduced in such a way that each operator $\mathcal{A}_{-1}$ and $\mathcal{A}_0$ is equivalent only to itself; this equivalency relation shall be designated by ε.

<u>A controlling graph of R-schema</u> is constructed upon $\bar{A}$ and 2^X; it is a finite directed graph with two distinct vertices: input a vertex with an empty set of incoming directed edges and output a vertex with an empty set of outgoing edges; both vertices are marked with operator $\mathcal{A}_0$; each remaining vertex is associated with either an operator from $\bar{A}$ different from $\mathcal{A}_0$ and $\mathcal{A}_{-1}$ or a sub-set of set X, no two vertices being associated with one and the same operator. A vertex associated with an operator is identified with this operator; a vertex associated with set $\alpha \subseteq X$ is called a filter and designated by $\tau(\alpha)$, and set α is called content of filter $\tau(\alpha)$. A controlling graph of R-schema shall be designated by G and called simply graph of R-schema. Each operator $\mathcal{A}_i \in \bar{A}$ different from $\mathcal{A}_0$ and $\mathcal{A}_{-1}$ shall be associated with a certain representation $s_i : X \to 2^X$, called a shift of operator $\mathcal{A}_i$. The correspondence described shall be called a <u>shift relation</u> if each time the equivalency

of $\mathcal{A}_i$ and $\mathcal{A}_j$ with respect to relation ε results in equality $s_i=s_j$. A shift relation shall be designated by S.

For R-schema we shall use the designation $\mathfrak{A}=(G,S,\varepsilon)$.

If $\mathfrak{A}=(G,S,\varepsilon)$ and the relation ε is such that the class of equivalency of each operator of R-schema $\mathfrak{A}$ with respect to relation ε consists only of this operator, then $\mathfrak{A}$ shall be called R-schema <u>with no recurring operators</u>.

Given the equivalence relation ε in $\bar{A}$ and shift relation S. The equivalency class of operator $\mathcal{A}_i \in \bar{A}$ with respect to relation ε shall be designated by $\hat{\mathcal{A}}_i$. The finite sequence

$$x_{i_1}\hat{\mathcal{A}}_{j_1}\; x_{i_2}\hat{\mathcal{A}}_{j_2} \ldots x_{i_t}\hat{\mathcal{A}}_{j_t} \quad , \qquad (1)$$

where

$$x_{i_l} \in X, \quad \mathcal{A}_{j_l} \in \bar{A} ,$$

shall be called a <u>configuration</u> if the following conditions are fulfilled:

1. Symbols $\hat{\mathcal{A}}_o$ and $\hat{\mathcal{A}}_{-1}$ may enter (1) only at the last place;
2. For all $l=1,2,\ldots,t-1$

$$x_{i_{l+1}} \in s_{j_l} x_{i_l} \ .$$

Number t shall be called the configuration length (1).

Let us introduce the notion of successor function of a graph G.

Let $\mathcal{A}_{k_1}, \mathcal{A}_{k_2},\ldots,\mathcal{A}_{k_n}$ be all operators of a graph G. We shall say that in graph G.

1. Operator $\mathcal{A}_j (j=0,k_1,k_2,\ldots,k_n)$ is accessible from operator $\mathcal{A}_i (i=0,k_1,k_2,\ldots,k_n)$ for information bit $x \in X$, if in G there is a path beginning in vertex $\mathcal{A}_i$ and ending in vertex $\mathcal{A}_j$, and even if this path contains other vertices, those are only filters, x belonging to the contents of each of them;

2. Operator $\mathfrak{A}_{-1}$ is accessible from operator $\mathfrak{A}_i (i=0,k_1,k_2,\dots,k_n)$ for information bit x, if in G there is a path beginning in vertex $\mathfrak{A}_i$, passing only through filters, x belonging to the contents of each of them and if at least one of these filters occurs twice.

Let α_{i_j} designate the set of all information bits for which operator $\mathfrak{A}_j$ is accessible from operator $\mathfrak{A}_i$ in graph G. Set

$$\{\alpha_{i_j},\ i=0,k_1,k_2,\dots,k_n;\ j=-1,\ 0,k_1,k_2,\dots,k_n\}$$

shall be called the <u>successor function</u> of graph G.

Graph G (and also R-schema (G,S,ε)) shall be called <u>determined</u> if for all i's and all unequal j's and l's $\alpha_{i_j} \cap \alpha_{i_l} = \emptyset$, and <u>non-determined</u> in the opposite case.

The <u>route of graph</u> G is the finite sequence

$$\mathfrak{A}_{j_o} = \mathfrak{A}_o \; {}^{x_{i_1}}\mathfrak{A}_{j_1} \; {}^{x_{i_2}}\mathfrak{A}_{j_2} \dots \mathfrak{A}_{j_{t-1}} \; {}^{x_{i_t}}\mathfrak{A}_{j_t} \,, \qquad (2)$$

satisfying the condition: for all $l = 1,2,\dots,t$ $\; x_{i_l} \in \alpha_{j_{l-1}\,j_l}$;
the route (2) of graph G shall be called the <u>route of R-schema</u> (G,S,ε), if for all $l = 1,2,\dots,t-1$ $\; x_{i_{l+1}} \in s_{j_l} x_{i_l}$ (here s_{j_l} is the shift of operator $\mathfrak{A}_{j_l}$).

If (2) is the route of R-schema $\mathfrak{O}\mathfrak{l}$, then the corresponding sequence

$$^{x_{i_1}}\hat{\mathfrak{A}}_{j_1} \; {}^{x_{i_2}}\hat{\mathfrak{A}}_{j_2} \dots {}^{x_{i_t}}\hat{\mathfrak{A}}_{j_t} \,, \qquad (3)$$

as it is easy to check, is a configuration; we shall say that (3) is a <u>configuration generated by R-schema $\mathfrak{O}\mathfrak{l}$</u> or a configuration of R-schema .

A route (2) of R-schema $\mathfrak{O}\mathfrak{l}$ (as well as configuration (3)) shall be called <u>finite</u> if $\mathfrak{A}_{j_t} = \mathfrak{A}_o$. The set of all configurations generated by R-schema $\mathfrak{O}\mathfrak{l}$ shall be designated by $K(\mathfrak{O}\mathfrak{l})$; the set consisting of all finite configurations of R-schema $\mathfrak{O}\mathfrak{l}$ and of all their beginnings shall be designated by $K^*(\mathfrak{O}\mathfrak{l})$.

Let G_1 and G_2 be graphs of R-schemata $\mathfrak{A}_1$, and $\mathfrak{A}_2$. Graphs G_1 and G_2 (as well as R-schemata $\mathfrak{A}_1$ and $\mathfrak{A}_2$) shall be called <u>similar</u> if their through-put capacities coincide.

R-schemata $\mathfrak{A}_1$ and $\mathfrak{A}_2$ having common shift relation and equivalency relation in $\bar{A}$ shall be called <u>equivalent</u>, if $K(\mathfrak{A}_1) = K(\mathfrak{A}_2)$ and partially equivalent, if $K^*(\mathfrak{A}_1) = K^*(\mathfrak{A}_2)$.

It is evident that the similar graphs and only they have equal sets of routes, that similarity of R-schemata results in their equivalency and the equivalency of R-schemata results in their partial equivalency.

It should be noted that any of Yanov's schemata allows construction of R-schema generating the same set of configurations as the Yanov's schema. In fact, the set of A operators used in constructing Yanov's schema is a sub-set of set $\bar{A}$; set X should be considered as the set of all ordered sequences of values of variables $p_1, p_2, \ldots, p_\kappa$; the equivalency relation ε in set $\bar{A}$ should be chosen so that each operator from A be equivalent only to itself. Shift s_1 of operator $\mathcal{A}_1 \in \bar{A}$ is constructed according to shift $P_{\mathcal{A}_1} \subseteq P$ as follows: set $s_1 x$, $x \in X$, consists of ordered sequences every one of which differs from set x, may be, by the values of variables from $P_{\mathcal{A}_1}$; each operator $\mathcal{A}_j$ not belonging to A can be associated to an arbitrary shift s_j. The controlling graph of R-schema is obtained from the controlling graph of Yanov's schema through the following procedure: each identifier of Yanov's schema is split into two filters: one is ascribed the truth zone of the identifier logical function; the other one is ascribed the zone of its falsity; from the first filter the marked directed edges of identifier are brought out, from the second filter the non-marked (the appearance of several marked and non-marked directed edges of the identifier is caused by the fact that each time the splitting of identifier into filters is accompanied by the splitting of each incoming directed edge of this identifier). Fig. 1a shows Yanov's schema and Fig. 1b shows the corresponding R-schema.

Investigation of R-schemata produced the following results. For a set of R-schemata of an arbitrary kind:

c 1. It has been proved that the problem of equivalence of R-schemata can be solved algorithmically; an algorithm has been constructed identifying equivalency of R-schemata;

c 2. It has been proved that the problem of partial equivalency of R-schemata is reducible to the problem of equivalency of R-schemata; an algorithm has been constructed identifying partial equivalency of R-schemata.

For a set of R-schemata with no recurring operators:

d 1. The existence and uniqueness has been proved of 1) the canonical representation of R-schema which is equivalent to this R-schema; 2) canonical representation of R-schema which is partially equivalent to this R-schema;

d 2. A complete system of equivalent transformations of R-schemata and a complete system of partially equivalent transformations of R-schemata have been constructed;

d 3. It has been proved that the problem of complete reducibility of R-schemata is reducible to the problem of paired equivalency of R-schemata belonging to specially constructed sets of R-schemata.

For determined R-schemata the notions have been introduced of the interpreted R-schema and the relation of functional dependence of R-schemata. It has been proved that the relations of partial and functional equivalencies of R-schemata are coincidental.

The last statement yields the interpretation of equivalency and partial-equivalency relations of Yanov's schemata, i.e. the solution of problem a; statements c 2 and d 4 give the solution of problem b, and statement d 2 the solution of problem c.

Let us consider the ideas and methods used in obtaining these results.

c 1. The base of algorithm identifying equivalency of R-schemata $\mathfrak{A}_1$

and $\mathfrak{A}_2$ consists in

<u>Theorem 1.</u> For each of R-schemata $\mathfrak{A}_1$, and $\mathfrak{A}_2$ we can specify such a natural number t, that

$$K(\mathfrak{A}_1) = K(\mathfrak{A}_2) \rightleftarrows K_t(\mathfrak{A}_1) = K_t(\mathfrak{A}_2) ;$$

here $K_t(\mathfrak{A}_i)$ is a sub-set of set $K(\mathfrak{A}_i)$, which consists of all its configurations having lengths not exceeding $t (i=1,2)$.

As soon as we have established the number t mentioned in Theorem 1, the algorithm checking equality $K_t(\mathfrak{A}_1) = K_t(\mathfrak{A}_2)$ will also become an algorithm for identifying equivalency of R-schemata $\mathfrak{A}_1$ and $\mathfrak{A}_2$.

While proving Theorem 1, it is found that for the number t we can take any number

$$\mathcal{N}(\mathfrak{A}_1)\mathcal{N}(\mathfrak{A}_2)\mathcal{M}(\mathfrak{A}_1)\mathcal{M}(\mathfrak{A}_2)\rho(\mathfrak{S}) + 1,$$

where $\mathcal{N}(\mathfrak{A}_i)$ is the number of all operators of R-schema $\mathfrak{A}_i$; $\mathcal{M}(\mathfrak{A}_i)$ is the number $2^{q_i}-1$, where q_i is the maximum number of operators belonging to R-schema $\mathfrak{A}_i$ and included into the same equivalency class with respect to relation ε ; $\rho(\mathfrak{S})$ is the maximum of operator shift characteristics whose operators belong to at least one of R-schemata $\mathfrak{A}_1$ and $\mathfrak{A}_2$; shift characteristic $s : X \to 2^X$ is determined as the maximum of lengths of sequences

$$(x_{i_1}, x_{j_1}), (x_{i_2}, x_{j_2}), \ldots, (x_{i_\kappa}, x_{j_\kappa})$$

consisting of ordered pairs of information bits and having the property that:

for all $\nu = 1,2,\ldots,\kappa$

$$x_{j_\nu} \in s x_{i_\nu} \;\&\; x_{j_\nu} \notin \bigcup_{t=1}^{\nu-1} s x_{i_t} .$$

c 2. Reducibility of the problem of partial equivalence of R-schemata to the problem of equivalence of R-schemata is established by

<u>Theorem 2.</u> There exists an algorithm $\mathfrak{b}$, which for any R-schema $\mathfrak{A}$

constructs such an R-schema $\mathfrak{b}(\mathfrak{A})$, that

$$K(\mathfrak{b}(\mathfrak{A})) = K^{*}(\mathfrak{A}).$$

Algorithm $\mathfrak{b}$ includes sub-algorithms $\mathfrak{b}^{\mu}$ and $\mathfrak{b}^{n}$; algorithm $\mathfrak{b}^{\mu}$ constructs a matrix R-schema similar to an R-schema of an arbitrary type; algorithm $\mathfrak{b}^{n}$ transforms the matrix R-schema into a saturated one. Let us define the notions used here. R-schema is called a matrix schema if 1) from each operator of R-schema and from its input there are exactly $\mathcal{N}+2$ outgoing directed edges where N is the number of operators of R-schema; 2) each of these $(\mathcal{N}+2)\times(\mathcal{N}+1)$ directed edges is leading to its own filter and there are not two directed edges coming into the same filter; 3) R-schema contains no filters other than those mentioned; 4) among the filters connected with the same vertex by the incoming directed edge (filters of a given vertex) there is one with a loop; beside the loop this filter has no other outgoing directed edges; each of the remaining filters of the vertex has exactly one outgoing directed edge; this edge leads either to the operator or to the output, no two edges leading to the same vertex. The filter of a matrix R-schema connected with vertex $\mathcal{A}_i$ by the incoming edge and with vertex $\mathcal{A}_j$ by the outgoing edge shall be designated by $\tau_{i_j}(\alpha_{i_j})$. Fig. 2 shows the matrix R-schema containing two operators.

The matrix R-schema $\mathfrak{A}$ shall be called a saturated schema if for each of its filters $\tau_{i_j}(\alpha_{i_j})$ the following condition is valid: for any $x \in \alpha_{i_j}$, R-schema has a route containing the triplet $\mathcal{A}_i \; x \; \mathcal{A}_j$. The following theorem is true:

Theorem 3. There is an algorithm, that for any matrix R-schema $\mathfrak{A}$ constructs a saturated R-schema having the same set of routes as R-R-schema $\mathfrak{A}$.

Such an algorithm is $\mathfrak{b}^{H}$. To describe $\mathfrak{b}^{H}$, we shall have to consider the passage of information along the matrix R-schema $\mathfrak{A}$. Here the term information is used for an arbitrary sub-set of set X and the process of its passage along R-schema is determined as follows. At the moment of time t=1 each directed edge going out of the input of R-schema receives information X; each of the remaining directed edges of R-schema holds information ∅. At any subsequent moment of time (assumed to be discrete) the edges going out of the input hold information ∅, and the remaining edges hold the information determined by the rules of its passage along the edges and through the vertices of R-schema. These rules are as follows. Along the edge information is passing only in the direction of the edge itself and with no time consumed for passage. If filter $\tau(\alpha)$ at the moment of time t received information β, then at the same time t the directed edge going out of $\tau(\alpha)$ shall receive information $\alpha \cap \beta$. If operator $\mathcal{A}_1$ at the moment of time t receives totally information β through all edges coming into $\mathcal{A}_1$, then at the moment t + 1 each edge going out of $\mathcal{A}_1$ shall receive information $\bigcup_{x \subseteq \beta} s_1 x$. Information along R-schema is infinite.

Let $\delta^t_{i_j}$ be the information, that at the moment t appeared on the edge going out of filter $\tau_{i_j}(\alpha_{i_j})$;
matrix $D_t=\{\delta^t_{i_j}\}$, $i=0,k_1,k_2,\dots,k_n$; $j=-1,0,k_1,k_2,\dots,k_n$; fixes the value of information flow in R-schema at the moment t; the process of information passage along R-schema $\mathfrak{A}$ is described by the series $\{D_t, t=1,2,\dots\}$ called the <u>matrix series</u> of R-schema $\mathfrak{A}$. Connection of matrix series with the set of routes of R-schema $\mathfrak{A}$ is established by

<u>Lemma 1</u>. Given any matrix D_t and its element $\delta^t_{i_j}$, unit x belongs to $\delta^t_{i_j}$ if and only if R-schema $\mathfrak{A}$ has a route where triplet of elements $\mathcal{A}_i \overset{x}{} \mathcal{A}_j$ occupies t-th place. Lemma 1 is proved through induction on t. Properties of the matrix series of R-schema are described by

<u>Lemma 2</u>. The matrix series of R-schema is periodic with some preperiod.

A saturated R-schema having the same set of routes as R-schema $\mathfrak{A}$ is constructed according to the initial section of the matrix row; the length of this section does not exceed the sum of lengths of pre-period and period of the series. Construction of this section of matrix series having a proper length is the principal purpose of algorithm $\mathfrak{b}^{H}$.

We shall now return to algorithm $\mathfrak{b}$ discussed in Theorem 2; it consists in sequential performance of five procedures:

1. Constructing matrix R-schema $\mathfrak{b}^{H}(\mathfrak{A}) \equiv \mathfrak{A}_1$ for R-schema $\mathfrak{A}$;
2. Constructing saturated R-schema $\mathfrak{b}^{H}(\mathfrak{A}_1) \equiv \mathfrak{A}_2$ for R-schema $\mathfrak{A}_1$;
3. Applying inversion operation giving matrix R-schema $\mathfrak{A}_2^{-1}$ to R-schema $\mathfrak{A}_2$;
4. Constructing saturated R-schema $\mathfrak{b}(\mathfrak{A}_2^{-1}) \equiv \mathfrak{A}_3$ for R-schema $\mathfrak{A}_2^{-1}$;
5. Applying inversion operation giving matrix R-schema $\mathfrak{A}_3^{-1}$ to R-schema $\mathfrak{A}_3$;

R-schema $\mathfrak{A}_3^{-1}$ is the result of applying algorithm $\mathfrak{b}$ to R-schema $\mathfrak{A}$.

The inversion operation of matrix R-schema (G,S,ε) used here is determined as follows: it results in matrix R-schema $(\tilde{G},\tilde{S},\varepsilon)$, where $\tilde{G}$ is a graph obtained from graph G by changing direction of all its edges except those leading to filters having loops and by assuming the contents of filters with a loop to be equal to an empty set; $\tilde{S}$ is the shift relation obtained from S through substitution of each shift by the one conjugate to it; by definition, shifts s and s^* are conjugate if for all $x,x' \in X \quad x' \in sx \rightleftarrows x \in s^*x'$.

The algorithm identifying partial equivalency of R-schemata $\mathfrak{A}_1$ and $\mathfrak{A}_2$ is reduced to applying algorithm $\mathfrak{b}$ to each of them and to the subsequent checking of equality $K_t(\mathfrak{b}(\mathfrak{A}_1)) = K_t(\mathfrak{b}(\mathfrak{A}_2))$, where t is defined as described above.

Let us consider R-schemata without recurring operators.

All results obtained here are based on the following statement: R-schemata without recurring operators are equivalent if and only if the sets of their routes are coincidental and are partially equivalent if and only if the sets of their finite routes are coincidental.

d1. Let us first consider equivalency relation between R-schemata. The set consisting of all equivalent R-schemata shall be called a <u>class</u>. Operator $\mathcal{A}_i$ ($i \neq 0$) belonging to R-schema shall be called a <u>non-essential</u> operator if not a single route of R-schema $\mathfrak{A}$ contains $\mathcal{A}_i$. Operator $\mathcal{A}_0$, by definition, is non-essential if and only if the set of finite routes of R-schema $\mathfrak{A}$ are empty.

R-schema $\mathfrak{A}$ is called <u>canonical</u> if it is saturated and does not contain non-essential operators. The following theorem is true

<u>Theorem 4.</u> Each class of R-schemata contains a single canonical R-schema (disregarding its isomorph transformations); there exists an algorithm of its construction according to any R-schema of a given class.

When proving singularity of the canonical R-schema use is made of

<u>Lemma 3.</u> If two canonical R-schemata are not isomorphic, they are not equivalent.

The algorithm constructing an equivalent canonical schema according to R-schema $\mathfrak{A}$ is split into three sequentially executed algorithms: $\mathfrak{b}^{\mu}$, $\mathfrak{b}^{h}$ and $\mathfrak{b}^{\circ}$; algorithm $\mathfrak{b}$ removes from the saturated R-schema the non-essential operators; this is possible through

<u>Lemma 4.</u> In saturated R-schema operator $\mathcal{A}_j$ is non-essential if and only if each filter τ_{i_j} has empty content.

Passing from equivalency relation to partial equivalency relation, by analogy with definition of class, saturated R-schema and non-essential R-schema, causes the appearance of definitions of (*)-class, (*)-saturated R-schema and (*)-non-essential operator of R-schema. For example, (*)-saturated schema is a matrix R-schema where all filters τ_{i_j} (α_{i_j}) satisfy the condition: if $x \in \alpha_{i_j}$, then there exists a finite route of R-schema containing the triplet of elements $A_i \; x \; A_j$.

R-schema $\mathfrak{A}$ is called (+)-canonical if it is (+)-saturated and does not contain (+)-non-essential operators.

In case of partial equivalency the theorem and lemma similar to Theorem 4 and Lemmas 3 and 4 will be true. Algorith transforming R-schema $\mathfrak{A}$ into (*)-canonical and partially equivalent R-schema consists in consecutive application of algorithms $\mathfrak{b}^{u}\mathfrak{b}^{*n}$ and $\mathfrak{b}^{o}$. Here $\mathfrak{b}^{*n}$ is an algorithm that according to matrix R-schema constructs (*)-saturated R-schema having the same set of finite routes as the initial matrix R-schema; algorithm $\mathfrak{b}^{*n}$ is a sequence of procedures 2 to 5 included in algorithm $\mathfrak{b}$.

d 2. We have considered system L of equivalent transformations of R-schema and system L^* of partially equivalent transformations of R-schema. Both systems are shown in Tables 1 and 2. Proof has been obtained of

Theorem 5. Transformations of system L can reduce any R-schema to a canonical R-schema equivalent to it.

From Theorem 5 and reversibility of each transformation it follows that system L is complete.

Completeness of system L^* is a consequence of

Theorem 6. Any R-schema can be reduced into (*)-canonical R-schema partially equivalent to it by transformations of system L^* owing to reversibility of each transformation of system L^*.

Both the systems are constructed as a calculus of R-schemata. Formulae of this calculus can be presented as $F_1 \sim F_2$, where F_1 and F_2 are fragments. The fragment notion is introduced in such a way that R-schema itself is a particular case of a fragment, and for each fragment F there exists such an R-schema $\mathfrak{A}$ whose part is fragment F.

Each of the systems L and L^* includes Axiom 1 and Derivation Rule 0, that have a technical character; beside these, system L includes sub-systems L^{u}, L^{H}, L^{O}, and system L^* includes sub-systems L^{u}, L^{*H}, L^{O}.

Let F_1 and F_2 be R-schemata; then sign $\sim$ called the symbol of equipotence is interpreted as follows: in system L^{u} it shows similarity of R-schemata; in systems L^{H} and L^{O} it shows the relation between R-schemata retaining the set of routes of R-schema; in system L^{*H} it shows the relation retaining the set of finite routes of R-schema. If fragments F_1 and F_2 are not R-schemata, formula $F_1 \sim F_2$ can be interpreted as an abbreviated way of writing the set of formulae $\mathfrak{A}(F_1) \sim \mathfrak{A}(F_2)$, where $\mathfrak{A}(F_1)$ is an arbitrary R-schema containing fragment F_1 and $\mathfrak{A}(F_2)$ is an R-schema obtained from $\mathfrak{A}(F_1)$ by substituting fragment F_1 with fragment F_2.

Let us consider Axiom 1 and Derivation Rule 0. According to Axiom 1 each fragment is equivalent to itself. Derivation Rule 0 provides the following: if formula $F_1 \sim F_2$ can be derivated within system L^{u}, then by substituting fragment F_1 with fragment F_2 in any R-schema $\mathfrak{A}(F_1)$ we shall obtain R-schema $\mathfrak{A}(F_2)$ similar to R-schema $\mathfrak{A}(F_1)$; if, however, $F_1 \sim F_2$ can be derived within system L^{*H}, then the R-schema $\mathfrak{A}(F_2)$ obtained shall have the same set of finite routes as R-schema $\mathfrak{A}(F_1)$, etc.

System L^{u} together with Axiom 1 and Derivation Rule 0 shall be designated by $\bar{L}^{u}$; system $\bar{L}^{H}$ and $\bar{L}^{*H}$ are obtained in a similar way.

The following Lemmas are true:

Lemma 5. Arbitrary R-schema can be reduced to a similar matrix R-schema by transformations of system $\bar{L}^{\mu}$.

Lemma 6. Arbitrary matrix R-schema can be reduced to an equivalent saturated R-schema by transformations of system $\bar{L}^{H}$ and into a partially equivalent (*)-saturated R-schema by transformations of system $\bar{L}^{*H}$.

Finally, axiom of system L^{o} and Axiom 2 of system L^{μ} provide for the removal of non-essential operators from the saturated R-schema and of (*)-non-essential operators from (*)-saturated R-schema.

d 3. Let (G,S,ε) be a matrix R-schema, where contents of all filters τ_{i-1} are empty; we shall call it R-schema having no empty cycles. The set of matrix R-schemata $(\tilde{G},S,\varepsilon)$, where graph $\tilde{G}$ may differ from graph G only by the contents of filters τ_{io}, shall be designated by $T(\mathfrak{A})$. The following theorem is true:

Theorem 7. R-schemata $\mathfrak{A}_1$ and $\mathfrak{A}_2$ having no empty cycles are equivalent if and only if, whatever be the R-schema of one of the sets $T(\mathfrak{A}_1)$, $T(\mathfrak{A}_2)$, the other set contains a partially equivalent R-schema.

Theorem 7 demonstrates connection between equivalency relation and partial equivalency relation in a set of R-schemata having no empty cycles.

Let us consider determined matrix R-schemata. Set $\bar{A}$ of operators, set X of information bits, shift relation S and equivalency relation ε in A are assumed to be fixed.

We shall say that on sets A and X interpretation is defined if

1) arbitrary set M is chosen;
2) representation $\mu : \mathcal{M} \to X$ is defined;
3) each operator $\mathbf{A}_i$ different from $\mathbf{A}_o$ and $\mathbf{A}_{-1}$ is associated with representation $f_i : \mathcal{M} \to \mathcal{M}$

We shall consider a determined matrix R-schema $\mathfrak{A}$, where for all $i=0,1,\ldots,n$ $\bigcup_{j=-1}^{n} \alpha_{i_j} = X$, and define <u>function</u> $f_{\mathfrak{A}}$ <u>realized by R-schema</u> $\mathfrak{A}$ in interpretation $(\mathfrak{M},\mu,f_i,\ i=1,2,\ldots)$.

Let m_o be an arbitrary element from M. Among sets α_{o_j} we shall find a single set $\alpha_{o_{j_o}}$, for which $\mu m_o \in \alpha_{o_{j_o}}$ is true. If $j_o=0$, then we shall assume $f_{\mathfrak{A}}(m_o) = m_o$; if $j_o = -1$, then the function $f_{\mathfrak{A}}$ shall be considered as not defined on m_o. In all the other cases element m_o shall be transformed into element $m_1=f_{j_o}(m_o)$ and for element m_1 among sets $\alpha_{j_{oj}}$ we shall find a single set $\alpha_{j_oj_1}$ satisfying condition $\mu m_1 \in \alpha_{j_oj_1}$. Just as in the previous step (considered as zero step) for $j_1=0$ we shall assume $f_{\mathfrak{A}}(m_o)=m_1$, for $j_1=1$ we shall assume that $f_{\mathfrak{A}}$ is not defined on m_o and in all the other cases we shall transform m_1 into $m_2=f_{j_1}(m_1)$; after this we shall find set $\alpha_{j_1j_2}$ among sets α_{j_1j}; for set $\alpha_{j_1j_2}$ $\mu m_2 \in \alpha_{j_1j_2}$, etc. Function $f_{\mathfrak{A}}$ shall be considered determined on m_o if on the k-th step the process described the element m_k satisfies the requirement $\mu m_k \in \alpha_{j_{k-1}},0$; in this case we shall assume $f_{\mathfrak{A}}(m_o)=m_k$.

Let I be a set of interpretations $(\mathfrak{M},\mu,f_i,\ i=1,2,\ldots)$. R-schemata, by definition, are <u>functionally equivalent</u> on a set of interpretations I, if for any interpretation from I the functions realized by these R-schemata are coincidental.

An interpretation $(\mathfrak{M},\mu,f_i,\ i=1,2,\ldots)$ shall be called <u>admissible for shift relation S and equivalency relation</u> ε, if the following conditions are fulfilled:

1) if operators A_i and A_j are equivalent on ε, then $f_i=f_j$;
2) each representation f_i has a property:

$$\forall_{m\in\mathfrak{M}} [\mu f_i(m) \in s_i \mu m] .$$

We have proved

<u>Theorem 8.</u> R-schemata (G_1,S,ε) and (G_2,S,ε) are partially equivalent if and only if they are functionally equivalent on a set of interpretations admissible for shift relation S and equivalency relation ε.

That is the interpretation of the formally introduced partial equivalency relation.

REFERENCES

I. Янов Ю.И. О логических схемах алгоритмов. Сб."Проблемы кибернетики". Вып.I. Физматгиз, М.,1958.

2. Ершов А.П. Об операторных схемах Янова. Сб."Проблемы кибернетики". Вып.20, изд. "Наука", М.,1968.

3. Подловченко Р.И. R -схемы и отношения эквивалентности между ними. Сб."Проблемы кибернетики". Вып.27 (в печати).

4. Подловченко Р.И. Полная система подобных преобразований R - схем. Сб."Проблемы кибернетики". Вып.27 (в печати).

5. Подловченко Р.И., Петросян Г.Н., Хачатрян В.Е. Интерпретации схем алгоритмов и различные типы отношений эквивалентности между схемами. Изв.АН Арм.ССР (в печати).

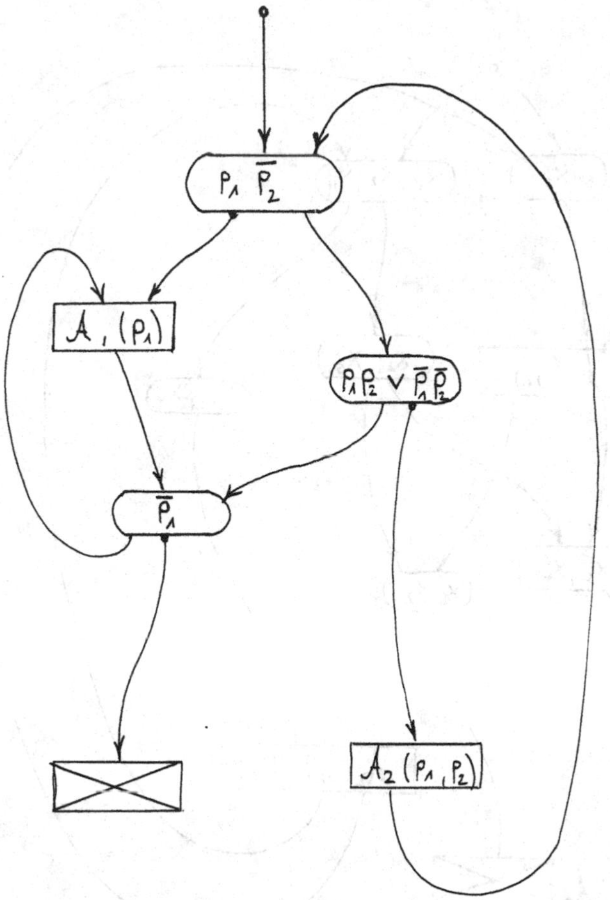

FIG. 1a

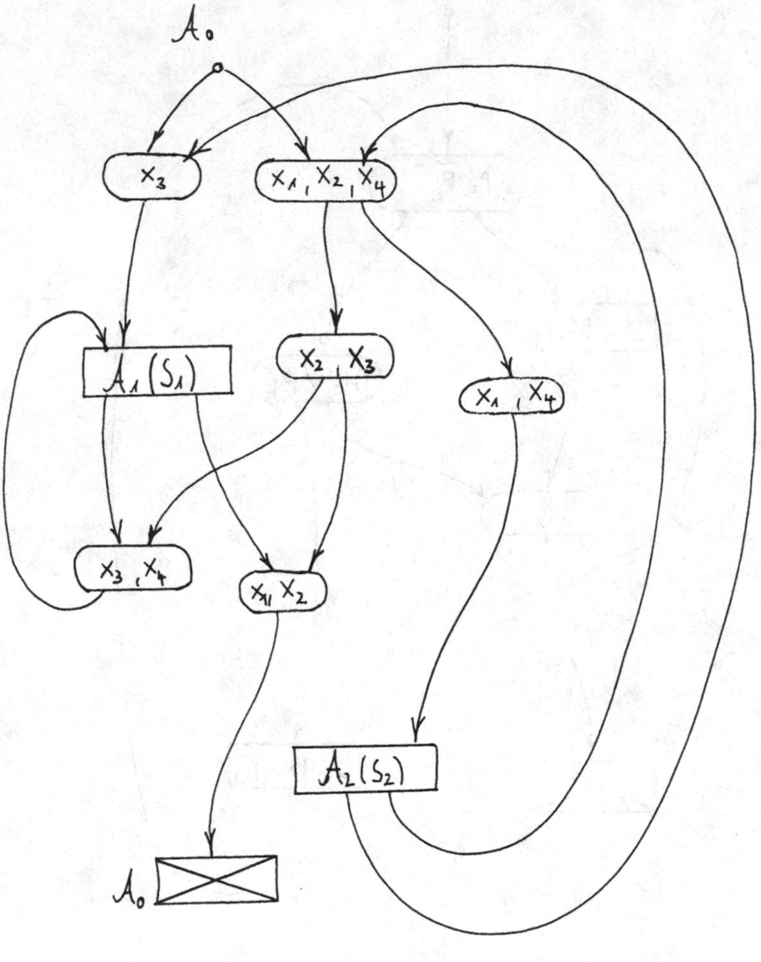

$$x_1 = (0,0) \qquad x_2 = (0,1) \qquad x_3 = (1,0) \qquad x_4 = (1,1)$$

$$S_1 : \begin{cases} x_1 \to \{x_1, x_2\} \\ x_2 \to \{x_2, x_4\} \\ x_3 \to \{x_1, x_3\} \\ x_4 \to \{x_2, x_4\} \end{cases} \qquad S_2 : \begin{cases} x_1 \to X \\ x_2 \to X \\ x_3 \to X \\ x_4 \to X \end{cases}$$

FIG. 1b

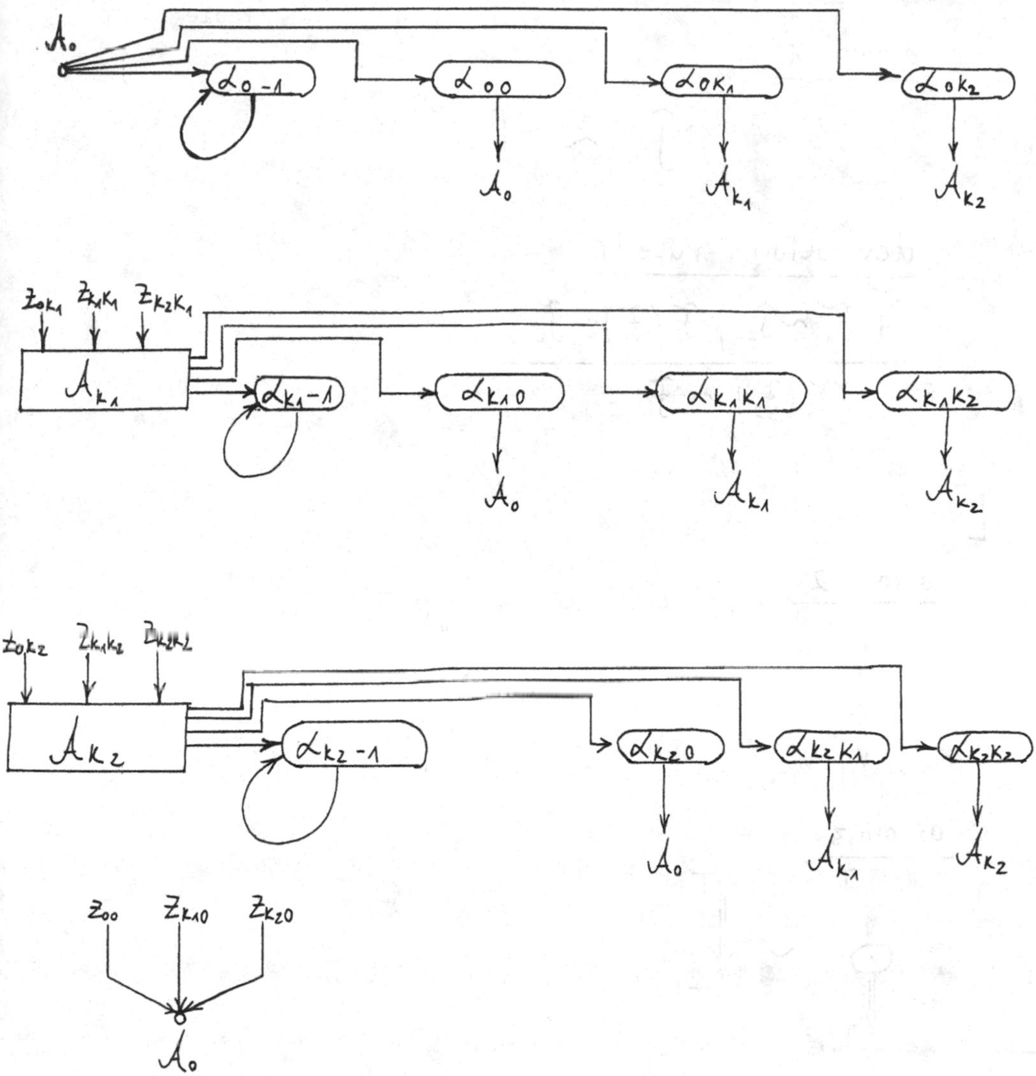

$\mathcal{A}_0$
$\alpha_{0\,-1}$
α_{00}
α_{0k_1}
α_{0k_2}
$\mathcal{A}_0$
$\mathcal{A}_{k_1}$
$\mathcal{A}_{k_2}$
z_{0k_1} $z_{k_1k_1}$ $z_{k_2k_1}$
$\mathcal{A}_{k_1}$
α_{k_1-1}
α_{k_10}
$\alpha_{k_1k_1}$
$\alpha_{k_1k_2}$
$\mathcal{A}_0$
$\mathcal{A}_{k_1}$
$\mathcal{A}_{k_2}$
z_{0k_2} $z_{k_1k_2}$ $z_{k_2k_2}$
$\mathcal{A}_{k_2}$
α_{k_2-1}
α_{k_20}
$\alpha_{k_2k_1}$
$\alpha_{k_2k_2}$
$\mathcal{A}_0$
$\mathcal{A}_{k_1}$
$\mathcal{A}_{k_2}$
z_{00} z_{k_10} z_{k_20}
$\mathcal{A}_0$

FIG. 2

Table 1

axiom 1

$$\mathcal{F} \sim \mathcal{F}$$

deviration rule 0

$$\frac{\vdash \mathcal{F}_1 \sim \mathcal{F}_2 \; , \; \mathcal{F}_3(\mathcal{F}_1) \sim \mathcal{F}_4}{\mathcal{F}_3(\mathcal{F}_2) \sim \mathcal{F}_4}$$

L^{n}:

axiom 2

axiom 3

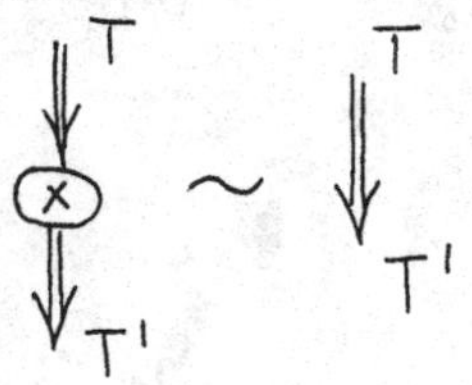

axiom 4

axiom 5

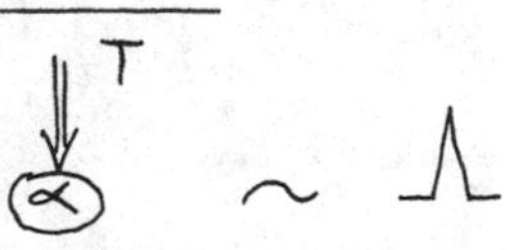

Table 1

axiom 6

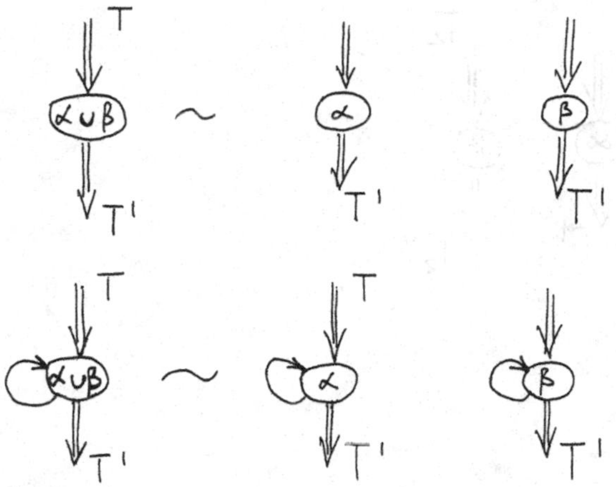

axiom 7

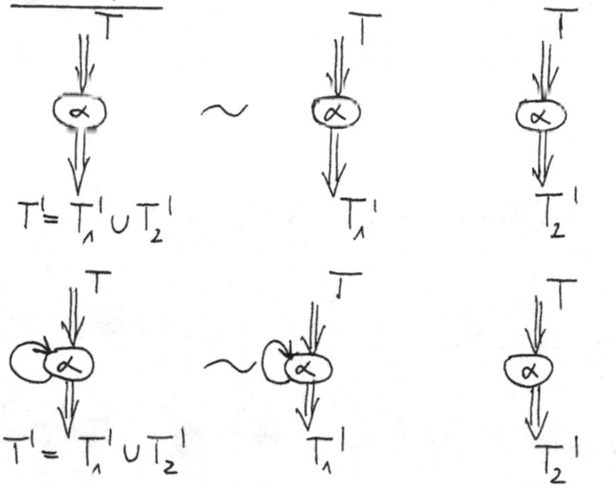

axiom 8

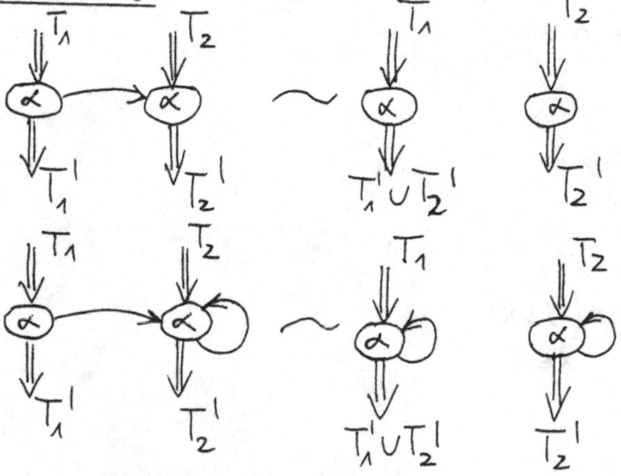

axiom 9 $\alpha \cap \beta = \emptyset$ Table 1

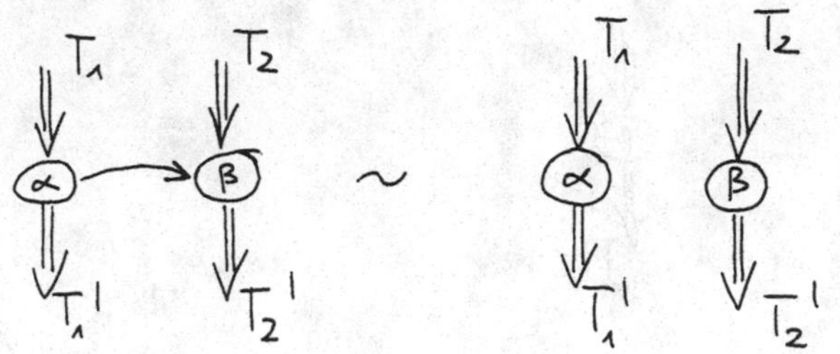

$L^{\#}$:

axiom 10

axiom 11

axiom 12

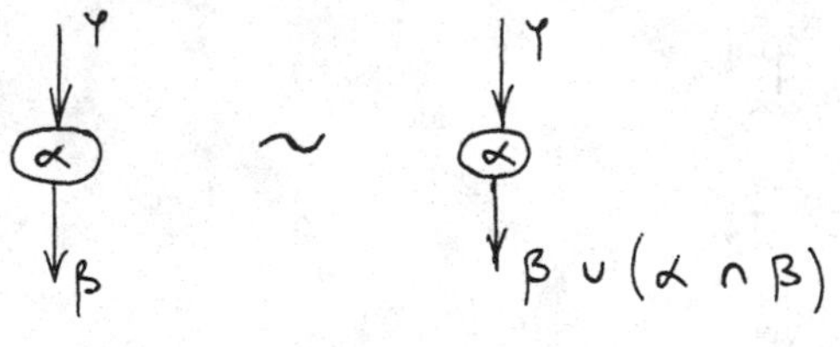

axiom 13

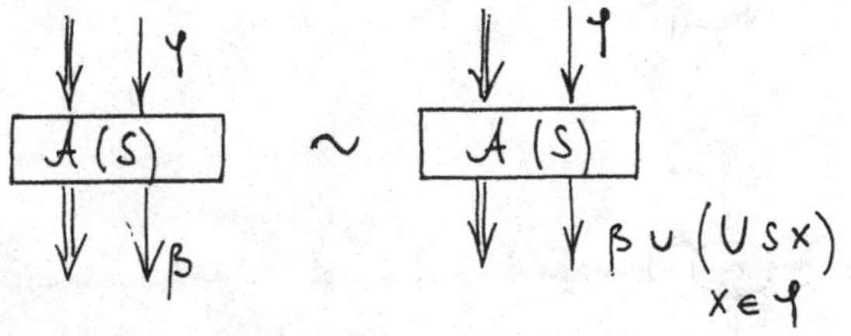

deviration rule 14

Table 1

$$\forall \left(\begin{array}{c} \downarrow^{\gamma} \\ \boxed{\alpha} \\ \downarrow \beta \end{array} \right) [\alpha \cap \gamma \subseteq \beta] \quad , \quad \forall \left(\begin{array}{c} \downarrow \quad \downarrow^{\gamma} \\ \boxed{\mathcal{A}(s)} \\ \downarrow \quad \downarrow \beta \end{array} \right) [\bigcup_{x \in \gamma} {}^{sx} \subseteq \beta]$$

$$\forall \left(\begin{array}{c} \downarrow^{\gamma} \\ \boxed{\alpha} \\ \downarrow \beta \end{array} \right) \left[\begin{array}{c} \downarrow^{\gamma} \\ \boxed{\alpha} \\ \downarrow \beta \end{array} \sim \begin{array}{c} \downarrow^{\gamma} \\ \boxed{\alpha \cap \gamma} \\ \downarrow \beta \end{array} \right]$$

L° :

axiom 15

$$\boxed{\mathcal{A}(s)} \qquad \sim \quad \Lambda$$
$$\downarrow$$

L^{*H} :

Table 2

axiom 10

$$\begin{array}{c} \mathcal{A}_{\circ} \\ \bigwedge \end{array} \qquad \sim \qquad \begin{array}{c} \mathcal{A}_{\circ} \\ \bigwedge {}^{x/\emptyset} \end{array}$$

$$\begin{array}{c} \bigvee \\ {}_{\mathcal{A}_{\circ}} \end{array} \qquad \sim \qquad \begin{array}{c} \bigvee {}^{\emptyset/x} \end{array}$$

axiom 11

$$\downarrow \qquad \sim \qquad \downarrow {}^{\emptyset/\emptyset}$$

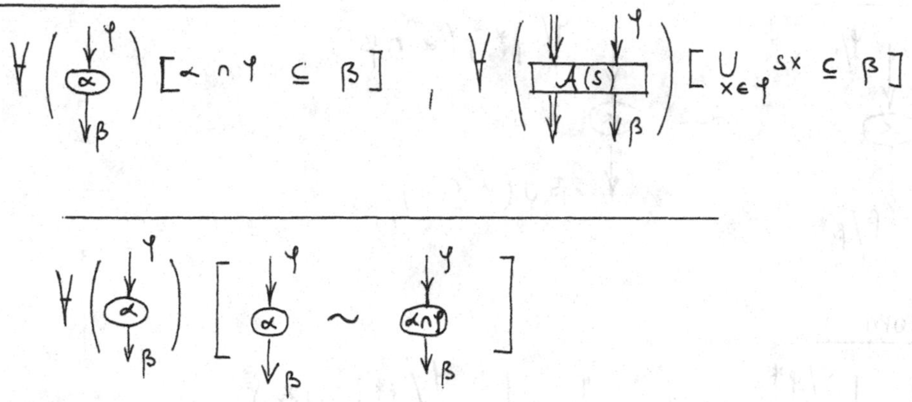

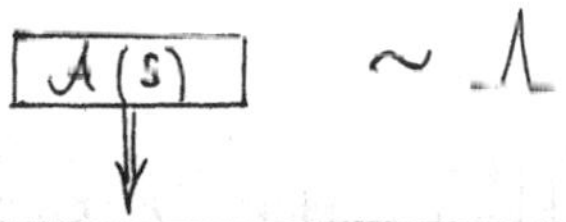

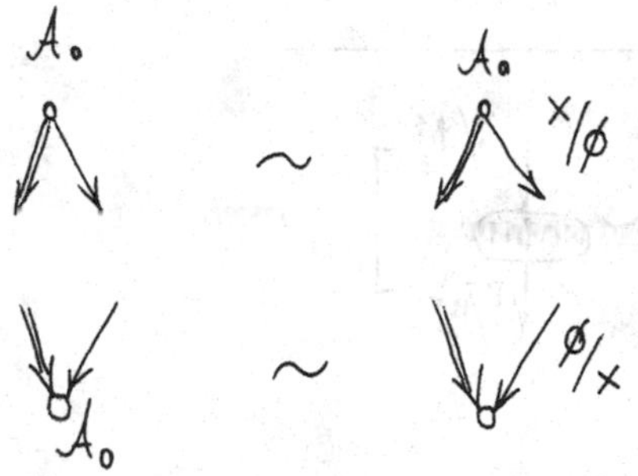

Table 2

axiom 12

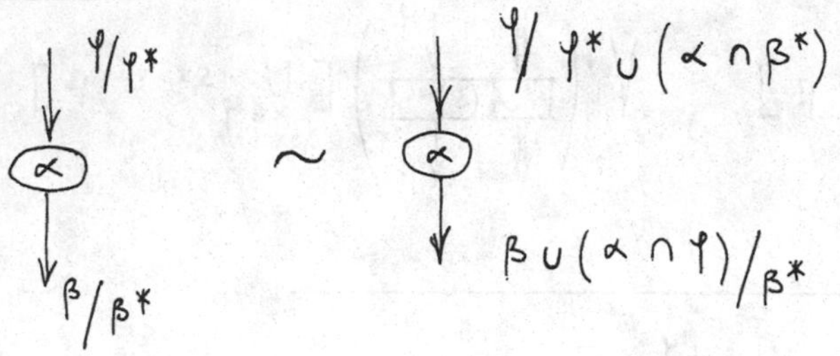

axiom 13

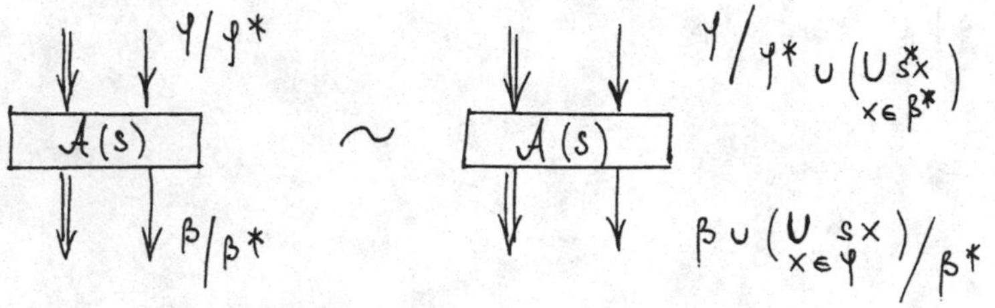

deviration rule 14

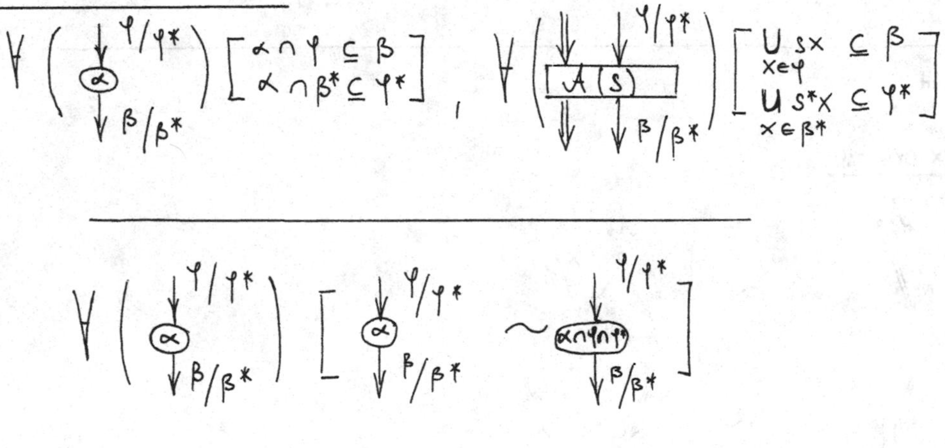

EQUIVALENCE AND OPTIMIZATION OF PROGRAMS

A.A.Letichevsky
Institute of Cybernetics
Ukrainian Academy of Sciences
Kiev - 28, U.S.S.R.

This paper treats basic methods used for speed (run time) optimization of programs. These methods cover most of those utilized in practice when constructing programming systems, for instance, described in [1,2], and contain a number of new concepts which may apply in practice. In particular, a link is shown between the optimization problem and the equivalence recognition problem and that of program stopping.

Program Schemata. Let $\mathcal{U}$ be the alphabet of elementary conditions, Y-alphabet of operators. $\mathcal{U}$-Y-scheme of program is an oriented graph whose arrows are marked by pairs (u,y), where u is a propositional function of variables in $\mathcal{U}$, $y \in Y$. Graph nodes are called states of the program scheme. The initial and final states are selected from a set of the states.

Deterministic program schemata will be dealt with only, i.e. such for which the following condition holds: If two arrows, marked by pairs (u,y) and (u',y') leave the node a, then $u \wedge u' = 0$. Stating the interpretation of operator symbols as transformations acting over some information set B, and the interpretation of conditions as predicates defined on the same set, it is possible to define, in a usual way(e.g. as in [3]), the action of schema A with the given interpretation, and to define (partial) transformation $f_{A,B}$ of set B, performed by scheme A. The scheme action follows the following rule: if, at some time instant, the scheme is in the state a and transforms element b, which satisfies condition u, and an arrow, that connects a to a', is marked by (u,y) then, at the next time instant, the scheme will transform element b' = y(b), being in state a'. Operation of the scheme begins with the initial state and ends at the final one. The program scheme together with the interpretation, i.e. with information set B over which operators act, and elementary conditions are defined, is called the program. The form of definition given differs from Yanov's classical scheme in some respects but it is close to the concept of a final state automaton (there corresponds to each $\mathcal{U}$-Y-scheme $2^{\mathcal{U}}$-Y-Mealy automaton), and the program concept is a particular case of the concept of a discrete processor. In view of such a correspondence, all results of the theory of discrete processors [4] may be interpreted in terms of programs and program schemata. Schemata A and A' are equivalent relative to B($A \sim A'(B)$) if $f_{A,B} = f_{A',B}$. A stronger equivalence is often used when optimization problems are stated more precisely, by considering interpretation class J and assuming that $A \sim A'(J)$ if $A \sim A'(B)$ for all B of J. In particular, in comparing programs A and A' equivalent relative to J, program A is better than A' if, with any interpretation B in J, any element $b \in B$, which A and A' are applied to, is transformed by program A earlier than by program A'; the program runtime thereby being calculated as a sum of times of work of operators acting in the process of transforming element b.

<u>Schemata on Memory</u>. The concept of the scheme on memory is obtained from examining a certain syntactic structure on a set of elementary conditions and operators. We shall discuss here the definition of the scheme on memory that is more general in comparison with the conventional [5]. This generalization is aimed at involving the concepts associated with arrays. Let R be a set of variables or names (memory), Ω-signature of operations.

Each operation ω is of the type that is defined by a set of symbols $(\alpha_1,\ldots,\alpha_n,\alpha)$, where α is 0 or 1. Let us define the set T(R) of terms and the set T'(R) of naming terms by means of the rules:

1. Any variable is a naming term.
2. Any naming term is a term.
3. If ω is an operation of the type $(\alpha_1,\ldots,\alpha_n,\alpha)$, $t_1,\ldots,t_n$ are terms such that it follows from $\alpha_i = 0$ that t_i is a naming term $(i = 1,\ldots,n)$, then $\omega(t_1,\ldots,t_n)$ is a term if $\alpha = 0$, or a naming term if $\alpha = 0$.

Thus the naming terms will be interpreted so that they will take on values not only in the set of values of variables but in set R. The expression of the form $(S_1 := t_1,\ldots,S_n := t_n)$, where $S_1,\ldots,S_n$ are naming terms and $t_1,\ldots,t_n$ are terms, will be referred to as an assignment operator. Signature Π of predicate symbols is considered to form conditions. Each symbol is of the type $(\alpha_1,\ldots,\alpha_n)$ where $\alpha_i = 0,1$. If π is a predicate symbol of the type $(\alpha_1,\ldots,\alpha_n)$, $t_1,\ldots t_n$ are terms, and if it follows from $\alpha_1 = 0$ that t_i is a naming term, then the expression $\pi(t_1,\ldots,t_n)$ is called the elementary condition (on memory).

The scheme on memory is a $\mathcal{U}$-Y-scheme such that $\mathcal{U}$ is a set of conditions on memory and Y - a set of assignment operators.

Interpretation of Schemata on Memory. Since the scheme on memory is simply a program scheme, any interpretations may be examined for it. However, the syntactic structure of operators and conditions imposes additional restrictions upon feasible interpretations. The interpretation of the schema on memory (of operators and conditions, to be more exact) is constructed on the base of some sets D and S (R S). Elements of set D are called data, elements of set S-variables (extended memory). Function $f_\omega : D_{\alpha_1} \times D_{\alpha_2} \times \ldots \times D_{\alpha_n} \to D_{\alpha_0}$, where $D_1 = D$, $D_0 = S$, is determined for each symbol of operation of the type $(\alpha_1,\ldots,\alpha_n,\alpha)$. Predicate $f_\pi : D_{\alpha_1} \times D_{\alpha_2} \times \ldots \times D_{\alpha_n} \to \{0,1\}$ is determined for each predicate symbol π

of the type $(\alpha_1,\dots,\alpha_n)$. Information set $\beta = D^S$ is a set of all mappings of S into D (memory states). Each memory state $1 : S \to D$ continues up to mapping $b_1 : T(R) \to D$ and generates mapping $b_o : T'(R) \to D$ by means of two conditions:

$$b_1(\omega(t_1,\dots,t_n)) = f_\omega(b_\alpha(t_1),\dots,b_\alpha(t_n)) \text{ if } \omega \text{ has type } (\alpha_1,\dots,\alpha_n,1),$$

$$b_1(\omega(t_1,\dots,t_n)) = b(f_\omega(b_\alpha(t_1),\dots,b_\alpha(t_n))) \text{ if } \omega \text{ has type } (\alpha_1,\dots,\alpha_n,0)$$

$$b_o(\omega(t_1,\dots,t_n)) = f_\omega(b_\alpha(t_1),\dots,b_\alpha(t_n)),$$

if ω has type $(\alpha_1,\dots,\alpha_n,0)$, $b_o(r) = r$, $r \quad R$.

The value f_u of the elementary condition $u = \pi(t_1,\dots,t_n)$ at memory state b is determined by the formula : $f_u = f_\pi(b_1(t_1),\dots,b_1(t_n))$. The transformation f_y that is performed by the operator $y = (s_1 := t_1,\dots,s_n := t_n)$ when the interpretation is stated consists in the simultaneous assignment of values $b_1(t_1),\dots,b_n(t_n)$ to variables $b_o(s_1),\dots,b_o(s_n)$, respectively. If $b_o(s_i) = b_o(s_j)$, the value $(b_1(t_{i}), (b_1(t_{i}),\dots, (b_1(t_{i}), b_1(t_{i}))\dots))$, where is a binary associative operation over D, $1 \le i_1,\dots,i_n \le n$ for all such subscripts that $b_o(s_i) = b_o(s_{i})$ $p = 1,\dots,k$, is assigned to variable $b_o(s_i)$. The interpretation constructed this way is said to be correct. The scheme of the program on memory together with the correct interpretation is called the program on memory or simply the program. Note that in using the foregoing formalism to describe existing programs, the n-dimensional array is referred to as the n-ary operation ω of the type (1, 1, ... 1, 0), i.e. as the operation which yields a variable (name) from S on the set of values of the subscripts (in region D). If the expression $\omega(i_1,\dots,i_n)$ corresponding to this operation is found in the left-hand member of the assignment operator, the variable $b_o(\omega(i_1,\dots,i_n))$ (subscribed variable) gets new value, and if the expression $\omega(i_1,\dots,i_n)$ is found in the right-hand member of the assignment operator, the value $b_1(\omega(i_1,\dots,i_n))$ of the variable $b_O(\omega(i_1,\dots,i_n))$ is utilized for calculation of values of the right-hand member.

Consider basic algebraic objects associated with particular interpretation, which are of great importance in solving the optimization problems. The data algebra D consists of a set of information objects and operations of signature Ω. Apart from operations acting on set D, operations also act in the data algebra a portion of arguments of which assumes values in set S, as well as operations assuming values in S. Such operations are external operations of the data algebra. The data algebra is said to be simple if all its operations are internal and there are no operations assuming values in S. This relates to the well studied case when there are no arrays and memory has a simple structure.

Set S is also an algebra of signature Ω-memory algebra. Algebras D and S which are considered together form a two-basic algebra or a pair of algebras of signature Ω. Relations in the data algebra and in the memory algebra represent one of the major sources of optimizing transformations of programs. Another source of transformations is relations in semigroup G_B of transformations of information set $B = D^S$ generated by $f_y (y \in Y)$. Sets T(R) and T'(R) also form a pair of algebras of signature Ω. These algebras are called the free data algebra and free memory algebra. Since each naming term is term ($T'(R) \subset T(R)$), one should distinguish between consideration of the naming terms as elements of the data algebra and those of the memory algebra. In order to distinguish between these two cases we shall use notation 't for naming term t being considered as an element of set T(R) (i.e. "'"denotes operation of embedding T'(R) into T(R)). Set R generates the pair of algebras (T(R),T'(R)). The pair of mappings $\varphi: R \rightarrow D$ and identical mapping $\psi: R \rightarrow S$ may be continued uniquely to a homomorphism of pair (T(R),T'(R)) into (D,S). Considering T(R) as being the data algebra , and T'(R) as the memory algebra it is possible to define the set $T(R)^{T'(R)}$ of memory states and semigroup G_F of transformations of this set, which semigroup is generated by operators $y \in Y$, as having been interpreted in a usual way.

Assume t_1 and t_2 to be terms or naming terms. Relation $t_1=t_2$ (symbolically $t_1=t_2(\beta)$) holds in memory state b D^S if $b_\alpha(t_1)=b_\alpha(t_2)$ (α=0 if naming terms, α=1 for terms are meant). Relation $t_1=t_2$ is an identity of the data algebra (memory algebra) if it is satisfied with any state of memory. Factorizing pair (T(R), T'(R)) in all identities of pair (D,S) we have pair (D_o,S_o). Also it is of interest to examine intermediate algebras (D',S') which are obtained by factorization of a free pair not in all, but in some identities only. A set of memory states may be formed for each of such a pair, and semigroup G' transforming this set may be built. Semigroup G' is a homomorphic image of G_F and is mapped homomorphically on G_β. Intermediate data algebras are useful when strong equivalences of program schemata are dealt with. For instance, having fixed algebra (D',S') we may consider a class of all correct interpretations with this algebra (predicate interpretation being varied in this case). If the free algebra is fixed, a functional equivalence will be obtained which coincides with the equivalence with respect to the class of all correct interpretations. This kind of equivalence is being actively investigated of late. Of great importance is a kind of equivalence representing a semi-group equivalence which is obtained if semi-group G' is fixed and a class is considered of all (not necessarily correct) interpretations for which the semi-group transforming the information set is isomorphic to semi-group G'.

We proceed now to discuss major techniques of optimizing the programs on memory.

<u>Optimization of Linear Segments</u>. Set $a_1,\dots,a_{n+1}$ of scheme states is said to be a linear segment if these states are connected by transisions $a_1 \; {}^{u_1/y_1} a_2,\dots,a_i \; {}^{1/y_i} a_{i+1},\dots,i=2,\dots,n$ and only one arrow is contained in state a_i (relation $a \; {}^{u/y} \; a'$ among a,u,y and a' means that state a is connected to state a' by an arrow marked by pair (u,y)). Word $y_1,\dots,y_n$ is called a word generated by linear segment $a_1,\dots,a_{n+1}$. The basic

transformation of linear segments implies the following. If words $y_1 \ldots y_n$ and $y'_1 \ldots y'_m$ are equal in semi-group G' (i.e. transformations of memory states defined by these words coincide) the linear segment which generates word $y_1 \ldots y_n$ may be replaced by the linear segment generating word $y'_1 \ldots y'_m$. Optimization of the linear segment, consequently, consists in searching for the shortest (with time of executing each operator taken into account) representation of a given element of semi-group G'. G_β or G_F or any intermediate semi-group for G' may be used. If schemes operating with simple data algebras are involved, the equality problem for semi-group G' is readily reduced to the equality problems in the data algebra. Also, this is the case for arbitrary algebras, the proof of the respective fact being though much more complex. It has been obtained by Malinovsky [6]. In common practice algorithms employ semi-group G' which is obtained with the use of commutativity and associativity (rarely of distributivity) relations in the data algebra. The optimum solution is obtained for such a semi-group by consideration of an information graph, and corresponds to the well-known economy method of expressions.

Of great importance also is a conditional optimization of linear segments. Relation $t_1=t_2$ is said to occur in state a of the program if $t_1=t_2(B)$ occurs each time when the program gets to state a and if it processes an element into the information set. Let R be a set of relations. Programs A and A' are equivalent to relation $R(A \sim A'(B,R))$ if f_A and $f_{A'}$ coincide on the set of those states $b \in B$ in which relations from R are satisfied. A notion of the relation may also be introduced for the program schemes with respect to a class of interpretations. This results in the equivalence with respect to the class of interpretations and a set of relations. Satisfaction of some relations at the beginning of the linear segment gives additional possibilities for optimization. For instance, if relation $\Gamma = s+t$ holds, operator $p:=(s+t)\times c$ may be replaced by operator $p:=\Gamma\times c$.

Search for Relations. A great number of relations need to be found in order to obtain additional possibilities for optimization of linear segments. It is very difficult to search for all relations and, say, for the case of functional equivalence, the problem of finding the satisfaction of relations Γ=s (Γ and s-variables) in a given state of the scheme is algorithmically insolvable. Sill there exist simple methods which make it possible to find a rather great number of relations. These methods are based on a simple fact that relation s=t holds upon execution of operator s:=t. Taking into consideration those relations that are preserved during execution of a given operator, it becomes possible to transfer information on relations along arrows of the program scheme up to complete saturation, which will be given by some number of relations. In this case the following important question arises. Each set of relations generates other relations that are consequences of given data. If two sets of relations are given, the question is, how do we know whether they generate one and the same set of consequences or not ? How shall we know relations which generate an intersection of sets of consequences of two specified systems of relations. Efficiency of methods of searching for relations according to a stated scheme of the program depends on the meaning of answers to these questions. These questions are dependent on a structure of the data algebra and their solutions seem to involve considerable difficulties. The complete answer may be obtained for the free data algebra. Here any set of relations satisfied in a given state has a unique final basis - the least set of relations which generate the same set of consequences as in the case of the given set of relations. A similar result is obtained for the data algebra provided with an addition operation with respect to which data forms Abelian group, whereas other operations do not participate in any relations. This case is of importance from the standpoint of transforming index expressions.

Estimation of Mergings. This transformation retains a strict equivalence of the program schemes, i.e. the equivalence with respect to the class of all interpretations. Its meaning is understood from the following figure:

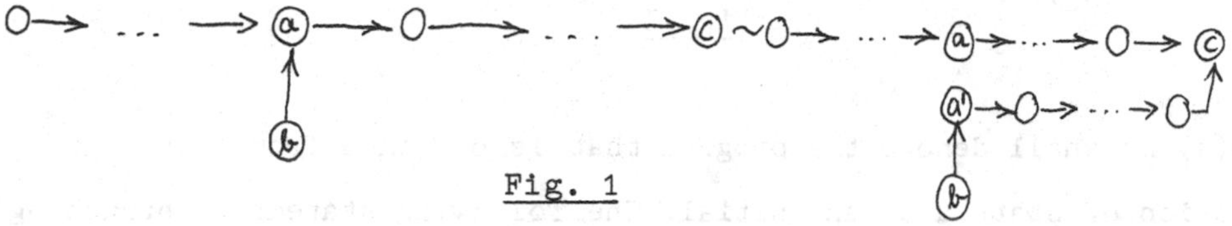

Fig. 1

If the scheme contains the fragment of the left-hand portion of the figure, it may be replaced by the fragment of the right-hand portion. A set of states from a to c should be a linear segment. All jumps of this segment are repeated in a chain of new states from a'. Elimination of mergings allows, on the one hand, to increase the length of the linear segment, and on the other hand, to increase the number of relations on the linear segments.

Elimination of mergings is usually carried out inside a linear segment. To go beyond the bounds of the linear segment it is sometimes useful to apply the transformation illustrated in the following figure (transfer of the merging beyond the boundary of the linear segment):

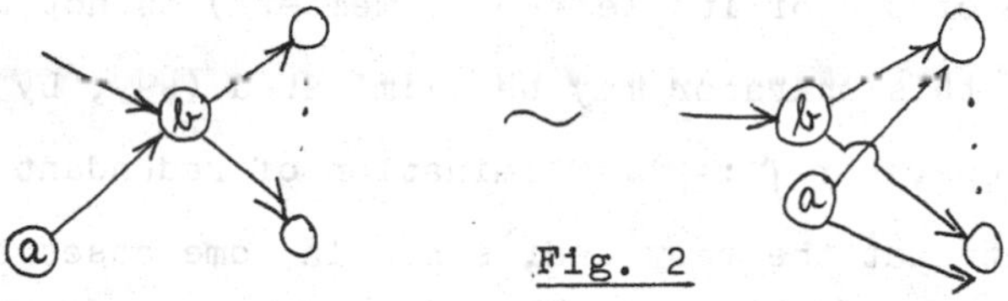

Fig. 2

Elimination of Branchings. Let a branching be present in state a of program A, i.e. there exist jumps a $\xrightarrow{u'/y'}$ b and a $\xrightarrow{u''/y''}$ c such that y' ≠ y" or b ≠ c.

Examine programs A' and A" which are obtained by substitution of the second and third fragments for the first fragment of Fig. 3 in program A, respectively.

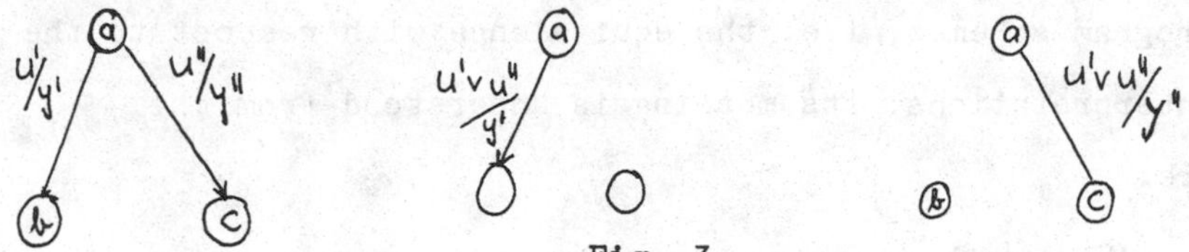

Fig. 3

By A(a) we shall denote the program that is obtained from A through selection of state a as an initial. The following statement (branching theorem) is available. Assume that relations R hold in state a of programs A, A'(a) and A"(a). Then, if A'(a) $\sim$ A"(a)(B,R), then A $\sim$ A'(B,R) The use of this suggestion enables us to rule out branchings in the program by substitution of A' for A. Elimination of branchings permits us to increase the lengths of the linear segments, and to attain additional possibilities of optimization.

<u>Elimination of Redundant Calculations and Jumps</u>. When considering the programs on memory it is useful to distinguish between input and output variables (or input and output naming terms in the general case). The program uses the initial values of only input variables and its result is examined only for output variables. If a result of an action of an operator (i.e. the value of one of its left-hand members) is not utilized in further calculations, this operator may be eliminated (say, by replacing it by identical operator $\rho:=\rho$). Elimination of redundant operators is to be effected at the very end, since in some cases a redundant calculation on one linear segment may be of use for transformations on others, and may cease to be redundant. In some cases it is even useful to introduce redundant calculations to obtain possibilities of program speed optimization.

A jump (i.e. an arrow with a pair which marks the arrow) is said to be redundant if any path from the initial state, feasible in calculations, does not cross this jump. Redundant jumps may be ruled out.

Recognition of redundancy of calculations and jumps is reduced to the recognition problem of reaching state B from state a (simply or with a set of R relations which hold in state a).

Sufficient Conditions of Program Equivalence and Accessibility. Checkout of program equivalence, necessary for application of the theorem about elimination of branchings, as well as checkout of accessibility (equivalence to a program with an empty set of arrows) are complex problems that are algorithmically insolvable even for the simplest (but infinite) interpretations. Therefore, in practice, one is confined to the application of sufficient conditions of equivalence and accessibility. The simplest sufficient conditions are attained by application of equivalence recognition algorithms of the program schemes [7], and others weaker but close to equivalence notions (e.g. relative strict equivalence of discrete transformers [8]). The theoretical-automaton methods [8-9] are of paramount importance here. The further weakening of equivalence, that is admitted by recognition algorithms, give conditions of semi-group equivalence [10]. Equivalence of interest has been treated by V.E. Itkin in [11]. Elimination of branchings make it possible to strengthen the existing criteria of equivalence in the following manner. A branching is said to be eliminable if the branching theorem is applicable to it. Let us have some sufficient criterion of equivalence. Look into the following checkout process of equivalence (branching elimination method). Assume that programs A_1 and A_2 are to be compared. We start from elimination of branchings in each of the programs. For this purpose all branchings are examined one after another and checked for eliminability. If a branching is eliminable, we eliminate it. Equivalence is to be checked in order to check eliminability. But this checkout is accomplished for automata A'(a) and A"(a) each of which has one branching less than the initial automaton. That is why, the branching elimination method applies recursively to such a check-up. Checking at the very internal stage of recursion is equivalent to branch free automata, which reduces to the problem of checking equality of words in a semi-group. After eliminable branchings in automata A_1 and A_2 have been cleared, the sufficient criterion of equivalence is applied to them.

The branching elimination method led to the proof of solubility of the equivalence problem of semi-groups with the left-hand cancellation and the insoluble unit [12], and to obtainment of the algorithm of constructing the best-speed automaton for these semigroups. The further generalization of the branching elimination method has allowed the study of the equivalence problem of relative semi-groups with the two-side cancellation [13].

The methods of solving the accessibility problem (not dependent on the equivalence problem) have been investigated a little. Solutions for relative strict equivalence (automaton case) are known. A.B. Godlevsky (Institute of Cybernetics of AS of Ukr.SSR) has managed of late to obtain an algorithm for the semigroup of assignment operators generated by operators $r:=\omega(r)$, $s:=\omega(s)$ and $\tau:=0$ (solubility of the equivalence problem for this semi-group is not yet proved). He also studied the accessibility problem for the whole class of semi-groups similar to the above.

General Method of Speed Optimization of Programs. Summarizing the foregoing, we suggest the following method of program optimization.

(1) Search for relations in program states.

(2) Optimization of linear segments with account taken of the relations.

(3) Estimation of mergings. The transfer to item (1) (new relations may appear upon elimination of mergings). When this item is repeatedly accomplished the mergings may be carried over beyond the boundaries of the linear segment, and such a procedure may be repeated a certain number of times, or until it ceases to yield new possiblities of optimization.

(4) Elimination of redundant calculations and jumps.

(5) Elimination of branchings with the use of a sufficient criterion of optimization. Transfer to item (1). Item (5) is repeated over again either a certain number of times or until it ceases to give new possibilities of optimization.

The described general scheme gives different algorithms of optimization if different methods are used for optimization of linear segments, and for searching for relations to check equivalence and accessibility.

Segments having no cycles may be optimized instead of examination of linear segments. The results obtained by Yu.G. Shukuryan [14] may be of use here. Alternate modifications of this method may be connected with reduction of run time of optimization algorithms owing to more reasonable organization of the results.

The described method covers the great part of known optimization methods. In particular, to optimize the program of matrix multiplication (in the line of the example considered in [15]) it is sufficient to calculate relations in the data algebra with group relations for the addition operation taken into account.

On the Average Speed of Automaton with Terminal State

Ju.H.Shukurian
Institute of Mathematical Machines, Yerevan - 33, USSR

In [1] A.A.Letichevskii shows, that functional equivalence of programs is reduced to an equivalence problem for automatons with terminal state - the operational automaton with varying label function.

This report deals with the optimization of automata with terminal state with respect to speed. An average speed of an automaton is introduced and for the case, when an operational automaton is considered to be composed of finite and loop-free automata, a theorem of solvability of problem optimization is proved.

Definitions Let X,Y be finite alphabets. An initial Mealy automaton A with input and output alphabets X and Y accordingly is called X-Y-automaton A with a terminal state if the terminal state is available in the set of states of A; all transitions of the automaton A are undetermined.

Let G be some completely determined initial automaton with an input alphabet Y (Y-automaton G), then Y-X-Moore automaton G_μ is Y-automaton G with label function $\mu: G \to X$.

The interaction between X-Y-automaton A and Y-X-automaton G_μ for each $\mu \in X^g$ is determined by connecting the input channel of one with the output channel of the other. If, during some time of interaction X-Y-automaton A attains its terminal state, then A is said to be applicable to G_μ and the state of G at this instant is identified with a result of the work of automaton A and is designated by $u_A(\mu)$. X-Y-automata A and A' are meant to be equivalent relative to Y-automaton G if $u_A(\mu) = u_{A'}(\mu)$ for each $\mu \in X^G$. Let N_A be the set of those $\mu: G \to X$, for which automaton A is applicable to G_μ.

By the absolute speed of X-Y-automaton A relative to Y-automaton G we mean a function $T_A : N_A \to \mathcal{N}$, where $T_A(\mu)$ is the time of work for A before it attains its terminal state; $\mathcal{N}$ is the set of natural numbers. A relation $\leq$ on the set of automata, which are equivalent relative to G is defined as follows: $A \leq A'$ if for each $\mu \in N_A = N_{A'}$,$T_A(\mu) \leq T_{A'}(\mu)$. Arelation "$A \leq A'$ & $A' \leq A$" is an equivalence.

The classes of this relation define a partially ordered set. The minimal (least) element of this set is called an optimal (highest) (relative to G) automaton with respect to absolute speed.

Let $(X^G, W, \mathcal{P})$ be a probability space, where W is a σ-algebra of the set X^G, which is generated by its subsets of the following type:

$$W_{\{(g_1,x_1),(g_2,x_2),\ldots,(g_k,x_k)\}} = \{\mu \in X^G \mid \mu \supset \{(g_1,x_1),(g_2,x_2),\ldots,(g_k,x_k)\}\},$$

$$g_i \in G,\ x_i \in X.$$

Let $N_A \neq \emptyset$, T_A be the absolute speed of A with respect to G. The <u>average speed</u> of automaton A with respect to G and measure $\mathcal{P}$ is defined by the formula:

$$\widetilde{T}_A = \frac{1}{\mathcal{P}(N_A)} \sum_{i \in \mathcal{N}} i\mathcal{P}(T_A^{-1}(i)),$$

if the series on the right converge.

Let G and $\mathcal{P}$ be fixed, $\mathfrak{A}$-class of equivalence of automaton with terminal state relative to G. An automaton A_0 is said to be optimal in $\mathfrak{A}$ if $\widetilde{T}_{A_0} = \min \widetilde{T}_A$.

The optimization problem relative to G and $\mathcal{P}$ is solvable if an algorithm exists which enables any finite X-Y-automaton A with terminal state to obtain a finite automaton, which is equivalent to A and optimal with respect to average speed.

Let G - direct product of Y'-automaton G' and Y''-finite automaton G'' $(Y = Y' \cup Y'',\ Y' \cap Y'' = \emptyset)$. The set $S(g') = \{(g',g'') \in G \mid g'' \in G''\}$ is called a series of G. The following conditions for $(X^G, W, \mathcal{P})$:

1) if $\sigma_1 \subset S(g_1')xX, \sigma_2 \subset S(g_2')xX, g_1' \neq g_2'$, then $\mathcal{P}(W_{\sigma 1}).\ = \mathcal{P}(W_{\sigma 1}).\ (W_{\sigma 2})$.

2) if $\sigma_1 = \{((g_1', g_i''), x_i) \mid i = 1,2,\ldots,n\} \subset S(g_1')xX,\ \sigma_2 = \{((g_2', g_i''), x_i) \mid i = 1,2,\ldots,n\} \subset S(g_2')xX$, $g_1' = g_2'$, then $\mathcal{P}(W_{\sigma 1}) = \mathcal{P}(W_{\sigma 2})$.

are called conditions of independence concerning the layers of G.

<u>Theorem</u> Let G' be a loop-free automaton. If all subautomatons of G' are isomorphic and $(X^G, W, \mathcal{P})$ satisfies conditions of independence concerning the layers of G, then the optimization problem relative to G and $\mathcal{P}$ is solvable. In the proof of this theorem, when G is a loop-free automaton, Letichevskii's result on highest automaton with respect to absolute speed, methods of removal of immaterial branches and the theory of Markov chains are used. In this case the problem of synthesis is reduced to the solving of the optimization problem of loop-free automata with terminal state. This is examined by the author in [2]. Let us note the following:

Corollary If G is an Y-automaton corresponding Y-semigroup G with left reduction and undecomposed unit and $(X^G, W, \mathcal{P})$ satisfy conditions of independence concerning the layers of G, then the optimization problem relative to G and $\mathcal{P}$ is solvable.

Application One of the uses of the theorem is the minimization of verification conditions of the average, whivh can be realized by program schemes. We can construct a large class of so called microprogrammed schemes, when the criteria of the optimization is given by linear functionals with coefficients determined from the system equations, together with the given schema. In the synthesis if a loop-free automaton with terminal state, we can use the method of branches and bounds for optimizing this functional.

References

1. A.A.Letichevskii. Functional Equivalence of Dicrete Processors. 1. Cybernetics. N 2, 1969; II. Cybernetics N 2,1970.

2. Ju.H.Shukurian. On Optimal Automaton with a Concluding State without Cycles with respect to average Speed Cybernetics, N 4, 1968.

Logical-Termal Equivalence of Program Schemata

V.E. Itkin (Novosibirsk)

Abstract

In this paper the logic - termal (LT) equivalence of some class of program schemata is introduced and the solvability of recognizing the problem of this equivalence is proved. To the LT -equivalence belongs, for example, the operator and recognizer decomposition, the translation and permutation of operators, the memory redistribution, "untwisting of cycles", economy due to coinciding parts of computations.

0 INTRODUCTION

Fig. 1 presents the standard schema. Let us call it V. Here x is the variable, c is the symbol of the constant, f is the functional symbol and p is the predicate one. 0 is the initial vertex, 0 is the final vertex, 1, 2, 4, 5, 8, are the operator vertices, 3, 6, 7, 9 are the logical ones. The operator and logical vertices are compared to some operators and some recognizers, respectively. x_1, x_2 play the role of the input schema variables and x_1, x_2, x_3 play the role of the output ones. The predicate symbol p plays an auxiliary role only. The arbitrary interpretation A of the symbols x, c, f, p brings the program V into correspondence with the program A(V).

Let us call the standard schemata V,V' to be R-equivalent if for any interpretation of A program A(V) and A(V') either give no results or give coinciding results. The program A(V) could give no result due to two reasons:

(1) The execution of the program follows an infinite path.

(2) The execution of the program follows some path L

where the "use" of some variable is not preceded by its "producted" value. In this case we take this path L not to be a c l o s e d one.

For example, the path

$$0123^{-}7^{+}89^{+}0$$

of the schema Fig. 1 is not a closed one due to the variable x.

LT - history of the path

$$L = 0123^{+}456^{-}89^{+}0^{*}$$

of the schema Fig. 1 is the expression

$$p_1(c_1,c_2)^{+}p_2(f_1(f_3(c_1,c_2)))^{-}p_2(f_1(f_2(c_1)))^{+}$$
$$p^{*}(f_3(c_1,c_2),f_1(f_2(c_1)),f_1(f_2(c_1))) ,$$

i.e. it is the sequence of the formulas for computation of recognizer values belonging to the path L. Each of these formulas has the sign ("+" or "-") labeling the graph arc which the flow from the corresponding logical vertex goes along. We shall call the standard schemata V,V' to be LT - equivalent if the set of all LT - histories of closed paths from the initial to the final vertex of one schema is equal to the set of LT - histories of such paths of the other schema.

The R - equivalence follows from LT - equivalence.

Let us make several general remarks.

(1) This investigation has been undertaken in connection with the attempts to get over some difficulties of the generalization of Yanov schemata [8], [3]. These difficulties are given in [a]. The equivalence of Yanov schemata is founded on the sequence of the executed operators while the LT - equivalence is founded on the sequence of executed recognizers.

(2) In the paper [7] it has been shown that the "interpretational" and "non-degenerate" equivalence of the standard schemata is unsolvable. The LT - equivalence is not the interpretational one.

(3) The LT - history notion and the technique of proving the solvability is founded on the notion of the informational communication r o u t e introduced in [4]. On Fig. 2 the schema (schema over distributed memory, [4]) is presented. In this schema the informational communications are shown explicitly. In [5] the set of routes is considered as an invariant of the schema relative to various memory distributions. The notion of route is analysed also in [6] in connection with the problem of program desequention.

Let us give an example of presentation of the predicate term in the form of an informational communication tree. Let us consider the sequence

$$x_1:=c_1;x_2:=c_2;x_1:=f_1(x_1,x_2);x_3:=f_2(x_1,x_2);p_1(x_3)$$

we denote L. For an arbitrary interpretation the recognizer value $p_1(x_3)$ after executing this sequence is calculated according to the formula

$$p_1(f_2(f_1(c_1,c_2))$$

which we define as e. The D(e) informational communication tree is shown in Fig. 3. In Fig. 4 the arcs designate the routes from L, corresponding to the tree D(e).

In the paper the problem of recognizing the LT - equivalence is considered only for "simple" schemata. Some remarks by B.A. Trakhtenbrot simplifying essentially the proof in this case are used here. The general case is presented in [9].

1. Simple Schemata

1.1 Definition of a simple Scheme

We shall call an arbitrary standard schema (see introduction) a simple one, if it satisfies the following restrictions:

(1) Each operator has either the form x:=c, or x:=f(x').
(2) Each recognizer has the form p(x).
(3) Each path of the schema, which begins with the initial vertex is closed (see introduction).

Below we shall consider only simple schemata. A simple schema is given in Fig. 5.

1.2 Denotations

Let us introduce some denotations and abbreviations relevant to the fixed schema.

(1) h is the schema vertex.
(2) b is the vertex entry into the schema path.
(3) b=h means that b is the h vertex entry.
(4) d is logical vertex entry into the path;
d=h means that d is the entry of the logical vertex h.
(5) L is the schema path.
(6) g is the schema path not containing entries of logic vertices (g may be empty).
(7) d^z means that for d entry into the path the further movement occurs along the arc marked as z (z is "+" or "-").
(8) R(h) is the operator or recognizer compared to the vertex h.

(9) $R_1(h)$ is the functional, predicate symbol, or symbol of the constant belonging to R(h).

(10) HK-path is the path from the initial to the final schema vertex.

(11) HB-path is the infinite path from the initial vertex.

(12) H-path is the HK- or HB-path.

(13) The vertex h uses the variable x, if R(h) is either the operator of x' := f(x) form, or the recognizer of p(x).

(14) The vertex h produces x if R(h) is the operator, having either the form x := f(x'), or x := c.

Let

$$L = g_1 d_1^{x_1} \ldots g_1 d_i^{z_i} \ldots$$

be the schema path.

(15) The sequence

$$z_1 \ldots z_i \ldots$$

is the direction of the path L.

(16) The sequence

$$R_1(\bar{d}_1) \ldots R_1(\bar{d}_i) \ldots$$

is the trace of the path L.

(17) |L| is the length of the path L, i.e. the number of the vertices entries into this path.

(18) ||L|| is the logical length of the path L, i.e. the number of entries of logical vertices into the path L.

For example, the path

$$0123^{+}45^{+}3^{-}673^{+}45^{-}0^{*}$$

of the schema Fig. 5 has the direction

$$++-+-,$$

the trace $p_1 p_2 p_1 p_1 p_2 p^{*}$,

the length 13, the logical length 6.

1.3 The Termal Value

The termal value of the recognizer is the formula for its calculating. More exactly.

Let the path L of V schema be called a route, if

$$L = hL'h'$$

where h' uses the same variable, which h produces and no vertex from L' produces this variable.

For example, the path $123^{-}6$

of the schema Fig. 5 is the route as the vertex 1 produces x_1, the vertex 6 uses x_1 the vertices 2,3 do not produce x_1.
Fig. 6a illustrates this route conditionally.

Let us consider the path L of V schema which opens the initial vertex and closes the logical vertex h, such that

$$R(h) = p(x).$$

Let the presentation

$$L = L_k b_k \dots L_0 b_0 \quad , \quad k \neq 1 \quad , \quad (*)$$

be called the <u>standard presentation</u> of the path L where each of the paths

$$b_1 L_0 b_0$$

$$* * *$$

$$b_k L_{k-1} b_{k-1}$$

is a route, and $R_1(b_k)$ is the symbol of the generator.

Let

$$R_1(b_1) \dots R_1(b_{k-1}) R_1(b_k) = f_1 \dots f_{k-1}{}^{c} \quad .$$

The predicate term

$$p(f_1(\dots f_{k-1}(c) \dots))$$

is the <u>termal value</u> of the recognizer p(x) for the path L.

The standard presentation (*) is conditionally shown on Fig. 6b. In Fig. 6c is conditionally shown the standard presentation of the path

$$0123^{-}673^{-}673^{-}673$$

the schema of Fig. 5. The recognizer termal value $p_1(x_1)$ for this path is equal to

$$p_1(f_2(f_2(f_2(c_1))))$$

1.4 LT - History

Let us consider the arbitrary HK - path

$$L = g_1 d_1{}^{z_1} \dots g_n d_n{}^{z_n} g_{n+1} d_{n+1}$$

of the schema V. The expression e_i(i, 1,...,n+1) is called the <u>LT - history</u> of the path L

$$e_1{}^{z_1} \dots e_n{}^{z_n} e_{n+1}$$

where e_i ($i = 1,\dots,n+1$) is the termal value of the recognizer $R(d_1)$ for the path

$$L(i) = g_1 d_1 \dots g_1 d_i$$

The predicate term e_i is denoted as $i(L)$.

1.5 LT - Equivalence

Let the set of all LT - histories of HK - paths of the schema V be det(V).
The schemata V,V' are called LT - equivalent if det(V) = det(V').

2. The Solution of the Problem

2.1 Causes of Non-equivalence.

H - paths of L, L' schemata V, V' are correspondingly called coordinated ones, if these path directions are either equal or if one of them is the beginning of the other.
For example, if the directions of the paths L_1, L_2, L_3 are equal

$$++-+, ++-, ++-- ,$$

then the paths L_1, L_2 are coordinated, the paths L_2, L_3 are coordinated, the paths L_1, L_3 are not coordinated. If a path has an empty direction it is coordinated with any one.
Assertion. The schemata V, V' are not LT - equivalent if and only if there are coordinated H-paths of L,L' of these schema, satisfying one of the following conditions:

(1) One of these paths is finite, the other is infinite.
(2) Both paths are finite, but have different logical lengths.
(3) Both paths are finite, have equal logical lengths, but their traces are different.
(4) Both paths are finite, have equal logical lengths and equal traces, but $i(L) \neq i(L')$ /see point 1.4/ for some i.

2.2 Denotations

Let us introduce some denotations and abbreviations.

(1) The pair L, L' satisfying the property i(i=1,2,3,4) from the statement 2.1 will be called i-pair.
(2) The minimum of the logical lengths of the paths L, L' will be called the logical length of L, L' paths.

(3) i-pair will be called <u>minimum</u> relative to the i property if the logical length of this pair is not greater than the logical length of any other i-pair paths of the same schemata (i is fixed).

(4) r is the maximum of the number of vertices in V, V' schemata.

(5) Path transformation

$$L = L_1 h L' h L_2$$

where h is the logical vertex, into the path $L_1 h L_2$ will be called reduction of the path L to the cyclic subpath hL'h.
Let us consider the standard presentation (*) of the L (see 1.3).

(6) Entries $b_1, \dots, b_n$ into presentation (*) will be called <u>terminals</u> of the path L. The terminal <u>rank</u> b_s is the number s, i.e. the number of terminals in the interval $b_s \dots b_0$.

(7) Let d be the entry of the logical vertex into the path L. An empty symbol is called the neighbour for d if there are not terminals to the left from d, or an operator vertex h, if the nearest to the left from d terminal b is such, that $\bar{b} = h$.

(8) The entries d, d' to the path L are <u>weak equivalent</u> if their neighbours are equal and $\bar{d} = \bar{d}'$.

Let

$$L = g_1 d_1 \dots g_k d_k; \dots$$
$$L' = g_1' d_1' \dots g_k' d_k' \dots$$

be H-paths of the V, V' schemata. Fig. 7 demonstrates pair conditionally.

(9) The pair of subpaths $d_k \dots d_j$, $d_k' \dots d_j'$ is called a <u>rectangle</u> and denoted as $d_k d_j d_k' d_j'$ and these subpaths are sides of the rectangle. We shall call this one <u>A-rectangle</u> if $d_k = d_j$, and $d_k = d_j'$.

Let us consider the pair of paths

$$L(i) = g_1 d_1 \dots g_i d_i$$
$$L'(i) = g_1' d_1' \dots g_i' d_i'$$

which are the initial interval of HK-paths of L, L'.

(10) The rectangle T belonging to this pair is called a free one if its sides do not contain terminals of paths L(i), L'(i), correspondingly. The rectangle $d_k d_j d'_k d'_j$ is called B-rectangle if the entries d_k, d_j and d'_k, d'_j are weak equivalent.

2.3 The Idea of Proving Solvability

It is readily seen that if we find the estimation Q depending only on r, such that the logical length of each minimum i-pair is not greater than Q then the problem of recognition of LT - equivalence will be reduced to a review of every possible variant.

2.4 Reduction of Paths

Note: As a result of reduction of coordinated H-paths by the corresponding sides of A-rectangle we shall obtain coordinated H-paths.

Note: Let d, d' be weakly equivalent entries of logical vertices into the path L (d is more left than d'); let the interval d...d' contain $m(m \geq 0)$ of the path L terminals; let the path L be obtained by reducing L for the subpath d...d'. Then the following is fulfilled:

(1) There are less terminals in L, on m, than in L;

(2) Each terminal of the path L, to the left from d transforms into the terminal of the path L, its rank being lowered on m;

(3) Each terminal of the path L to the right from d' transforms into the terminal of the same rank of the path L_1.

Fig. 8 depicts all the situations of mutual location of the d, d' entries and the nearest from the left terminals.

2.5 Evaluation of logical lengths of minimum 1-,2-,3-pairs

It is easy to see that the minimum 1-pair as well as the minimum 2-pair contains no one rectangle which is A-rectangle. The estimate for these pairs is r^2.

For the minimum 3-pair there exists a pair (d_k, d'_k) such that $R_1(d_k) \neq R_1(d'_k)$, there are no A-triangles either to the right or to the left from (d_k, d'_k). Here the estimate is $2\ r^2$.

6 Estimation of Logical Length of the Minimum 4-pair

te: Let L, L' be coordinated HK-paths of V,V', schemata having equal aces. The pair L, L' is the 4-pair if and only if there are such i, s at the following property is satisfied: for the terminals b_s, b'_s of e paths L(i), L'(i) is fulfilled

$$R_1(b_s) \neq R_1(b'_s) ,$$

ere terminals b_s, b'_s have one and the same rank s. We shall mark this operty as C(i,s).

is easy to see that if the paths L(i), L'(i) have unequal numbers of rminals, there exists s, at which C(i,s) is carried out.

g. 9 demonstrates the 4-pair satisfying the property C(i,s). In this gure d_k is the nearest to the right from b_s entry of the logical vertex, is the nearest to the left from b_s entry of the logical vertex. We ppose for simplicity that

$$b_s \ldots b_{n+1} \qquad b'_s \ldots b'_{n+1} \quad .$$

shall make some remarks on the evaluation of logical length the pair results from

) There is no one triangle, being A-triangle, in the $d_1 d_j d'_1 d'_j$ triangle well as in $d_1 d_{n+1} d'_n d'_{n+1}$ triangle. The estimate for these triangles is

$$Q_1 = r^2 \ .$$

2) There are no two "uncrossed" B-triangles (i.e. there are not two -triangles, located as in Fig. 10) in the triangle L, L'. Indeed, pposing the opposite, after reducing the paths L, L' by the sides one or both triangles we shall again obtain the 4-pair that contra-cts to the minimum of the 4-pair L, L'. Here it is necessary to con-ider the following cases. Let m, m' be the numbers of terminals in e paths L, L' correspondingly; m_1, m'_j be the numbers of terminals in e upper and lower sides of the triangle T_1 (see Fig. 10); m_2, m'_2 be e numbers of terminals in the upper and lower sides of the triangle T_2.

Case 1 Either $m_1 = m'_1$, or $m_2 = m'_2$.

Case 2 $m_1 \neq m'_1$ and $m_2 \neq m'_2$.

Case 2(1) $m - m_1 \neq m' - m'_j$.

Case 2(2) $m - m_1 \quad m' - m'_1$. In this case due to

$m_2 \neq m_2'$, is fulfilled $m - (m_1 + m_2) \neq m' - (m_1' + m_2')$.
After reducing for the side of one of B-triangles in the cases 1, 2(1), and for the sides of both B-triangles in the case 2(2), we shall again obtain the 4-pair. The estimate of the logical length of the $d_k d_1 d_k' d_1'$ triangle is

$$Q_2 = 2 \cdot r^2 \cdot (r + 1)^2 .$$

(3) The arbitrary terminal b_u from the interval $d_j \ldots b_s$ will be called <u>"non-essential"</u> one if the number of terminals of L'(i) path is less than u. The other terminals from the $d_j d_k d_j' d_k'$ triangle will be called <u>essential</u> ones. The arbitrary triangle T, belonging to $d_j d_k d_j' d_k'$, will be called a <u>nearly free</u> one, if it is either free or each terminal it contains, is a non-essential one. It is easy to see that $d_j d_k d_j' d_k'$ does not contain nearly free A-triangles.

(4) In the section $b_s' \ldots d_k'$ there are no more terminals than entries of operator vertices into $b_s \ldots d_1$. In the section $d_1 \ldots b_s$ there are no more essential terminals than entries of the operator vertices into $a_0' \ldots b'$ (a_0' is the initial vertex of the schema V'). We shall mark the estimate of the quantity of essential terminals in the $d_j d_k d_j' d_k'$ triangle as Q_3.

$$Q_3 = r \cdot (Q_1 + {}''2^{+2}) .$$

(5) The estimate of the logical length of $d_j d_k d_j' d_k'$ triangle follows from the preceding remarks. We shall denote it as Q_4.

The value Q of the logical length of the minimum 4-pair follows from the preceding remarks:

$$Q = 2 \cdot Q_1 + {}''2^{+Q_4} .$$

Now from 2.3 and derived estimates it follows that the problem of recognition LT - equivalence in the class of simple schemata is solved.

REFERENCES

[1] A.P. ERSHOV, Theory of Program Schemata, IFIP Congress, 71, Lubljana, August 23-28, 1971.

[2] A.P. ERSHOV, A.A. LIAPOUNOV, On Formalization of the Program Concept, Kibernetika (Kiev) 5 (1967).

[3] A.P. ERSHOV, On Yanov Program Schemata, Cybernetics Problems, 20 (Nauka, Moscow, 1967).

[4] A.P. ERSHOV, On Program Schemata Over Common and Distributed Memory, Kibernetika (Kiev) 4 (1968).

[5] A.P. ERSHOV, Reducing the Problem of Memory Allocation when Compiling Programs to the one of Colouring the Vertices of Graphs, Dokl. Akad. Nauk SSSR, 142, IV.4 (1962).

[6] V.E. KOTOV, Transformation of Program Schemata into Asynchronous Programs, Dissertation autoreferate (Comp. Center Siberian Div. Ac. Sci. Novosibirsk, 1970).

[7] V.E. ITKIN, Z. ZWIENOGRODSKY, On Equivalence of Program Schemata, J. Comp. Syst. Sci. 5 (1971).

[8] Yu.I. YANOV, On Logical Algorithm Schemata, Cybernetics problems 1, (Fizmatgiz, Moscow, 1958).

[9] V.E. ITKIN, Logic-Thermal Equivalence of Program Schemata, Kibernetika (Kiev) 1 (1972).

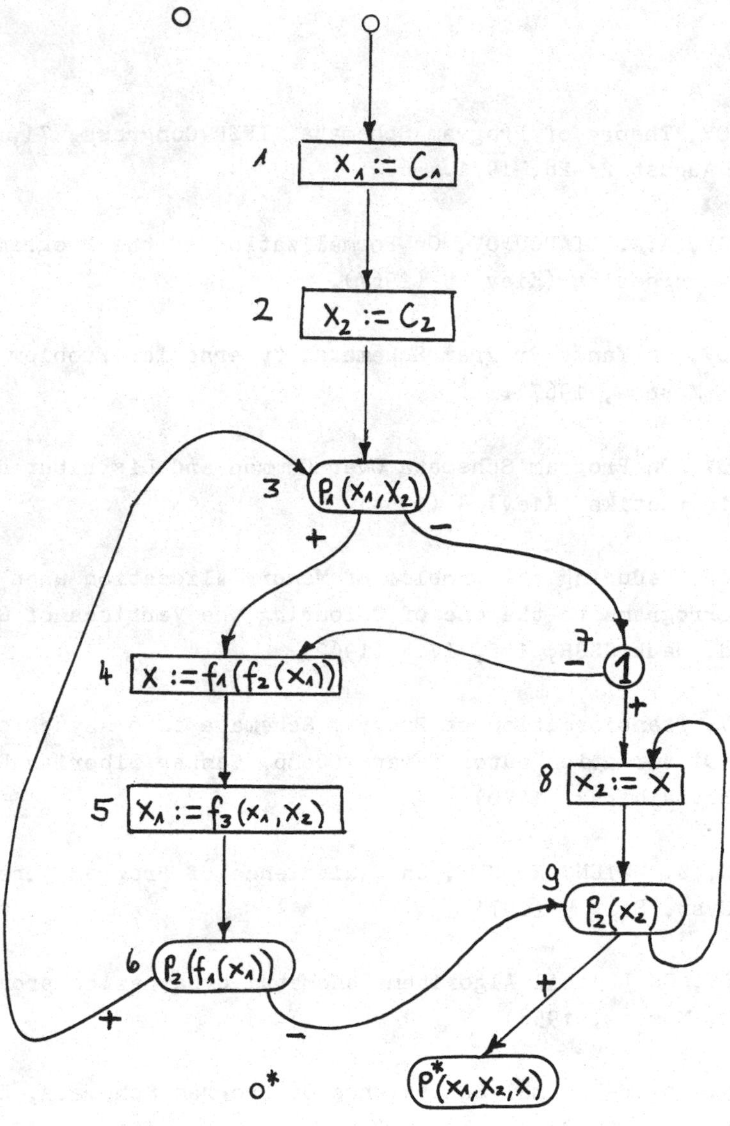
o
o
1
$x_1 := C_1$
2
$x_2 := C_2$
3
$p_1(x_1, x_2)$
+
−
4
$x := f_1(f_2(x_1))$
7
−
1
+
8
$x_2 := x$
5
$x_1 := f_3(x_1, x_2)$
9
$p_2(x_2)$
6
$p_2(f_1(x_1))$
+
−
+
o*
$p^*(x_1, x_2, x)$

Fig. 1

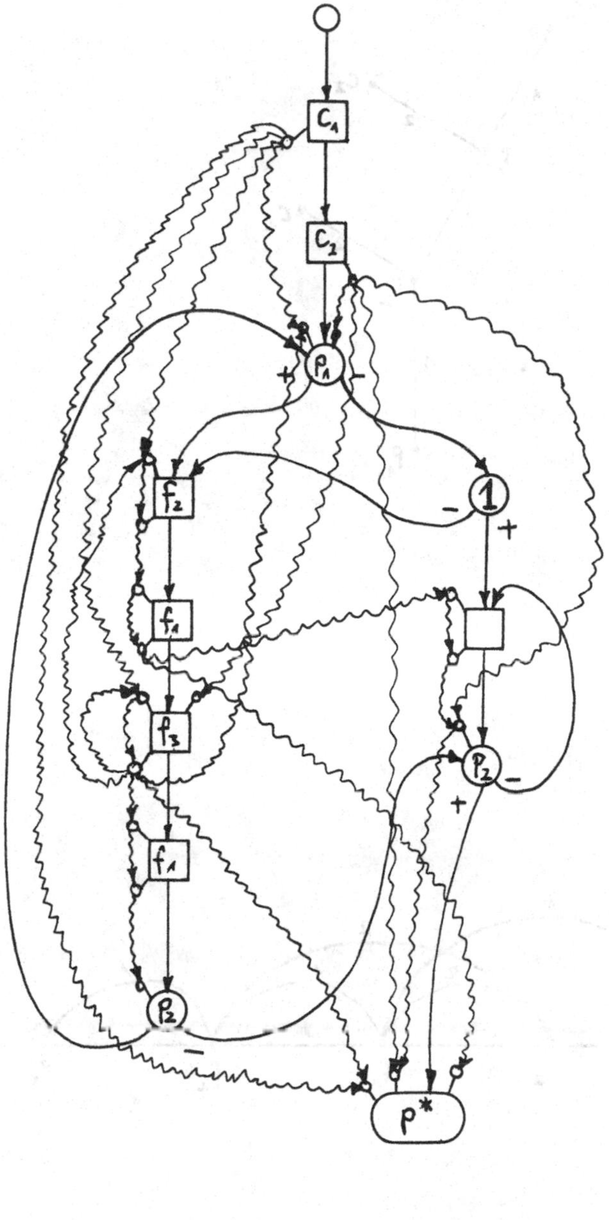

Fig. 2

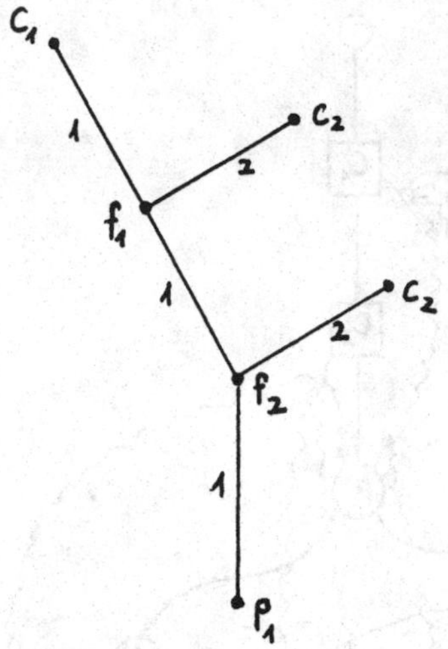

Fig. 3

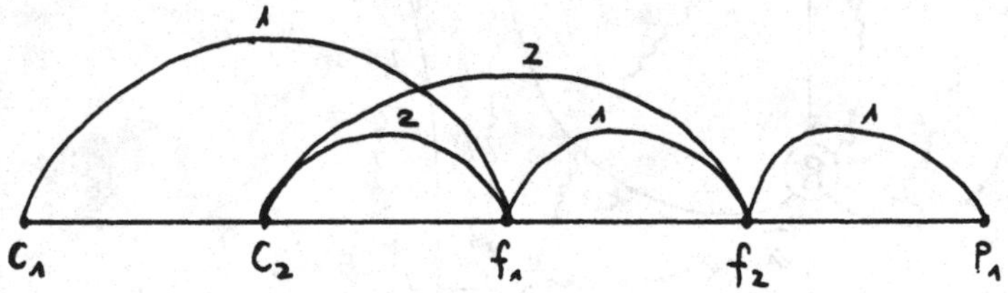

Fig. 4

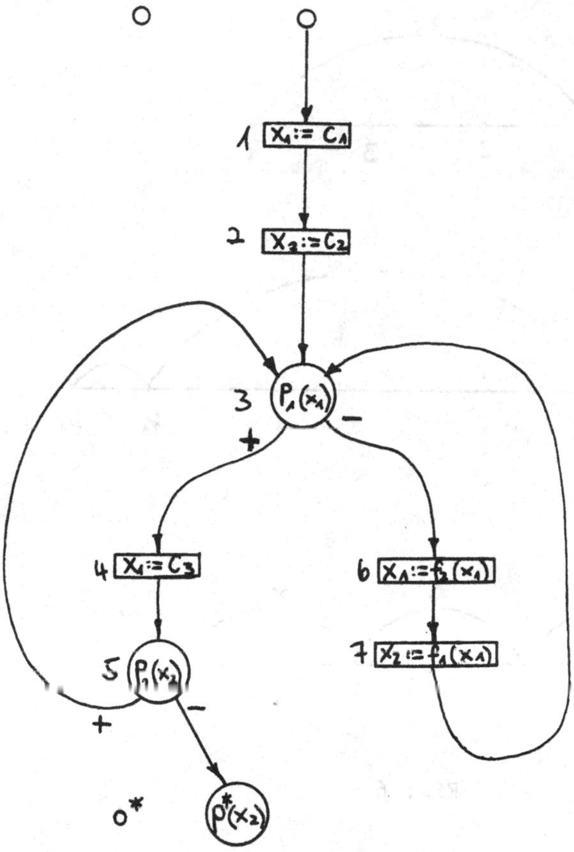

Fig. 5

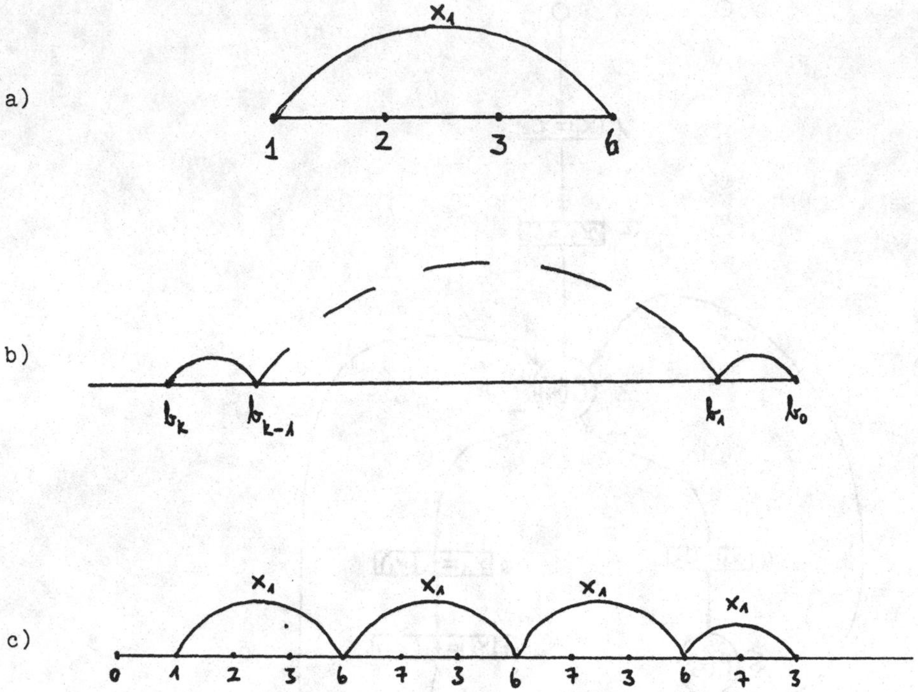

Fig. 6

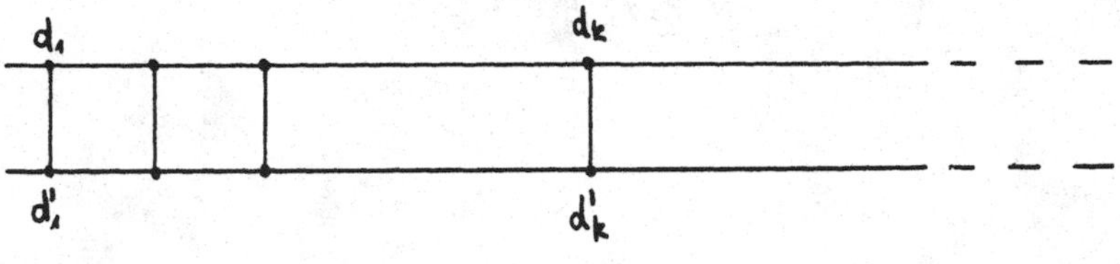

Fig. 7

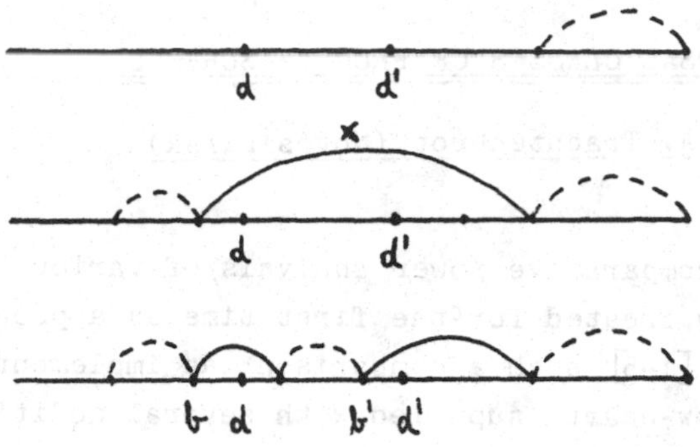

Fig. 8

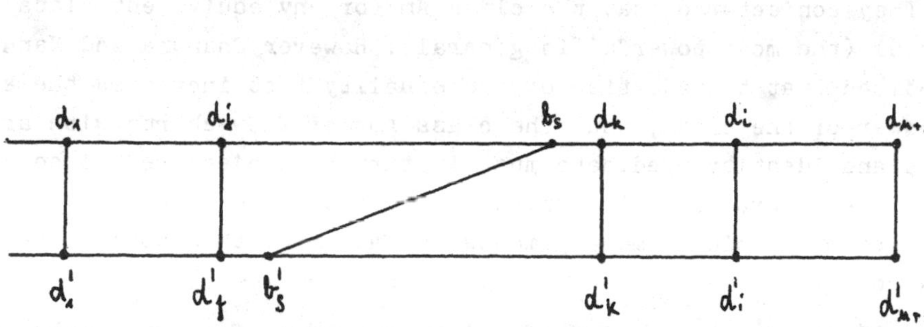

Fig. 9

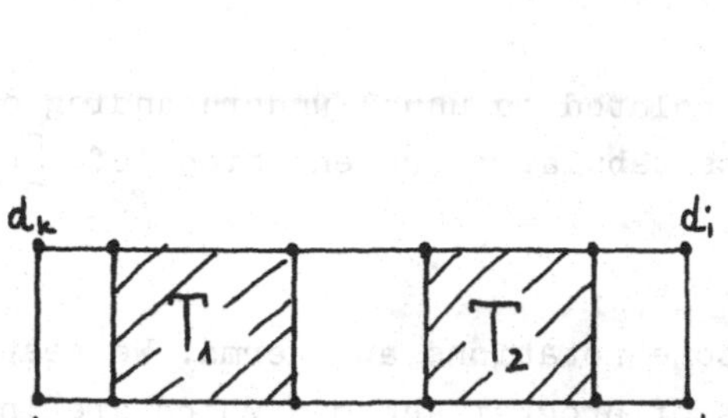

Fig. 10

ON UNIVERSAL CLASSES OF PROGRAM SCHEMAS

B.A. Trachtenbrot (Novosibirsk)

Introduction

In [1] the problem of comparative power analysis of various programming languages is apparently treated for the first time as a program schemas comparison problem. In [1-5] such a comparison was implemented for recursive schemas and flow-charts supplied with several additional programming devices such as arrays, counters, markers, equality test etc. Constable and Gries proved in [4] that the class Am of flow-charts with arrays and markers is the most powerful among the classes considered by them. They conjectured that the class Am (or any equivalent class) is universal (the most powerful in general). However Chandra and Manna in [5] noticed that the addition of the equality test increases the expressive power of the class; thus the class Am= of flow-charts with arrays, markers and identity predicate must in turn be conjectured to be universal. Thus a natural question arises whether this conjecture is final. In this communication some arguments in favour of this conjecture are suggested.

It is evident that the notion of universal class of program schemas (universal language) becomes exact only after a proper formalization of the notions "program schema" and "program schema class (language)". In §1 axioms are stated which we suppose must be satisfied at a reasonable definition of the notions mentioned above. In §2 it is shown that from these axioms the existence of universal classes follows, in particular Am= is one of them.

Our approach is closely related to usual understanding of effective (recursive) operator and its tabular representation (cf. [6]).

§1.

First of all we recall some notations and terms. We restrict our considerations to the class of program schemas which are intended for programming and computation of one-argument functions.

Program schemas in contrast to programs may contain both interpreted symbols (constants, functions, predicates, labels etc.) and uninterpreted ones. These last symbols form the signature of the schema (more precise, the uninterpreted part of it) which has the form:

$$\sigma = < x; \varphi_1,\dots,\varphi_k; P_1,\dots,P_m >,$$

where

a) x is the initial object symbol,
b) $\varphi_1,\ldots,\varphi_k$ are functional symbols with various numbers of argument places,
c) $P_1,\ldots,P_m$ are predicate symbols with various numbers of argument places.

Let R be a schema in the signature σ, and $\mathcal{J}$ be a model in the same signature with some object domain $\mathfrak{D}$. Thus the schema R becomes (completely interpreted) program $\langle R,\mathcal{J}\rangle$, which prescribes a definite computation process. If the process is finite and a result $y^o \in \mathfrak{D}$ is obtained (notation - $Exec(R,\mathcal{J}) = y^o$) then we say that the schema R is applicable to the model (interpretation) $\mathcal{J}$. Otherwise we say that R is not applicable to $\mathcal{J}$, and we denote it as follows:

$$Exec(R,\mathcal{J}) = \omega ,$$

where ω is the "undefined value" symbol.

Let us stress the following:

(I) In models $\mathcal{J}$ the functions φ_i and the predicates P_j are assumed to be total. The presence of partial functions and predicates is of a great interest but causes specific difficulties. (This situation is cleared up in [1] and [4]).

(II) The domain $\mathfrak{D}$ contains no interpreted objects associated a priori (i.e. before the choice of the model $\mathcal{J}$) with the schema R. This assumption prevents from possible collisions which result from the coexistence of interpreted and uninterpreted objects.

Two schemas R_1 and R_2 in the same signature are considered to be equivalent (notation $R_1 \approx R_2$) under the following condition

$$\forall \mathcal{J}.\ Exec(R_1,\mathcal{J}) = Exec(R_2,\mathcal{J}) .$$

The subject of investigation is generally a class of schemas, in other word - a schema language. A class of schemas (a Schema language) is usually described in syntactic or semantic terms, and join all the schemas of a given type in any signature.

Class $\mathcal{K}_1$ is translatable into a class $\mathcal{K}_2$ if:

$$\forall R_1 \in \mathcal{K}_1\ \exists R_2 \in \mathcal{K}_2 [R_1 \approx R_2] .$$

The class $\mathfrak{K}_1$ is effectively translatable into the class $\mathfrak{K}_2$ if there exists an algorithm which gives for any R_1 the corresponding schema R_2. Of course, when we compare the concrete classes of schemas in terms of translatability relation, the exact definition of notions of "program schema" or "class of program schemas" are redundant. However, we need exact definitions when setting a problem on the existence of universal (effectively universal) class of schemas. Let us consider the following natural definition. "The class $\mathfrak{K}$ is universal (effectively universal) if any other class is translatable (effectively translatable) into $\mathfrak{K}$". This definition calls for preliminary refinement of the notions of schemas and class of schemas or at least for refinement of those of their properties which are relevant in this situation. The axioms formulated below formalize explicitely the properties which must have the two-argument function Exec(R,$\mathfrak{J}$) when R and $\mathfrak{J}$ form any schema-model pair (in the same signature) and when R "ranges" over some schema class.

A. Let λ be an isomorphic mapping of a model $\mathfrak{J}$ onto a model $\mathfrak{J}'$ ($\lambda(\omega)=\omega$). Then

$$\lambda(\text{Exec}(R,\mathfrak{J})) = \text{Exec}(R,\mathfrak{J}') \quad .$$

Note that in this axiom the remark (II) on the object domain $\mathfrak{D}$ is contained implicitely.

Any restriction $\mathfrak{J}'$ of a model $\mathfrak{J}$ to a subset $\mathfrak{D}' \subseteq \mathfrak{D}$ containing the initial object x^o we call a fragment of the model $\mathfrak{J}$. Particularly the fragment of the model $\mathfrak{J}$ may happen to be a submodel of it (when $\mathfrak{D}'$ is f_1-closed). All the axioms to follow are formulated in terms of fragments and submodels.

The notation

$$\mathfrak{J}' \leq \mathfrak{J}$$

has the sense : $\mathfrak{J}'$ is a fragment of $\mathfrak{J}$.

B. Let $\delta(\mathfrak{J})$ be the least submodel of the model $\mathfrak{J}$ such that its object domain $\delta(\mathfrak{D}) \subseteq \mathfrak{D}$ contains x and is closed under the functions $f_1,\ldots,f_k$. Then

$$\forall \mathfrak{J}.\ \text{Exec}(R,\mathfrak{J}) = \text{Exec}(R,\delta(\mathfrak{J})) \ .$$

The sense of this demand is quite evident. During an implementation of a (completely interpreted) program <R,$\mathfrak{J}$> only such elements of $\mathfrak{D}$ may be used which are generated by signature functions from the elements available to a moment in $\mathfrak{D}$. In other words, the program implementation process prevents from occasional generating of any irrelevant elements*).

Let $T\sigma$ denote the set of all terms obtainable from the object symbol x and the functional symbols $\varphi_1,\dots,\varphi_k$ in σ. From the axioms A-B it follows that the behaviour of a schema R in all the models is completely determined by its behaviour in the factor-termal models only (an analogue of the Löwenheim-Skolem theorem for the formulas of the first-order predicate calculus**)). These axioms have pure model theoretic nature. They do not mirror the natural features of effectiveness which are specific to any resonable notion of the program implementation process.

Partially these effectiveness features become apparent in the following. Since every terminative computation process is finite, it may use the information contained only in a finite fragment $\mathfrak{J}'$ of the model $\mathfrak{J}$. This is expressed in the following axiom:

C_1. Let $\mathrm{Exec}(R,\mathfrak{J}) = y^{o} \in \mathfrak{D}$. Then there exists a finite fragment $\mathfrak{J}' \subseteq \mathfrak{J}$ such that

$$\forall \mathfrak{J}_1 \{\mathfrak{J}' \subseteq \mathfrak{J}_1 \to \mathrm{Exec}(R,\mathfrak{J}_1) = y^{o}\} .$$

Let us consider the constructive object $\mathfrak{R}$ which is a finite set of terms from $T\sigma$ with identity relation and signature predicates defined consistently on it. It is evident that there exists a (not unique in general) factor-termal model $\tilde{\mathfrak{R}}$ such that $\mathfrak{R}$ is its fragment (notation $\mathfrak{R} \subseteq \tilde{\mathfrak{R}}$). Let τ be one of the terms in $\mathfrak{R}$. It may happen that the information contained in $\mathfrak{R}$ is sufficient for an execution of R with the result equal to τ; in this case we say that the pair $\langle \mathfrak{R}, \tau \rangle$ is consistent with regard to R. Formally the consistency property of the constructive object $\langle \mathfrak{R}, \tau \rangle$ means that $\mathrm{Exec}(R,\tilde{\mathfrak{R}}) = y^{o}$ for any factor-termal model $\tilde{\mathfrak{R}}$ such that $\mathfrak{R} \subseteq \tilde{\mathfrak{R}}$.

---

*) M.S. Paterson and D. Park drew the author's attention to the fact that this restriction excludes some types of "nondeterministically" functioning schemas.

**) In a free termal model with the signature σ (called also free interpretation) the object domain coincides with $T\sigma$. In a factor-termal model the object domain is derived from $T\sigma$ by the partition into equivalence classes according to the identity relation.

C_2. The set of all the pairs $\langle \mathfrak{A}, \tau \rangle$ consistent with regard to R is recursively enumerable.

At least let us formulate the requirement for a well-defined class $\mathfrak{K}$ of the program schemas.

D. There exists an algorithm which for any schema $R \in \mathfrak{K}$ gives an effective enumeration of all the pairs consistent with R.

Commonly in real classes $\mathfrak{K}$ this property is verified as follows. For a terminative computation process the notion of its length (that is the number of its steps) is introduced in a natural way. Let the predicate

$$T(R, \mathfrak{A}, \tau, n)$$

denote: "The schema $R \in \mathfrak{K}$ being applied to $\mathfrak{A}$ terminates its computation with the result τ no later than after n steps". This predicate proves to be effective; its value may be computed at least by finite searching through all the possible variants.

§2.

THEOREM: (I) The class Am= is effectively universal;
(II) The class A= is universal but not effectively universal.

Proof. In [4] the class Am is proved to be translatable but not effectively translatable into the class A. The same proof is suitable for the comparison of the classes Am= and A=. Hence it is sufficient to show that the class Am= is effectively universal, therefore it is sufficient to prove the following fact:

Let M be a recursively enumerable set of pairs $\langle \mathfrak{A}, \tau \rangle$ in some signature σ (for example a Turing machine $\mathfrak{M}$ which carries out an enumeration of M is given). In this case one can effectively construct a program schema $R \in$ Am= in the signature σ which has the following property:

If M coincides with the set of all the pairs consistent with some schema R' in the signature σ then R' is equivalent to R.

The construction of R is carried out in two stages. The first stage depends only on the signature σ and does not depend on the set M. The second stage takes into account the information of the set M. We outline both stages of the construction dropping all the details of programming by means of Am=. Point (b) in the stage I and points (d) and (e) in the stage II deal with constructions in Am=. Other points deal with encoding and are not related to any specific programming techniques.

Stage I.

a) Encoding of all the possible pairs $<\mathfrak{A},\tau>$.
Assume that for a given signature σ an enumeration of the terms from $T\sigma$

$$\tau_1, \tau_2, \ldots, \tau_n, \ldots \qquad (\#)$$

and enumeration of the pairs of terms

$$<\tau_1', \tau_1''>, <\tau_2', \tau_2''>, \ldots \qquad (\#\#)$$

of the triples, the quadruples and so on are fixed.

With the help of the marker system $\{\wedge, |, *, ', t, f\}$ the encoding may be carried out which is clear from the following examples:

a_1) $\wedge\wedge\wedge\wedge|$ encodes the term τ_5;

a_2) $*\wedge\wedge t \wedge f \wedge t$ means: one-place (one occurence of $*$) predicate P is defined on the terms τ_3, τ_5, τ_7 so that: $P(\tau_3)$ is true, $P(\tau_5)$ is false, $P(\tau_7)$ is true (the terms $\tau_1, \tau_2, \tau_4, \tau_6$ are dropped, which is pointed out by the corresponding occurences of the symbol $\wedge$);

a_3) $**\wedge\wedge t \wedge f \wedge t$ (differs from the previous example by additional occurence of the symbol $*$) denotes: two-place predicate P is defined on the pairs $<\tau_3', \tau_3''>$, $<\tau_5', \tau_5''>$, $<\tau_7', \tau_7''>$ and takes the values true, false, true correspondingly.

Now let the signature σ contain for example one one-place predicate P_1, one two-place predicate P_2, and two three-place predicates (P_3 and P_y). Then the code of the pair $<\mathfrak{A},\tau>$ has the form "$\tilde{P}_1\tilde{P}_2\tilde{E}_q\tilde{P}_3\tilde{P}_y \rightarrow$ code (τ)", where $\tilde{P}_i$ stands for the code (in the sense of the examples a_2-a_3) of the information on the predicate P_i on the set of terms under consideration, $\tilde{E}_q$ stands for the same kind of information about the identity predicate.

b) In [4] it is proved that by means of a flow-chart with arrays a repititionless listing of all the terms from $T\sigma$ and the location of their values into the members of some array B_1 may be carried out. Therefore, we get some definite enumeration of the terms in $T\sigma$, namely τ_k is the term whose value is kept in $B_1[k]$.

Similarly we may fill an array B_2 by values of all the possible pairs of terms, an array B_3 - by values of all the possible triples of terms and so on (locating the elements of the first pair into B_2 [1], B_2 [2], the elements of the second pair into B_2 [3], B_2 [4], etc.).

We may consider the enumerations (#), (##), ... used for encoding the pairs of the form $<\mathcal{R},\tau>$ to be just those described by means of arrays B_1, B_2, ...

Stage II.

c) The enumeration $\mathfrak{M}$ may be based on an encoding which differs from that described above. In this case $\mathfrak{M}$ carries out first of all necessary recoding. Henceforth we suppose that $\mathfrak{M}$ is a Turing machine which on one of its tapes lists one after another all the pairs from the given set M.

d) It is well known how to similate computations of p-tape s-letter Turing machine by means of a flow-chart supplied by p arrays and s markers. This permits us to supply the schema R to be constructed with an array Γ destined for storing the codes of pairs from M.

e) After the next pair $<\mathcal{R},\tau>$ is transmitted to the array Γ, the schema R starts in dovetail manner to compute the predicates $P_1, P_2, \ldots$ and the identity predicate for the values stored in B_1, for pairs of values stored in B_2 etc., and to compare the results of the computations with the values encoded in R. If at some moment this comparison does not find any contradictions, the computation is completed successfully obtaining the value of τ (chosen in the array B_1).

[1] M.S. Paterson, C.E. Hewitt, Comparative schematology. Record of Project MAC, ACM, N.Y., pp. 119-128.

[2] S.J. Garland, D.C. Luckham, Program schemes, recursion schemes, and formal languages. UCLA-ENG-7154, University of California, Los Angeles, June 1971.

[3] H.R. Strong, Translating recursion equations into flow-charts. Jour. Comp. Syst. Sci., v.5 (1971), pp. 254-285.

[4] R.L. Constable, D. Gries, On classes of program schemata. TR71-105, Computer Science Dept., Cornell University, August 1971.

[5] A.K. Chandra, Z. Manna, Program schemas with equality. Stanford Artificial Intelligence Project MEMO AIM-158, Stanford, December , 1971.

[6] **Б.А.Трахтенброт. Табличное представление рекурсивных операторов. ДАН, IOI(I955),стр. 4I7-420.**

Certain decompositions of Gödel Numbering and the Semantics of Programming Languages

B. Buchberger *)

N o t a t i o n :

N ... set of natural numbers including o.

$N^k := \underbrace{N \times \ldots \times N}_{k \text{ times}}$

The whole treatment will be over the natural numbers. Thus, by a function (predicate) we normally mean an arithmetical function (predicate). Of course, all what follows could be done over arbitrary (effectively given) denumerable domains using an appropriate version of recursive function theory (ASSER 6o, SHOENFIELD 71 etc.).

$\bar{A}$ ... complement of the set A.

$A \subset_{+} B$ means $A \subset B$ and $A \neq B$.

If f, g denote functions then we often write fg(x) for f(g(x)) and $f^{(t)}(x)$ for $\underbrace{f \ldots f}_{t \text{ times}}(x)$. In addition, $f^{(o)}(x) := x$.

(x), (Ex) ... universal and existential quantification over N.

Let f be a function, $A \subset N$. We define $f(A) := \{y \mid (Ex \in A)(f(x) = y)\}$.

An analogous notation will be used for n-ary functions.

$|C|$ ... cardinality of the set C.

$|C| = \infty$ ... C is an infinite set.

P_n ... set of all n-ary partial recursive functions.

R_n ... set of all n-ary total recursive functions.

*) Inst. f. Num. Mathematik und Elektronische Informationsverarbeitung, Universität Innsbruck, A6020 Innsbruck, Austria/Europe.

1. A certain type of universal functions and the semantics of universal programming languages

Definition 1.1:

τ is a pairing function: $\Longleftrightarrow$ $\tau \in R_2$, τ is 1-1, and $\tau(N,N)$ is decidable.

Notation: Let τ be a pairing function. By τ_1, τ_2 we denote total recursive functions for which

$$\tau_1\tau(x,y) = x, \quad \tau_2\tau(x,y) = y,$$

$$z \in \tau(N,N) \rightarrow \quad \tau(\tau_1(z),\tau_2(z)) = z.$$

Further, $<x,y>$ stands for $\tau(x,y)$, where τ is an arbitrary pairing function that remains fixed throughout the following.

Definition 1.2. (ROGERS 58, USPENSKIİ 60):

Ψ describes a Gödel numbering of the unary partial recursive functions (in short: Ψ "is" a Gödel numbering) $:\Longleftrightarrow$

(GN1) $\Psi \in P_2$,

(GN2) for all $\Psi' \in P_2$ there exists a $\sigma \in R_1$ such that

$$\Psi'(p',x) = \Psi(\sigma(p'),x).$$

Remarks: The relevance of Gödel numberings for a semantical theory of universal programming languages has been pointed out in various papers (see, for instance, SCHWENKEL 66; the earliest investigation in this direction is due to USPENSKI I 56). Briefly summarized, this relevance relies on the following observations:

(L1) We could content ourselves with the knowledge we obtain on the semantics of a programming language L by knowing the result ${}^{L}\Psi(p,x)$ of the application of the program p to the data x for all p,x. Otherwise stated, we could conceive the semantics of a programming language to be given by the correspondence

$$p \longmapsto (\lambda x)({}^{L}\Psi(p,x)),$$

where p ranges over all programs of the language L.

(L2) The result ${}^{L}\Psi(p,x)$ should be effectively computable form p and x.

(L3) $\{ (\lambda x)({}^{L}\Psi(p,x)) \mid p \in N \} = P_1$ should hold for a universal language L.

(L4) Given a description p' of a function g in some standard mathematical notation, e. g. in some other programming language (that could be equally well characterized by some binary function Ψ'), a program p for g in L should be effectively obtainable from p'.

It is clear that requirement (L2) is guaranteed by (GN1) and requirements (L3) and (L4) are simultaneously guaranteed by (GN2). Hence, if we accept (L1) the theory of Gödel numberings would just coincide with the semantical theory of universal programming languages.

However, what makes the concept of (L1) unsatisfactory is, first, the total absence of a notion of "computation in the language L" (i. a. all intermediate stages between input of data and output of the result remain unspecified); and second, the impossibility of seperating the role which input/output coding plays for the determination of the Gödel numbering associated with a given language. Thus, Rogers isomorphism theorem (ROGERS 58) can be viewed as telling that by suitable program coding every universal language can determine every possible Gödel numbering. The data input/output coding has a similarly severe influence. Our Definition 1.4 is intended to give a precise version of a semantical concept for universal programming languages that takes into account both the stepwise work of programs and the role of input/output. Definition 1.3 is preparatory.

<u>Definition 1.3:</u> Let $\bar{\Psi}$, $\kappa \in R_1$. We say that Ψ^* is obtained by "conditioned iteration" from $\bar{\Psi}$ and κ, if $\Psi^*(\xi)$ is defined to be the first $\bar{\Psi}^{(t)}(\xi)$ in the sequence $\xi, \bar{\Psi}(\xi), \bar{\Psi}^{(2)}(\xi), \ldots$ for which $\kappa\bar{\Psi}^{(t)}(\xi) = 0$. More formally,

(CI)
$$\Psi^*(\xi) = \begin{cases} \xi, & \text{if } \kappa(\xi) = 0 \\ \Psi^* \cdot \bar{\Psi}(\xi), & \text{otherwise.} \end{cases}$$

<u>Notation:</u> We write $[\Psi,\kappa]$ for the function which is obtained form Ψ,κ by conditioned iteration.

<u>Remarks:</u> $[\bar{\Psi},\kappa](\xi)$ can be viewed, for instance, as defining the terminal state which an (infinite) automaton with transition function $\bar{\Psi}$ and "termination criterion" κ, eventually, assumes when started in state ξ . Of course, $[\bar{\Psi},\kappa](\xi)$ may be undefined for certain ξ . Thus, $[\bar{\Psi},\kappa] \in P_1$ for $\bar{\Psi},\kappa \in R_1$.

<u>Definition 1.4:</u> $\bar{\Psi},\kappa$ define a universal automaton (in short: $\bar{\Psi},\kappa$ "are" universal) : $\Longleftrightarrow$

(U1) $\bar{\Psi},\kappa \in R_1$

(U2) there exist $\rho \in R_1$ and $\gamma \in R_2$ such that $\rho[\Psi,\kappa]\gamma$ is a Gödel numbering.

<u>Remarks:</u> In BUCHBERGER 72 we give a detailed exposition of the intuitive reasons why we think that this notion of "universal" $\bar{\Psi},\kappa$ is an adequate precise substitute for the notion of a universal programming language. We briefly summarize the discussion given there:

1. The semantics of a programming language can be given by telling, first, what is done during one "step" of a computation according to a program of the language (i. e. by giving the successor "state" $\bar{\Psi}(\xi)$ for every possible state ξ that may arise in a computation in the language) and, second, which states are "terminal" (this is the role of κ). Of course, $\bar{\Psi}$ and κ should be total recursive. One "component" of the state is the program. By the Definition 1.4. it is not excluded that the program is altered during the computation. Hence, this concept is wide enough to encompass, for instance, machine languages.

2. Of course, also functions Ψ^* that are not defined in terms of two functions $\bar{\Psi},\kappa$ by the scheme (CI) can be used to define the semantics of programming languages by giving the terminal "state" $\Psi^*(\xi)$ corresponding to every possible initial state met in the computations of the language (see, for instance, the function apply [fn;x;a] for LISP in McCARTHY 62, or the flow chart interpreter $\mathfrak{V}(d)(\sigma)$ in SCOTT 71).
   However, as long as the available hardware essentially functions in the way given by the scheme (CI), at some stage of the implementation of a language its semantics must be given by a function of the form $[\bar{\Psi},\kappa]$ (compare, however, Remark 4. in Section 3).

3. Infact, a review of the relevant literature schows that most "programming languages" (including the various computability formalisms of recursive

function theory) are (informally) given in the form $[\bar{\Psi},\kappa]$. Thus, for instance, the Vienna method (LUCAS/LAUER/STIGLEITNER 68) uses essentially this form. Also, our concept (even that given in Definition 1.5 below) is still wide enough to embrace the concepts given in SCOTT 67.

4. We would not like to dispense universal programming languages from being capable of defining a Gödel numbering for <u>some</u> suitable input/output conventions. This is guaranteed by (U2). The restriction laid onto admissable input/output functions ρ,γ (namely their recursiveness) seems to be very wide. However, it is difficult to require additional properties for these functions without excluding, perhaps, interesting cases prematurely. An important special case is singled out by the following

<u>Definition 1.5:</u> $\bar{\Psi},\kappa$ define a normal universal automaton (in short: $\bar{\Psi},\kappa$ "are" normal universal"): $\Longleftrightarrow$

(NU1) $\bar{\Psi},\kappa \in R_1$

(NU2) there exists a pairing function τ and a $\bar{\bar{\Psi}} \in R_2$ such that

$$\kappa\tau(p,n) \neq 0 \rightarrow \bar{\Psi}\tau(p,n) = \tau(p,\bar{\bar{\Psi}}(p,n))$$

(NU3) there exist $\rho,\gamma \in R_1$ such that

$(\lambda p,x)(\rho\tau_2[\bar{\Psi},\kappa]\tau(p,\gamma(x)))$ is a Gödel numbering.

<u>Remarks:</u> The above definition characterizes those "interpreters" (automata) $\bar{\Psi},\kappa$ that do <u>not</u> change the program during execution time. Whether or not an interpreter changes the programs by execution also depends on how we split the states ξ in a program component $p:=\tau_1(\xi)$ and a working store compo-

ponent $\eta := \tau_2(\xi)$. In order that some given $\bar{\Psi},\kappa$ define a normal universal automaton (NU2) requires that $\bar{\Psi}$ does not alter the program for some possible splitting of the states. Given such a splitting it is natural to require that input/output should refer to the working store component only. This is just what is expressed in (NU3).

2. Propositions on the decompositions of Gödel numberings given in the Definitions 1.4 and 1.5.

In this section we state some theorems concerning the decompositions of Gödel numberings that appear in the Definitions 1.4 and 1.5. Partly, their proofs are quite elaborate and will be given in detail in BUCHBERGER/ ROIDER 72, if not stated otherwise.

First ist is good to know that every Gödel numbering has a decomposition of the form given in Definition 1.4:

Theorem 2.1: Every Gödel numbering Ψ can be written in the form

$$\Psi(p,x) = \rho\tau_2[\bar{\Psi},\kappa]\tau(p,\gamma(x)),$$

where

$$\bar{\Psi}\tau(p,\xi) = \tau(p,\bar{\bar{\Psi}}(p,\xi))$$

with suitable $\rho,\kappa,\gamma \in R_1$, $\bar{\bar{\Psi}},\tau \in R_2$, τ being a pairing function.

Remarks: Theorem 2.1 is a consequence of Corollary 2.6 in BUCHBERGER 71, where it is shown that suitable ρ, κ, γ, $\bar{\bar{\Psi}}$, τ can be obtained by mere substitution from arbitrary functions α,σ that satisfy

(ST1) $(E\varepsilon)(a)\cdot(\alpha(\varepsilon,a) = \varepsilon)$ ("empty-storage assumption")

(ST2)

$$\alpha(\sigma(s,a,c),b) = \begin{cases} c, & \text{if } b = a \\ \alpha(s,b), & \text{otherwise} \end{cases}$$ ("component-wise change of storage").

(For $\bar{\Psi}$, in addition to α, σ, the successor function is needed). Of course, some versions of functions α, σ appear frequently in recursive function theory and studies on storage models. However, it is noteworthy that one can do without any further assumptions on α, σ which appear elsewhere (for instance "finite storage assumption" etc. in BEKIČ/WALK 71, or assumptions (3.9), (3.1o) in McCARTHY/PAINTER 67). Theorem 2.1 may be viewed as a kind of normal form theorem which, for our purposes, is more suitable than Kleene's.

Second, the following equivalence theorem gives an intimate connection between Blum's complexity theory(BLUM 67) and the concept in Definition 1.4.

Theorem 2.2a: **Let Ψ be a Gödel numbering and**

$$\Psi(p,x) = \rho[\bar{\Psi},\kappa]\gamma(p,x)$$

for certain ρ, $\bar{\Psi}$, $\kappa \in R_1$, $\gamma \in R_2$. Define

$$\Phi(p,x) := (\mu t)(\kappa\bar{\Psi}^{(t)}\gamma(p,x) = o),$$

then Φ is a step counting function for Ψ in the sense of Blum, i.e.

(S1) $\Phi(p,x)$ defined $\longleftrightarrow$ $\Psi(p,x)$ defined

(S2) $\Phi(p,x) = m$ is decidable.

<u>Theorem 2.2b</u>: If Ψ is a Gödel numbering and Φ a step counting function for Ψ (i.e. (S1), (S2) hold) then one can find ρ, $\bar{\Psi}$, $\kappa \in R_1$ and $\gamma \in R_2$ such that

$$\Psi(p,x) = \rho[\bar{\Psi},\kappa]\gamma(p,x), \quad \text{and}$$

$$\Phi(p,x) = (\mu t)(\kappa\bar{\Psi}^{(t)}\gamma(p,x) = o).$$

<u>Remarks</u>: It is easy to check Theorem 2.2a. For the proof of Theorem 2.2b choose

$$\gamma(p,x) := \langle p,x,o\rangle,$$

$$\bar{\Psi}(\langle p,x,t\rangle) := \langle p,x,t+1\rangle,$$

$$\kappa(\langle p,x,t\rangle) := \begin{cases} o, & \text{if } \Phi(p,x) = t, \\ 1, & \text{otherwise,} \end{cases}$$

$$\rho(\langle p,x,t\rangle) := \begin{cases} \Psi(p,x), & \text{if } \Phi(p,x) = t, \\ o, & \text{otherwise.} \end{cases}$$

Here $\langle\ \rangle$ is the notation for a pairing function which, in addition, is onto. Subsequently, these functions ρ, $\bar{\Psi}$, κ, γ will serve as an interesting example.

By Theorem 2.2a we can use all the information given in Blum's theory to investigate universal $\bar{\Psi}$, κ. By Theorem 2.2b we can conclude that the intuitive concept of a computation according to some program (and, hence, of the semantics of programming languages), which lies behind Blum's complexity theory, is just the same as that which has been made precise in Definition 1.4. This is yet another reason for maintaining the adequacy of this definition.

Next, we shall give some propositions on the "possible" ρ, κ, γ in Definition 1.4. First, a characterization of the possible γ:

<u>Theorem 2.3:</u> Let $\gamma \in R_2$.
There exist ρ, $\bar{\Psi}$, $\kappa \in R_1$ such that $(\lambda p,x)(\rho[\bar{\Psi},\kappa]\gamma(p,x))$ is a Gödel numbering $\Longleftrightarrow$ there exists an $f \in R_1$ such that $(\lambda p,x)(\gamma(f(p),x))$ is 1-1.

<u>Remarks:</u> The intuitive meaning of this theorem is that "possible" input functions γ, though not 1-1 everywhere, turn out to be 1-1 at least on an effectively constructible "cylinder". The proof of "$\Longrightarrow$" would be slightly easier if one knew that every $\Psi^* \in P_1$ can be written in the form

$$\Psi^* = \rho[\bar{\Psi},\kappa]$$

for suitable ρ, $\bar{\Psi}$, $\kappa \in R_1$. However one can show

<u>Theorem 2.4:</u> $\{\Psi^* \mid \Psi^* = \rho[\bar{\Psi},\kappa] \text{ for some } \rho, \bar{\Psi}, \kappa \in R_1\} \subset_+ P_1$.

<u>Remark:</u> This theorem also tells us that we should not expect that every Ψ^* which might define a programming language in the manner described in Remark 2. (after Definition 1.4) can immediately be given in the form $[\bar{\Psi},\kappa]$. Some input (and output, see Theorem 2.7) will be necessary, in general.

Theorem 2.3 still admitts a wide class of possible input functions. One might suspect that γ already could do "most of the computational work". However, Theorem 2.2a and the theorems of Blum's complexity theory (for instance the compression theorem) tell us that however complex (total re-

cursive!) input functions may be, the number of applications of $\bar{\Psi}$ (counted by the Φ of Theorem 2.2a) may be arbitrarily large for certain computations. In this respect the following theorem might be of some interest, too.

<u>Theorem 2.5:</u> Let $(\lambda p,x)(\rho[\bar{\Psi},\kappa]\gamma(p,x))$ be a Gödel numbering, where ρ, $\bar{\Psi}$, $\kappa \in R_1$, $\gamma \in R_2$. Then we can find a pairing function τ, such that

$$\rho[\bar{\Psi},\kappa]\gamma(p,x) = \rho[\bar{\Psi},\kappa]\tau(p,x).$$

<u>Remark:</u> Whenever $\bar{\Psi}$, κ are universal, then by this theorem they are so with respect to an input function τ that defines the initial states of the computations such that the program and data involved can uniquely be reconstructed from the initial state. Thus, prior to the "execution" the information contained in the program has not yet been used to alter the data and vice versa.

<u>Theorem 2.6:</u> Let $\rho \in R_1$.
There exist $\bar{\Psi}$, $\kappa \in R_1$, $\gamma \in R_2$ such that $(\lambda p,x)(\rho[\bar{\Psi},\kappa]\gamma(p,x))$ is a Gödel numbering $\Longleftrightarrow$ ρ is onto and $|\{\xi \mid (E\xi')(\rho(\xi') = \rho(\xi) \;\&\; \xi' < \xi)\}| = \infty$.

<u>Remarks:</u> This is a characterization theorem for the possible output functions ρ. In BUCHBERGER 72 we have shown that these ρ must not be 1-1, that every ρ of "large oscillation" is suitable, and furthermore that there exist suitable ρ which are not of large oscillation^{+}). The condi-

---

$^{+}$) ρ is of large oscillation $:\Longleftrightarrow$ $(y,z)(Ex)(x > z \;\&\; \rho(x) = y)$. The total recursive functions of large oscillation are exactly the possible τ_1 (or τ_2) for paring functions τ. In MARKOV 47 it is shown that these functions are just the functions suitable as "output" functions in Kleene's normal form theorem.

tion in the theorem defines a class of functions which "lies between" the class of 1-1 functions and those of large oscillation.

Theorem 2.7: $\{ \psi^* \mid \psi^* = [\bar{\Psi},\kappa]\gamma$ for some $\bar{\Psi},\ \kappa \in R_1,\ \gamma \in R_2\} \subsetneq P_1$.

Remark: Compare Theorem 2.4.

Theorem 2.8: Let $\kappa \in R_1$.

There exist $\rho,\ \bar{\Psi} \in R_1,\ \gamma \in R_2$ such that $(\lambda p,x)(\rho[\bar{\Psi},\kappa]\gamma(p,x))$ is a Gödel numbering $\iff$ $|\{ \xi \mid \kappa(\xi) = o \}| = |\{ \xi \mid \kappa(\xi) \neq o\}| = \infty$.

Remark: This gives a characterization of the possible κ.

Next we examine the functions γ which might occur in Definition 1.5.

Theorem 2.9: Let $\rho,\ \bar{\Psi},\ \kappa,\ \gamma \in R_1$, $\quad \bar{\bar{\Psi}} \in R_2$, τ be a pairing function,

$$\kappa\tau(p,\eta) \neq o \rightarrow \bar{\Psi}\tau(p,\eta) = \tau(p,\bar{\bar{\Psi}}(p,\eta)), \text{ and}$$

$(\lambda p,x)(\rho\tau_2[\bar{\Psi},\kappa]\tau(p,\gamma(x)))$ be a Gödel numbering, then γ is 1-1 and $|\overline{\gamma(N)}| = \infty$.

Remarks: By Theorem 2.3 one might suspect that γ can be onto. However, this is excluded by the above theorem which even shows that infinitely many states of the working store must be"preserved for computation only". They cannot be met by the input function (in perfect correspondence to our experience with concrete languages).

Theorem 2.1o: Let $\gamma \in R_1$ be such that γ is 1-1, $|\overline{\gamma(N)}| = \infty$ and $\gamma(N)$ is decidable. Then γ may possibly occur in decompositions of the form given in (NU3).

Remarks: We have not been able to prove Theorem 2.1o without the assumption "$\gamma(N)$ decidable". Nor was it possible to derive "$\gamma(N)$ decidable" as a necessary condition in Theorem 2.9.

We still don't have a nice characterization of the possible ρ in Definition 1.5.

We next concentrate on the possible $\bar{\Psi}$. The study of the $\bar{\Psi}$ deserves our special interest since, intuitively, a programming language is most strikingly characterized by its $\bar{\Psi}$. However, the characterization we can present still suffers from a nonsymmetry (details of the proof and a discussion of the result appeared in BUCHBERGER 72):

Theorem 2.11: $\bar{\Psi}$, κ universal $\Longrightarrow$ there exists an infinite sequence $\xi_o, \xi_1, \ldots$ (all $\xi_i \in N$) such that

($\bar{\Psi}$1) $$(i,j,t_1,t_2)(i \neq j \vee t_1 \neq t_2 \rightarrow \bar{\Psi}^{(t_1)}(\xi_i) \neq \bar{\Psi}^{(t_2)}(\xi_j)).$$

Remarks: Condition ($\bar{\Psi}$1) tells that if $\bar{\Psi}$, κ are universal then $\bar{\Psi}$ must contain infinitely many "tracks" that don't run into a "cycle" and don't "meet" each other.

Theorem 2.12: Let $\bar{\Psi}$ be such that for some $f \in R_1$

($\bar{\Psi}$1') $$(i,j,t_1,t_2)(i \neq j \vee t_1 \neq t_2 \rightarrow \bar{\Psi}^{(t_1)} f(i) \neq \bar{\Psi}^{(t_2)} f(j)),$$

$(\bar{\Psi}2)$ $\{\ddot{\Psi}^{(t)}f(i) \mid t,i \in N\}$ is decidable.

Then one can find ρ, $\kappa \in R_1$, $\gamma \in R_2$ such that $(\lambda p,x)(\rho[\bar{\Psi},\kappa]\gamma(p,x))$ is a Gödel numbering.

Remark: In addition to the necessary condition $(\bar{\Psi}1)$ we need some assumption on the effective constructibility of the "tracks" to obtain sufficient conditions for "universal" $\bar{\Psi}$.

Until now we looked to the possible ρ, $\bar{\Psi}$, κ, γ separately. What would of course be most interesting is the interplay of $\bar{\Psi}$ and κ for universal $\bar{\Psi}$, κ. We give some necessary conditions. For this we introduce the following

Definition 2.1: Let $\xi_1,\xi_2 \in N$.

$$\xi_1 \overset{\bar{\Psi},\kappa}{\sim} \xi_2 :\leftrightarrow (Et_1,t_2)(\bar{\Psi}^{(t_1)}(\xi_1) = \bar{\Psi}^{(t_2)}(\xi_2) \;\&$$
$$(\tau < t_1)(\kappa\bar{\Psi}^{(\tau)}(\xi_1) \neq o) \;\&$$
$$(\tau < t_2)(\kappa\bar{\Psi}^{(\tau)}(\xi_2) \neq o)).$$

Remark: $\overset{\bar{\Psi},\kappa}{\sim}$ is an equivalence relation on N. (Even for universal $\bar{\Psi}$, κ it may happen that this relation is decidable, see example after Theorem 2.2).

Notation:

$[\xi]$... equivalence class of ξ with respect to $\overset{\bar{\Psi},\kappa}{\sim}$. In the notation $[\xi]$ we don't make any reference to the $\bar{\Psi}$, κ used any more since, in the following, no confusion will arise. Also, we trust that the twofold use of the brackets in $[\xi]$ and $[\bar{\Psi},\kappa]$ will not trouble the reader.

$[N]$ ... set of all equivalence classes with respect to $\overset{\bar{\Psi},\kappa}{\sim}$.

Remarks: All $[\xi]$ are recursively enumerable. There are examples (see example after Theorem 2.2) where all $[\xi]$ are even recursive. $[N]$ divides into three disjoint subsets:

$[N] = [N_+] \cup [N_c] \cup [N_\infty]$, where

$[N_+] := \{ [\xi] \mid (E\xi')(\xi' \in [\xi] \;\&\; \kappa(\xi') = o) \}$,

$[N_c] := \{ [\xi] \mid [\xi] \notin [N_+] \;\&\; (E\xi',t)(\xi' \in [\xi] \;\&\; t \neq o \;\&\; \bar{\Psi}^{(t)}(\xi') = \xi') \}$,

$[N_\infty] := [N] - [N_+] - [N_c]$, i.e.

$[N_+]$ consists of all $[\xi]$ that contain terminal states ξ', $[N_c]$ consists of all $[\xi]$ that contain "cycles" and $[N_\infty]$ collects the remaining $[\xi]$. Although one's experience with the usual programming languages might not suggest it, there are examples of universal $\bar{\Psi}$, κ where $[N_c] = \emptyset$ (see example after Theorem 2.2).

Definition 2.2: Let $[X] \subset [N]$.

A function f is $[X]$-generating $:\Longleftrightarrow [X] = \{ [f(i)] \mid i \in N \}$.

Remarks: For $\bar{\Psi}$, $\kappa \in R_1$ there exist f_+, $f_c \in R_1$ such that f_+ is $[N_f]$-generating and f_c is $[N_c]$-generating.

<u>Theorem 2.13:</u> Let $\bar{\Psi}$, κ be universal. Then

($\bar{\Psi}$,κ1) there does not exist a recursive $[N_\infty]$-generating function

($\bar{\Psi}$,κ2) for all n:

there exist infinitely many distinct equivalence classes

$[\xi_o], [\xi_1], \ldots$ in $[N_+]$ such that

$(i)(E\xi')(\xi' \in [\xi_i] \; \& \; (\tau<n)(\bar{\Psi}^{(\tau)}(\xi_i) \in [\xi_i])).$

<u>Remarks:</u> ($\bar{\Psi}$,κ1) is easily deduced from Rice's Theorem (see, for instance, ROGERS 67), ($\bar{\Psi}$,κ2) needs simple results of Blum's complexity theory which, by Theorem 2.2, are available for our investigation. Intuitively ($\bar{\Psi}$,κ2) says that $\bar{\Psi}$ must contain enough "tracks" of every length that lead to a terminal state.

We have a strong feeling that for $\bar{\Psi}$, $\kappa \in R_1$ the conditions ($\bar{\Psi}$,κ1) and (an effective version of) ($\bar{\Psi}$,κ2) are also sufficient for guaranteeing the universality of $\bar{\Psi}$, κ. However, we have not been able to prove this.

Finally, we want to give an interesting result on the reducibility of universality to normal universality.

<u>Theorem 2.14:</u> Let f be $[N_\infty]$-generating and $\bar{\Psi}$, κ universal. Then one can find $\rho, \gamma \in R_1$ and an f-pairing function τ such that

$(\lambda p,x)(\rho\tau_2[\bar{\Psi},\kappa]\tau(p,\gamma(x)))$ is a Gödel numbering, and

$\bar{\Psi}\tau(p,\eta) = \tau(p,\bar{\bar{\Psi}}(p,\eta))$ for $\bar{\bar{\Psi}}(p,\eta) := \tau_2\bar{\Psi}\tau(p,\eta)$.

Remarks: By an f-pairing function we mean a 1-1, binary, f-recursive function τ for which $\tau(N,N)$ is f-recursive. Thus, Theorem 2.14 says that the states of a "universal automaton" $\bar{\Psi}$, κ can always be decomposed in such a way that one component (which plays the role of the "program") is not altered during execution. Unfortunately, Theorem 2.4 is not constructive in that the τ obtained depends on the non-recursive f (see Teheorem 2.13). It is open whether one could find a constructive version of this theorem.

3. Future problems

A further investigation on the topics given in this note will center around the following problems:

1. A further detailed study of universal $\bar{\Psi}$, κ, especially of the questions left open by the Theorems 2.11 - 2.14. Construction of simple examples of universal $\bar{\Psi}$, κ.

2. An exact definition of the concepts "compilation", "simulation", "dependence of syntax on semantics" etc. in terms of the concept of an automaton based on the recursion scheme (CI).

3. Study of the whole hierarchy of possible notions of universal functions between the general notion of a Gödel numbering and our notion of universal $\bar{\Psi}$, κ and such notions which may be obtained by further specializing our notion.

4. Study of automata whose basic action principle is a more complicated recursion scheme than (CI), e.g. such that they could "directly" function according to a definition like that of "apply" in McCARTHY 62. Such automata would have to consist of infinitely many universal automata. Thus the cellular automata in CODD 68 would probably not suffice. Also Gilmore's "computer with a LISP-like machine language" is not such an automaton. However, a detailed examination of Gilmore's work reveals that his computer essentially functions still according to our recursion scheme (CI).

5. Recently it has been pointed out (MOSCHOVAKIS 71, FENSTAD 72) that generalized recursive function theories should include notions like "computation", "length of computation", "subcomputations", "computational steps" etc. as primitive notions. We think that a better understanding of the power contained in one step of an ordinary computability formalism (reflected by the power of $\bar{\Psi}$ in our terminology) could help in reasonably axiomatizing these notions.

Acknowledgement: Most of the material in Section 2. was obtained by a constant and most pleasing collaboration with Dr.B.Roider (Univ.Innsbruck). To him I want to express my sincere gratitude.

References:

ASSER 6o, G.Asser, Rekursive Wortfunktionen, Zeitschrift für mathematische Logik und Grundlagen der Mathematik 6, pp.258-278.

BEKIČ/WALK 71, H.Bekič, K.Walk, Formalization of storage properties, in: Symposium on Semantics of Algorithmic Languages (E.Engeler ed.), Springer Lecture Notes 188, 1971.

BLUM 67, M.Blum, A machine-independent theory of the complexity of recursive functions, J.ACM 14/2, 1967.

BUCHBERGER 71, B.Buchberger, Associating functions and the operator of conditioned iteration (Russian), Communications of the JINR Dubna, P5-5788, (English translation: Bericht Nr.71-1, Inst.f.num. Math., Univ.Innsbruck, 1971).

BUCHBERGER 72, B.Buchberger, A basic problem in the theory of programming languages, Bericht Nr.72-1, Inst.f.num.Math., Univ.Innsbruck, 1972.

BUCHBERGER/ROIDER 72, B.Buchberger, B.Roider, A study on universal functions, Bericht Nr.72-5, Inst.f.num.Math., Univ.Innsbruck, to appear.

CODD 68, E.F.Codd, Cellular automata, Academic Press, 1968.

FENSTAD 72, J.E.Fenstad, On axioms for computation theories, Lecture given at the conference on mathematical logic, Oberwolfach, Germany, April 1972.

GILMORE 67, P.C.Gilmore, An abstract computer with a LISP-like machine language, in: Computer Programming and Formal Systems (P.Braffort/D.Hirschberg ed.), North-Holland, 1967.

LUCAS/LAUER/STIGLEITNER 68, P.Lucas, P.Lauer, H.Stigleitner, Method and notation for the formal definition of programming languages, TR 25.o87, IBM Laboratory Vienna, 1968.

McCARTHY 62, J.McCarthy, LISP 1.5 programmer's manual, MIT Press, 1962.

McCARTHY/PAINTER 67, J.McCarthy, J.Painter, Correctness of a compiler for arithmetic expressions, Proc.of Symp.in Applied Math. 19 (J.T. Schwartz ed.), Amer.Math.Soc., pp.33-41.

MARKOV 47, A.A.Markov, On the representation of recursive functions (Russian), Doklady Ak.Nauk SSSR, n.s.58, pp.1891-1892.

MOSCHOVAKIS 71, Axioms for computation theories - first draft, in: Logic Colloquium '69 (R.O.Gandy, C.M.E.Yates ed.), North-Holland, 1971.

ROGERS 58, H.Rogers, Jr., Gödel numberings of partial recursive functions, J.Symbolic Logic 23/3, pp.331-341, 1958.

ROGERS 67, H.Rogers, Jr., Theory of recursive functions and effective computability, McGraw-Hill 1967.

SCHWENKEL 66, F.Schwenkel, Semantische Theorie der Programmiersprachen, Dissertation, Univ.Tübingen, Germany, 1966.

SCOTT 67, D.Scott, Some definitional suggestions for automata theory, J.Comp.System Sci. 1, pp.187-212, 1967.

SCOTT 71, D.Scott, The lattice of flow diagrams, in: Symposium on Semantics of Algorithmic Languages (E.Engeler ed.), Springer Lecture Notes 188, 1971.

SHOENFIELD 71, J.R.Shoenfield, Degrees of unsolvability, North-Holland/ American Elsevier, 1971.

USPENSKII 56, V.A.Uspenskii, Computable operators and the notion of program (Russian), Uspehi Mat.Nauk 11/4, pp.172-176.

USPENSKII 6o, V.A.Uspenskii, Lectures on computable functions (Russian), Gos.Izd.Fiz.Mat.Lit., Moscow, 196o.

CRITERIA FOR THE ALGORITHMIC COMPLETENESS

OF THE SYSTEMS OF OPERATIONS

by

V.A. Nepomniaschy

(Novosibirsk)

1. Introduction

In different theories of discrete mathematics the problem arises of finding criteria for completeness, i.e. conditions by which from a finite system of constructive objects with the help of given means one may arrive at the principal class of constructive objects. The solution of the problem plays an important role in the theory as well as in its applications. Thus, Post's theorem on functional completeness is of fundamental value in the algebra of logics. In the theory of recursive functions the study of complete systems of recursive functions (basis) from which one may derive all n-ary recursive functions (n = 1, 2, ...)

by means of recursive operators (superpositions and others) plays an important role. For example, the conditions of completeness in the classes of monadic partial-recursive and primitive-recursive functions are shown in [1] - [3].

Operator algorithms defined by means of sets of variables, corresponding to memory cells of computers and by means of elementary operations, corresponding to systems of computer operations are considered in [4]. A system of operations is complete if, by means of the operations, one can program a computation of any recursive function. The completeness of a system of operations with numbers, which involves an identical operation, addition of a unity and recognition of the inequality, is established in [4]. Similar results are presented in [5] - [8] for the notions of the algorithm which are similar to those of the operator. In [8] it is also found that the problem of recognition of the completeness of an arbitrary system of operations is unsolvable.

The problem of finding the criteria for the completeness of an arbitrary system of operations is discussed in [8] and [9]. In [10] and [11] we begin to study the problem for a special subclass of the operator algorithms. In particular, some necessary and some sufficient conditions are established for completeness of systems which involve two arbitrary monadic operations: functional and predicate. The results follow from the criteria given in the present paper. In the recent paper [12] some necessary and sufficient conditions are given for the Gödel numberings of all partial-recursive functions to be obtained from the initial functions (which correspond to a definite notion of the algorithm) by means of a special operator of conditioned iteration.

2. General Notions

Let us describe the subclass $\mathfrak{R}$ of operator algorithms we use. $\mathfrak{R}$ is similar to the subclass of operator algorithms $\mathfrak{b}\ (\mathfrak{V},\mathfrak{C})$ ([4] 3.5), to the class of graph-schemes with memory [8] and to the class of programs from [13]. The main difference between $\mathfrak{R}$ and the above classes of algorithms is as follows: the algorithms from $\mathfrak{R}$ are designed for computation of functions defined only on k-tuples from N = 0, 1, 2, ... while the algorithms from the above classes can compute functions defined on arbitrary domains. The $\mathfrak{R}$ algorithms will be determined in two ways:

(1) in terms of the simplest statements of ALGOL-60 (linear form);

(2) by means of the Kaluzhnin graph-scheme [14] (graph form). Let us turn to the definition of algorithms from in the linear form. The algorithm M consists of finite sets of memory locations $x = \{x_1,\dots,x_n\}$, operations $K = \{f_1,\dots,f_\mu;\ p_1,\dots,p_\nu\}$ and statements $\mathcal{O} = \{O_1,\dots,O_s\}$.

Numbers from N are stored in the locations. The operations are of two kinds: functional $f_i(i=1,\dots,\mu)$ and predicate $p_j(j=1,\dots,\nu)$. f_i is a function (generally, partial) representing the k-tuples from N into N. p_j is the predicate defined on all k-tuples of N (of corresponding dimensionality). p_j is not identically true and p_j is not identically false. m-ary functional or predicate operation g will be denoted by $g(y_1,\dots,y_m)$. Note, that the operations can be noneffective as well. The statements are of three kinds: assignment, conditional and ending. The statement of assignment has the form:

(a) $< x_m := f_i(x_\tau,\dots,x_\eta)$ <u>go to</u> $O_\kappa >$ $(x_m,x_\tau,\dots,x_\eta \in X;\ f_i \in K, O_\kappa \in \mathcal{O})$,

(b) $< x_m := 0$ <u>go to</u> $O_\kappa >$ $(x_m \in X, O_\kappa \in \mathcal{O})$.

Under execution of the statement of assignment of the form (a) the value f_i is written into location x_m. From the contents of the locations $x_\tau,\ldots,x_\eta$. For the form (b) a zero is written into the location x_m (the location is cleared). Then one proceeds to the execution of the statement O_κ. Note that although the statement of assignment of the from (b) is a special case of the statement of the form (a), it is singled out and given an idependent form to avoid insertion of clearing locations in the set of operations K (i.e. the operation $f_i(y_1,\ldots,y_m)=0$ for all $y_1,\ldots,y_m$). The conditional statement has the form <if $p_j(x_\delta,\ldots,x_\lambda)$ then go to O_u else go to O_v>$(x_\delta,\ldots,x_\lambda\in X;\ p_j\in K;\ O_u,O_v\in\mathcal{O})$. Under execution of the conditional statement the value p_j is computed from the location contents $x_\delta,\ldots,x_\lambda$; if p_j is true (false) then a jump to the execution of the statement O_u (O_v) is performed. The statement of ending has the form <stop> or <stop i> (i=0,1). The set of statements $\mathcal{O}$ has one statement of ending <stop>, or two statements of ending <stop 0> and <stop 1>.

Now, let us describe the graph form of the algorithm M. Given is a set of statements $\mathcal{O}$, the oriented graph Γ is built in the following way. The nodes Γ are identified with the symbols of the statements $O_\kappa(\kappa=1,\ldots,s)$. The node O_1 is called an input node. If O_τ is the statement of assignment <$x_m := f_i(x_\tau,\ldots,x_\eta)$ go to O_κ> (respectively <$x_m := 0$ go to O_κ>), then the expression <$x_m := f_i(x_\tau,\ldots,x_\eta)$> (<$x_m := 0$>) is related to the node O_τ, and an arrow extends from the node O_τ to the node O_κ. If O_τ is a conditional statement <if $p_j(x_\sigma,\ldots,x_\lambda)$ then go to O_u else go to O_v> then the expression <$p_j(x_\sigma,\ldots,x_\lambda)$> is related to the node O_τ, and two arrows extend from the node O_τ, one of them entering O_u (denoted by the symbol "+"), the other entering O_v (denoted by the symbol "-"). If O_τ is the statement of ending <stop> (<stop i>, i=0,1) then the expression <stop> (<stop i>) is related to the node O_τ, no arrows extend from the node O_τ in this case.

Define the computation of the function or predicate $g(y_1,\dots,y_\ell)$ by the algorithm M. Locations of memory $x_1,\dots,x_\ell$ $(\ell < n)$ are called input locations. Let the numbers a_i $(i=1,\dots,\ell)$ be written in the locations x_i at the initial moment $t = 0$; the remaining locations are clear. The configuration M at the moment t is $\rho_t=(\alpha_t,q_t)$ where α_t is the symbol of the statement M, which is being executed at the moment t and q_t is the state of the memory M at the moment t (e.g. $q_t=(q_t(x_1),\dots,q_t(x_n))$, $q_t(x_i)$ is the contents of the location x_i at the moment t. Formal definition of the sequence of configurations ρ_t $(t=0,1,2,\dots)$ is as follows: $\rho_o=(0_1,q_o)$ where $q_o=(a_1,\dots,a_\ell,\ 0,\dots,0,\dots,0)$. Let $\rho_o, \rho_1,\dots,\rho_{t-1}$ be already defined. The following cases are possible:

(1) $\alpha_{t-1} = \langle x_m := f_i(x_\tau,\dots,x_\eta)$ <u>go to</u> $0_\kappa\rangle$, then $q_t(x_j)=q_{t-1}(x_j)$ if $j \neq m$ and $q_t(x_m)=f_i(q_{t-1}(x_\tau),\dots,q_{t-1}(x_\eta))$, $\rho_t=(0_\kappa,q_t)$. If $f_i(q_{t-1}(x_\tau),\dots,q_{t-1}(x_\eta))$ is not defined, then $\rho_t=\rho_{t-1}$.

(2) $\alpha_{t-1} = \langle x_m := 0$ <u>go to</u> $0_\kappa\rangle$, then $q_t(x_j):=q_{t-1}(x_j)$ if $j \neq m$ and $q_t(x_m)=0$, $\rho_t=(0_\kappa,q_t)$.

(3) $\alpha_{t-1} = \langle$ <u>if</u> $p_j(x_\sigma,\dots,x_\lambda)$ <u>then go to</u> 0_u <u>or else go to</u> $0_v\rangle$, then $q_t=q_{t-1}$, and $\alpha_t=0_u$ (respectively $\alpha_t=0_v$), when $p_j(q_{t-1}(x_\delta),\dots,q_{t-1}(x_\lambda))$ - is true (respectively false).

(4) α_{t-1} - is the statement of ending, then ρ_t is not defined.

If the set of statements M contains a statement <stop>, then M computes the function $\phi_M(y_1,\dots,y_\ell)$, which for $y_i=a_i$ $(i=1,\dots,\ell)$ is defined as follows. The location x_τ is called an output location. In the case of infinite configuration the sequence $\phi_M(a_1,\dots,a_\ell)$ is considered to be undefined. Let the configuration sequence M be finite and equal to $\rho_o,\dots,\rho_t$, where $\alpha_t=$ <stop>. Then $\phi_M(a_1,\dots,a_\ell)=q_t(x_\tau)$. If the set of statements M contains statements <stop 0> and <stop 1>, then M computes the predicate $\mathfrak{R}_M(y_1,\dots,y_\ell)$ which for $y_i = a_i$ $(i=1,\dots,\ell)$ is defined in the following way. Let the configuration sequence M be finite and equal to $\varrho_0,\dots,\varrho_t$. Then $\mathfrak{R}_M(a_1,\dots,a_\ell)$ is true (respectively false) at α_t = <stop 1> (respectively, α_t = <stop 0>). In the case of infinite configuration sequence M $\mathfrak{R}_M(a_1,\dots,a_\ell)$ is considered to be undefined. Memory locations which are neither input nor output ones are called temporary.

Consider an example. Let the algorithm M be given by sets $X = \{x_1,x_2,x_3,x_4\}$, where x_1, x_2 are input locations, and x_3 is an output location,

$$K = \{y, y+1; y_1=y_2\}, \quad \sigma = \{O_1,O_2,O_3,O_4,O_5\}$$

where O_1 = <$x_3:=x_1$ <u>go to</u> O_2>, O_2 = <<u>if</u> $x_2 = x_4$ <u>then go to</u> O_3 <u>else go to</u> O_4> O_3 = <stop>, O_4 = <$x_3:=x_3+1$ <u>go to</u> O_5>, O_5 = <$x_4:=x_4+1$ <u>go to</u> O_2>. The graph Γ has the form

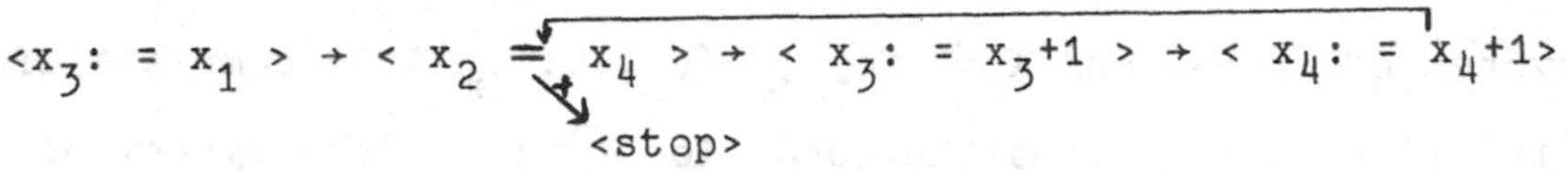

It is easy to see that $\Phi_M(y_1,y_2) = y_1 + y_2$.

Denote by $\mathfrak{R}[K]$ the class of all algorithms from $\mathfrak{R}$, given by means of the system of operations K. The system of operations K is called complete if for any partial-recursive function $\psi(y_1,\dots,y_\ell)$ there exists an algorithm $M \in \mathfrak{R}[K]$ such that $\Phi_M(y_1,\dots,y_\ell) = \psi(y_1,\dots,y_\ell)$ (i.e. the function Φ_M and ψ have the same domain of definition in which their values coincide). The function (or predicate) $g(y_1,\dots,y_\ell)$ is computable over the system of operations K, if in $\mathfrak{R}[K]$ there exists an algorithm, computing $g(y_1,\dots,y_\ell)$.

3. The Reduction Theorem

We say that the function $f(y)$ satisfies the condition $\sqcap$ if $\forall_m \exists_\kappa f^\kappa(0)=m$, where $f^o(0)=0$, $f^{i+1}(0)=f\,(f^i(0)$ $(i=0,1,2,\ldots)$. Note that $f(y)$ satisfies the condition $\sqcap$ if and only if $f^y(0)$ is a rearrangement $N = \{0,1,2,\ldots\}$. For example, the function

$$h(y) = \begin{cases} y+1, & \text{if } y \text{ is odd,} \\ y-3, & \text{if } y = 4+6\kappa \; (\kappa=0,1,2,\ldots), \\ y+3, & \text{in other cases,} \end{cases}$$

satisfies the condition $\sqcap$, since

$$h^y(0) = \begin{cases} y+2 \text{ if } y = 1+6\kappa \text{ or } y = 2+6\kappa, \\ y-2 \text{ if } y = 3+6\kappa \text{ or } y = 4+6\kappa, \\ y \text{ in other cases,} \qquad (\kappa=0,1,2,\ldots) \end{cases}$$

is a rearrangement N.

Denote the predicate $P(f^{y_1}(0),\ldots,f^{y_m}(0))$ by $P_f(y_1,\ldots,y_m)$.

<u>Theorem 1</u> (Reduction)

The system of operations $K = \{f(y); P(y_1,\ldots,y_m)\}$ is complete if and only if (1) $f(y)$ satisfies the condition $\sqcap$; (2) the system of operations $K' = \{y+1; P_f(y_1,\ldots,y_m)\}$ is complete; (3) $f(y)$ is computable over the system K'.

If $P(y_1,y_2) = (y_1 = y_2)$ and $f(y)$ satisfies the condition $\sqcap$, then $P_f(y_1,y_2) = (f^{y_1}(0) = f^{y_2}(0) = (y_1 = y_2)$. But then $K' = \{y+1;\ y_1 = y_2\}$ is complete. Thus,

<u>Corollary 1</u>. The system of operations $K = \{f(y);\ y_1 = y_2\}$ is complete if and only if $f(y)$ is a total recursive function satisfying the condition $\sqcap$.

4. Criterion of Completeness of Operation System $\{y+1; P(y)\}$

Fix the predicate P(y). A "true" symbol ("false" symbol) will be identified with unity (zero). Denote the infinite sequence of zeros and unities P(0) P(1) P(2) ... P(i) ... by {P}.

Consider the multihead finite automata of a special kind related to the predicates P(y). Automaton A_P has:

(a) states $\tau_0, \tau_1, \dots, \tau_\kappa$ (τ_0 is initial, τ_κ is halting);

(b) reading heads $\Gamma_1, \dots, \Gamma_m$ (Γ_{λ_0} is a special head);

(c) two tapes consisting of squares which contain symbols 0 or 1; the first (main) tape is made up of $\delta + 1$ squares contains words of the kind $P(\mu)\, P(\mu+1) \dots P(\mu+\delta)$; the second (auxiliary) tape which is (semi-) infinite on the right side contains {P};

(d) a program consisting of 2κ instruction of the form

(*) $\tau_i \xi \to \tau_{i'}\, S_\nu\, \Gamma_j$ ($i \in \{0,\dots,\kappa-1\}$, $i' \in \{0,\dots,\kappa\}$, $\xi \in \{0,1\}$,

$N \in \{0,\dots,m\}$, $j \in \{1,\dots,m\}$; any two instructions of a program do not have same left parts).

At the initial moment automaton A_p is in the state τ_0, head Γ_1 scans the leftmost square of the main tape, heads $\Gamma_2, \Gamma_3, \dots, \Gamma_m$ scan the leftmost square of the auxiliary tape, the special head λ_0 being considered active. Let A_P at moment t be in the state τ_i, and the active head Γ_{λ_t} scans symbol ξ . Then A_P executing the instruction (*) changes its state into $\tau_{i'}$, and moves the active head one square to the right if $\nu = 0$ or places Γ_{λ_t} into that square of the corresponding tape which the head Γ_ν ($\nu=1,\dots,m$) scans at moment t. The head Γ_j is considered to be active at moment t + 1 (i.e. $\lambda_{t+1}=j$). A_P stops in halting τ_κ as well as when one of the heads leaves the main tape. We say, that automaton A_P accepts the word $Z = P(\mu) \dots P(\mu+\delta)$ which is on the main tape if A_P goes into τ_κ and in this case the head Γ_1 leaves the main tape.

Let us denote the set of subwords {P} which the automaton A_P accepts by $G(A_P)$. Say A_P accepts the set $G(A_P)$. Let us consider an example. Let $\eta(y)$ be the predicate "y is the exact square". Automaton A_η has states τ_o, τ_1, τ_2 (τ_o is initial, τ_2 is halting), one head Γ_1 and the program including four instructions

$$\tau_o 0 \to \tau_o S_o \Gamma_1, \quad \tau_o 1 \to \tau_1 S_o \Gamma_1, \quad \tau_1 0 \to \tau_1 S_o \Gamma_1, \quad \tau_1 1 \to \tau_2 S_o \Gamma_1.$$

Then $G(A_\eta) = \{0^{i_j} 1\ 0^j 1 \mid j = 0,2,4,6,\dots, i_j = 0,1,2,\dots,j \mid 2\}$.

We may need special functions $\gamma(y)$ which map numbers y into subwords { P }. Denote by $\mathcal{V}_y$ the set

$$\{ P(y)\ P(y+1) \dots P(y+\kappa) \mid \forall Z (Z \neq y \to$$
$$P(Z)\ P(Z+1) \dots P(Z+\kappa) \neq P)y)$$
$$P(y+1) \dots P(y+\kappa)),\ \kappa = 0,1,2,\dots\},$$ i.e.

$\mathcal{V}_y$ is the set of all words of kind $P(y)\ P(y+1) \dots P(y+\kappa)$, which occur only once in {P}; it is easy to see that for every y $\mathcal{V}_y$ is either empty or infinite. In the last case there exists such κ_y that $P(y) \dots P(y+\kappa_y+j)$ $\mathcal{V}_y$ for all $j=0,1,2,\dots$. Denote by F_P the set of toal functions $\gamma(y)$ such that for every y $\gamma(y) \in \mathcal{V}_y$. It is easy to see that F_P is empty if and only if there exists y for which $\mathcal{V}_y$ is empty. For example, for the above predicate $\eta(y)$ $\gamma(y) = 0^{i(y)} 1\ 0^{j(y)} 1$ where $i(y) = \mu Z(\eta(y+Z) = 1)$, $j(y) = 2\sqrt{y+i(y)}$ belongs to F_η.

<u>Theorem 2</u>. The system of operations { y + 1; P(y)} is complete if and only if there exist automaton A_P and a function $\gamma(y) \in F_P$ such that A_P accepts the range of the function $\gamma(y)$.

Thus, it follows from theorem 2, in particular, that in the case of the empty set F_P the system of operations is not complete. For example, {y + 1; y is an even number} is not complete for this reason. The system of operations y + 1; $\eta(y)$} is complete, since the above automaton A_η accepts the range of the above function $\gamma(y)$.

This follows immediately from theorems 1 and 2.

Corollary 2. Let f(y) be a partial-recursive function. The system of operations {f(y); P(y)} is complete if and only if

(1) f(y) satisfies the condition ⊓,

(2) there exist a automaton A_π and a function $\gamma(y)$ such that A_π accepts the range of $\gamma(y)$, where $\pi(y) = P_f(y)$.

From theorem 2 follow simple sufficient conditions for completeness of operation system {y + 1; P(y)}. Note, that if {P} has a finite number of units then F_P is empty and, hence, {y + 1; P(y)} is not complete. For a predicate P(y) having {P} with an infinite number of units we determine a function $\psi_P(Z)$. Let $\psi_P(0)$ be the number of zeroes in the biggest initial segment {P}, containing only zeroes. Let $\psi_P(Z)$ (Z=1,2,...) be the number of zeroes which are in {P} between Z-th and (Z + 1)-th units. For example,

$$\psi_\eta(Z) = \begin{cases} 0, \text{ if } Z = 0 \\ 2(Z - 1), \text{ if } Z \geq 1 \,. \end{cases}$$

Corollary 3. Let P(y) satisfy one of the conditions

(a) $\psi_P(Z)$ is a function which assumes different values,

(b) $\psi_P(Z)$ is an unbounded, monotonic-increasing function.

Then {y + 1; P(y)} is complete.

5. Applications of the Reduction Theorem

With the help of the reduction theorem we establish the following sufficient condition for completeness of the system of operating $\{f(y);\ P(y)\}$.

Theorem 3. Let

(1) $f^y(0)$ be such a rearrangement N that the sequence
$f^1(0) - f^o(0),\ f^2(0) - f^1(0), \ldots, f^{i+1}(0) - f^i(0), \ldots$
is periodic beginning from some place;

(2) $\psi_P(Z)$ be an unbounded monotonic-increasing function. Then the system of operations $\{f(y);\ P(y)\}$ is complete.

For example, from theorem 3 follows the completeness of the operation system $\{h(y);\ \eta(y)\}$ (these operations are determined in sections 3,4). Indeed, the sequence is periodic with a period +3, +1, -3, +1, +3, +1;

$$\psi_\eta(Z) = \begin{cases} 0, & \text{if } Z = 0, \\ 2(Z-1), & \text{if } Z \geq 1, \end{cases}$$

is the unbounded, monotonic-increasing function.

The predicate $P(y_1, \ldots, y_m)$ will be called maximally-complete if for any function $f(y)$ satisfying condition $\sqcap$ the operation system $\{f(y);\ P(y_1, \ldots, y_m)\}$ is complete. By means of theorems 1 and 2 we can prove the following:

Theorem 4.

(1) The predicate $y_1 = y_2 + 1$ is maximally complete.

(2) There are no monadic maximally complete predicates.

Function $f(y)$ is called suitable for completeness if there exists a predicate $P(y)$ such that the system $\{f(y);\ P(y)\}$ is complete. Predicate

P(y) is called suitable for completeness if there exists a function f(y) such that the system {f(y); P(y)} is complete. Predicate P(y) is called finitely - defined if there exists a constant C such that $\forall y \geq C$ P(y) is true or $\forall y \geq C$ P(y) is false.

Theorem 5.

(1) The function f(y) is suitable for completeness if and only if f(y) satisfies the condition $\sqcap$.

(2) The predicate P(y) is suitable for completeness if and only if P(y) is not a finitely-defined predicate.

6. Discussion of Results

The main results of the paper are criteria for completeness of the following operation systems:

(a) {f(y); P(y)} in case of effective functions f(y) (corollary 2);

(b) {f(y); $y_1 = y_2$} (corollary 1);

(c) {f(y); $y_1 = y_2 + 1$} (theorem 4 (1)).

Though, these criteria are non-effective they allow us to solve the problem of completeness of many particular operation systems as well as to study the structure of the set of complete operation systems. Theorem 5 shows that the completeness of the system {f(y); P(y)} imposes more significant restrictions on f(y) than on P(y). Corollary 1 answers the question raised by A.P. Ershov to which conditions are to be satisfied by the function f(y) to replace the function y + 1 together with the predicate of equality. The function f(y) should be effective and satisfy the condition $\sqcap$. The requirement of effectiveness is due to invariance of the equality predicate with regard to rearrangements (i.e. $(f^{y_1}(0) = f^{y_2}(0)) = (y_1 = y_2)$ if $f^y(0)$ is a rearrangement N).

The reduction theorem plays the main role in the proof of the above criteria for completeness. For the proof of the reduction theorem it is essential that the function f is monadic. An attempt to generalize the reduction theorem for n-ary functions ($n > 1$) results in bulky conditions in terms of numbers of n-tuples.

Among the open problems we note the following one: it is interesting to find criteria for completeness of operation systems for other notions of algorithms (operator algorithms of arbitrary rank, partial-recursive functions, etc.). This would allow us to compare different notions of algorithms with respect to the structure of sets of complete operation systems.

In conclusion the author thanks A.P. Ershov and V.A. Uspensky for their interest and advice throughout the work.

REFERENCES

[1] Zakharov, D.A., Recursive Functions, A special course for students of the Novosibirsk State University, Novosibirsk, 1970.

[2] Lavrov, I.A., The Use of Arithmetic Progressions of k-th Order For Building Basis of Algebra of Primitive-Recursive Functions, Doklady AN SSSR, v. 172, N 2, 1967, pp. 279-282.

[3] Polyakov, E.A., Algebras of Recursive Functions, Algebra and Logika, Collection of papers of the Institute of Mathematics of the Sib.Br. of the USSR Acad. Sci., v. 3, publ. 1, 1964, pp. 41-56.

[4] Ershov, A.P., Operator Algorithms 1, Problemy Kibernetiki, 3, 1960, pp. 5-48.

[5] Peter, R., Graphschemata und rekursive Funktionen, Dialectica, 12, 1958, pp. 373-388.

[6] Kaphengst, H., Eine abstrakte programmgesteuerte Rechenmaschine, Zeit. Math. Logik und Grund. d. Math., 5, 1959, pp. 366-379.

[7] Sheperdson, J.C. and Sturgis, H.E., Computability of Recursive Functions, Journal of the ACM, v. 10, N 2, 1963, pp. 217-255.

[8] Zaslavsky, I.D., Graph Schemes with Memory, Trudy Math. Instituta AN SSSR, 72, 1964, pp. 99-192.

[9] Ershov, A.P. and Liapounov, A.A., On the Formalization for the Notion of Program, Kibernetika, 5, 1967, pp. 40-57.

[10] Nepomniaschy, V.A., Conditions for the Algorithmic Completeness of the Systems of Operations, Preprints IFIP Congress 71, TA-2, 7-11, 1971.

[11] Nepomniaschy, V.A., On Completeness of the Systems of Operations, Doklady AN SSSR, 199, N 4, 1971, pp. 780-782.

[12] Buchberger, B., A Basic Problem in the Theory of Programming Language, Institut für Numer. Math. und Elektron. Information, Universität Insbruck, Bericht N 72-1, Febr. 1972.

[13] Manna, Z., The Correctness of Programs, Journal of Computer and System Sciences, 3, N 2, 1969, pp. 119-127.

[14] Kaluzhnin, L.A., On the Algorithmization for the Mathematical Problems, Problemy Kibernetiki, 2, 1959, pp. 51-67.

DATA FLOW SCHEMAS

J.B. Dennis, J.B. Fosseen and J.P. Linderman

Massachusetts Institute of Technology
Cambridge, Mass., July 27,1972

INTRODUCTION

A data flow schema is a representation of the logical scheme of a program in a form in which the sequencing of function and predicate applications and the flow of values between applications are specified together. In a data flow schema, application of a function or predicate is free to proceed as soon as the values required for its application are available and the need for application of the function or predicate is determined. Since the availability of one computed value may simultaneously enable the application of several functions or predicates, concurrency of action is an inherent aspect of a data flow schema.

We present here some basic properties of a class of data flow schemas which model the logical schemes of programs that compute with unstructured values. These schemas are a variation and extension of the program graphs studied by Rodriguez [12]. A related data flow model for computations on structured data has been described informally by Dennis [3]. The material of the present paper is based largely on a recent thesis by Fosseen [5].

We introduce the reader to data flow schemas by means of an example. Consider the following program expressed in an Algol-like notation:

```
begin
     y := x; v := h(x);
     while p(w, v) do
     begin
          if q(v) then v := f(v);
          y := g(y);
     end
     z := y;
end
```

This research was done at Project MAC, MIT, and was supported in part by the National Science Foundation under grant GJ-432 and in part by the Advanced Research Projects Agency, Department of Defense, under Office of Naval Research Contract Nonr-N00014-70-A-0362-0001.

Variables w and x are input variables of the program and z is the output variable.

A data flow schema for this program is given in Figure 1. The arcs of a data flow schema should be thought of as channels through which tokens flow carrying values between nodes that perform function application (drawn as square boxes with function letters written inside) and nodes that evaluate predicates (drawn as diamonds with predicate letters written inside). The arcs are data arcs that carry arbitrary values and control arcs with open arrowheads that carry <u>true</u>/<u>false</u> values. Decisions made as a result of predicate evaluation are used to control the flow of data values by means of <u>gate</u> nodes drawn as circles and <u>merge</u> nodes drawn as ellipses. A gate node passes a value on or discards it according as the truth value received matches or does not match the inscribed letters. A merge node passes on the value received at its T or F input according to the truth value received at its control arc. Values received at the unselected input are not discarded.

In the representation of a program loop, merge nodes pass initial values into the body of the loop from their <u>false</u> data input arcs. Values for subsequent repetitions of the body of the loop are passed in through the <u>true</u> data input arc. As shown in the figure, the control arcs of these <u>merge</u> nodes hold a <u>false</u> value in the initial condition of the schema to enable the first cycle of the body. Note that the value of input variable w is replicated by a combination of merge and gate nodes for use in the successive evaluations of predicate p.

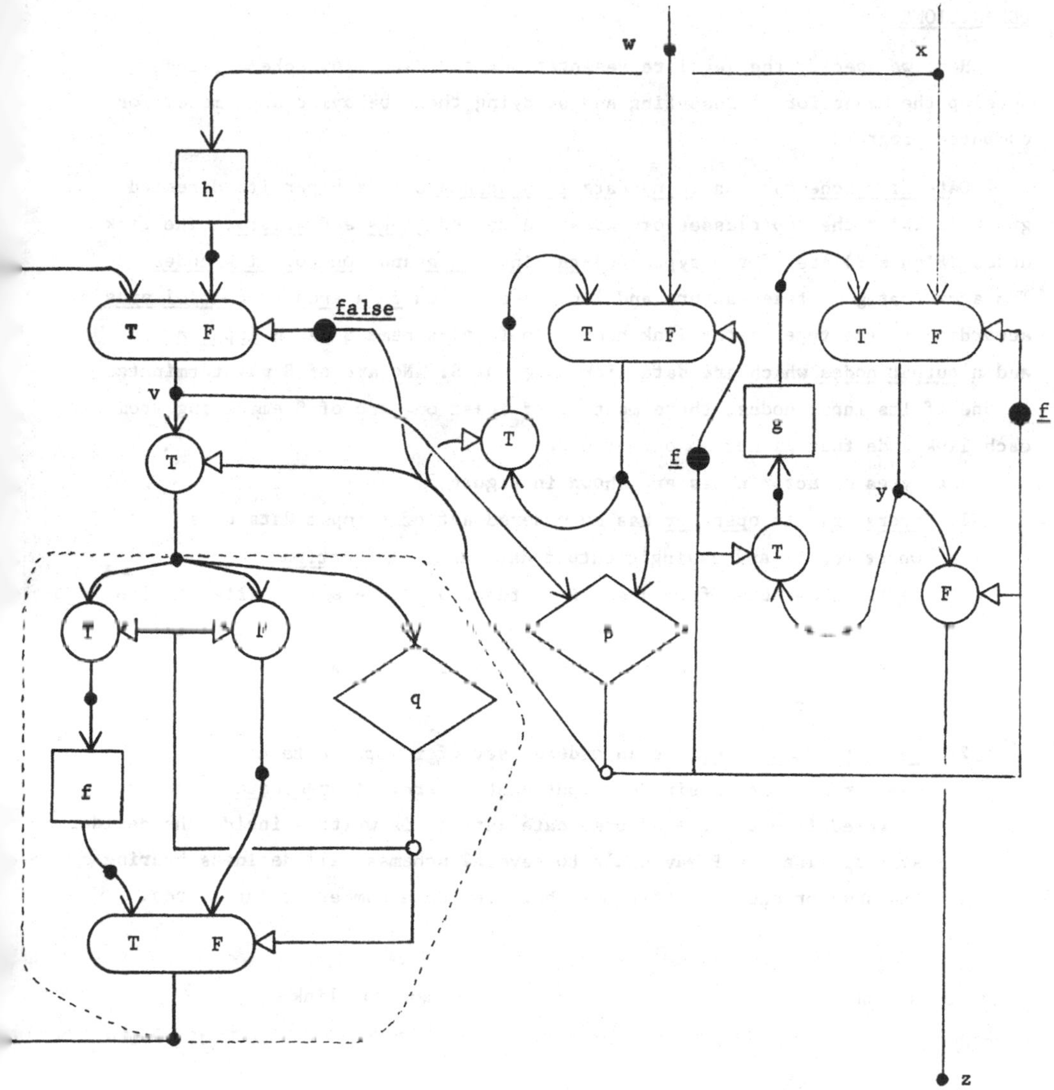

Figure 1. A data flow schema.

DEFINITIONS

Here we specify the legal representations for data flow schemas, and develop the means for representing and studying their behavior as a model for computer programs.

Data flow schemas: An (m,n)-data flow schema S is a bipartite directed graph in which the two classes of nodes are called links and actors. The link nodes (Figure 2) are of two types: data link nodes and control link nodes. The arcs that go between actors and links are called data arcs or control arcs according to the type of the link node. An (m,n)-schema S has m input nodes and n output nodes which are data link nodes of S. No arc of S may terminate on one of its input nodes; there must be at least one arc of S emanating from each link node that is not an output node.

The types of actor nodes are shown in Figure 3.

1. operator: An operator has an ordered set of r input data arcs where $r \geq 1$, and a single output data arc. A function letter f selected from a set F of function letters is written inside the operator symbol. The set F may apply to several schemas; all operators bearing the same function letter must have the same number of input arcs.

2. decider: A decider has an ordered set of r input data arcs where $r \geq 1$, and a single output control arc. A predicate letter p selected from a set P of predicate letters is written inside the decider symbol. The set P may apply to several schemas; all deciders bearing the same predicate letter must have the same number of input arcs.

(a) data link (b) control link

Figure 2. Types of link nodes and arcs in data flow schemas.

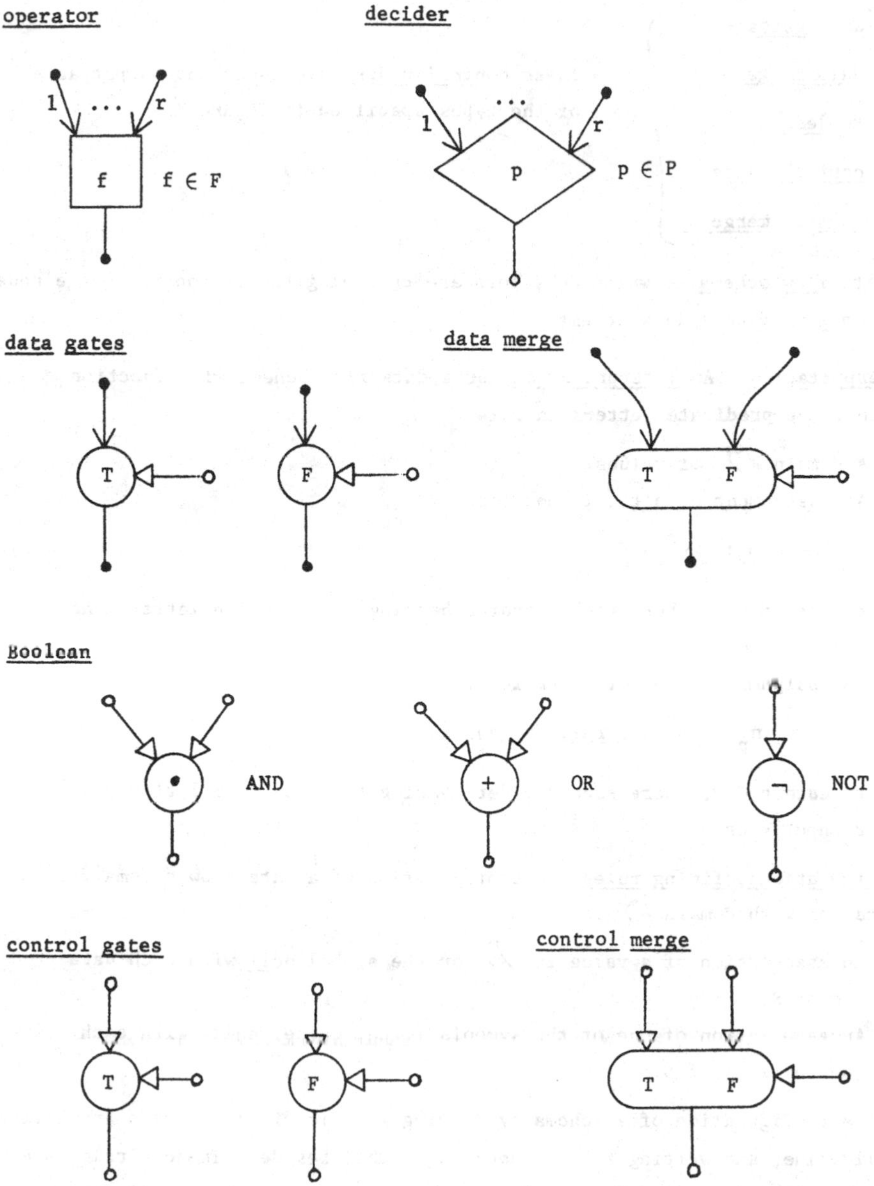

Figure 3. The actor nodes of data flow schemas.

3. data gates
4. data merge
5. Boolean
6. control gates
7. control merge

These control nodes have input and output arcs of the types specified in Figure 3.

A data flow schema in which no actors are control gates or control merge nodes is called a simple data flow schema.

Interpretation: An interpretation for a data flow schema with function letters in F and predicate letters in P is:

1. A domain $\mathcal{D}$ of values.
2. An assignment of a total function

$$\varphi_f: \mathcal{D}^r \to \mathcal{D}$$

to each $f \in F$, where each operator bearing the function letter f has r input arcs.

3. An assignment of a total predicate

$$\pi_p: \mathcal{D}^r \to \{\underline{\text{true}}, \underline{\text{false}}\}$$

to each $p \in P$, where each decider bearing the predicate letter p has r input arcs.

Configurations; firing rules: A configuration of a data flow schema for an interpretation with domain $\mathcal{D}$ is:

1. An association of a value in $\mathcal{D}$ or the symbol null with each data arc of S.
2. An association of one of the symbols {true, false, null} with each control link of S.

We depict a configuration of a schema by drawing a solid circle on each arc having a non-null value, and writing a value denoting symbol beside. These circles are called data tokens, true tokens or false tokens according to the associated value.

A data flow schema S progresses through a sequence of configurations $\gamma_0, \gamma_1, \ldots$ through the firing of nodes. The rules of firing for each type of actor and link are given in Figure 4. Conditions for which a node is enabled are shown on the

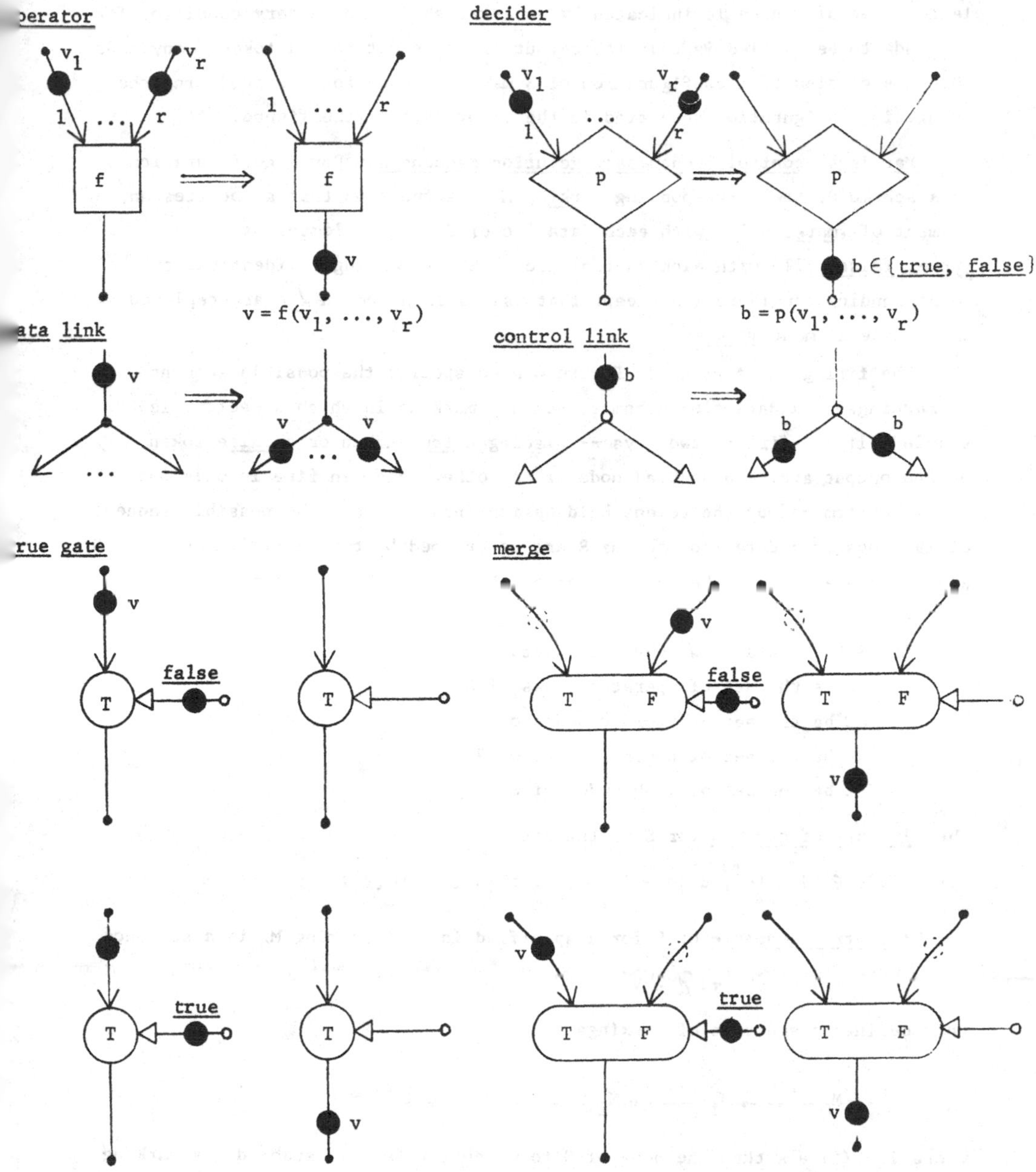

Figure 4. Firing rules for data flow schemas.

left (an enabled node is indicated by an asterisk). A necessary condition for any node to be enabled is that its output arc does not hold a token. Any node which is enabled in a configuration of S may be chosen to fire producing the change in configuration specified in the right part of the figure.

Markings; control sequences; execution sequences: For a configuration γ of a schema S, the corresponding marking M is a function that associates an element of {mark, null} with each data arc of S and an element of {true, false, null} with each control arc of S. A marking is identical to the corresponding configuration except that values in a domain $\mathcal{D}$ are replaced by the single element mark.

The firing rules given in Figure 4 also specify the possible sequences of markings of a data flow schema. For any marking in which a decider is enabled, it may fire in two ways -- placing a true token or a false token on its output arc. An enabled node of any other type can fire in only one way -- determined by the tokens held by its input links. The possible sequences of markings of a data flow schema S are determined by the initial marking of S and are independent of the interpretation chosen for the function and predicate letters of S.

Let S be a data flow schema and let:

A be the set of operator nodes of S

D be the set of decider nodes of S

C be the set of control nodes of S

L be the set of link nodes of S

The alphabet of actions for S is the set

$$V = \{a \mid a \in A\} \cup \{d^T, d^F \mid d \in D\} \cup \{c^T, c^F \mid c \in C\} \cup \{\ell \mid \ell \in L\}$$

A control sequence of S for a specified initial marking M_0 is a sequence*

$$\tau : \mathcal{N} \rightarrow V$$

that defines a sequence of markings of S

$$M_0 \xrightarrow{\tau(0)} M_1 \xrightarrow{\tau(1)} M_2 \longrightarrow \cdots\cdots \xrightarrow{\tau(k-1)} M_k$$

where if $\tau(i) = x$ then the node of S to which x refers is enabled for marking M_i and M_{i+1} is the result of firing node x. If τ is a finite control sequence of

---

*$\mathcal{N} = \{0, 1, \ldots\}$ is the set of natural numbers.

k elements then no node may be enabled in the final marking M_k. The symbols d^T and d^F are used to distinguish firings of a decider with <u>true</u> outcome and <u>false</u> outcome, and c^T, c^F are used to distinguish firings of control nodes in response to <u>true</u> and <u>false</u> tokens on their input control arcs.

Let $\gamma_0, \gamma_1, \ldots$ be a sequence of configurations of a data flow schema S for some interpretation, and let $M_0, M_1, \ldots$ be the corresponding sequence of markings of S. Let $\omega: \mathcal{N} \to V$ be a control sequence that yields the marking sequence $M_0, M_1, \ldots$, where for any configuration γ_i in which a decider d is enabled, application of the predicate associated with the predicate letter of d yields <u>true</u> or <u>false</u> according as $\omega(i)$ is d^T or d^F. Then ω is an <u>execution sequence</u> of S for the initial configuration γ_0.

<u>Well behaved data flow schemas</u>: Let S be an (m,n)-data flow schema and let M_0 be a marking of S in which no data arc has a token. Let S' be S with added data arcs as shown in Figure 5. Schema S is <u>well behaved</u> for marking M_0 if and only if each finite control sequence starting from the marking in Figure 5a leaves S' in the marking shown in Figure 5b, in which the marking of S is again M_0.

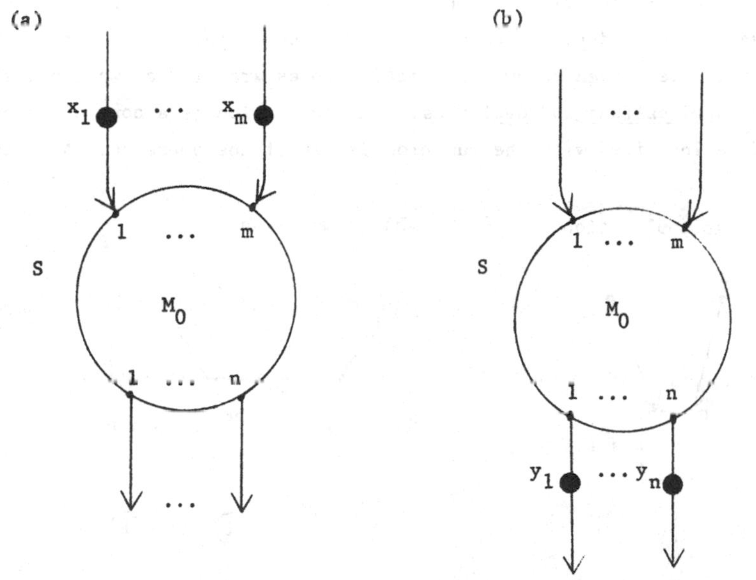

Figure 5. Definition of a well behaved schema.

A data flow schema is a system of interconnected elements that intercommunicate according to a strict discipline. Patil [11] has studied such systems and his work shows that the actors of data flow schemas are determinate systems and that since a data flow schema is a well formed interconnection of determinate subsystems, any data flow schema is a determinate system.

Therefore, a well behaved (m,n)-data flow schema S defines a function

$$\varphi_S : \mathcal{O}^m \to \mathcal{O}^n$$

Two such schemas S and S' are *weakly equivalent* if and only if for every interpretation φ_S and $\varphi_{S'}$ yield the same value $\underline{y} \in \mathcal{O}^n$ for every $\underline{x} \in \mathcal{O}^m$ at which both are defined; S and S' are *strongly equivalent* if and only if S and S' are weakly equivalent and $\varphi_{S'}$ is defined for $\underline{x} \in \mathcal{O}^m$ if and only if $\varphi_{S'}$ is defined for $\underline{x}$.

In the remainder of this paper we will be concerned only with data flow schemas that have specified initial markings for which they are well behaved. We will use the term *schema* henceforth to mean a well behaved, marked data flow schema.

Data dependence graphs: A *data dependence graph* (*dadep graph*) of a well behaved (m,n)-schema S is a finite, directed, acyclic, bipartite graph having *value nodes* and *action nodes*, and constructed from some control sequence of S according to the rules given below. The action nodes are of the two types shown in Figure 6 -- *applications* and *decisions*. An application is a copy of an operator node of S and is inscribed with the function letter of the operator. A decision

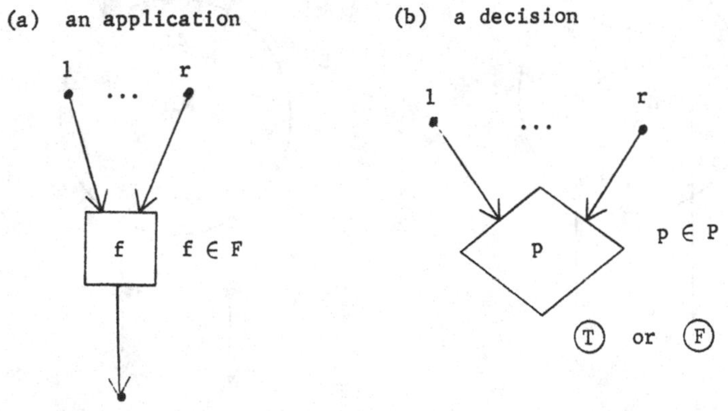

Figure 6. Components of a dadep graph.

is a copy of a decider node of S inscribed with the predicate letter of the decider, and labelled either (T) or (F) .

Given a control sequence ω of S, the corresponding dadep graph is constructed as follows: For each prefix $\omega(0), \omega(1), \ldots, \omega(i-1)$ of ω we define a partial dadep graph G_i and a partial labelling function ξ_i. The domain of ξ_i is certain data link nodes of S and its values are value nodes of G_i.

<u>Basis</u>: G_0 consists of m value nodes, and $\xi_0(u_j)$ is the jth <u>input node</u> of G_0 if u_j is the jth input node of S.

<u>Induction</u>: Let $x = \omega(i)$ be the ith element of ω, where $x \in V$. If $x \in L$ then $G_{i+1} = G_i$ and $\xi_{i+1} = \xi_i$. If $x \in A$ or $x \in \{d^T, d^F\}$ for some $d \in D$, then G_{i+1} is obtained from G_i by adding an action node y which is a copy of the actor of S to which x refers. If u_j is the jth input node of x in S then $\xi_i(u_j)$ is the jth input value node of y in G_{i+1}. If x is an operator, a new value node w is included in G_{i+1} and made the output node of application y. The new labelling function ξ_{i+1} is ξ_i with the exception that $\xi_{i+1}(v) = w$ where v is the output node of x in S. If y is decider d, then y is a decision and is labelled (T) or (F) according as x is d^T or d^F.

If x is an action by a control node c with output node v, then $G_{i+1} = G_i$ and ξ_{i+1} is defined as follows: If c is a Boolean node, a control gate, a control merge, a data F-gate where $x = c^T$ or a data T-gate where $x = c^F$, then $\xi_{i+1} = \xi_i$. If c is a data T-gate (F-gate) with data input node u and $x = c^T (x = c^F)$, then ξ_{i+1} is ξ_i with the exception that $\xi_{i+1}(v) = \xi_i(u)$. If c is a data merge with data input node u^T and u^F, then $\xi_{i+1} = \xi_i$ with the exception that $\xi_{i+1}(v) = \xi_i(u^T)$ if $x = c^T$, or $\xi_{i+1}(v) = \xi_i(u^F)$ if $x = c^F$.

<u>Termination</u>: If ω has k elements, then $G = G_k$ is the corresponding dadep graph. The jth <u>output node</u> of G is $\xi_k(v_j)$ where v_j is the jth output node of S. The values of ξ_i used in the construction are defined because any actor x in a well behaved schema S must lie on some data path from an input node of S. Each node on all such paths must fire at least once for x to be enabled. Also ξ_k must be defined for every output node of S because each output node of S must fire exactly once in any control sequence.

The <u>labelling relation</u> ψ for a dadep graph G of a schema associates each value node of G with the data nodes of S that handle the value. It is defined by

$$(u,w) \in \psi \quad \text{iff} \quad \xi_i(u) = w, \text{ any } i \in \{0, \ldots, k\}$$

Similarity and consistency: Suppose G and G' are dadep graphs of (m,n)-schemas using the same sets G and P of function and predicate letters.

A value node w of G is similar to a value node w' of G' if and only if either

1. w is the jth input node of G and w' is the jth input node of G' for $1 \leq j \leq n$.
2. w is the output node of an application x in G, w' is the output node of an application x' in G', x and x' bear the same function letter f, and corresponding input nodes of x and x' are similar.

Dadep graph G is similar to dadep graph G' if and only if corresponding output nodes of G and G' are similar.

A decision y in G is similar to a decision y' in G' if and only if y and y' bear the same predicate letter, and corresponding input nodes of y and y' are similar.

Decisions y in G and y' in G' are inconsistent if and only if they are similar and one is labelled T and the other F . Decisions y and y' are strongly consistent if they are similar but not inconsistent.

Two dadep graphs G and G' are strongly consistent if and only if for each decision in one there is a strongly consistent decision in the other. Two dadep graphs G and G' are weakly consistent if and only if there is no pair of decisions y in G and y' in G' which are inconsistent.

Two (m,p)-schemas S and S' are strongly similar if and only if for each dadep graph of one there is a similar, strongly consistent dadep graph of the other. Two (m,p)-schemas S and S' are weakly similar if and only if for each dadep graph of one there is a similar, weakly consistent dadep graph of the other.

Free and liberal schemata: A data flow schema S is free if and only if each dadep graph of S has no pair of inconsistent decisions. A data flow schema S is liberalif and only if each dadep graph of S has no pair of similar value nodes. These definitions are Paterson's notions of free and liberal [9, 10] applied to data flow schemas.

Proposition: Two free, well behaved (m,n)-schemas are strongly (weakly) equivalent if they are strongly (weakly) similar.

This result is applied in the transformations of well formed schema discussed in later sections of this paper.

WELL FORMED DATA FLOW SCHEMAS

In this section we define a class of simple, well behaved schemas having a hierarchical structure.

Well formed data flow schemas: A well formed data flow schema is any acyclic interconnection of operators, conditional subschemas and loop subschemas (these latter will be recursively defined later). No schema input or output nodes occur within conditional or loop subschemas, although they may be input or output nodes of such subschemas. Input nodes are precisely those data link nodes having no data arcs incident upon them. Output nodes include all data link nodes having no data arcs emanating from them. This restriction will ensure that well formed schemas containing no conditional or loop subschemas will be well-behaved. The definition of the subschemas will be such that all well formed schema will be well behaved. (The converse is not true. That is, there are well behaved schemas which are not well formed.)

To facilitate the definition of conditional subschemas and loop subschemas, we introduce two useful structures.

A decider subschema is an acyclic interconnection of deciders and boolean actors with the property that exactly one control link node has no emanating control arc. This node is the output of the decider subschema. Inputs to the schema are simply the data link nodes from which the deciders take their input data arcs. A decider subschema will be used to represent a single boolean expression involving the deciders it contains. A decider subschema is pictured in Figure 7.

We also have use for a representation of k data arcs emanating from $j(\leq k)$ data link nodes. Unless otherwise specified, the only constraint is that at least one data arc emanate from each link node. Such a representation is shown in Figure 8.

Conditional subschemas: Given two well formed schemas having the same number of output nodes, we can construct a conditional subschema as shown in Figure 9. No data arcs or control arcs are marked in the initial marking.

The effect of a conditional subschema is to set its outputs using S_1 if D is true and using S_2 if D is false. It is not difficult to see that if S_1 and S_2 are well behaved, the specified interconnection is also well behaved.

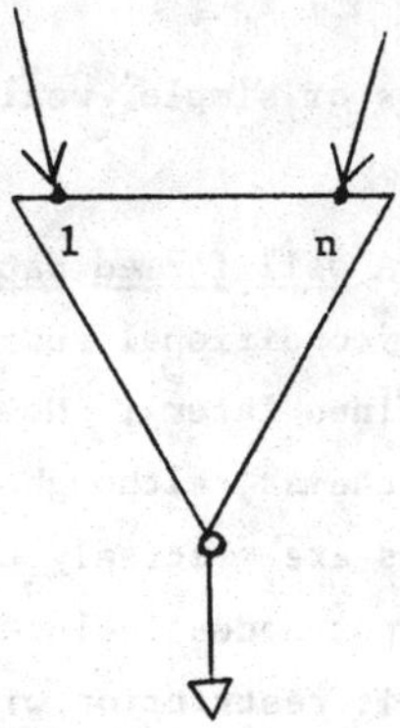

Figure 7. Decider subschema.

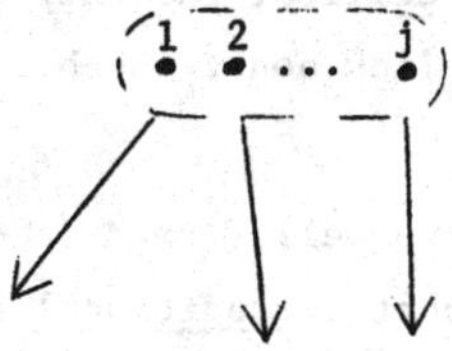

Figure 8.

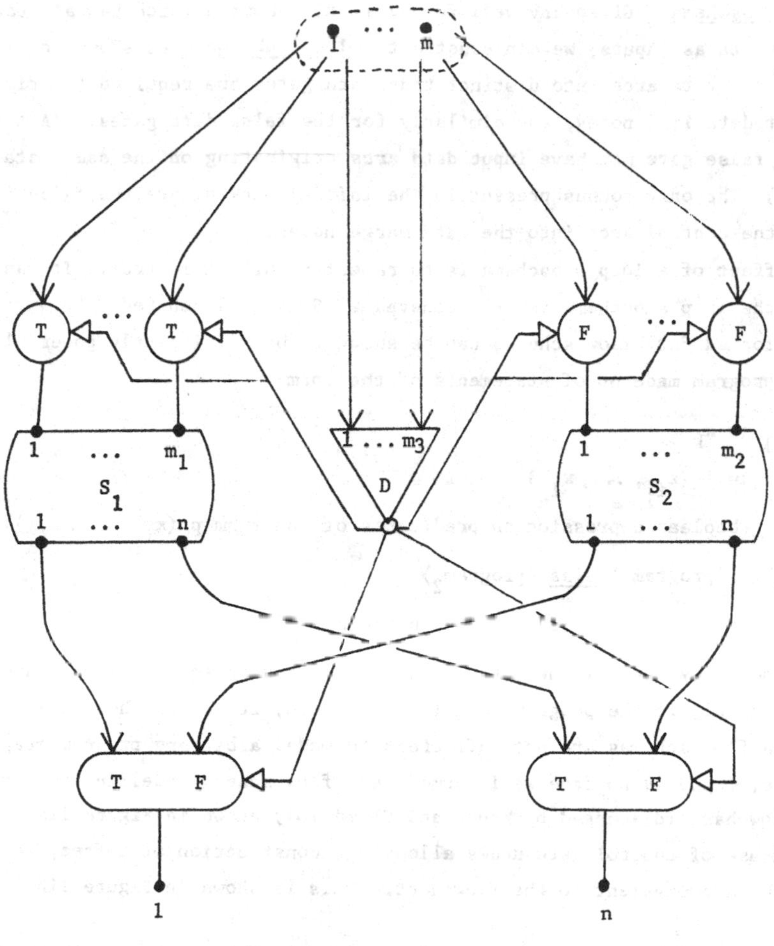

S_1 is a well formed (m_1,n)-schema

S_2 is a well formed (m_2,n)-schema

D is an m_3-input decider subschema

Figure 9. Well formed (m,n)-conditional subschema.

Loop subschema: Given any well formed (m,n)-schema S which has at least as many outputs as inputs, we can construct a loop subschema as shown in Figure 10. Data arcs into distinct true data gates are required to originate on distinct data link nodes, and similarly for the false data gates. (A true gate and a false gate may have input data arcs originating on the same data link node.) The only tokens present in the initial marking are the false tokens on the control arcs into the data merge nodes.

The effect of a loop subschema is to repeat S while Ð is true. It can be seen that the loop subschema is well behaved if S is well behaved.

Well formed data flow schemas can be shown to be sufficiently powerful to model any program made up of statements of the form

a) $x_j := x_k$

b) $x_j := f_k(x_{i_1}, \ldots, x_{i_n})$

c) if ⟨boolean expression on predicates of the form $p_k(x_{i_1}, \ldots, x_{i_n})$⟩ then ⟨$\text{program}_1$⟩ else ⟨$\text{program}_2$⟩

d) while ⟨boolean expression⟩ do ⟨program⟩

By "model" we include the notion that the data flow schema be free and liberal precisely if the program is. In this sense, it can be shown that well formed data flow schemas are not sufficient to model arbitrary program graphs. For example, there is no free well formed data flow schema modelling the free program flowchart (discussed by Knuth and Floyd [8]) shown in Figure 11a. Permitting use of control gate nodes allows the construction of a free, well behaved schema equivalent to the flowchart. This is shown in Figure 11b.

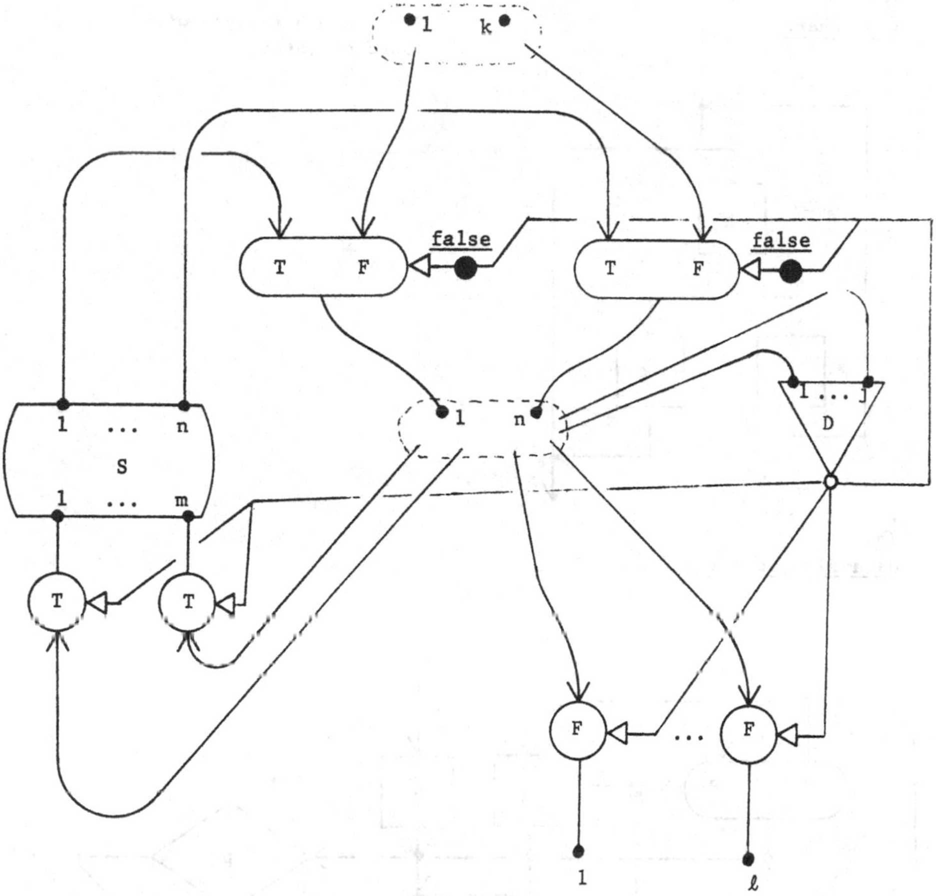

S is a well formed (m,n)-schema (n ≥ m)

D is a j-input decider subschema

Figure 10. Well formed (k, ℓ)-loop subschema

(a)
flow chart

Floyd-Knuth example with added operator

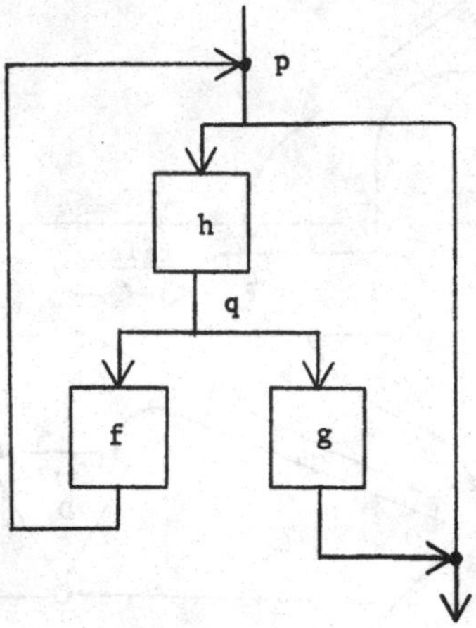

(b)
data flow schema

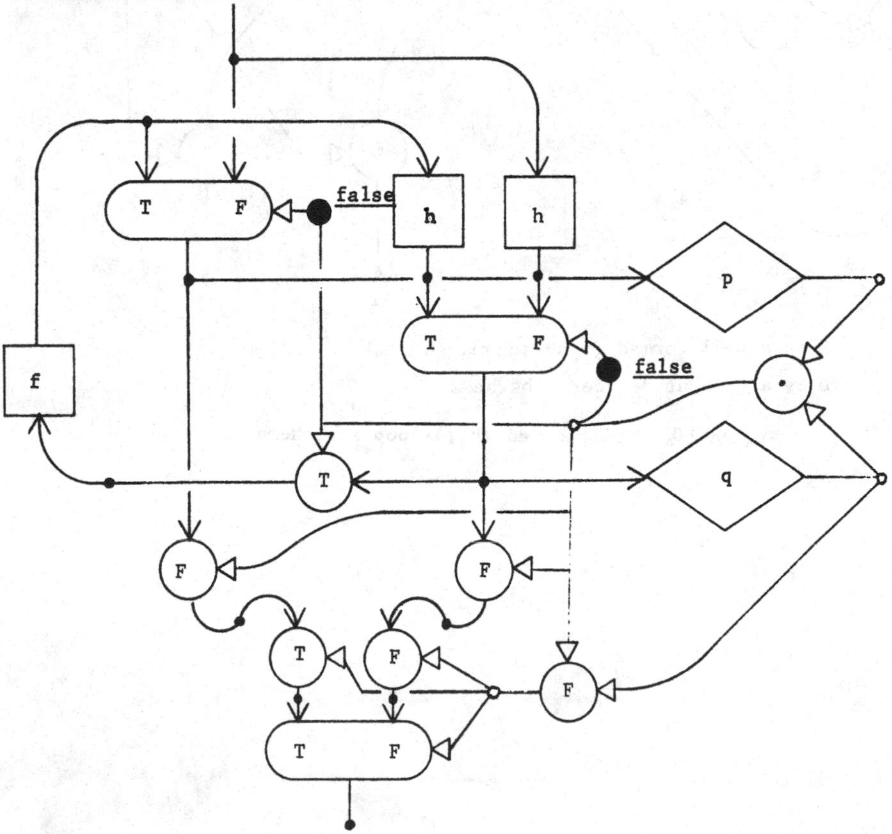

Figure 11. A free data flow schema for a multiple exit flowchart.

EQUIVALENCE OF DATA LINKS

In this section we show how to transform any well formed schema into a weakly equivalent well formed schema in which no pair of data link nodes are weakly equivalent. Such a schema is said to be irredundant.

Definition: Two data link nodes v_1 and v_2 of a well formed schema S are (weakly) equivalent if and only if, for every interpretation of S, the sequences of data values associated with v_1 and v_2 by any finite execution sequence of S are equal.

Definition: A well formed schema S is irredundant if and only if any distinct output links v_1 and v_2 of a well formed subschema of S are not equivalent.

The transformation of a free well formed schema S into an irredundant well formed schema is done in two phases: We first modify S so that operators, whose execution is required regardless of the action taken by a decider are not part of the subschema controlled by the decider unless they are within one of its subschemas. Performing this modification simplifies the problem of testing for the equivalence of data link nodes.

Definition: A modified well formed schema S is a well formed schema such that for any output link p of a loop subschema L of S either: 1) there exist partial dadep graphs G and G' of S with value nodes v and v' that correspond to data node p in S and v and v' are output nodes of operator applications bearing different function letters; or 2) there is a partial dadep graph G of S with a value node v that corresponds to data node p and also to some input node of S.

A well formed schema is put into modified form by moving operators past gate and merge nodes wherever this may be done without changing the function defined by the schema.

The transformation of a schema into modified form involves directed acyclic paths in the schema that contain only data link nodes, gate nodes, and merge nodes. Such a path is called an empty data path.

Transformation T: Let u be an output node of some loop subschema L of a free, well formed schema S. Let $X = \{a_1, \ldots, a_k\}$ be the set of all operator nodes of S such that for each $a \in X$ there is an empty data path from the output node of a to node u. Suppose each $a \in X$ bears the same function letter f. Transform S into S' as follows:

1. Let R be the subgraph of S defined as follows: For each $a \in X$, every empty data path from the output node of a to node p is a path in R. For each true (false) gate in R with data input and control input nodes that are also input nodes of a false (true) gate of S, the false (true) gate, its output node and its input and output arcs are elements of R.
2. A data node is an output node of R if it is an input node of any actors of S other than those actors in R. Let these distinct nodes (including u) be $u_1, \ldots, u_\ell$. Let the input nodes of a_i be $u_{i1}, \ldots, u_{ir}$ which need not be distinct.
3. Schema S' is obtained by making r copies of R and rearranging the operators of X as shown in Figure 13.

Lemma 1: Transformation T yields a well formed schema S' when applied to a well formed schema S. Furthermore S' and S are strongly equivalent and S' is free if S is free.

Proof: 1. (S' is well formed.) Deciders are associated with loop and conditional subschemas in S' exactly as in S. Each control node of S' is part of the same subschema as the deciders to which it is connected by paths of control arcs. The gate and merge nodes of S' define boundaries of loop and conditional subschemas having the same nested structure in S' as the corresponding subschemas have in S. Thus S' is well formed.

2. (S and S' are strongly equivalent.) This is clear from the construction of S' from S.

3. (S' is free if S' is free.) Each decider performs the same function in S' as in S.

Theorem 1: Given any free well formed schema S one can construct a free, modified well formed schema S' strongly equivalent to S.

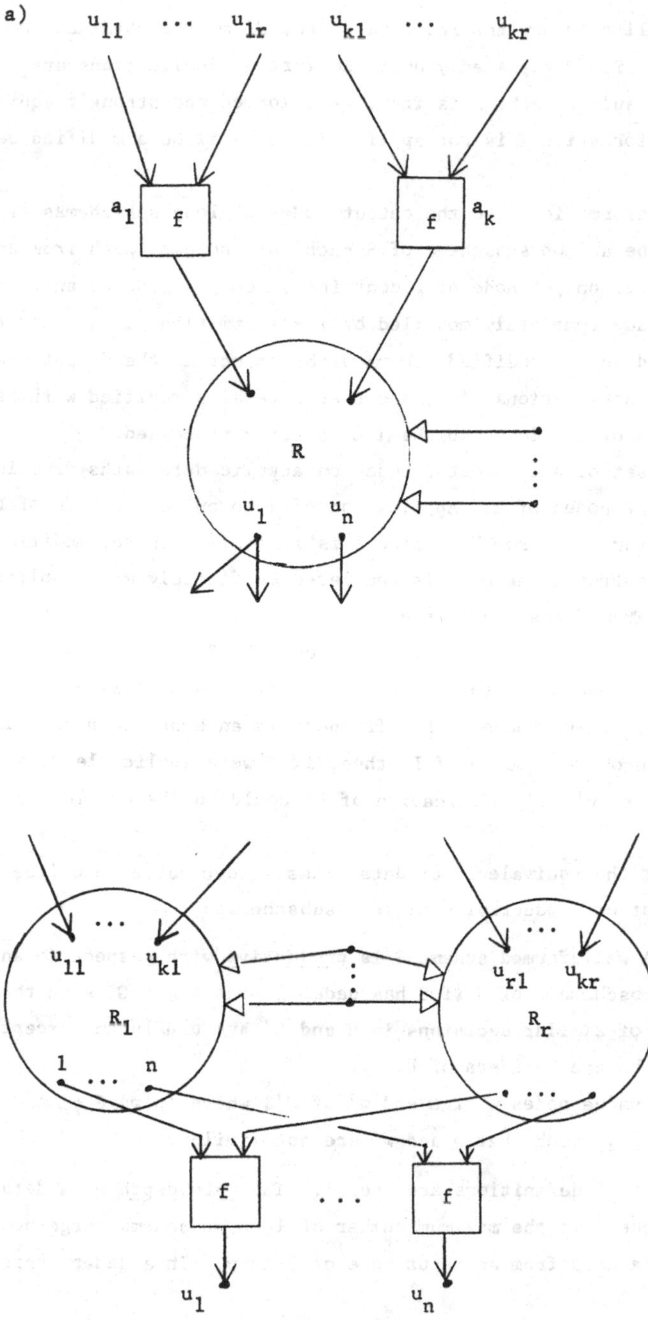

Figure 13. The transformation T.

Proof: We will show how the required schema S' may be obtained from S by applying Transformation T repeatedly until no further applications are possible. By Lemma 1 the resulting schema is free, well formed and strongly equivalent to S. Since Transformation T is not applicable, S' will be a modified well formed schema.

We apply Transformation T to the output nodes of loop subschemas of S one at a time. Let L be a loop subschema of S such that no data path from an input node of S to an output node of L contains an output node of another loop subschema not already completely modified by Transformation T. We show that S will be converted into a modified schema with respect to the output nodes of L in finitely many applications of T, and that S remains modified with respect to the output nodes of any loop subschema L' already processed.

Let X be the set of all operator nodes on acyclic data paths from input nodes of S to output nodes of L. Application of T to an output node of L removes at least one operator node from X. Since X is initially finite, modification of S with respect to output nodes of L is completed by finitely many applications of T.

Suppose that Transformation T is being applied to a loop subschema L, and that loop subschema L' has already been modified. If S contains no empty data path from an output node of L' to an output node of L then L' is unaffected by application of T to output nodes of L. If there is an empth path from an output node v' of L' to an output node v of L, then, if T were applicable to v it would also be applicable to v' and modification of L' could not be complete contrary to assumption.

Our proof that the equivalence of data links is decidable in a free schema involves the concept of productivity of loop subschemas:

Definition: A well formed schema S is productive with respect to an output link pfof a loop subschema L of S if S has dadep graphs G and G' such that:

1. All pairs of similar decisions in G and G' are consistent except decisions by the deciders of L.
2. There are value nodes w of G and w' of G', where $(p,w) \in \psi_G$ and $(p, w') \in \psi_{G'}$, such that w and w' are not similar.

Several additional definitions are useful. The path depth of a data link p in a well formed schema is the maximum number of loop subschema merge nodes on an acyclic path of data arcs from an input node of S to p. In a dadep graph G of a schema S, two paths are <u>similar</u> if they have equal numbers of operator applications, the ith operator on each path has the same function letter, and, if a and b are the ith applications on the two paths, the input arcs of a and b that lie on the two paths have the same index. If x is a path in a dadep graph G, a path x' is a <u>proper subpath</u> of x if x' is contained in x, x and x' terminate on the same value node, and x' has fewer applications than x.

We first state the theorem and give the structure of its proof. Then we state and prove the necessary lemmas.

<u>Theorem 2</u>: Let S be a free, modified, well-formed schema. It is decidable whether any two data links p_1 and p_2 of S are equivalent.

<u>Proof</u>: The proof is an induction on the maximum path depth of data links p_1 and p_2.

<u>Predicate of induction</u>: P_k: Let p_1 and p_2 be two data links of S such that no acyclic data path from an input node of S to either p_1 or p_2 passes through more than k merge nodes of loop subschemas of S. Then it is decidable whether p_1 and p_2 are equivalent.

<u>Basis</u>: If there are no merge nodes of loop schemas on any data path from input node of S to p_1 or p_2, then equivalence of p_1 and p_2 is decidable because the sequences of values at p_1 and at p_2 are defined by a finite set of partial dadep graphs.

<u>Induction</u>: Assume P(k) to be true and we prove P(k + 1).

Let X be the subgraph of S that contains all acyclic data paths to nodes p_1 and p_2 that contain only operators and gate or merge nodes of conditional subschemas of S. The input data nodes of X will be

1. output links of loop subschemas
2. output links of true gates of loop subschemas
3. input nodes of S.

The second and third categories are mutually exclusive. Not all input nodes of X can be input nodes of S if either of p_1 or p_2 has path depth k + 1.

<u>Case I</u>: Suppose some input link of X is an output link p_i of some loop subschema L. Then, if p_1 and p_2 are equivalent, X must also contain a path from some output link p_j of L to p_2. Since the input links of L are of path depth k or less, they may be partitioned into equivalence classes, and by Lemma 2 we can modify S so that every output link of L is productive.

Lemma 3 proves that the equivalence of any pair of output links of L is decidable. If the input nodes of X include output nodes of distinct loop subschemas, these nodes cannot be similar because S is assumed to be free. If some input node u of X is an output link of a true gate of some loop schema L', then L' must contain the loop subschemas for which some output link is an input link of X. Hence u must be of path depth k or less and the equivalence of u with other input nodes of X is decidable by our hypothesis of induction. Input nodes of X that are input nodes of S are not equivalent to each other and cannot be equivalent to output nodes of productive loop subschemas. Thus the input nodes of X may be partitioned into equivalence classes. By Lemma 4 the equivalence of p_1 and p_2 is decidable.

<u>Case II</u>: Suppose every input link of X is the output link of true gate node of some loop subschema. Since every path in X must be inside the loop schema of the gate node at which it originates, all merge nodes from which paths in X lead to p_1 must belong to the same loop subschema, and similary for p_2. If p_1 and p_2 are equivalent, these two loop subschemas must be one and the same. Since the equivalence of input nodes of this loop subschema L is decidable, Lemmas A and B show that we may assume that L is productive and that the input nodes of X may be partitioned into equivalence classes. Then Lemma 4 shows that the equivalence of p_1 and p_2 is decidable.

<u>Lemma 2</u>: Let L be a loop subschema of a free, modified, well formed schema S. If the equivalence of the input links of L is decidable, then it is decidable whether S is productive with respect to any output link p of L.

<u>Proof</u>: Construct a subgraph X of L using the following procedure:

1. Include output node p in X.
2. If the output link of a gate node or merge node x in L is in X then x and its data input node or nodes are also in X.

The input nodes of X are output links of operators contained in L and certain input links of L. A necessary and sufficient condition that S is not productive with respect to p is that all input nodes of X are input links of L and are mutually equivalent.

<u>Sufficiency</u>: If all input links of X are equivalent, the sequence of values produced at output link p will be exactly the sequence presented on each of the input links regardless of the decisions made by the deciders of L. In this case, S is not productive with respect to p and p may be identified with any input node of X, yielding a new schema, weakly equivalent to S, in which subschema L has one less unproductive output node.

<u>Necessity</u>: Suppose S is unproductive with respect to link p, and suppose that one or more input links to X are output links of operators $a_1, \ldots, a_k$ inside L. Since S is free and L is unproductive, operators $a_1, \ldots, a_k$ must bear the same function letter f. Also, every empty data path in S leading to an input node of L that is an input node of X must originate at an operator bearing function letter f. This contradicts our assumption that S is a modified well formed schema. If all input nodes of X are input nodes of X, then S is clearly not unproductive with respect to p unless these input nodes are mutually equivalent.

<u>Lemma 3</u>: If L is a loop subschema of a free, modified, well formed schema S, and the equivalence of input links of L is known, then the equivalence of output links of L is decidable.

<u>Proof</u>: We prove the following proposition by an induction on the number of nested loop subschemas in L.

Proposition: Let p_i and p_j be output nodes of a loop subschema L of S. Either p_i and p_j are not equivalent for any partition of the input nodes of L into groups of equivalent nodes, or one can construct a partition P of the input nodes of L such that p_i and p_j are equivalent if and only if P is a refinement of the partition of the input nodes of L into groups of equivalent nodes.

Basis: Let the body of L be the well formed (q,r)-schema R which has no loop subschemas, as shown in Figure . Construct a series of partitions of input links $p_1', \ldots, p_r'$ of L as follows:

1. Partition P_0 contains the part (p_i', p_j') where p_i' and p_j' are the input links of L from which data paths lead to output nodes p_i and p_j, respectively, without passing through R. Each remaining input node of L forms a separate part of P_0.
2. Given a partition P_i of the input links of L, let P_i^1 be the partition of the output nodes of R defined by P_i and the connection from merge outputs to inputs of R.

   A necessary and sufficient condition that p_i and p_j are equivalent is that the input nodes in each part of P be mutually equivalent. The sufficiency of this condition is clear. The necessity depends on S being a modified, well formed schema, because only then can we claim that links in the same part of P_i must be equivalent if any links in the same part of P_i are to be equivalent.
3. Construct a partition P_i^2 of the input nodes of R as follows: Since R has no loop subschemas, the dadep graphs of R are finite in number and size. For each dadep graph G of R, construct the finest partition of input nodes of R such that x and x' are in the same part whenever output nodes y and y' are in the same part of P_i^1 and G has similar paths from x to y and x' to y'. Let P_i^2 be the union of these partitions. (The union P of partitions P_1 and P_2 is the finest partition such that two elements are in the same part of P if they are in the same part of P_1 or in the same part of P_2.)
4. P_{i+1} is the union of P_i and the partition of the merge node output links corresponding to P_i^2.
5. Continue the construction until $P_{i+1} = P_i$. If the construction fails (by the absence of similar paths where required in a dadep graph of R), then there is no partition of the input nodes of L into groups of equivalent

nodes such that p_i and p_j are equivalent. Otherwise, the construction must terminate because there are finitely many distinct partitions of the input nodes of L. Let $P = P_i$.

Induction: Suppose the body of L is the well formed (q,r)-schema R which contains K or fewer nested loop schemas. Construct a series of paritions of the input nodes of L as in the basis.

Let G be a dadep graph of R and suppose y and y' belong to the same part of P_i^1. Trace backwards from y and y' along similar paths in G. If one path strikes the boundary of a dadep graph H' of a loop subschema L' of R there are two cases to consider according as 1) the other path strikes the boundary of H' at the same distance from y and y'; or 2) the other path either strikes the boundary of a different loop subschema of R, or does not strike any loop subschema boundary. In case (2) S must be unproductive with respect to the output node of L'. This requirement, if it can be met at all, determine a partition of the input links of L' such that links in the same part must be equivalent if y and y' are equivalent. In case (1), the output nodes of L' on the two paths must be equivalent. By the induction hypothesis, this requirement determines a partition of the input links of L' into groups of links that must be equivalent. This process is continued unless it fails due to absence of similar applications, unproductive loop subschemas, or the impossibility of a loop subschema having the required equivalent output links. If it does not fail, the paths will reach input nodes x and x' of G and require that x and x' be equivalent if y and y' are equivalent. There are only a finite number of cases to be considered in constructing P_i^2 from P_i^1 because the procedure does not involve the structure of dadep graphs of the loop subschemas of R.

Lemma 5: Let X be an acyclic data subgraph of a free, modified, well formed schema S such that:

1. X contains only operators and gate or merge nodes of conditional subschemas of S.
2. X has two output nodes p and p'.
3. Each input node p_i of X is either a productive output node of a loop subschema, the output node of a true gate of a loop subschema or an input node of S, the last two cases being mutually exclusive.

If the equivalence of input links of X is decidable then the equivalence of p and p' is decidable.

Proof: Let R be the body of the smallest loop subschema of S that contains X, or let R be S if X is not contained in any loop subschema. Let G be any dadep graph of R in which value nodes w and w' correspond to data nodes p and p' and value nodes $w_1, \ldots, w_r$ correspond to input nodes of X. This correspondence is unique because R has no loop subschemas. Then for each path in G from some w_i to w there is a similar path in G from some w_j to w', and nodes p_i and p_j are equivalent.

Sufficiency: The sufficiency of the condition is clear.

Necessity: Let G be any dadep graph of R in which value nodes w and w' correspond to nodes p and p'. Let x be a path in G from a value node w_i that corresponds to input node p_i of X. We consider three cases as p_i is a productive output node of a loop subschema of S, the output node of some true gate of a loop subschema of S, or an input node of S.

Case I: Assume p_i is a productive output link of a loop subschema L. Assume p and p' are equivalent. Then G contains a path x' from w_j to w' such that x is similar to a proper subpath of x', x' is similar to a proper subpath of x, or x and x' are similar. Since L is productive and p is equivalent to p', p_j must be an output link of L. Now consider the two cases of similarity of proper subpaths.

(a) If x' is similar to a proper subpath of x, there is a value node w_k in x which must always be similar to the corresponding appearance of value node w_j of x' in any dadep graph of S in order for p to be equivalent to p'. However, since S is in modified form there is a dadep graph D of S such that corresponding appearances of w_j and w_k in D are output nodes of operators with different function letters -- contradiction.

(b) A similar argument as outlined in (a) shows that x is not similar to a proper subpath of x'. Therefore x and x' must be similar and p_i and p_j must be equivalent.

<u>Case II</u>: Assume p_i is a output link of a true gate of loop subschema L, and assume p and p' are equivalent. Then G contains a path, x', from w_j to w' such that x is similar to a proper subpath of x', x' is similar to a proper subpath of x, or x and x' are similar. Since p and p' are equivalent, p_j cannot be the output link of a productive loop subschema or an input link of S. Therefore p_i and p_j must both be output links of true gates of the same loop subschema. By the same argument as is used in Case I we can show that x and x' are similar, and p_i is equivalent to p_j.

<u>Case III</u>: Assume p_i is an input link of S and p and p' are equivalent. Then G contains a path, x', from w_j to w' such that x is similar to a proper subpath of x', x' is similar to a proper subpath of x, or x and x' are similar. Since p and p' are equivalent, p_j cannot be an output link of a productive loop subschema or a true gate of a loop subschema, and therefore it must be an input link of S. Since p_i and p_j are input links of S and since p is equivalent to p', x and x' are similar, and p_i and p_j are equivalent.

ACKNOWLEDGEMENT

We acknowledge the help of James E. Rumbaugh and Paul J. Fox for providing us with many useful ideas and counter examples.

REFERENCES

1. Ashcroft, E., and Manna, Z. The translation of 'go to' programs to 'while' programs. Information Processing 71, Ljubljana. 1971.

2. Cooper, D. C. Programs for mechanical program verification. Machine Intelligence, Vol. 6, Edinburgh University Press, 1970.

3. Dennis, J. B. Programming generality, parallelism and computer architecture. Information Processing 68, North-Holland, Amsterdam 1969, pp 484-492.

4. Engeler, E. Structure and meaning of elementary programs. Symposium on the Semantics of Algorithmic Languages, 1970

5. Fosseen, J. B. Representation of Algorithms by Maximally Parallel Schemata. M.S. Thesis, Massachusetts Institute of Technology, Cambridge, Mass., June 1972.

6. Karp, R. M., and Miller, R. E. Parallel program schemata. J. of Computer and System Sciences, Vol. 3, No. 2, May 1969, pp 147-195.

7. Keller, R. M. On maximally parallel schemata. IEEE Conference Record, Eleventh Annual Symposium on Switching and Automata Theory, October 1970, pp 32-50.

8. Knuth, D. E., and Floyd, R. W. Notes on avoiding "go to" statements. Information Processing Letters 1, North-Holland Publishing Co., Amsterdam 1971, pp 23-31.

9. Luckham, D. C., Park, D. M. R., and Paterson, M. S. On formalised computer programs. J. of Computer and System Sciences, Vol. 4, No. 3 (June 1970), pp 220-249.

10. Paterson, M. S.. Equivalence Problems in a Model of Computation. Ph.D. Thesis, Trinity College, University of Cambridge, 1967.

11. Patil, S. S. Closure properties of interconnections of determinate systems. Record of the Project MAC Conference on Concurrent Systems and Parallel Computation, ACM, New York 1970, pp 107-116.

12. Rodriguez, J. E. A Graph Model for Parallel Computation. Report MAC-TR-64, Project MAC, M.I.T., Cambridge, Mass., September 1969.

13. Slutz, D. R. The Flow Graph Schemata of Parallel Computations. Report MAC-TR-53, Project MAC, M.I.T., Cambridge, Mass., September 1968.

OPERATION PATTERNS

by A. Bährs

A. INTRODUCTION

The control in computers during the program run passes successively from one instruction to another. Similarly, elaboration of programs, written in any algorithmic language, is defined by flow of control from one statement to another. Following them the existing program models called usually program schemata have in its base a graph of transitions [1]. Information links between the shema statements are either not reflected in it, or are set implicitly by the mark of statements inputs and outputs, or if the information graph of the shema is set play a subordinate role. The basic links between the statements are defined by the transition graph, and the elaboration of the statement starts, when the control is passed on it.
The operation patterns defined in this paper are based unlike shemata on flow of data. Data units called from here on objects, are yielded on outputs of action units called statements. Any statement of the operation pattern starts to elaborate only when a full set of objects it needs will come to its inputs. The elaboration of several statements may be started simultaneously due to such start condition being localized in each statement. The completion of statement elaboration results in yielding an object on its output. Through the links this object comes to all the statement inputs connected by links with the particular output. This offers conditions for starting elaboration of some other statements and so on. In this manner the OPs are fitted, for describing parallel or, as it is often called, collaterally elaboration of program.

The objects the OP works at may be of different kinds defined by their mode. The statement inputs and outputs and the OP links are adjusted to definite modes of objects related to them.
The objects are received and yielded by the statements and transfered to the links as a whole irrespectively of their inside composition which may be complex. The range of any object is that totality of links connected to the output the object yielded.
In other words, the operation patterns express the "structure of operations" the program executes on some data. Operation patterns do not describe the "data structure" to be set in addition.
The statements are composed of a small number of basic element kinds having quite simple features. Selection of these features was done in such a way, to divide between various basic elements, if possible the responsibility for such important characteristics of programs and their

tribution and so on. Later on this will allow to examine the effect of each property on the course of the program elaboration.

Composition of statements out of basic elements is going on by systematic applying the extension mechanism, which allows to replace certain operation patterns by some new elements.

In particular, various memory elements are defined by extension. They have a definite mode predetermining the mode of objects, which may be stored in a given memory element.

Apart from using extensions for building statements, the extensions are used also to determine the function or predicate performed by the statement by a suitable OP which may be arbitrary complex. Such a recursive definition allows to increase greatly the set of routines performed by the statements starting with a small number of initial functions and predicates.

In this case the features of the construction and elaboration of the OP are not changed at any level of consideration. This feature of "built in varying enlargement" makes the OP convenient for theoretical investigation of program features, as well as for constructing on their basis a convenient expansible programming language.

The statements in the OP possess of closeness i.e. the statement elaboration independence of other statement elaboration, and wholeness that means that the statement does not effect the elaboration of the OP in any other way but yields an object at its output. In other words the full information about the statement environments explicitely denoted and localized in totality of links which are connected to its inputs and outputs. This feature of operation patterns makes them convenient for program transformations which are used, for example, for program optimization.

Acknowledgements

The author considers the end of the Introduction to be a suitable place for thanking his colleagues at the Department of Informatics of the Computing Center of the Sib.Br. of the USSR Acad. of Sci. for their attention to this work. I would like to express my particular gratitude to A.P.Ershov for his support and guidance and also to V.V.Grushetzky, whose daily collaboration stimulated the advance of the paper and improved its style.

B. BASIC OPERATION PATTERNS

Basic operation patterns (BOP) consist of basic elements, having outputs and inputs, and links connecting them.
Elaboration of BOP consists of a set of events either related to changes of basic element states or to objects the BOP deals with. Some partial relationships are defined between these events and the BOP elaboration generates a course of events partially ordered by these relationships.

A formal description of basic elements and the manner of their joint into a basic operation pattern is given in this section. The relationship between the events, elaboration of the basic operation pattern and the general features of the objects which are set by the basic patterns are also defined there.

B.1. Objects

All these objects are divided into three non-overlapping classes. The first class objects are called values. It is supposed that a mode from the value mode set is related to each value. In this conection a value is said to have a definite mode or it is a value of this mode.
According to the definition, a set of unitary objects is assigned to values, a unitary object is denoted by $\mathcal{E}$ and the mode of a unitary object is denoted by u - 0 and belongs, according the definition, to the value mode set. Which other objects belong to the value class and what are other modes constituting the value mode set is left undefined.
The second class objects are called infors. The infors class is divided into subclasses each of them being related to a mode c - i , for each integer $i \geq 1$, integral numbers I_1, I_2, ... , I_i are only objects of c - i mode.
The third class objects are called strobs, all of them have the same mode s - p (synchropulse).
Below the expressions "value mode object" or "signal mode object" will stand for arbitrary value (value or infor) respectively.

When describing BOPs all the objects are considered to be quasielementary (though values unlike the unitary object may be stowed, for example, arrays or structures).The objects yielded in whole on the element outputs are transfered as a whole through the links and received at the element inputs. The range of any object is a totality of links, joined to the output of the element this object yields.

B.2. States and Events

There are two states for basic elements: free and busy. Each element may be in one of these states.
When the basic element state is changed from "free" to "busy" the event relevant to this element called the start of its elaboration occurs. When it is changed from "busy" to "free" another event occurs called the finish of its elaboration. There are no other events relevant to the elements.
There are two events relevant to the objects: an object comes to the element input and the object is yielded on the element output. There are no other events relevant to the objects.
The effect of the events on changing the element states and on each other is considered when describing proper basic elements.
Following partial binary relationships are defined between the events:
$x \mathrel{|\!\!=\!\!|} y$ - the events x and y are simultaneous. The relationships $\mathrel{|\!\!=\!\!|}$ is the equivalency relation of that allows to speak about simultaneity of several events as about the event occuring simultaneously with them.
$x \vdash y$ - the event y occurs after the event x. The relation $\vdash$ is a strict order one, i.e. it is transitive and non-reflexive.
$x \models y$ - the event y occurs just after the event x. The relation $\models$ is defined by $\forall (x,y)\ (x \models y) \rightarrow (x \vdash y) \& (\overline{\exists} z)((x \vdash z) \& (z \vdash y))$
therefore it is non-reflexive. Moreover $(x \models y \models z) \rightarrow (x \vdash z)$ holds.
The events are considered to have no duration, and the intervals between events are not supplied by any measure of duration as it is seen from the above relationships.

B.3. Basic Elements

Each input and output of basic elements is related to some mode. The input (output) mode may be either <u>c - i</u> for some $i \geq 1$, or <u>s - p</u>, or a union of some modes of the value mode set. The mode of input (output) predetermines the mode of objects which may come (be yielded) to this input (output). The input (output) is also said to have a proper mode.

The basic elements belong to one of the following three classes: transformers, distributors and a gate.

B.3.1. Basic Transformers

Basic element having one output and $k \geq 1$ inputs is called a basic k-transformer. All the transformers have only one output and differ in the number of inputs and input and output modes. Each k-transformer is related to a function of k-variables this transformer performs.

At $k > 1$ all inputs and the output of basic k-transformer must have a value mode, the coordination of inputs and output modes being not obligatory.

There exist five types of basic 1-transformers at $k = 1$:

a. basic 1-transformer, performing the function of one variable, that differs from the identity one. Its input and output must have the value mode, the coordination of modes being not obligatory;

b. identity transformer, performing an identity function. Its input and output must have a coinciding signal mode;

c. basic predicate, performing a monadic k-fold predicate. Its input must have the value mode and its output must have a c-i mode for some $i \geq 1$;

d. generator, its input must have a s-p mode, and the output -- a signal mode;

e. indicator, its input must have a signal mode, and the output -- a s-p one.

When a strob (signal) comes to the input of generator (indicator) the the signal (strob) is yielded simultaneously at its output. Therefore, the generator (indicator) start and finish of the elaboration are simultaneous events.

When a signal comes to the input of the identity transformer the start of its elaboration occurs. Just after that a signal is yielded at its output and the elaboration finish occurs simultaneously.

Elaboration of the basic predicate and basic k-transformer at $k \geq 1$ which performs the non-identity function, defined as following:

a. If the transformer (predicate) is free then:

-- the simultaneous values coming to all its inputs forces a simultaneous start of its elaboration;

-- if the values come to some but not all its inputs then the following its elaboration is undefined;

b. If the transformer (predicate) is busy, then:

-- the value coming to its inputs, no events occurs, and the values are lost;

-- the finish of the transformer (predicate) elaboration forces simultaneously the yielding of value (infor) at its output;

c. The finish of transformer (predicate) elaboration always occurs after its start.

The basic elements will be denoted by large triangles in BOP drawings. The denotation of the function or predicate, performed by the element is placed inside it. Signal inputs and outputs of elements are denoted by small triangles. Light triangles will be used for value inputs (outputs) and dark ones will be used for infor inputs (outputs). Small light circles will be used for strob inputs (outputs). Fig. 1 shows the denotations for various kinds of basic transformers.

B.3.2 Basic Distributors

Basic element having one main input, $k \geq 1$ outputs and one auxiliary input which mode is c-i is called the basic k-distributor. The main input and all outputs of each basic k-distributor must be of the same mode, called the mode of the distributor. Any basic distributor has signal mode.

Elaboration of the basic k-distributor for any $k \geq 1$ is defined as following:

a. If the distributor is free then:

-- when the signal comes to the main input and simultaneously the infor I_1 comes to its auxiliary input the start of elaboration of the distributor is forced. The signal that came to the main input is yielded at its i-th output simultaneously. Just after that the distributor becomes free and its elaboration is completed;

-- when the signal comes only to the main input of the distributor its elaboration start is forced simultaneously, therefore, it becomes busy and stores the signal;

-- if only an infor comes to the auxiliary input no events occur, and the infor is lost;

b. If the distributor is busy, then:

-- if a signal comes to the main input then the further elaboration is undefined;

-- if only the infor I_1 comes to the auxiliary input then the signal which stores the distributor is yielded at its i-th output simultaneously, just after that the distributor becomes free and its elaboration is completed.

B.3.3 Gate

Basic element having one main input, one braking input and one output, all of them having the s-p mode, is called gate. The strob at gate output is yielded simultaneously with the strob coming to its main input provided that the strob does not come simultaneously to the gate braking input. The simultaneous coming of strobs to both inputs or a strob only to the braking input does not force any events and the strobs are lost.

Distributors and gate denotation is given in Fig. 2.

B.4. Poles and Links

Each basic operation pattern must have at least one input and one output poles. Each pole is related to a mode according to the same rules as to elements inputs (outputs).

The links connect the input poles (basic element outputs) to the inputs of basic elements or output poles. Output (input pole) at which some link begins and an input (output pole), at which it ends must have the same mode, which is called the link mode.

Several links ending at different inputs (poles) may begin at an output (pole). The object yielded at this output (pole) comes simultaneously to all the inputs (output poles) which is connected with it. In other words there occurs object copying through all the links beginning at the output (pole).

Several links may end at an input (pole) which is called a multiple input (pole).

If two or more signals come simultaneously to the multiple input of a basic element then the further elaboration of this basic element is undefined.

If several strobs come simultaneously to the multiple input then it is equivalent to the coming any one of them.

Any signal (strob) coming to an output pole is lost indopondontly of other signals (strobs) coming simultaneously with it.

A denotation of a link is an arrow directed from the output (pole) to the input (pole). Pole denotations are similar to those of inputs or outputs of basic elements.

B.5. Join

Two operation patterns may be joined in a resulting one by identifying some output poles of the first OP with some input poles of the second one. In particular an operation pattern may be joined with itself.

Let P and Q be BOP for which are additionally defined:

a. P^+ stands for a subset of the output pole set in P, and Q^- stands for a subset of the input pole set in Q;

b. P^+ separation into classes called join sources and denoted by S_p^1, $S_p^2,\dots,S_p^m$ and Q^- separation into classes called join destinations and denoted by D_Q^1, $D_Q^2,\dots,D_Q^m$. All the poles belonging to the same source (destination) must have the same mode called the mode of the source (destination);

c. φ stands for one-to-one mapping between the sources and destinations which have the same mode.

For operation patterns P and Q marked in such a way their join by mapping φ is done as follows:

a. the sources are considered in turn and for the source:

aa. there is considered a set of all outputs of basic elements and input poles, connected in P by links to poles belonging to this source. Let $P^{\bullet}$ stand for the set;

ab. there is considered a set of all inputs of basic elements and output poles, connected in Q links to the poles belonging to corresponding destination. Let $Q^{:}$ stand for the set;

ac. each output (pole) belonging to $P^{\bullet}$ is connected by links to all the inputs (poles) belonging to $Q^{:}$;

b. all the poles belonging to P^+ and Q^- with all incident to them links are deleted from the resulting basic operation pattern.

Fig. 3 shows a join of basic operation patterns A and B by φ. The resulting BOP C joined by φ' with itself gives the resulting BOP E.

B.6. Basic Operation Patterns

Basic operation patterns consisting of any basic element and corresponding mode poles connected one-to-one to the inputs and outputs of this basic element will be called elementary BOP. Moreover two elementless BOP shown in Fig. 4 will also be called elementary.

Any BOP may be designed on the basis of elementary BOP by a proper join sequence. The proof of this assertion is easily seen from the join definition and from the fact that by elementary BOP, shown in Fig. 4, one may increase the amount of the input and output poles to the desired quantity.
The set of states of all basic elements of BOP is called the state of this BOP.

The elaboration of BOP is defined relative to its initial state and some order of object yielding at its input poles. Usually, if there are no other notes, the initial state of BOP is the state in which all its basic elements are free. The objects yielded at the input poles come through links to the input of corresponding basic elements. In this case some of basic elements are busy according to their elaboration rules. When the elaboration of an element is finished a new object is yielded at its output. These objects, in their turn, come to inputs connected to these outputs and so on. A partially ordered event set arises. This set generates a course of elaboration of BOP for its given initial state and given objects yielded at its input poles. The course may be either infinite or complete if no basic element of the BOP may start.

C. EXTENSIONS AND STANDARD CONSTRUCTIONS

> "The sneezing neuron equivalent is a volume the cover of which has to be opened by a crane".
> SUMMA TECHNOLOGIAE, St. LEM

To transform the basic operation patterns into a programming language in which practical program may be written it is necessary to define additionally:

first, the class of values having described the actual set of values permitted by this language and to include their modes into the value mode set. Thus are defined modes of poles, inputs and outputs of basic elements.

second, an actual set of functions and predicates performed by basic transformers and dealing with introduced values.

However, it is easy to imagine that writing programs in such a language founded just on BOPs would be a laborious job, and the programs themselves even for comparatively simple interesting cases would be extremely bulky.

To prevent the above difficulties we shall now turn from BOPs to operation patterns of general mode introducing a mechanism of extensions.

C.1. Extensions

Each extension is a substitution of a definite BOP which may satisfy some conditions by a special denotation which is to be considered as an operation pattern element and which elaboration coincides with the elaboration of the substituted BOP. The use of special denotations for definitely organized systems of links is also an extension.

The use of extensions enables to simplify the picture of operation patterns and the description of their elaboration. The extensions permit to hidden for often used and rather complex fragments of operation pattern numerous fine details of their construction and elaboration proving an increase in look round and clearness for them.

Though each extension may be given by its BOP when describing extensions it is convenient to use previously introduced extensions. Similarly sometimes it is convenient to describe the elaboration of new operation pattern elements introduced by extensions from outside fixing only events occuring on the poles of the corresponding BOP and omitting all the details of its inside elaboration.

Some new kinds of distributors with less restrictions for the kind of distributed by them objects and synchronization conditions than for previously introduced basic distributors will be defined with the help of extensions. New elements: some kinds of memory elements and the most important for further applications statements and recognizers will be described with the help of extensions. Finally, extensions are used for simplification and ordering the system of links between the operation pattern elements in drawing them graphically.

C.1.1 Denotation of Links System

A well known difficulty in drawing graphs is the appearance of a great number of "extra" crossings of their arcs in the graphs with a great number of vertices. A considerable decrease of in the number of such crossings and an improvement of general clearness of the picture is reached by the use of so-called collector technique described in [2] and used in the edition of syntactic charts of ALGOL 68 [3]. We shall use the collector technique when giving examples of operation patterns as an extension for the initial non-sticked system of links. Fig.5 shows an example of operation pattern with and without collector technique

C.1.2 Extensions for Indicators

In many cases, we need not the object yielded at an output but only the knowledge of the fact that the object is yielded. For this purpose it is useful to connect an indicator to the corresponding output and to use the strob yielded by it for representing the event "the object is yielded". Fig. 6 shows how to simplify the indicator denotation in this often employed case.

C.1.3 Extensions for Distributors

All the basic distributors have signal mode. The distributor of s-p mode may be designed from a basic distributor of u-o mode, the generator yielding a unitary object and unitary object indicators. This element is shown in Fig. 7. Here the token "$\Longleftrightarrow$" is the extension symbol indicating that the element denoted at his left may be replaced by a BOP on the right and vice versa.

The extension, shown in Fig. 8, introduces a new element called a distributor controlled by strobs. In it the object coming to the main input or stored by the distributor is yielded at the output corresponding to that auxiliary input the strob comes to. If strobs come simultaneously to several auxiliary inputs then the further elaboration of such a distributor is undefined. Such a replacement of "quality" distinctness of the controlling signal by "space" distinctness is often useful.

Of course, the combination of the both extensions gives a new element -- the strob distributor controlled by strobs (Fig. 9). Later on such natural combinations of introduced extension will be used without special reserves if it does not lead to ambiguity.

All the distributors defined till now assured the storage only of the object coming to their main input. The extension shown in Fig. 10 introduces as a new element the distributor which stores also the infor come to its auxiliary input. For any pair of an object and an infor coming to the proper inputs in any order one by one, the object coming to the main input is yielded at the output that is defined by the infor. For all other cases of signals coming to the inputs the distributor elaboration is undefined.

C.1.4 Extension for Transformers

Let us consider some operation pattern having $k \geq 1$ input value poles and one output value pole. Let the elaboration of this operation pattern be defined at simultaneous yielding of objects at all its input poles. Then is relates to each value tuple yielding at its input poles a value coming to its input pole. Therefore the mapping of k-tuples set of input values on the set of output values is a function called a function performed by the given operation pattern.

The first defined extension for the transformers enables to replace the operation pattern under consideration by a basic transformer which inputs and outputs have appropriate modes, and the function performed by it is the function performed by the given operation pattern.

Now, let us consider an operation pattern having one input value pole and one output c-i pole for some $i \geq 1$. Let the elaboration of this OP be defined at value yielding at its input pole. Then we may relate to it as above a i-fold predicate, called the predicate performed by the given OP.

The second defined extension for the transformers enables to replace the OP under consideration by a basic predicate which input and output have appropriate modes, and the predicate performed by it is the predicate performed by the given OP.

The extensions introduced for transformers play an important role, as they enable to enlarge function and predicate set performed by basic elements in recursive way.

The requirement of simultaneous value coming to all the transformer input enveloped in the definition of basic k-transformers is, of course, hard for practical program writing with the help of OPs.

Therefore, our nearest goal is to introduce new elements working as the transformers but without the above restriction by means of proper extensions.

First, various memory elements will be defined by means of extensions of BOP. Next, after defining some standard constructions main elements of OP called statements will be described.

The OP considered at describing extensions are examples elucidating various features of operation patterns.

C.2. Memory Elements

The computer main memory unit consists of cells having addresses. As it is known each memory cell has the following features:

a. in practice the cell is storing its contents during unlimited time between addressings;

b. when writing new contents into a cell its previous contents is superseded and lost;

c. when reading the cell contents it is regenerated and, therefore, conserved.

Present programming languages simulate a memory by means of variable notion. The variables (together with assignation) reproduces literally the above features of the computer memory cells.

The stack is another memory element often used. Besides another manner of treating the objects when writing and reading the stack shows explicitly one more feature of memory elements -- it may be empty.

Two features may be considered as characteristic memory element features:

a. contents storing between addressings

and b. no additional information to the signal "reading" is required.

According to the feature b. a based-variable of PL/1 [4], for example, cannot be considered as a memory element.

Among the basic element features described in the section D.3. only the basic distributor ability to store the object coming to its main input is the feature related to the memory. Therefore, the basic 1-distributor may be considered as a simplest memory element called a nest. If the nest is free then it receives the object coming to its main input and stores it. If the nest is busy, then the signal coming to its auxiliary input forces the stored object yielding at the output of nest which becomes free. The nest has neither the feature of superseding the previous object when writing a new one nor the one of the object conserving when reading.

Another memory element shown in Fig. 11 having more features is called a semicell. It provides superseding of the previous object when writing a new object into the semicell. The second of two successive objects cannot come through links before than "just after" the first. This fact is essentially used in this OP. Always when the next successive object comes to the input of identity transformer of the operation patterns this transformer is already free, therefore, the object will not be lost. The action of this OP is founded on the following: the strob "indicating" its distributor about the object coming to be written comes to its auxiliary input before the object comes to its main input. The gate used here provides the elaboration of this OP when the signals of writing and reading come simultaneously. In this case the elaboration takes place as if the writing signal comes just after the reading signal. To be noted, the considered OP would be used without any changes and with such a distributor for which the signal coming to its main input is lost if the distributor is busy.

The extension in Fig. 12 shows the construction of a memory cell which has all the above features. As in the previous case the gates provide the elaboration of this OP when the signals of writing and reading come simultaneously. In this case the regeneration is cut off and an object to be written replaces a yielded one.

Fig. 13 shows an extension introducing a new memory element called a finite stack of depth p. Its operation pattern does not contain any new pecularities. Note, that actually the semicell is the finite stack of depth one.

Indeed, the common stack having potentially an infinite depth cannot be described by any OP. It would be possible if the OPs had a growth feature which in this article, however, they are not supposed to have. Note, inter alia, that all stacks implemented into computers are also finite.

The memory elements introduced in this section may be used not only as self-dependent elements in OP, but will constitute an important part of the extension defining the statements.

Before introducing the statement extensions some more auxiliary elements to be used in the extensions will be designed.

C.3. Some Auxiliary Constructions

The strob at the indicator output is yielded simultaneously with coming to its input an object which is yielded at the output of some other element or the input pole which is connected to the indicator. Therefore the strob may be used for representation of the event "the output has yielded an object". Only events of this kind may be represented by strobs. It is said that the events of some set are represented on an input of an OP element if the indicator outputs yielding the strobs representing the events are connected to the input of the element.

The extension shown in Fig. 14, defines a new element called an accumulator of events. Its purpose is to register that events represented on every of its inputs have taken place. The accumulator has n inputs and one output all of them having s - p mode. The strob at the accumulator output is yielded if and only if strobs independently of their order come to all accumulator inputs. Just after the output strob is yielded the accumulator turns into its initial state at which the first distributor of the chain A stores ε and each distributor of the group B stores the infor I_1.

The accumulator and the memory elements will serve as a material of which the OP for the extension giving a new element called a starter is designed. The extension is shown in Fig. 15. The starter inputs are divided into permitting and auxiliary information. All the information inputs must have the value mode; the coincidence between input modes is not obligatory. There exist three groups of information inputs. The first group of inputs are inputs of memory semicells. The second group of inputs are inputs of finite stacks, each of them may have a proper depth, the third group of inputs are memory cell inputs. The general number of the starter information inputs must be at least one, and the distribution of their number among the groups may be arbitrary.

All the permitting inputs and the auxiliary input of the starter have the same mode - s - p. the number of the starter permitting inputs may be any one (e.g. none), but if all the starter information inputs belong to the third group, i.e. all of them are memory cell inputs then the starter must have at least one permitting input.

The number and modes of the starter outputs must have one-to-one mapping to the number and modes of its information inputs.

In the starter initial state all its semicells and stacks, if any, are free, and its accumulator has its initial state.

The starter accumulator registers the object writing into its memory elements and strobs coming to the auxiliary and permitting inputs. The strob yielded by the accumulator is used for reading values from all memory elements, and all values come simultaneously to the starter outputs.

Thus, the starter solves the problem of accumulation of values coming to its inputs and their synchronous yielding when a full staffing of objects comes and by condition that some, previously specified events have taken place.

The second kind of starter, the extension which is shown in Fig. 16 differs from the previous one in not having an auxiliary input and in having only two information inputs. One of these inputs has the value mode, and the second the c - i mode. The second kind of the starter will be used with basic distributors.

C.4. Statements

Fig. 17 shows an extension introducing a transformer-statement with k information and m permitting inputs. For completeness the three groups of information inputs are assumed existing though it is not necessary for each transformer-statement to have them. The strob from the basic k-transformer output comes to the starter auxiliary input. Due to this the finish of the transformer elaboration is a part of the event set forcing the simultaneous arrival of the objects at its inputs. To enable the transformer-statement to start the elaboration for the very first time just after object generation at its input poles, a following assumption is adopted:

> Before the start of the elaboration of any operation pattern having at least one transformer-statement, a strob, indicating that in the initial state of the operation pattern all the basic transformers of its statements are free, is sent to the starter auxiliary input of each transformer-statement.

Fig. 18 introduces an extension for a distributor-statement, and Fig. 19 introduces an extension for a recognizer-statement.

By introducing extension for statements the process of operation pattern definition is finished. We shall recall only that the introduction of new extensions is common to the principle of the offered model and that by using extensions for transformers defined in C.1.4 one may increase the assortment of functions and predicates performed by the basic transformers.

D. USE OF OPERATION PATTERNS

To illustrate the use of equipment described in the above sections we shall give an operation pattern for the following algorithm calculating the real polynom coefficients by its zeros :

```
   proc p = (ref[1:] compl z) union ([ ]real , u - 0):
1  begin [0: upb z] real a;
2  a [0] : = 1;
3  int i : = 1;
4  while i ≤ upb z do
5  begin compl zi = z[i];
6  a[i]: = 0;
7  if im zi = 0
8  then for k from i by -1 to 1 do
9  a[k]- : = re zi * a[k - 1]
10 else if i = upb z then error fi;
11 if zi ≠ conj z[i + : = 1] then error fi;
12 real s = re zi * * 2 + im zi * * 2,
13       t = 2 * re zi; a[i]: = 0;
14 for k from i by -1 to 2 do
15 a[k]- : = t * a[k-1]- s * a[k-2];
16 a[1]- : = t
17 fi; i + : = 1;
18 end a.
19 error : u - o
   end
```

This routine-denotation is taken with small changes from [5]. The difference from the original is that at invalid initial data the procedure will yield a unitary object and will not go to the label in the other block. The line numbers written to the left do not belong to the procedure text, but are intended to make easier for comparison the given ALGOL 68 program with its OP shown in Fig. 20. In this OP the statements performing the functions F1 and F2 correspond to the program lines 8-9 and 12-16, respectively. Their transformers are described by their operation patterns which are shown in Fig. 21 and 22. A distributor-statement R, a memory cell and gates provide the check of validness of the initial zero vector and the completion of the operation pattern elaboration when discovering an unpaired complex zero. The operation tokens and modes are taken from ALGOL 68. For convenience in comparison with the initial program some links are marked by variables, corresponding to the yielded objects. In this operation pattern is also used a statement with three [ ] real, int and real inputs and [ ] real output performing the function denoted by [ ]: =. This statement is designed to write a coming real number into the vector element, defined by an integer and to yield the modified in this way vector at the output.

As a second example let us consider the method of constructing an operation pattern for a recursive procedure.

If the procedure is recursive then it contains, at least, one call of itself. Besides, to enable its elaboration to be performed, it must contain a condition that allows "to avoid" the elaboration of its inside call at some moment. Let us call this condition the procedure critical point.

To make the following presentation concrete we shall assume that p is a recursive procedure proc (int, int) int having only one inside call of itself and a critical point, denoted by C. Let us assume that some operation pattern is designed for this procedure and its inside call p is denoted proforma by one statement. Now let us reconstruct this OP in the following way (see Fig. 23).

The output set of those statements which elaboration does not depend on the call p will be called a crossing defined by the inside call. In Fig. 23 the crossing defined by the call p consists of outputs of statements X_1, X_2, X_3 and X_4. The set of statements between the input poles and the crossing including the crossing statements will be called the left part of OP and its all remaining statements, but inside call p the right part of this operation pattern. Naturally, the critical point of the procedure will be in the left part. Redistribute the links connecting the left part with the call and the right part in the following way: (see Fig. 24)

-- links connecting X_1 and X_2 to the call p will be transported to the statement inputs connected to the input poles of the OP,

-- to the outputs X_3 and X_4 will be connected a distributor-statement with two outputs. The first outputs of the distributors will be connected to those inputs in the right part to which were connected the outputs of statements X_3 and X_4, and their second outputs will be connected to the stack inputs having a sufficient depth q,

-- connect the operation pattern output to the inputs of those statements or the right part the call p output was connected, and connect the strobs from the OP output to the stack reading inputs.

After that delete the inside call from the operation pattern and connect to the critical point a predicate yielding the infor I_2, if during the elaboration the inside call p must act, and yielding the infor I_1 in the opposite case. Connect this predicate output to the auxiliary inputs of the introduced distributor-statements. As a result we shall get the proper OP for the recursive procedure.

Indeed when the values come to the input poles the left part statements start its elaboration and under predicate Q elaboration it clears up if a recursive call must take place. If a recursive call must be performed then Q yields the infor I_2 and, therefore, all the objects which are yielded in the crossing will arrive of the stacks and new argument values will come to the input poles of the OP. It will be going on until the predicate Q will yield the infor I_1 then the right part statements will be able to start the elaboration. When the value will be yielded at the output pole of the OP the reading from stacks occurs. Then enables the right part statements of OP to continue their elaboration and so on till the completion.

REFERENCES

[1] A.P. Ershov, Theory of Program Shemata, IFIP Congress 71, Lubljana, August 1971.

[2] A.A. Bährs, A.P. Ershov, and A.F. Rar, On Descriptions of Syntax of ALGOL 68 and its National Variants, ALGOL 68 Implementation edited by J.E.L. Peck, North-Holland, Amsterdam-London, 1971.

[3] A.A. Bährs, and V.V. Grushetsky, Syntactic Charts of ALGOL 68, J. "Kibernetika" No. 6 1969 and No. 1 1970.

[4] PL/1 Language Specification, IBM, GY33-6003-2, June 1970.

[5] J.E.L. Peck, An ALGOL 68 Companion, Vancouver, October 1971.

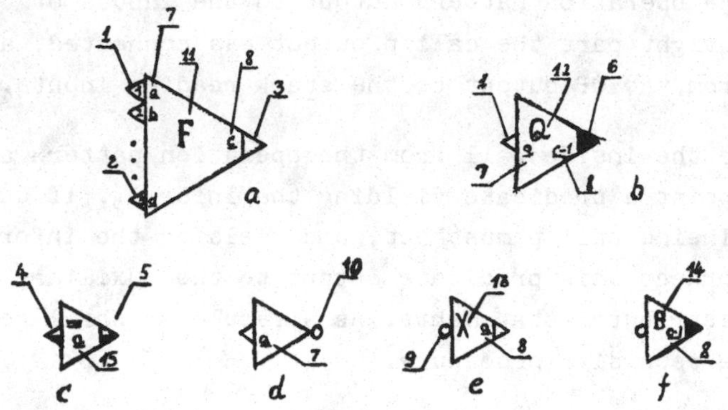

Fig. 1 - Basic Transformers

a) Basic k-transformer, b) Basic predicate,
c) Identity transformer, d) Indicator, e)-f) Generators

1 - value input, 2 - input's number, 3 - value output,
4 - signal input, 5 - signal output, 6 - infor output,
7 - input's mode, 8 - output's mode, 9 - strob input,
10 - strob output, 11 - performed function, 12 - performed predicate, 13 - generated value, 14 - generated infor
(s $\leq$ i), 15 - mode.

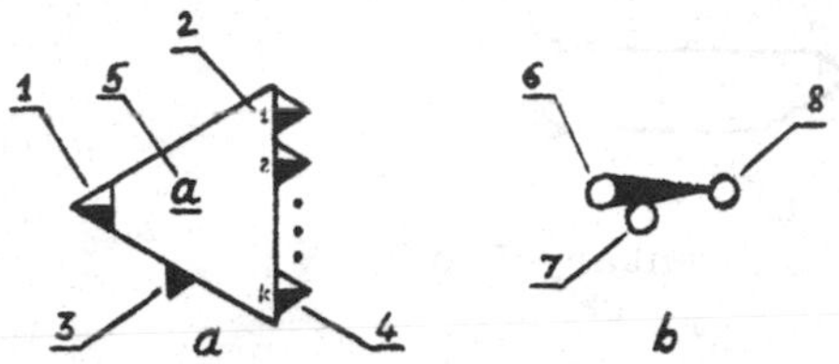

Fig. 2 - a) Basic Distributor
b) Gate

1 - signal main input, 2 - output's number, 3 - infor auxiliary input, 4 - signal output, 5 - mode, 6 - strob main input, 7 - strob braking input, 8 - strob output.

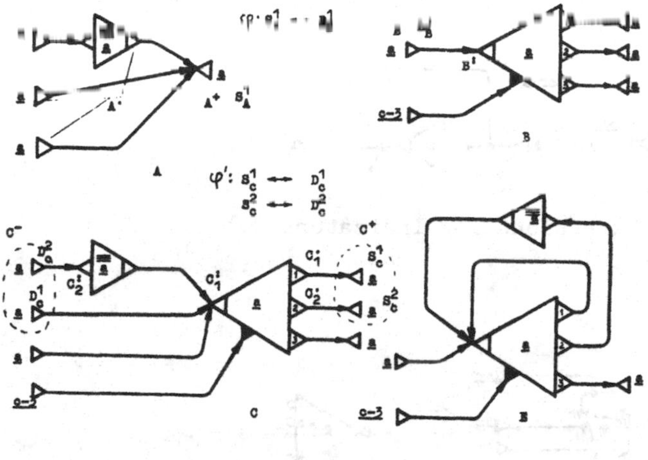

Fig. 3 - Join of Bop

Fig. 4 - Elementless Elementary B o p

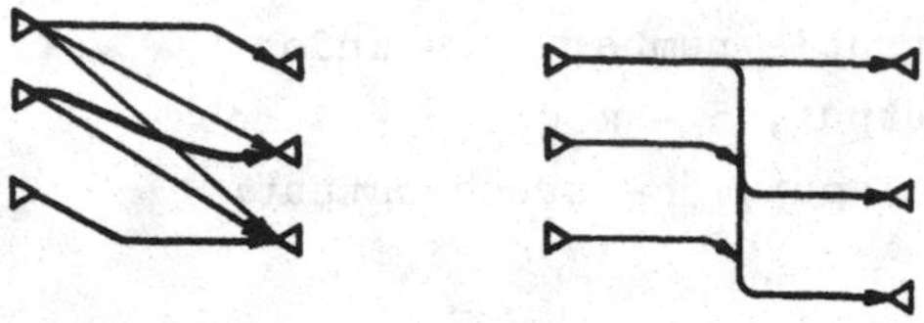

Fig. 5 - Use of Collector Technique

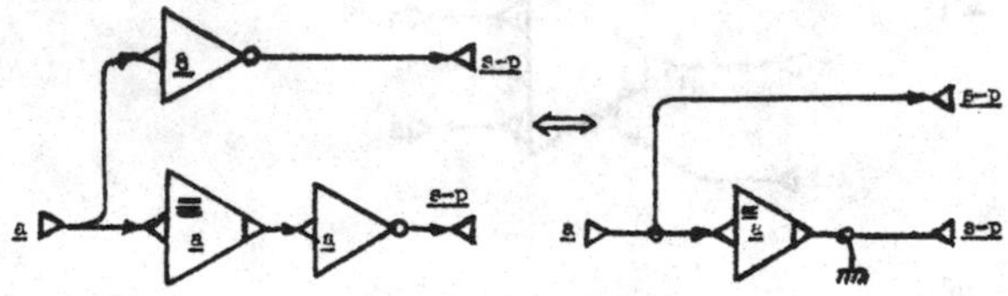

Fig. 6 - Extensions for Indicators

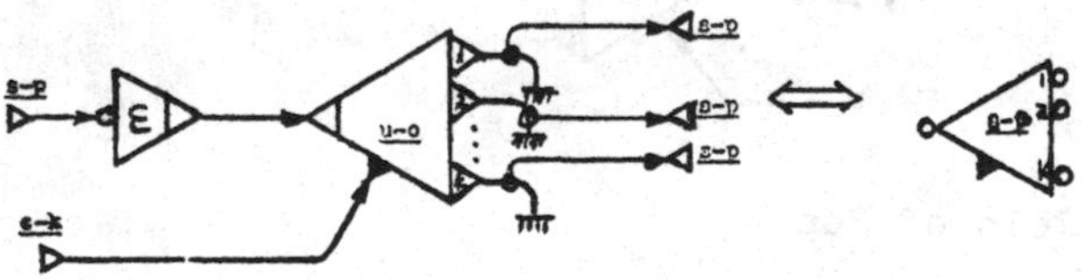

Fig. 7 - Strob Distributor

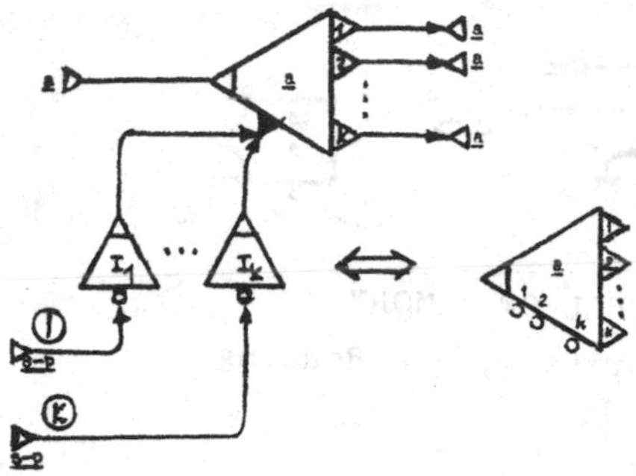

Fig. 8 - Signal, Distributor Controlled by Strobs

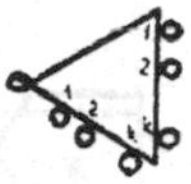

Fig. 9 - Strob Distributor Controlled by Strobs

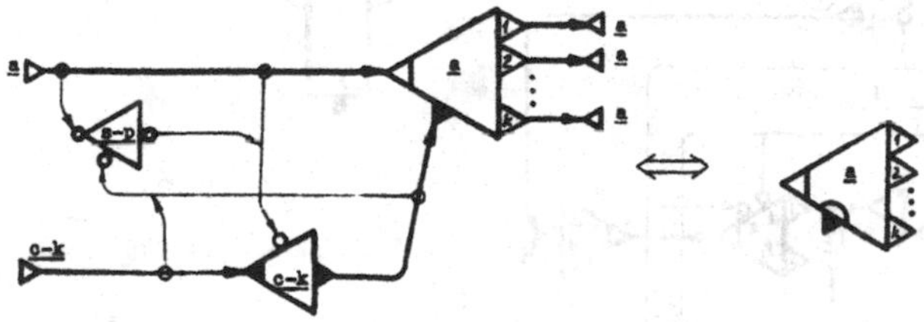

Fig. 10 - Distributor With Stored Infor

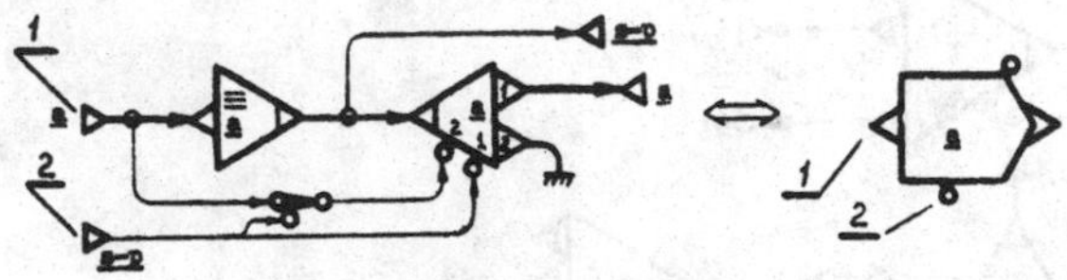

Fig. 11 - SEMICELL OF MEMORY
1 - Writing, 2 - Reading

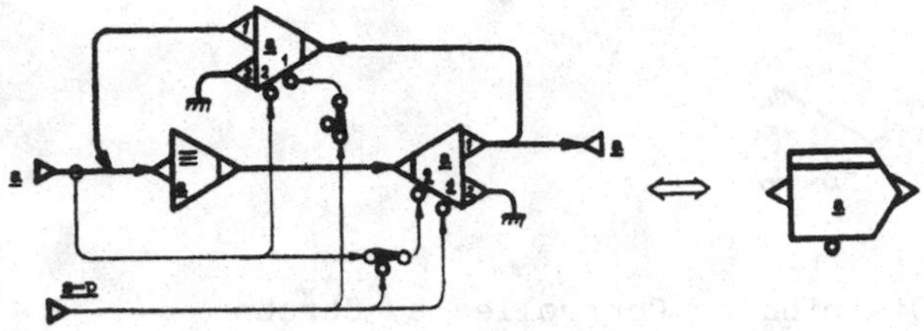

Fig. 12 - CELL OF MEMORY

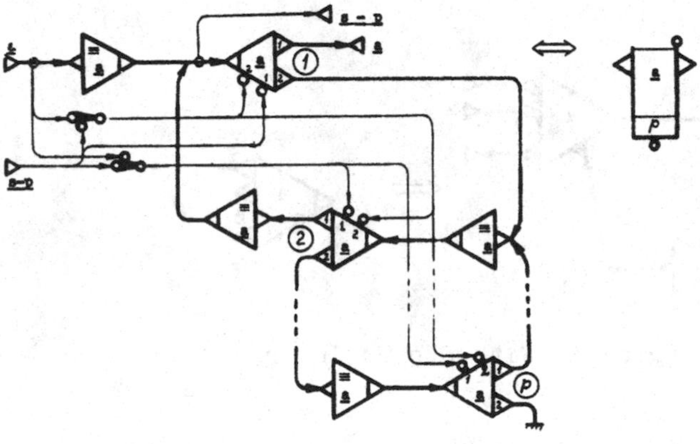

Fig. 13 - Finite Stack of Depth p

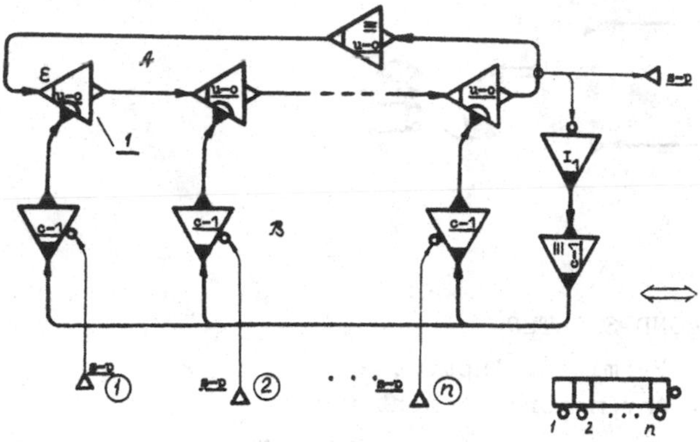

Fig. 14 - ACCUMULATOR OF EVENTS

1 - In initial state the distributor stores

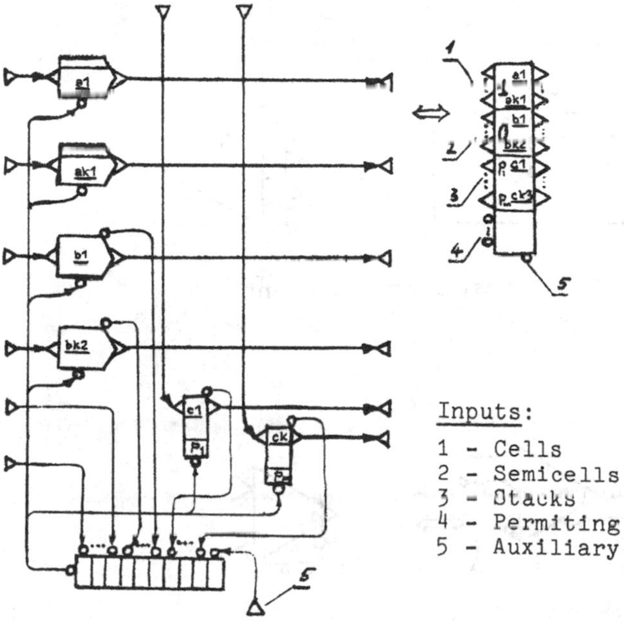

Fig. 15 - THE STARTER

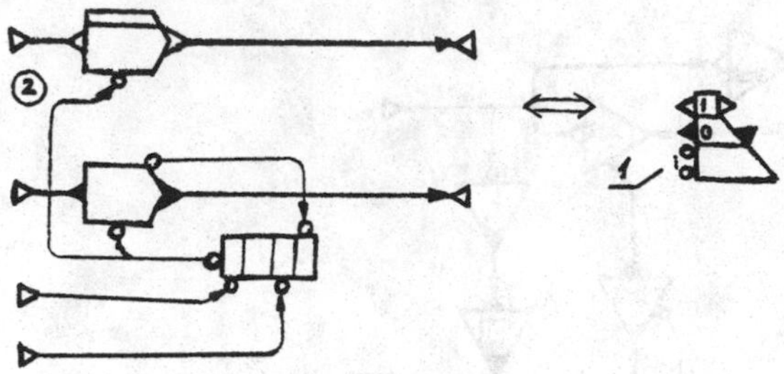

Fig. 16 - SECOND STARTER
1 - Permiting inputs,
2 - Any memory element may be related to each information inputs

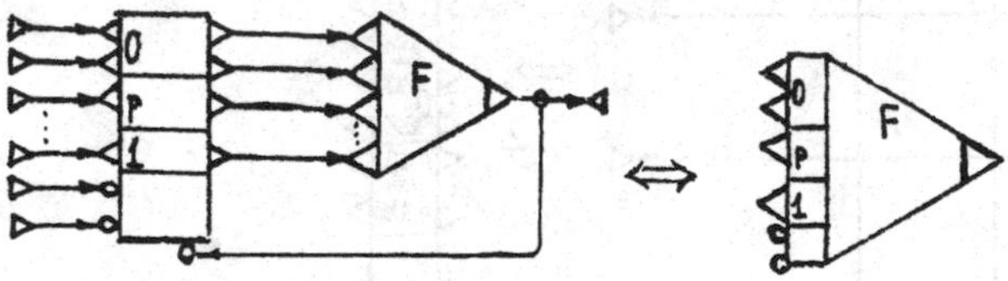

Fig. 17 - Transformer-statement

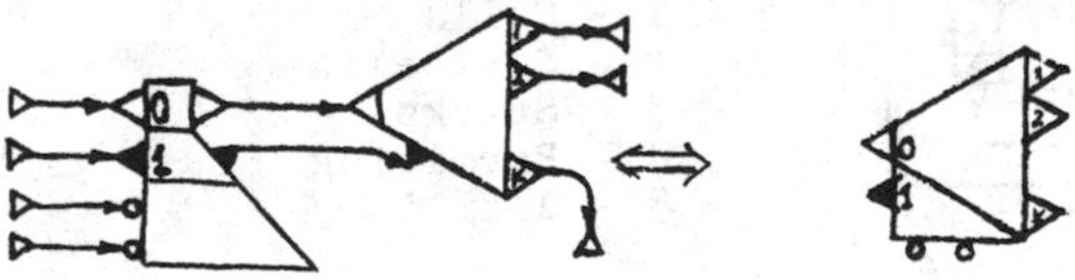

Fig. 18 - Distributor-statement

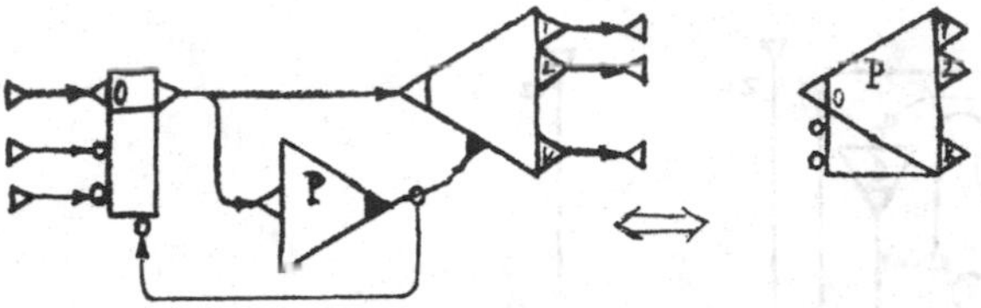

Fig. 19 - Recognizor-statement

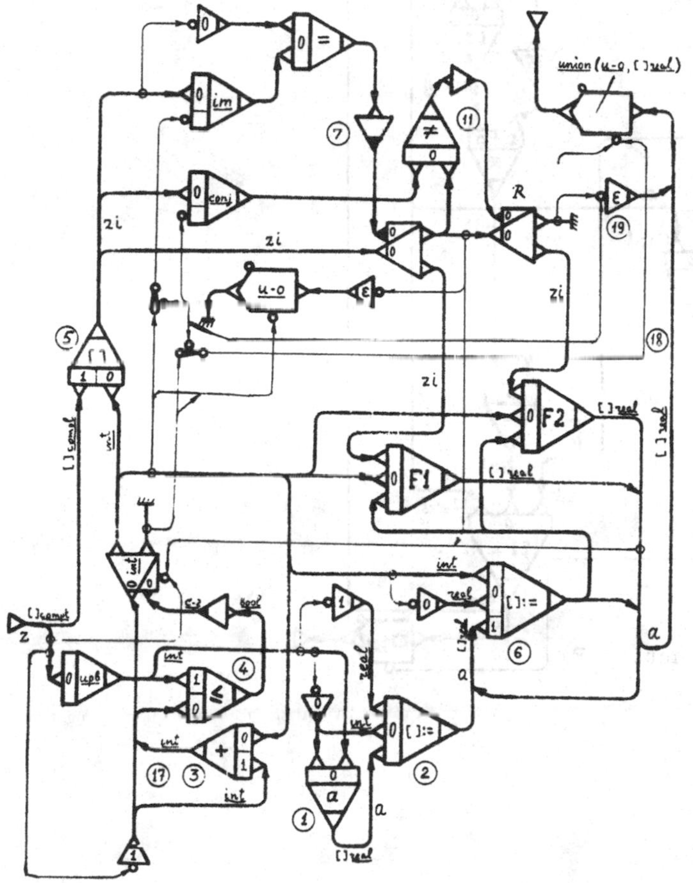

Fig. 20 - Example of Operation Pattern

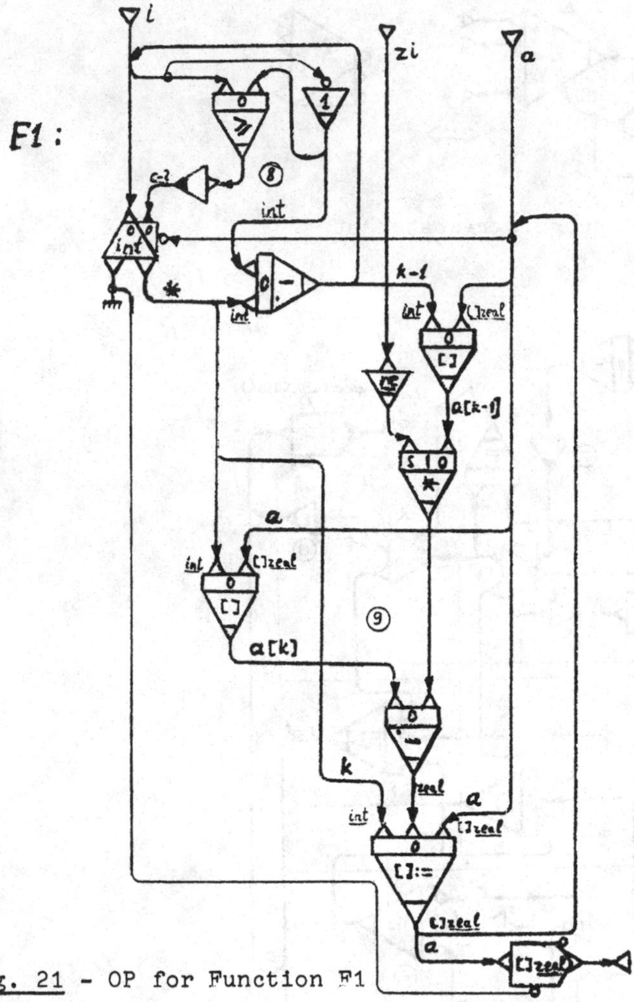

Fig. 21 - OP for Function F1

F2:

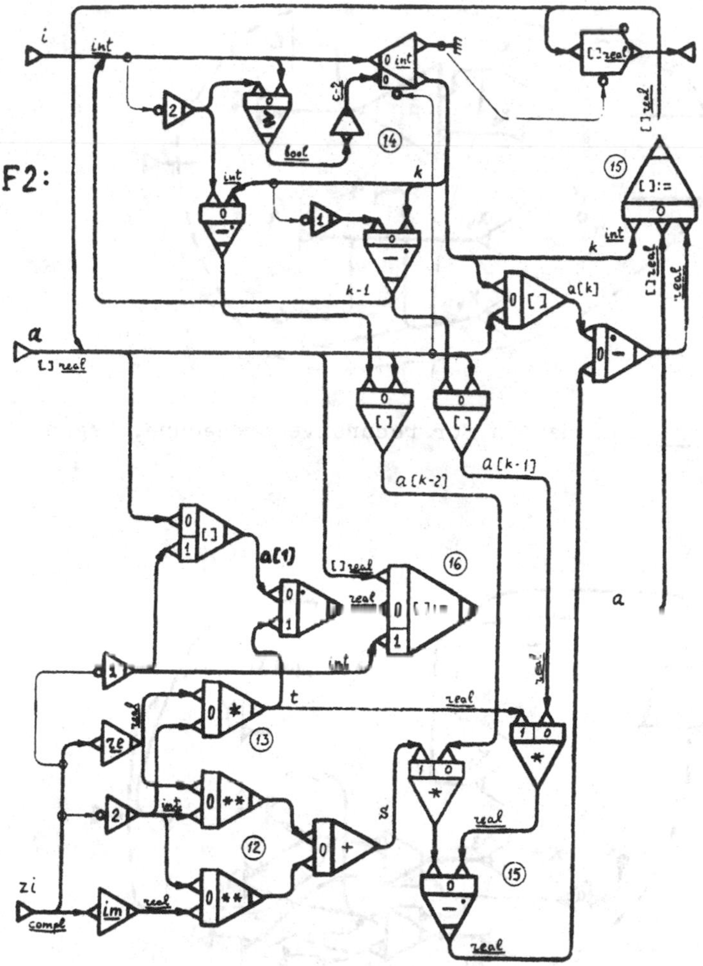

<u>Fig. 22</u> - OP for Function F2

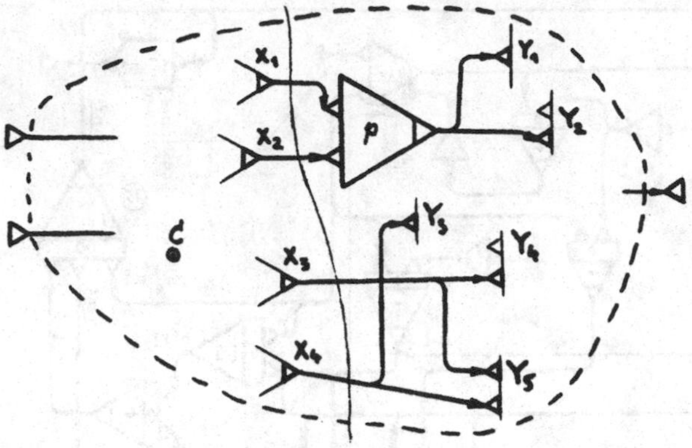

Fig. 23 - OP design for recursive procedure, begin

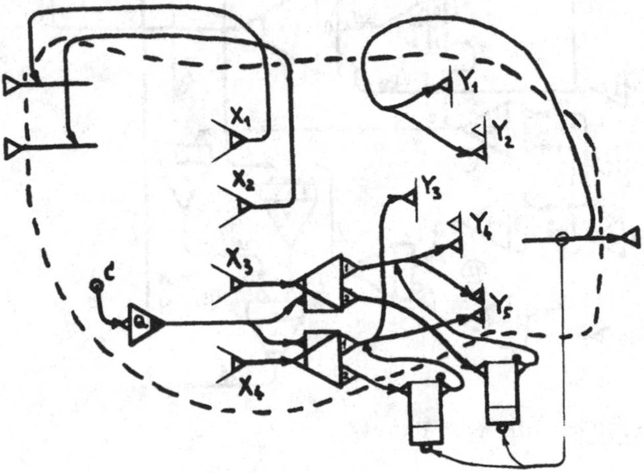

Fig. 24 - OP design for recursive procedure, end.

LOOKING FOR AN APPROACH TO A THEORY OF MODELS FOR PARALLEL COMPUTATION

by

A.S. Narinyani

(Novosibirsk)

Introduction

The Theory of Parallel Computations is not quite a theory yet. As usual in early stages of development, the range of conceptions here is narrow; they are rather simple and there are not accepted goals, common standards or a general language. Each author begins by building his model "from the very beginning" and as it grows complex, he becomes a prisoner of his own constructions. Fencing himself off from the rest of the world, he is often forced to resort to tricks in order to peek into the next yard.

Each successive model offers a language generating a class of programs (schemata, algorithms), a definition of a computational process (chain, configuration, time diagram) and a performance system-rule to unroll a program into a computational process. The author of each model evidently has his reasons for his choice of a particular language, process and system. But usually these reasons are perfectly personal and in the absence of a general method of classification and comparison of models, there are no ways to estimate the objective value of a model and of results.

Thus, we have the situation that makes it possible to add to the numerous works already available infinitely many new ones, introducing in each of them a new model and proving for it an arbitrary number of new theorems. Thus, the theory has an unusual opportunity to extend itself indefinitely without any sizable advance.

The situation is hardly acceptable. It is obviously necessary to generalize the available material by means of an adequate metamodel to make it possible to consider the existing models as particular cases of a general construction and to interpret individual results in a general context.

We have no intention to deal with immensity. So, from the beginning we set a number of limitations - let us assume that every particular model must satisfy the following:

(a) The computations are executed on some <u>memory</u>*, consisting of certain <u>elements</u>.

(b) Every process takes place in <u>discrete time t</u> having values of 0,1,2, etc; at the moment t=0 the memory is in <u>initial state</u>.

---

* The terms used in the introduction are defined more accurately in the text of the report.

(c) A memory state can be changed only by individual actions of <u>operators</u> from some fixed (may be, infinite) set. Thus, the memory state is a function of time.

Restricted by limitations /a/-/c/ a general sketch of a computation looks as follows: there is a model (for the time, it may be considered as a Black Box or a certain automaton presenting "a program" and "a system" at the same time). In the model we distinguish a memory <u>M</u>, fixed set A of operators and some imaginary button "START". We choose a certain initial state for the memory and push the "START". The discrete time which has had the value "0" up to the moment, starts running through the moments in consecutive order beginning from "1". Synchronously with the moments the model forms a process, which is as a matter of fact a time-table of functioning of operators from A.

If a model under examination is non-deterministic* (the type we are interested in) then the process at tis output is not in unique correspondence with the initial state M_o. If we return the Black Box to its initial state, the memory to the state M_o and press START again, then in the general case the new process at the output will be different from the previous one. In other words, every non-deterministic model X brings each M_o into correspondence with not only one but a certain set of computational processes $\mathcal{P}[X,M_o]$. Thus, some internal freedom is specific for our Black Box, but the freedom is a restricted one as set $\mathcal{P}[X,M_o]$ is not the set of all processes using operators A, but defined by the pair X,M_o.

An arbitrary set of computational processes will be called here a <u>codex</u>. It is evident that we are not interested in arbitrary codices, but we certainly are interested in output codices of our Black Box.

---

* The term is chosen by analogy with non-deterministic automata.

It is time to introduce here the next limitation:

(d) We suppose, that the Black Box is finite, i.e. the information needed for introduction of a codex $\wp[X,M_0]$ for all initial M_0 has a limited volume. It is obvious that the condition does not demand finiteness of memory, set A or the codex itself.

Thus, an output codex is rather "well-formed" as it could be represented in the form of tuple $\langle \underline{M}, M_0, A, X \rangle$.

It is interesting to note the following paradox: in many papers considering models with rather complex and detailed programming languages*, the definitions specifying the main classes of models are given as limitations for codices generated by these programs rather then requirements for the programs structure. For example, a <u>determinate</u> program is a program whose codex includes only equivalent processes, a <u>serial</u> program is one with the codex including sequential processes, etc. All the basic notions: such as persistent, conflict-free, repetition-free, permutable, commutative schemata are defined through their codices rather than through the structure of schemata.

For this reason some results of these papers could be reformulated directly in terms of codices, effect of corresponding theorems growing more general as they are valid in this case for every model with the same class of codices.

We come here to our first thesis:

1. The significant part of general results in the theory of models of computation can be obtained through direct investigation of codices, i.e. ignoring the model structure even in its most general form.

---

* Below we call them the models with advanced syntax.

It is natural that the present theory can not be restricted to codices as, first of all, it is interesting in the mechanism of organisation of computation, and at the level of codices the structural properties of original models are almost wholly (not quite) deleted. Thus we need a metamodel to describe the model at the arbitrary level of generality preserving if desired some of its structure properties but ignoring all the others. The metamodel has to allow realization of the second thesis:

2. The level of a model generality is to be adapted for the problem. Stated differently, consideration is to be conducted at the level provided preserving only those model properties which are essential for the problem; this will allow us to formulate the results in the most general form.

Finally, one more requirement for the metamodel - it must allow us to consider different models at the same level of generality, to compare individual results and to interpret them, if possible, for other models of the same level. The requirements will ensure realization of our third thesis:

3. General problems can be solved for the whole classes of models rather than for every individual model. This will allow us to choose a model which is more suitable and simple for the given problem, to obtain an appropriate result "at a lower cost", and then to interpret it for other models using the opportunity to consider these models as particular cases of some general construction.

Undoubtedly, the enumerated conditions and theses would have remained purely ornamental if they had not been supported by the reasonably concrete construction - some possible variants of the metamodel, satisfying to a certain degree, the above requirements is considered in paragraph 3 of the report. The first two paragraphs are devoted to introduction of some notions used for the metamodel definition. The corresponding problems are discussed in the remaining part.

* * *

In the report any symbol underlined, for example $\underline{m}$, is used for a memory element (of a variable) either a tuple of memory elements and the very symbol without underlining means a value or a state of the element (of a variable).

If a term is introduced without a definition, it means that a corresponding notion will be used in the text as undefined, the semantics of its use being quite clear from the context.

1. MEMORY AND OPERATOR DATA BASE

1.1. A Memory is usually considered a fixed set of storage elements. It is possible to introduce such universal presentation of a storage element that permits us to consider special types of elements (a cell, queue, etc.) as particular cases. Using the universal presentation allows us to treat an heterogeneous memory (i.e. the one being composed of elements of different types) as a homogeneous one, i.e. as a set of universal elements. To introduce the universal element it is necessary to use rather complex constructions so we omit here corresponding definitions. Further, we shall deal with just a memory without specifying such peculiarities as homogeneity or heterogeneity and the type of elements.

Interpretation of Memory $\underline{M}$ is a mapping that brings every element $\underline{m} \in \underline{M}$ into correspondence with its domain (set of values $v(\underline{m})$. (The domain of an arbitrary subset $\underline{M}' \subseteq \underline{M}$ is the cartesian product of domains for all elements of $\underline{M}'$.) Further, we assume for simplicity that domains for all elements are similar.

Every memory interpretation fixes for each element m M a set of all its possible *states*: every state is a pair <h,j> where h is a *history* of element m, i.e. a finite sequence of values from domain v(m) and j is a non-negative integer specifying the position of a *reading value* in the history h. A set of memory states is the cartesian product of sets of states for all its elements.

Below the memory is described in discrete time t and at every time moment each element of the memory corresponds with one of its states. The element state can be changed only as a result of *reading* or *storing*. While storing some value into an element this value is joined to the history h, while reading the history is not changed. The rule for change of j while reading and storing is determined by the element type (for a cell storing changes j for j+1 and reading leaves j unchanged; for the queue the rule for j is more complicated). Thus, every reading is uniquely associated with some reading value indicated in the history by the current value of j.

Here and below many interesting properties of the memory are neglected (such as the structuring of data) since these properties are not directly connected with the theme we are interested in.

For simplicity we assume that for *initial* states of the memory (i.e. state corresponding to the moment t=0) only states with the history including a single value can be used.

1.2. Wishing not to overload the presentation we define here the operator and base merely for the common memory (see [1]). These constructions may be extended rather simply to a distributed memory too. This extension can be carried out in such a manner that a distinction of these memory types becomes inessential for further treatment so that it will be ignored in the next paragraphs. Let us introduce a set of operation symbols each of which corresponds with a pair of non-negative integers.

A operator on a memory M is a tuple <f,in,out, In, Out> where f is an operation symbol (with the pair m,n assigned), in and out are tuples of inputs and outputs (of the length m and n respectively) being in one-to-one correspondence with the given operator; In and Out are tuples of elements from M also of the length m and n. Elements of In are input elements, these of Out are output elements, and the triple <f,In,Out> is an operation of the given operator.

The interpretation of memory M defines a set of allowable interpretations for every operator on M: the operator interpretation is unique mapping from the domain of In into the domain of Out.

A data base (or simply a base) on memory M is a fixed set of operators on this memory. The base never includes two similar operators, but the same operation may correspond to different operators of the base.

An interpretation of the base A on memory M is a pair $<I_M, \mathfrak{J}_A>$: I_M is a memory interpretation, and $\mathfrak{J}_A$ - is a set of interpretations of base operators which includes for every operator some allowable interpretation, the same interpretation corresponding to all operators with the similar operation symbols.

2. COMPUTATIONAL PROCESS

In the introduction we have intended to consider our model as a Black Box. But the only real information about a Black Box is its behaviour - a computational process in our case. It is quite natural, thus, to pay special attention to the notion as the choice of its definition influences essentially generality and specific properties of the model.

Our definition below has a number of limitations, but being rather simple and general, it allows us to treat most of the process definitions in other papers as particular cases.

2.1. Let *t* be a discrete *time* and A be a data base. A *computational process* P on the base A is a non-empty set of triples $\langle a,\bar{t},\bar{\bar{t}}\rangle$ where a is an operator from A, and $\bar{t},\bar{\bar{t}}$ are time moments satisfying $0<\bar{t}\le\bar{\bar{t}}$.

Each triple $\langle a,\bar{t},\bar{\bar{t}}\rangle$ (we call it a *computational act*) corresponds to a single use of operator a, $\bar{t}$ being the initiation, and $\bar{\bar{t}}$ termination of the given use. We say that at moment $\bar{t}$ the operator is *switched in*, at moment $\bar{\bar{t}}$ - *switched off*, and in the interval $\bar{t}+\bar{\bar{t}}$ it is in a *working state*.

Limitation 2.1.: for the simplicity of further presentation we assume every pair of triples $\langle a,\bar{t},\bar{\bar{t}}\rangle$ and $\langle a',\bar{t}',\bar{\bar{t}}'\rangle$ in a computational process satisfies the condition

$$(a=a' \rightarrow \bar{t}+\bar{t}' \;\&\; \bar{\bar{t}}\neq\bar{\bar{t}}') \;\&\; (\underline{\text{Out}}\ a \cap \underline{\text{Out}}\ a' \neq \emptyset \rightarrow \bar{\bar{t}}\neq\bar{\bar{t}}').$$

The above definition means that:

(a) for every act $\langle a,\bar{t},\bar{\bar{t}}\rangle$ at moment $\bar{t}$ reading takes place for elements of *In* , the reading values are used as arguments for the operator a, and computed results are written into the corresponding elements of *Out* at moment $\bar{\bar{t}}$.

(b) At every moment first all readings, and then, all writing take place. The succession of reading has no effect upon the resulting state either for common* or for distributed memory, the succession of writing has no effect either under limitation 2.1.

---

* We mean here the homogeneous common memory with elements of a cell type.

Thus, any computational process on memory <u>M</u> under fixed interpretation of its base specifies for every intial memory state M_o some function $M(t)$ satisfying condition $M(t=0)=M_o$.

2.2. Our definition allows us to specify some special classes of computational processes. First of all, we note that instant execution of an operator is formally permitted. A computational process with all of its acts executed instantly is called <u>reduced</u>. For further consideration it is useful to discuss the formal presentation of a process. According to the definition, a computational process is a set of individual acts of computation; however, sometimes it is more convenient to consider this process as a sequence of events - ones of switching in and switching off of operators of its base.

Indeed, for every moment t the operators of the base of any process can be divided into four intersecting subsets:

(2.1.)

$^{+}A_t$ - ones switching in at moment t,

$^{-}A_t$ - ones switching off at moment t,

$^{p}A_t$ - ones being at moment t in a working state,

$^{o}A_t$ - ones being at moment t not in a working state.

Thus, every computation corresponds to some sequence $A, {}^{+}A_1, {}^{p}A_1, {}^{-}A_1, {}^{p}A_2, {}^{+}A_2, \ldots$. Evidently such a sequence is excessive, since it can always be restored from the sequence $A, {}^{+}A_1, {}^{-}A_1, {}^{+}A_2, \ldots$. The latter is called a <u>linear form</u> of a computational process.

(A). The definition of point 2.1. permits in the process pairs of acts $\langle a,\bar{t},\bar{\bar{t}}\rangle$ and $\langle a',\bar{t}',\bar{\bar{t}}'\rangle$ satisfying condition $a=a' \& \bar{t}<\bar{t}' \leq \bar{\bar{t}}$, i.e. allows a switching in of an operator at a moment when it is already working (we shall call such a process <u>autoparallel</u>). Moreover, the number of such switchings-in, i.e. the number of <u>copies</u> of the operator, being simultaneously in processing is not limited.

It is interesting to note that for the non-autoparallel processes a correspondence between the process and its linear form is one-to-one, while several autoparallel processes may corresponded to the same linear form. To escape the ambiguity one usually makes the class of autoparallel processes limited: for instance, Karp and Miller [4] allow only such processes in which every pair of acts $<a,\bar{t},\bar{\bar{t}}>$ and $<a,\bar{t}',\bar{\bar{t}}'>$ condition $\bar{t}<\bar{t}' \rightarrow \bar{\bar{t}}<\bar{\bar{t}}'$ holds.

(B). Let us consider one more class of computational processes: <u>one-dimensional</u> are processes satisfying the condition

$$(\forall t)(|{}^{+}A_{t}\cup{}^{-}A_{t}| \leq 1 \ \&\ {}^{+}A_{t}\cap{}^{-}A_{t} = \emptyset) \quad \text{, i.e.}$$

those in which every moment not more than one switching in or switching off takes place (the process of a common type is <u>two-dimensional</u>.

For one-dimensional processes linear form is excessive: usually in corresponding models time is formally eliminated and the process is defined as a sequence of switching in and switching off of base operators.

(C). And finally, our last special class of computational processes - sequential ones, i.e. non-autoparallel processes in which the set ${}^{p}A_{t}$ always consists of only one operator (the process of a general type is <u>parallel</u>). The sequential process also quite naturally permits time elimination, yielding in this case a simple sequence of executed operators, i.e. <u>a chain</u>. The class of models using chain processes covers all models known in the theory of sequential programming (for example, Ianov schemata), being at the same time far more broad to limited itself to these ones.

2.3. Let us call the model by the name of the class of computational processes it deals with. Then, due to the above classification we have specified the following model types:

Parallel and sequential
General type and reduced
Two-dimensional and one-dimensional
Autoparallel and non-autoparallel.

In all four cases the type on the right is a particular case of the one on the left. Under this classification not all combinations are permissible as is obvious from the diagram:

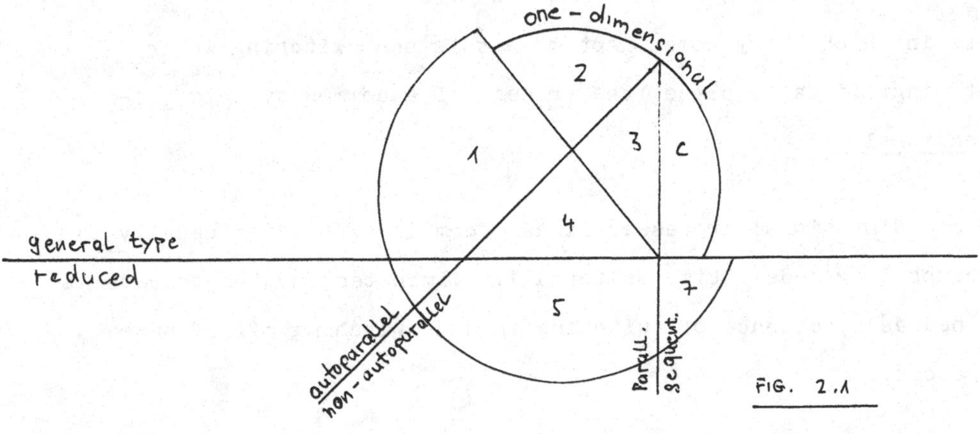

FIG. 2.1

Evidently, other things being equal the autoparallel two-dimensional model /1/ will be of the most general type, while the narrowest models are /6/ and /7/, i.e. sequential one-dimensional and sequential reduced.

2.4. Generally speaking we want to study not classes of computational processes but classes of codices fixed by one or another model. For example, the Karp-Miller model [4] generates a class of one-dimensional autoparallel codices, for any codex $\wp$; thus (a) for every process $P \in \wp$ each moment t and any operator $a \in {}^{p}A_t$ remaining after t moments in the working state there exists $P' \in \mathcal{P}$ coinciding up to moment t with P and satisfying condition $\bar{A}_t = a$.

Compared to the given model, for example, Slutz model [5] generates a broader class of codices since for these codices the condition (a) is not necessary.

Here, we are confronted with one of the most essential model characteristics. If earlier in papers on deterministic sequential models the foremost issue was the model generality in the sense of completeness of the class of functions represented by this model then, for non-deterministic models it is more essential to what extent syntactical properties of the model limit the class of codices generated by it, and to what extent these limitations reduce the generality of certain results for this model.

The more detailed discussion of the theme requires specifying what we mean here by a model and what type of a model we are interested in.

3. METAMODEL

Due to space limitation we shall have to omit a detailed consideration which influenced the character of the metamodel proposed below. We shall emphasize just the main property of it - the pair program-system is represented in it as an integer object. This may cause bewilderment as program and system are the main objects in theoretical programming and any formal model deals with them in one form or another. The principle reason of "indivisibility" of the given metamodel is pretension to sufficient generality - it is not possible to present formal definition of the program and system adequate to the whole variety of objects we mean by these terms. The more so as in reality the boundary between the program and the system exists only relatively and is established in the models rather arbitrarily.

At the same time it seems possible to give a rather general and formal description of the pair program-system as an integer construction. The way of presentation of a new object (we shall call it metasystem), allows us to vary the level of consideration since it permits us to give precisely the main functions of the pair program-system to any degree of generality.

3.1. We are interested in a non-deterministic metasystem. A memory and an data base on the memory are meant to be fixed for every metasystem; being given an initial memory state, the metasystem generates a computational process at its output. In the general case the process is not only a possible one but is "one of allowable" processes for this metasystem and this initial state.

Thus, the metasystem performance for every moment t is composed of the following standard actions:

(a) From the set A of base operators the set ${}^{+}A_t$ of operators being switched in at the moment is selected in some way. These are joined to the operators which have been switched in up to the moment t and they form together the set ${}^{p}A_t$ of working operators. (For auto-parallel metasystems the set ${}^{+}A_t$ may contain the operators which have been in working state up to the moment t. In this case one more "copy" of the given operator starts to take part in the computations.)

(b) From the set ${}^{p}A_t$, the set ${}^{-}A_t$ of operators being switched off is selected in some way.

(c) The determined part of the computational process which includes now also the moment t (the prefix of process P up to the moment t, it is denoted by $P\|_t$) defines the new memory state M_t.

3.2. As it has been noted in the introduction for the performance of non-deterministic metasystem a "restricted freedom" is inherent:

(a) On the one hand the selection of ${}^{+}A_t$ out of A and ${}^{-}A_t$ out of ${}^{p}A_t$, at least for some moments, is not defined uniquely by the process prefix $P\|_t$ and the initial M_o; if so, the model would be deterministic with the process being a single one.

(b) On the other hand the arbitrariness of selection of ${}^{+}A_p$ and ${}^{-}A_p$ is limited or else the metasystem would always generate a total set of computational processes with the given base.

It is naturally to assume that the metasystem has a current state of its own, - we denote it by q_t (Q is the set of all metasystem states). Immediately, there arise two alternative treatments of this state:

(a) The prefix $P\|_{t-1}$ and the initial M_o define q_t uniquely, in this case the dependence of selection of sets ${}^{+}A_t$ and ${}^{-}A_t$ on q_t remains non-unique.

(b) State q_t is "one of possible" at this prefix and M_o, i.e. it depends on them non-uniquely. But being selected this state determines the selection of ${}^{+}A_t$ and ${}^{-}A_t$.

As a rule the variant (a) is used in models, so we shall follow here the general example.

3.3. Let us pass directly to the metasystem. To simplify our description every operator $a_i \in A$ is put into correspondence with the counter c_i with the initial value 0. The current value of the counter fixes the difference between the number of switchings in and switchings out of the operator a_i (for non-autoparallel metasystems the value of these counters cannot exceed 1). All the above considered, we can present the metasystem as a set of recurrent relations:

$$(3.3.1)\quad \begin{aligned} q_t &= \Psi(P\|_{t-1}, M_o) \\ {}^{+}A_t &= \varphi'(A, q_t) \quad (c_i := c_i + 1 \ \text{ for all } a_i \in {}^{+}A_t) \\ {}^{p}A_t &= \{a_i / c_i > 0\} \\ {}^{-}A_t &= \varphi''({}^{p}A_t, q_t) \quad (c_i := c_i - 1 \ \text{ for all } a_i \in {}^{-}A_t \ . \end{aligned}$$

In this case Ψ is an unique (variant (a) !) function defining the new state of the metasystem in accordance with the prefix $P\|_{t-1}$ and the initial M_o, and φ is the non-unique mapping of $A^! \times Q$ in $A^{!*}$ satisfying the condition $(\forall A' \subseteq A)(\forall q)(\forall \varphi(A,q))(\varphi(A',q) \subseteq A')$, i.e. bringing into correspondence with every set $A' \subseteq A$ some of its subsets in accordance with the state q.

It is rather obvious that while one or another concrete method of realization for functions Ψ , φ' and φ'' and specifying the "structure" of state q, the metasystem (3.3.1) turns into a model of corresponding type. However, this metasystem describes a too broad class of models while below we shall be interested only in models of <u>asynchronous</u> type. It is natural that the metasystem describing this type of model is a particular case, - it is obtained by adding to the metasystem (3.3.1) some additional information on the character of the functions φ' and φ''.

3.4. The informal description of performance of any asynchronous metasystem for every moment t looks as follows:

(a) The initial memory state M_o and the prefix $P\|_{t-1}$ define the current state q_t.

(b) State q_t defines <u>uniquely</u> some set ${}^{*}A_t$ - they are the operators which are given a <u>permission for switching in</u>.

---

* $A^!$ is the set of all subsets of the set A.

(c) From ${}^{*}A_t$ <u>arbitrarily</u> is chosen subset ${}^{+}A_t$.

(d) Set ${}^{p}A_t$ as in the general case unites operators remaining switched in from the previous moment and ones of set ${}^{+}A_t$.

(e) From ${}^{p}A_t$ in accordance with the state q_t the set ${}^{-*}A_t$ of those operators which at the given tact are allowed <u>switching out</u> is <u>uniquely</u> selected.

(f) From ${}^{-*}A_t$ the set ${}^{-}A_t$ is <u>arbitrarily</u> selected.

To formulate the corresponding recurrent relations we shall introduce necessary notations:

$Q - \{q\}$ is a set of metasystem states with the initial state q_o fixed for every metasystem.

F is a unique (in contrast to φ) mapping $A' \times Q$ into A' satisfying the condition

$$(\forall A' \subseteq A)(\forall q)(F(A',q) \subseteq A')$$

ψ is just as above the function bringing every pair $P\|_{t-1}, M_o$ into correspondence with some state q_t.

These notations allow us to write down the asynchronous metasystem as the following set of recurrent relations:

$$
\begin{aligned}
&q_t = \psi(P\|_{t-1}, M_o)\\
&{}^{*}A_t = F_1(A, q_t)\\
(3.4.1) \qquad &{}^{+}A_t \quad {}^{*}A_t \quad (c_i := c_i + 1 \quad \text{for all } a_i \in {}^{+}A_t)\\
&{}^{p}A_t = \{a_i / c_i > o\}\\
&{}^{-*}A_t = F_2({}^{p}A_t, q_t)\\
&{}^{-}A_t \subseteq {}^{-*}A_t \quad (c_i := c_i - 1 \quad \text{for all } c_i \in {}^{-}A_t)
\end{aligned}
$$

Here the function F_1 defines operators which are allowed switching-in, and the function F_2 defines the ones which are allowed switching off. The selection of ${}^{+}A_t$ from ${}^{*}A_t$ and ${}^{-}A_t$ from ${}^{-*}A_t$ is done arbitrarily with only limitation in form of the <u>finite-delay condition</u>: "situation $a \in {}^{*}A_t \setminus {}^{+}A_t$ (or $a \in {}^{-*}A_t \setminus {}^{-}A_t$) may take place only in the limits of the finite interval of time <u>t</u> ".

3.5. However considering the relations (3.4.1) we come to the conclusion that this metasystem gives us (while fixing arbitrary functions Ψ, F_1 and F_2) models of the most general type, i.e. two-dimensional and autoparallel ones; it is not possible, for example, to obtain an arbitrary one-dimensional model by metasystem (3.4.1). We are certainly interested in more universal metasystems.

To find a way out, it suffices to remember that every special subclass of processes listed in 2.3 satisfies the same definite condition:

For non-autoparallel processes the limitation $(\forall a_i \in A)(c_i \leq 1)$ holds. This condition is true iff $(\forall t)({}^{+}A_t \subseteq {}^{o}A_t)$(${}^{o}A_t$ - see 2.1) for relations (3.4.1) is equivalent to the condition

(a) ${}^{*}A_t \subseteq {}^{o}A_t$

Every reduced process satisfies condition

(b) ${}^{+}A_t = {}^{-}A_t$ $(= {}^{p}A_t)$ (note that for a reduced process always ${}^{o}A_t = A$ as at every tact all working operators are switched off; therefore, though reduced processes belong to subclass of non-autoparallel ones, condition (a) for them becomes unnecessary).

For one-dimensional processes the condition

(c) $|{}^{+}A_t \cup {}^{-}A_t| \leq |\& {}^{+}A_t \cap {}^{-}A_t = \emptyset$ holds.

And finally for sequentional processes the condition

(d) $|{}^{p}A_t| = 1 \& {}^{*}A_t \subseteq {}^{o}A_t$ holds.

So, if we want to describe some special type of asynchronous metasystem we have to add a predicate Π, which has a concrete form for every class of processes, to the relations (3.4.1).

1. For the metasystem of the most general type Π is identical to "true" and is excluded from the set of relations.
2. For the one-dimensional case Π coincides with condition (c).
3. For the one-dimensional, non-autoparallel metasystem, Π unites condition (c) and (a).
4. For the two-dimensional, non-autoparallel case Π coincides with condition (a).
5. For reduced two-dimensional metasystems of a general type Π coincides with condition (b).
6. For sequentional metasystems of a general type Π coincides with condition (d).
7. For sequentional reduced metasystems Π unites conditions (d) and (b) and may be represented as: $|{}^{+}A_t| = |{}^{-}A_t| = 1$

3.6. The recurrent writing of metasystem with the set of "replaceable" predicates looks rather cumbersome, however, one should remember that this relations describe the class of metasystems essentially distinct from each other. As it will be seen more specialized metasystems are much simpler. (Thus, for example, in all models but that of Slutz [5], function F_2 has a trivial form $(\forall A', q)(F_2(A', q) = A')$ so the relation with F_2 in such models will be omitted further without reserve).

Let us consider several examples of metasystems, which describe certain models known in literature:

1) The model of Adams [6] (two-dimension, autoparallel one with trivial

function F_2) is described by the metasystem

$$\begin{aligned}
&.q_t = \Psi(P\|_{t-1}, M_o) \\
&.{}^{*}A_t = F_1(A, q_t) \\
&.{}^{+}A_t \subseteq {}^{*}A_t \\
&.{}^{p}A_t = \{a_i / c_i > o\} \\
&.{}^{-}A_t \subseteq {}^{p}A_t
\end{aligned}$$

2) The Karp-Miller model [4] (one-dimension, autoparallel) coincides with the previous one including, in addition, the predicate for one-dimensional processes (3.4 (c)).

3) The model of Slutz [5] is also one-dimensional and autoparallel. It differs from the previous model by the non-trivial function F_2 :

$$\begin{aligned}
&.q_t = \Psi(P\|_{t-1}, M_o) \\
&.{}^{*}A_t = F_1(A, q_t) \\
&.{}^{+}A_t \subseteq {}^{*}A_t \\
&.{}^{p}A_t = \{a_i / c_i > o\} \\
&.{}^{-*}A_t = F_2({}^{p}A_t, q_t) \\
&.{}^{-}A_t \subseteq {}^{-*}A_t
\end{aligned}$$

4) The model of Kotov [3] and Narinyani [2] (two-dimensional and non-autoparallel) :

$$\begin{aligned}
&.q_t = \Psi(P\|_{t-1}, M_o) \\
&.{}^{o}A_t = {}^{o}A_{t-1} \setminus {}^{+}A_{t-1} \cup {}^{-}A_{t-1} \\
&.{}^{*}A_t = F_1(A_t^{o}, q_t) \\
&.{}^{+}A_t \subseteq {}^{*}A_t \\
&.{}^{p}A_t = {}^{p}A_{t-1} \setminus {}^{-}A_{t-1} \cup {}^{+}A_t \\
&.{}^{-}A_t \subseteq {}^{p}A_t
\end{aligned}$$

5) One more metasystem from [2] is two-dimensional and reduced :

$$\begin{aligned}
&.\ q_t = \Psi(P\|_{t-1}, M_o) \\
&.\ {}^{*}A_t = F_1(A, q_t) \\
&.\ {}^{+}A_t \subseteq {}^{*}A_t \\
&.\ {}^{-}A_t = {}^{+}A_t (= {}^{p}A_t)
\end{aligned}$$

3.7. Schemata : the metasystem base is interpreted, however, for some problems it is convenient(and sometimes necessary) to consider models with an uninterpreted base. Such a model constructed similar to the metasystem is usually called a schema. Any schema S:

a) generates some set $\mathcal{P}[S]$ of uninterpreted processes.

b) Together with any interpretation I_A of the base it forms a metasystem S, I_A which in its turn, for any initial M_o generates $\mathcal{P}[S, I_A, M_o]$.

In the ideal case for every process $P \in \mathcal{P}[S]$ there exists a pair I_A and M_o (the pair is called the schema interpretation) with respect to which $P \in \mathcal{P}[S, I_A, M_o]$; however, one usually has to be satisfied with schemata more or less close to the ideal, it being defined, first of all, by the metasystem class and the method of realization of control functions Ψ, F_1 and F_2.

Further, we shall consider metasystem only. The problems and corresponding notions can be easily extended to schemata.

4. CONTROL

4.1. In accordance with the second thesis of the introduction, the method of description must allow us to vary the level of generality while studying the model of a chosen type. In this sense the writing of metasystem (3.4.1) is a description of the highest level: the model does not concretize the apparatus of realization of control functions Ψ, F_1, F_2 but simply considers them to be reflections of a certain type. We can decrease the level of the model in two ways:

(a) semantically: with the help of general limitations for functions Ψ, F_1, F_2. For example, "for any M_o $\Psi(P\|_t, M_o) = \Psi(P'\|_{t'}, M_o)$ if prefixes $P\|_t$ and $P'\|_{t'}$ are equivalent (say, by data flow graph)" or condition of <u>persistence</u> of the metasystem $(\forall a \in A)(\forall t)(a \in {}^*A_t \setminus {}^+A_t \rightarrow a \in {}^*A_{t+1})$.

(b) syntactically: by specifying the method of realization for all or some control functions. For example, in the paper of Karp and Miller [4] the model is considered at three levels: upper almost coinciding with the metasystem 3.6.(2) (parallel program schemata), middle, much more concrete (counter schemata) and lower representing a particular type of counter schemata (parallel flow charts).

It is quite natural to expect that general necessary and/or sufficient conditions will be formulated as symantical limitations for control functions in order that each concrete model consideration be reduced to the demonstration of the fact that syntactical properties of the control functions apparatus for the model imply (or, vice versa, do not imply) some or other symantical limitations.

Most of authors carry out their researches just in this way, and it helps further to use their results for investigation of other models with similar symantical limitations. However, in many papers the model is considered only at one, the most concrete level, so the results obtained in this case remain "thing in itself" - their use for other models may turn out to be non-paying because of the need for a special apparatus of reinterpretation.

4.2. Let us consider the well-known flow-chart as an illustration. The metasystem for an interpreted flow-chart is like a usual (sequentional) deterministic automaton:

$$(A) \quad \begin{aligned} q_t &= \widehat{\Psi}(q_{t-1}, M_{t-1}, {}^{p}A_{t-1}) \ / \ \widehat{\Psi}: Q \times \{M\} \times A \to Q \\ {}^{p}A_t &= \widetilde{F}({}^{p}A_{t-1}, q_t) \ / \ \widetilde{F}: A \times Q \to A \ . \end{aligned}$$

Thus, the metasystem defines a directed graph with vertices operators from A. Each vertex a_i A corresponds to a function $\varphi_i : Q \times \{M\} \to Q \ / \ (\forall_q, M)(\varphi_i(q,M) = \widetilde{\Psi}(q,M,a_i))$ and every arc from a_i to a_j to the set $Q^{ij} / (\forall_{q \in} Q^{ij})(\widetilde{F}(a_i,q) = a_j)$.

Limitation 1: The state q is a value of the fixed tuple of logical variables, and Q is the set of all values of this tuple, respectively. Every operator $a_i \in A$ is brought into correspondence with a subset $\underline{V}^i \subseteq \underline{V}$ and a function $\varphi_i : Q \times \{M\} \to Q$ such that $\varphi_i(q,M)$ may differ from q only by values of variables $\underline{V}^i$. For each pair of operators $a_i, a_j \in A$ the predicate $\Pi_{ij} / (\forall_i)(j \neq j' \to \Pi_{ij} \wedge \Pi_{ij'} = \text{false}$ of the values of variables $\underline{V}$ (may be identically true or identically false) is defined. In this case the metasystem has the form:

$$\begin{aligned} q_t = V_t &= \varphi_i(V_{t-1}, M_{t-1}) / a_i = {}^{p}A_{t-1} \\ \widetilde{F}(a_i, V_t) &= a_j \leftrightarrow \Pi_{ij}(V_t) = \text{true}. \end{aligned}$$

Limitation 2: Predicates Π_{ij} are realized by a fixed set of logic functions (for example $\wedge, \vee, \neg, 1$).

It is easily seen that the simultaneous introduction of limitations 1 and 2 (the lower level of consideration) leads us directly to the classical (interpreted) flow-chart. The limitation 1 taken individually (middle level) gives us a free choice of predicate Π_{ij} representation; for example, they can be realized by means of threshold functions from variables $\underline{V}$. Naturally, the choice of method for predicate Π_{ij} representation effects essentially the set of equivalent transformations. Consideration at the middle level allows us to separate the transformations resulting from the very character of the model from transformations which are a result of the method of predicates representation. As a rule, the latter transformations are a reformulation of axioms of algebra of logic for the corresponding basis.

Elemenating limitation 1, i.e. passing to metasystem (A) directly allows us to consider every operator $a_i \in A$ as a transformer of state q, and each arc $a_i a_j$ as a filter allowing the transit along this arc only in the case if the state of the metasystem after a_i belongs to the set Q^{ij}. As a convincing example of efficiency of flow-chart consideration at such a general level, one can refer to Podlovchenko's report [7] in the present symposium.

4.3. HYPEROPERATOR: in concluding this paragraph we shall consider one more construction which can be used for realization of control functions.

The operator notion in the form it is introduced above is generally accepted and widely used in theory because of its simplicity and convenience for formal considerations. However, more complex objects (statements with indices and conditions, etc.) are used in practice in programming, which demands introduction of a universal adequate construction into the formal apparatus.

A triple <<u>in</u>, , > is called a <u>hyperoperator</u> on memory <u>M</u> where <u>in</u> is an tuple of elements from <u>M</u>. $\mathcal{A}$ is a fixed set of operators on <u>M</u> and L is a mapping of the set of values of <u>in</u> onto $\mathcal{A}$.

It is important to note that the role of hyperoperator is not limited to its use as a universal element of computation. Indeed, let us consider the arbitrary determined (see 5.1.(A)) metasystem X: for each initial M_o the metasystem X realizes (independent of the selecting process from $\mathcal{P}[X,M_o]$) an operator, which uses the initial values of certain memory elements as arguments and places into some memory elements, values which are results of computations performed for the given arguments. However, in the general case for different initial memory states the metasystem realizes various operators, being in reality not an operator but a hyperoperator.

Thus, introduction of hyperoperators is a natural step to hierarchy structures for programs and metasystems (as it allows us to consider one metasystem to be a hyperoperator used in the other); it simplifies the consideration of procedures, etc. It is not by chance that a similar construction is used in Adams paper [6], paying special attention to procedures. The hyperoperator is one of the basic notions in the author's paper [2] and is used also by Kotov [3]; Lukoni operator [8] is, as a matter of fact, also a hyperoperator.

The use of a hyperoperator instead of an operator in the definitions of a metasystem and a computational process enables us to widen the potentiality of the corresponding constructions with respect to modelling real computational systems and programming languages.

5. PROBLEMS

5.1. All of the above dealt mainly with the apparatus itself: a model character, its generality, its position with respect to others, etc. But evidently, as are interested not only in the model itself, - it is, as a rule, a means of solving problems of one or another type. What are the main problems for the investigation of which we have now so impressive an amount of stored constructions and notions? Setting aside special, so to say "inside" problems connected with particular features of individual models, we give a short consideration of general problems:

(A) Let us consider an arbitrary asynchronous model: memory M, an initial value M_o, metasystem X, codex $\mathcal{P}[X,M_o]$ which is put into correspondence by metasystem X to a given M_o. As a non-deterministic model with given M_o can choose any process from $\mathcal{P}[X,M_o]$, naturally, there arises a question, if all the processes from $\mathcal{P}[X,M_o]$ are equivalent, i.e. if computations made by the metasystem (model) at M_o are in this sense determinate and independent of choice of the concrete process from $\mathcal{P}[X,M_o]$.

From the given question the more general one immediately follows. What are the conditions of determinacy for metasystems of the given class ? This general question demands specification as to what kind of processes equivalency we mean and investigation of dependency between choice of definition of processes equivalency and existence of effective conditions and/or an algorithm of determinacy examination for metasystems of one or another class.

(B) The theory can not restrict itself to the passive study of models. Its traditional purpose is learning methods whereby one actively works with them, first of all, optimizing transformations. The problem of existence of optimizing transformations is a part of a general item of equivalent transformations which, in its turn, is closely connected with a choice of equivalency definitions for metasystems.

This choice has an absolute influence upon the character of obtained results: decidability of recognizing equivalency for the given class of models, existence of the complete system of equivalent transformations, existence of directed transformations for optimization criteria, etc.

(C) While a problem of equivalency is common for all types of models, the subject of this point is connected only with the non-deterministic ones:

Let us fix some definition α of metasystem equivalency. Let metasystems X' and X" from one equivalency class be such that under any initial conditions M_o, $\mathcal{P}[X',M_o] \subset \mathcal{P}[X",M_o]$. For example, X" allows execution of the operators a and b both simultaneously and sequentially in any order, but X' executes them only in the sequence a,b. It is quite evident that X" has in the sense of α an advantage over X' obtaining the same results but having more freedom in choice of strategy of processing. Metasystems X" is in this respect more flexible, more asynchronous.

It is possible to introduce a relation allowing us to compare metasystems by the "degree of asynchronity". Such a relation partially orders metasystems of one or another class allowing us to put a question in this class of maximally asynchronous metasystems of existence of decidability of the problem to recognize if the given metasystem is maximal, of existence of equivalent transformations permitting us to increase the original metasystem asynchronity, etc.

(D) In close connection with the above items is the task of "parallelizing". Given some class Υ^A of asynchronous metasystems and some class Υ^d of usual sequential deterministic metasystems (e.g., flow-charts), it is necessary to find an algorithm allowing us to construct for every metasystem from Υ^d an equivalent determinate and maximally asynchronous metasystem from Υ^A. (The algorithm for parallelizing or to be more exact, asynchronizing the original sequentional metasystem was named desequentor as suggested by A.P. Ershov.) The existence of desequentor, its complexity, and possible limitations are dependent directly on the original classes of metasystems Υ^A and Υ^d, on the definition of metasystem equivalency, on the definition of a relation comparing metasystems by asynchronity.

(E) Finally, we pass to the item which has been ignored in the literature almost completely. As it has been said in the introduction every work, as a rule, is associated with an individual model and does not try to extend its results to other models and to connect the model properties with regard to specificity of "refraction" with some general problems. We would like to dedicate a special paragraph to the corresponding item, but before passing to it we return again to the problems of points (A)+(D).

5.2. DETERMINACY: as it follows from 5.1 (A) the choice of the definition of equivalency of computational processes is the key point in the investigation of determinacy. It would be possible to enumerate more than ten essentially differing definitions of equivalency used in the literature and the spectrum remains "open", i.e. it can be expanded further.

Let ω be a definition of equivalency of computational processes. The metasystem X will be called -determinate at the given initial M_o if all the processes from codex $\wp[X,M_o]$ are equivalent by this definition. Considering some class $\mathfrak{X}$ of metasystems of the choosen definition ω there arises a question if all the metasystems from $\mathfrak{X}$ are ω-determinate. If the class $\mathfrak{X}$ permits also non-determinate metasystems there arise further questions:

/a/ Is the problem of recognizing ω-determinacy decidable for an arbitrary metasystem from class $\mathfrak{X}$.

/b/ What conditions are necessary and/or sufficient for ω-determinacy of a metasystem from class $\mathfrak{X}$.

Among the models known from the literature only a few guarantee the determinacy. In general case the investigation is connected, as a rule, with attempts to consider questions /a/ and /b/. In this respect, the works known to us have not advanced beyond the results being "rather close to the surface". For question /a/ the answers are usually reduced to to statements that for one or another class $\mathfrak{X}$ a determinacy problem is decidable for the finite-state metasystems and undecidable for the general case. As to question /b/ the works present some or other sufficient and/or necessary conditions of determinacy for some or other classes of metasystems, but these conditions, as a rule, are of non-effective character, i.e. verification of them is an undecidable problem.

It is interesting to note that non-effectiveness here is connected, first of all, with the fact that conditions of determinacy are formulated not as requirements for control functions of a metasystem but as limitations for its code (i.e. limitations of a semantic type - see 4.1 /a/). In this respect point /b/ (mostly determining by the way the results of point /a/) could be divided into two stages:

/1/ Investigation of determinacy for codes of one or another type. In many cases such an investigation may be executed without a metasystem, the use of it is only necessary for those classes of codes which can not be introducted directly, but only by means of a corresponding metasystem.

/2/ The formulation of requirements on control functions of metasystems under investigation providing given properties for its code.

We should like to emphasize that every definition of process equivalency is connected, as a matter of fact, with invariants of a certain type The preliminary investigation of the correspondence between characteristics of the invariant and class of equivalency in many respects will help us, as it seems, to make /1/ more complete and exhaustive.

5.3. METASYSTEMS EQUIVALENCY: The scope of definitions of equivalency for metasystems does not yield to the variety of definitions of equivalency for processes. The most natural is a functional equivalency, though the recognition problem for this equivalency for most classes of metasystems is undecidable. So we are forced to consider the more narrow definitions, which on the one hand, guarantee similar results for equivalent metasystems, and on the other hand allow the existence of recordition algorithms, systems of equivalent transformations, etc. .

Just the choice of such a more narrow definition turns out to be decisive, the situation is quite similar to the one observed for problems of determinacy (the identity is not incidental as definitions of equivalency here and there are very closely connected). In this sense, the definitions used now are evidently far from being perfect as it is evident from available results. The latter ones are mainly reduced to establishing undecidability of equivalency recognition for one or another class of metasystems; sometimes this problem is decidable for rather special classes of finite-state metasystems.

---

*/ For functional equivalency, for example, such an invariant is a mapping from a set of values for the input element of the process on to a set of(terminal) values for output elements.
In other cases this is a set contents sequence of cells in memory (see [4]), a data flow information graph (see [2],[3]), etc.

In a number of papers systems of equivalent transformations are considered, but, as a rule, these systems are linked with a model with developed syntax, and due to this fact they are of doubtful importance on a larger scale.

In our opinion really interesting results can be expected in this field only after the investigations turn from concrete models to metasystems of rather general type. Another essential condition of success is finding the "limit" definition of equivalency. On the one hand this permits in the most interesting cases to remain within the bounds of decidability, on the other hand providing maxially broad classes of equivalency of Itkin [9] or rather an equivalency " a little more general".

3.4. ASYNCHRONITY. Insufficient development of problems of equivalency quite evidently influences the level of papers devoted to asynchronity investigation. Let us consider the simplest variant of a relation allowing us to compare the metasystems by asynchronity:
let $\mathfrak{X}$ be a set of equivalent metasystems on the same memory (the equivalency character is not significant here). For any pair $X, X' \in \mathfrak{X}$ one of the following statements may be true:

a. $(\forall M_o)(\mathcal{P}[X,M_o] = \mathcal{P}[X',M_o])$

in this case we say that metasystems X and X' <u>are equal by asynchronity</u>.

b. $(\forall M_o)(\mathcal{P}[X,M_o] \subseteq \mathcal{P}[X',M_o]) \& (\exists M_o)(\mathcal{P}[X,M_o] \subset \mathcal{P}[X',M_o])$

(X' <u>more asynchronous</u> than X^E).

If /a/ or /b/ is true then X and X' are <u>comparable by asynchronity</u>, otherwise <u>non-comparable</u>. We say that metasystem X^* is <u>maximal asynchronous</u> (or just <u>maximal</u>) in $\mathfrak{X}$,if it is comparable with all other metasystems in $\mathfrak{X}$, neither of them being more asynchronous than X^*.

This relation was considered in the paper of Keller [10] and Slutz [5], established the decidability of recognition of maximality for some (rather narrow) classes of metasystems and formulated the necessary and sufficient conditions of maximality for these classes.

This definition is quite simple and pictorial but the possibilities of its use are rather limited. For example, it allows one to compare only metasystems with the same base while in practice most interesting are equivalent transformations changing the memory allocation, in particular transformations in frames of equivalency by data flow graph.

The author [2] changed this definition correspondingly. The new definitic expands the class of equivalency covered by the relation that allows us in the general case to increase the asynchronity of the maximal metasystem with the help of optimal memory allocation. It is also worth mentioning a rather interesting class of metasystems not containing a maximal one. In [2] metasystems of "imperative" type which involve metasystems realized by the majority of the existing programming languages, including a considerable part of programming languages were considered. In imperative metasystems each switching off of an operator indicates some set of operators which have to be switched in irrespectively of the effect of the other working operators.

It was demonstrated in [2] that any class of equivalent (by the dataflow graph) metasystems of imperative type contains no maximal metasystem if the data flow graph for this class is different from the simple tree. In other words in the case of a more complex data flow graph the realization of maximal asynchronous metasystems (i.e. programs) is impossible in imperative languages. Metasystem comparison by asynchronity and following from here the notion of maximal asynchronous metasystem is a necessary basis for the development of equivalent transformations increasing asynchronity. Right now the natural limits of consideration one frames of data flow graph. One can surely say that these frames are too narrow, the corresponding notions must be expanded to more general definitions of equivalency, possibly up to functional one.

5.5. DESEQUENTION: As far as we know most detailed investigation of desequention was done in Kotov's paper [3].
We have to note that this work due to its scope and results essentially cover all the other papers dealing with desequention.
One may consider it to be a valid base for further development of the subject, though, of course, the progress here depends largely on a state of allied fields mentioned above.

6. PROGRAM AND SYSTEM

The title of this paragraph may raise bewilderment as above (§3) we have based the introduction of a metasystems notion on the impossibility of giving formal and general definitions of a "program" and "system" notion. But the contradiction here is quite apparent as in the same paragraph we have restricted the possible variety of models to a class of asynchronous metasystems.

Specific features of this class allow us to present some problems (considered usually for individual models) in rather general form very close to traditional decomposition of the model into a program and a system.

For any fixed class metasystem (3.4.1) a system will be called a set of recurrent relations (including predicate $\sqcap$) describing this metasystem and a program - the cortege $\underline{M}, M_0, Q, q_0, A, \Psi, F_1, F_2$.

(For simplicity in this paragraph we assign to the program also the initial state M_o - thus the pair "program-system" defines the metasystem together with the initial M_o).

Let us denote by $\mathcal{P}[X,Y]$ the codex defined by the pair "program Y - system X". We say that the system X is <u>more rigid</u> than the system X' (and X' respectively <u>less rigid</u> than X) on some set $\mathcal{J}$ of programs, if for each program $Y \in \mathcal{J}$ $\mathcal{P}[X,Y] \subseteq \mathcal{P}[X',Y]$ and there exists at least one $Y' \in \mathcal{J}$ for which $\mathcal{P}[X,Y] \subset \mathcal{P}[X',Y]$. If for X and X' $\mathcal{P}[X,Y] = \mathcal{P}[X',Y]$ for all $Y \in \mathcal{J}$ then these systems are <u>equal in rigidity</u>.

As an illustration to the introduced relation we shall give a diagram showing the relation by rigidity of systems for some models known from the literature. Systems comparable by rigidity are connected, the arrows are directed from less rigid to more rigid ones.

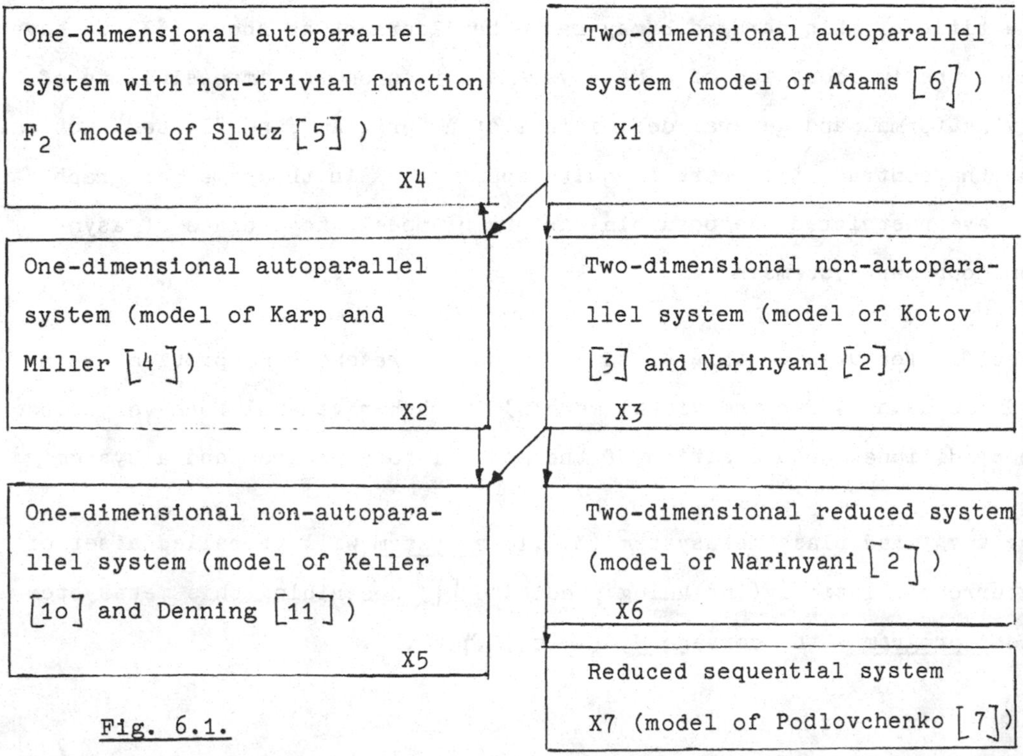

<u>Fig. 6.1.</u>

It is obvious that for the programs with the trivial function F_2 the systems X2 and X4 are equal w.r.t. rigidity as well as systems X2 and X5 are equal w.r.t. rigidity for programs which give non-autoparallel metasystems in the pair with X2. For the programs of this type system X3 is less rigid than X2, though in general they are not comparable.

It is easy to see that for any program Y and system X. A sufficient condition of determinacy Y for each system more rigid than X holds, and the necessary condition of determinacy Y for every system less rigid than X holds.

Thus, considering the problem of determinacy for some individual model we simultaneously obtain definite results with respect to some other models. Let us introduce one more definition:

We shall say that system X and X' are <u>tantamount by ω-determinacy</u> in some class $\mathcal{Y}$ of programs if for any program $Y \in \mathcal{Y}$-determinacy of the pair Y,X is a necessary and sufficient condition ω-determinacy of the pair Y,X' (similarly, one may introduce tantamounty of systems by ω-equivalency and ω-maximality).

Evidently, if the systems X and X' are equal by rigidity they are always tantamount by determinacy, equivalency and maximality. However, for two systems to be tantamount it is not necessary to be equal in rigidity: moreover, the most interesting results are expected for investigation of tantamouncy of systems not equal in rigidity. For example, let γ be a unique mapping bringing every process into correspondence with some other one. We say that the system X γ-<u>models</u> the system X' on the set of programs $\mathcal{Y}$ if for every program $Y \in \mathcal{Y}$ following the conditions $\mathcal{P}[X,Y] = \gamma(\mathcal{P}[X',Y])$.

Evidently, if P and $\mu(P)$ are always ω-equivalent then any system will be tantamount by ω-determinacy to every system μ-modelling it.

The notions introduced in this paragraph provide certain means for realizing the third thesis of the introduction. E.g. it is possible to demonstrate the tantamouncy by determinacy (data flow graph) of systems X3, X6 and X7 (see Fig. 6.1) for a rather wide class of programs. The same systems are tantamount also by equivalency for a definition choosen in a due way. Now, it suffices to remember that the computational processes for X7 - are well studied chains to see the convenient sides of this situation, e.g. the results of investigation of equivalent transformations for comparatively simple models using the system X7 can be directly extended to similar models using systems X3 and X6.

CONCLUSION

The range of practical problems dealing with parallel and asynchronous computation is rather broad; in its turn it leads to a variety of models becoming subjects of mathematical research. Up to now corresponding researches have dealt with every model individually, the main attention, as a rule, being paid to structures realizing the control functions. Thus, in a sense, the model itself has not been investigated rather the syntactical means of its realization choosen by the author. The short-comings of this approach are evident.

Further progress in the theory demands that we create an apparatus allowing us to describe each model in the most general form and study it in the context of the sufficiently broad class of similar models.

The system of notions presented in this report can be looked upon as some sketchy variant of such an apparatus, which to our opinion can serve, to a certain degree, as a basis for tis further development.

REFERENCES

[1] Ershov, A.P., Flow-charts on Common and Distributed Memory, J. "Kibernetika", Kiev, N 4, 1968.

[2] Narinyani, A.S., Asynchronous Computational Processes on Memory, Thesis, Novosibirsk, 1970.

[3] Kotov, V.E., Transformations Flow-charts in Asynchronous Programs, Thesis, Novosibirsk, 1970.

[4] Karp, R.M. and Miller, R.E., Parallel Program Schemata, Journal of Computer and Systems Sciences, v. 3, N 2, May 1969.

[5] Slutz, D.R., Flow Graph Schemata, Rec. of the Project MAC conf. on Concurrent Systems and Parallel Computations, Woods Hole, Mass., June 1970.

[6] Adams, D.A., A Computation Model with Data Flow Sequencing, CS-117, Computer Science Dept., Stanford Univ. Calif. Dec.1968.

[7] Podlovchenko, R.I. Non-Determined Algorithm Schemata or R-Schemata, Report at the present Symposium.

[8] Luconi, F.L., Asynchronous Computational Structures, MAC-TR-49, Thesis, Mass. Inst. of Technology, Cambridge, Mass. Feb. 1968.

[9] Itkin, B.E., Logic-termal Equivalence of Program Schemata, Kibernetika, Kiev, N 1, 1972.

[10] Keller, R.M., On Maximally Parallel Schemata, IEEE Conference Rec. of the 11-th Annual Symposium on Switching and Automata Theory, Oct. 1970.

[11] Denning, P.J., On the Determinacy of Schemata, Rec. of the Project MAC conf. on Concurrent Systems and Parallel Computations, Woods Hole, Mass., June 1970.

Configurable Computers: A New Class of General Purpose Machines

Raymond E. Miller and John Cocke

I. INTRODUCTION

Since the advent of electronic digital computers in the late 1940's and early 1950's, the main organizational concept has been that of a stored program. By means of the program a machine is sequenced through its instructional steps by successively fetching instructions from memory into a control unit which then decodes the instructions and sequences the operational units. The use of the same memory for instructions and data has given great flexibility to such machines, and was a major advance over earlier calculators using manual operations, plugboards, tape loops, or other predetermined and fixed sequencing of steps. Since the earliest stored program machines the basic organization of computers has remained the same. Certainly many innovations have been made, for example; special devices such as channels and multiplexors to control the input/output of machines, terminal devices, pipelined operational and control units, paging systems, and memory heirarchies. Generally speaking, however, the notion of stored program, instruction sequencing, and the memory -- cpu -- control -- I/O organization has prevailed. The innovations were essentially additions to this basic organization, removing the bottlenecks and improving performance by matching existing technologies with the basic stored program machine organization.

The configurable computer organizations which we briefly describe in this report are a major departure from the past stored program computer structure. Surprisingly, however, the notions of program, high level languages, compiler techniques, and the like, that have been built up over the years readily carry over to this new class of machines. This feature, provides an easy transition to configurable computers, and is a major contrast with previous attempts for obtaining new computer structures such as iterative array computers, modular computers, or "Holland Type" machines which have all failed, in large part, due to the inability to successfully program such machines.

The main concept of configurable computers is that the machine structure should attain the natural structure of the algorithm being performed. This contrasts with stored program machines in which the algorithm must be molded to the fixed structure of the machine through the program. In configurable computers a programming language of ones choice may be used to express the algorithm. The main difference is that the program is not used in the conventional way to sequence the computer operation. This difference in approach will become more obvious as we describe the two basic types of configurable computers, the search mode configurables and the interconnection mode configurables, in the next sections.

When proposing such a drastic departure from conventional computer organizations as we are doing, one must consider what potential gains can be attained, as well as the ease or difficulties imposed in adopting to the new machine organization. As we just noted, the ability to use existing programming languages and systems programming concepts in configurable computers overcomes most of the transitional difficulties. The most striking advantage seen for configurable computers is that they can achieve the speed advantages enjoyed by special purpose machines, but also have the general purpose capabilities not possible in special purpose machines through the dynamic reconfigurability features proposed. Another important advantage is that by having the machine structure itself to fit the algorithm, the natural and inherent parallelism of the algorithm is exposed and exploited during algorithm execution. No additional sequencing constraints due to program instruction sequencing or machine control limitations are imposed. Other advantages of configurable computers include: the same basic structure is suitable over a line of machines of varying performance; a machine can be readily upgraded in performance, the systems are resistant to unit failures, complex control units are not required, individual instruction fetching and storing is not required so memory utilization is simplified, natural data structure can be used to increase memory performance, and some aspects of the systems programming problem are simplified. We discuss this further as the configurable computer organizations are described in the next sections.

II. THE SEARCH MODE CONFIGURABLES

The search mode configurable computers consist of a memory unit, a collection of "active" operational units, and a searcher. This basic organization is depicted in Figure 1.

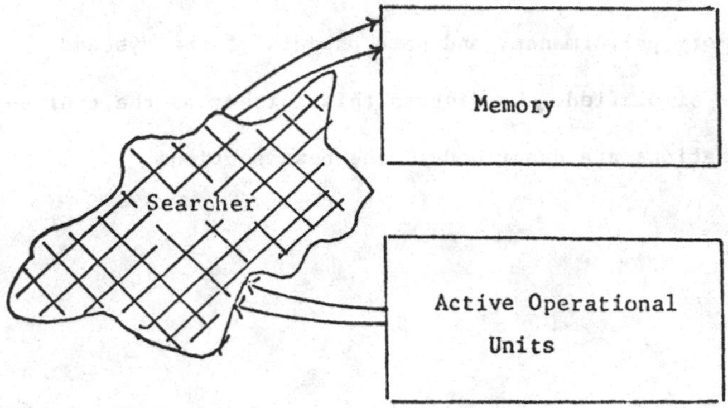

Figure 1: Search Mode Configurable Computer

The basic operation of this machine consists of an operation unit, when having completed a task of its type, asking (through the searcher) for a new task to perform. The searcher will inspect the memory, or suitable portions thereof, for a new task for the operational unit to perform. Operational units will consist of such devices as adders, multipliers, conditional testers, macro-operation modules, input-output devices, and the like. The capabilities of the machine will depend upon the types and number of operational modules in the system, the effective speed of the memory, and the capabilities of the searcher.

To describe the operation in more detail it is useful to discuss a typical format for an item in memory. An item may be stored in a single word or in a small block of words, but in each case will be considered to be a single entity in our discussion. Figure 2 illustrates a typical format for an item associated with an arithmetic operation having two operands and one result.

operation code	tag bits	first operand	second operand	"address" for result

Figure 2: Memory Item Format -- Search Mode Configurable

In this kind of item the operation code is used to specify the operation to be performed. The first and second operand fields are thought of as "registers" to hold operands and the address for the result is used to define the location into which the result is to be stored. The result normally will be stored into an operand field of some other item. The tag bits are used for status and sequencing information, and these, along with the operation code, are inspected by the searcher when it is looking for operations that are ready to be performed by operation units. For example, the tag bits would specify a condition that both operands had been produced and stored in the first and second operand fields and that the address for the result was set. Upon such a condition, when a suitable operational unit became available and the searcher designated this item to be performed, the item (or whatever parts are required) would be sent to the operation unit for performance. This would update the tag information indicating that the data from the operand fields had been removed (thus freeing these areas for future results of other operations) and indicating that the operation was no longer ready to be performed. As operations are performed, new items become eligible for performance, and in this way the sequencing of the algorithm is primarily dependent upon the availability of operands and the basic data sequencing requirements of the algorithm.

Without going into detail, it should be clear that formats of a similar nature can be specified for nonarithmetic operations such as testing and conditional branching, inputting and outputting -- where blocks of results could be specified, and also for macro and micro operations, as desired. In all cases the execution of the algorithm (or algorithms) would proceed in parallel, sequenced by the inherent data flow of the algorithms. The fetching and storing of information in memory would be done in these natural blocks of information specified as items. Paging techniques and a directed search for items could be used, based upon the algorithm structure.

The transformation of programs into such an item formatted structure is quite straightforward. Algorithms were developed by Miller and Rutledge for a data flow model transformation [4], and much of this analysis is already performed in the compiling processes, especially when code optimization is being considered [1, 2, 3]. The particular item formats would, of course, have to be set up to match the types of operational units one proposes to have in the machine.

The description of this search mode configurable computer organization has been given at a conceptual, rather than a detailed, level so that the basic concept can be most clearly emphasized. Obviously, many different approaches can be investigated and evaluated as more detailed design is considered. For example, the active modules may be partitioned into different classes according to their type and capability. That combined with specifying a certain subregion of the memory that contains items of a special type would tend to simplify the searcher design and speed up the performance. Also, one could have the searcher working ahead of the actual performance so that items would be immediately ready for operation when an operation unit finishes a previous task. In this way the items could be visualized as "streaming" through the operation units.

The machine performance is highly dependent upon the effectiveness of the searcher. and it is this part of the machine that leaves the most room for innovative design. There are many variations of approach possible here. One might be that the searcher always keeps one, or several, items which are ready to be performed available so that when an operational unit becomes available the searcher can immediately supply it with another task. These items could be physically located near the respective operational units so there is not an inordinate delay in information transfer. Another approach would be to use an associative memory in the searcher to keep track of potential items that may be -- or soon will -- become ready to be performed. Clues for being ready are supplied ahead of time by the loading of new operands into an item and the updating of result addresses. These clues could be used to have the memory supply the items to the searcher as they become available to be performed. Some care must be exercised in any such approach, however, so that the number of items available stays within reasonable bounds for the system.

Finally, let us return to some of the advantages claimed in the introduction. Clearly, parallel operation of units in the machine, and operations within the algorithm, are a natural outcome of this structure. With suitable speed in the searcher, the operations would be performed nearly at the speed of the operational units as if they were directly interconnected as a special purpose device. Yet, the representation of the algorithm as described by the item formats provides the desired general purpose capability. If an operational unit is found to be failing it can be turned to an inactive status so that it no longer performs any function in the algorithm execution. Thus, other units of the same type perform the tasks which would have been done by this unit, and this happens with no need for respecifying any part of the algorithm or its execution. Of course, the loss of a unit in this way degrades the performance of the machine. Also, new units -- memory, search, or operational -- can be added to the machine to upgrade the performance as required. If new, or more complex, types of operational units are added to the machine there could be extensive changes required in the format of items, the compiling process, and in required additional capabilities of the searcher. Finally, whether one or several algorithms are being performed simultaneously plays little role in how the machine operates, so this should simplify some of the systems programming problems in multiprogramming systems.

III THE INTERCONNECTION MODE CONFIGURABLES

As in the case of the search mode configurable computers, the interconnection mode configurable computers use the philosophy of having the computer reconfigure itself to suit the particular algorithm being performed. For interconnection mode configurables, however, the reconfiguration is performed in a more direct way by actually interconnecting operational units into the form of an algorithm or part of an algorithm. For this purpose an n×n interconnection network becomes a central part of the machine. An elementary block diagram of an interconnection mode configurable computer is shown in Figure 3.

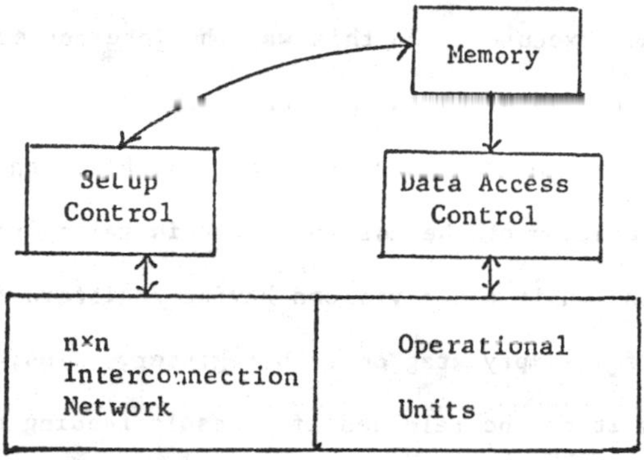

Figure 3: Interconnection Mode Configurable Computer

The interconnection network is used to create direct interconnections between outputs of operational units and inputs to other operational units in a manner consistent with the data flow model structure.

Having an algorithm specified in a high level language this program is first compiled into blocks of program which are of suitable size to utilize the operational units of the machine. For each block the compiler determines a setup (or interconnection) of the operational units that represent the data flow paths in the algorithm. This setup is coded and stored as a setup instruction in the memory. The setup instruction for the block including the start point of the program is used first -- sent to the setup control which interconnects the operational units. Then, this block is started in execution. Operands and results as required from memory are accessed as needed by the data access control. During execution, however, no instructions need be fetched from memory. Looping within a block is accomplished by direct interconnections with suitable synchronization between parallel parts of the same logical loop. Upon completion of the block execution the exit specifies the next block to be set up and executed. In this way the interconnection mode configurable computer appears as a special purpose machine during any block execution. With suitable control the setup for the next block may start to be processed while the execution of the current block is taking place.

Within each operational unit one envisions having registers for operands and results along with a full-empty tag on each register. Thus, when an operand register is empty it can be reloaded if a result feeding this register is available. Thus, these tag bits enable asynchronous transfer of temporary data between the interconnected operational units. The speed of execution follows the natural speeds of the operational units and the information transfer speeds.

An important facit of this organization is that both temporary data and instructions are eliminated as traffic over the memory access busses. This decrease in memory utilization, itself, reduces one of the annoying bottlenecks of a computing system. Also, of course, since the flow of data is all that occurs to and from memory during execution of a block any structure of the data, such as arrays, trees, etc., can be advantageously used to increase the rate of transfer.

Some words about the feasibility of such an interconnection network: Techniques exist for creating n×n interconnection networks in around n log n rather than n^2 switches, and these networks have a very uniform structure, highly suitable for integrated circuit structures. Also, they are logically constructed out of smaller k×k interconnection networks. It may be possible to distribute the various k×k networks among the operational units in order to substantially decrease the time needed to transfer a result to an operand register. Other savings in switches would be possible by organizing the data transfer as serial by bit or byte rather than in parallel a word at a time.

The appropriate transformation of a program into the blocks for setup and execution is a topic for further investigation. The compiler optimization techniques, data flow model transformation, methods of transforming in and out of recursive form, and analysis of loop free structures, are important stepping stones to make such a transformation feasible.

IV CONCLUSIONS

Although this report provides only a sketchy view of the concept of configurable computers, it is easy to visualize a number of other variations and applications of such structures. One could operate either of these machines in an incremental compile and run mode as a problem is being fed into the machine. Special types of operational units such as digital differentiators and integrators could be added to create a programmable digital differential analyzer. Special "often used" subroutines or macro-instructions could be semi-permanently installed -- possibly using read-only memories -- and the compiler would then assume these units existed. For simulation of proposed new machine organizations these machines would be almost ideal because the interconnection of units could then be made so as to directly mimic the proposed organization. The speed of simulation would increase and it would be easy to test slight variants in organization. For instructional purposes in machine design and organization such a machine should serve as almost an ideal laboratory model.

Another variation that could be investigated is the adding of special mechanisms to stack or queue data or procedures. Such a facility would aid in exposing additional parallelism in algorithms and might be especially useful in recursions.

Both the search mode and the interconnection mode configurable computers are sequenced by the basic data sequencing of the algorithm being performed. On the other hand, ordinary machines are sequenced through a program and machine control. There is a wide region of possible designs that fit somewhere between the complete data sequencing or complete control sequencing machines. For example, one might consider using ordinary instructions and control to sequence the normal arithmetic and logical operations but to use a separate data sequenced structure to determine the "flow" of the algorithm through tests and conditional branches. The opposite approach would be another possibility. At this point in the development of these ideas it is not clear which approaches would be most promising for actual machines, and some experimental studies are probably required to aid in such a determination.

REFERENCES

1. Allen, F. E., "Program Optimization" <u>Annual Review in Automatic Programming</u> , Vol. 5, Pergamon, New York, 1969.

2. Allen, F. E. and John Cocke, "A Catalogue of Optimizing Transformations" IBM Research Report RC-3548, September 1971.

3. Cocke, J. and J. T. Schwartz, "Programming Languages and Their Compilers" Preliminary Notes, Courant Institute of Mathematical Sciences, New York University, New York, April 1970.

4. Miller, R. E. and J. D. Rutledge, "Generating a Data Flow Model of a Program" IBM Technical Disclosure Bulletin, Vol. 8, No. 11, 1966, pp. 1550-1553.

A Method for Determining Program Data Relationships

F.E. Allen
IBM Thomas J. Watson Research Center
Yorktown Heights, New York

INTRODUCTION

Fundamental to the information required for program optimization, for the automatic detection of parallelism in programs, for the solution of some problems in extensible languages and for other related problems in the analysis and transformation of programs, is a knowledge of the data flow of the program being analyzed and transformed. The purpose of this paper is to outline a method for the automatic derivation of the data flow relationships which appear to exist in programs written in a high level, algorithmic language. Before presenting the derivation of the relationships we need to establish more precisely what data flow relationships we are interested in and how they are to be expressed.

CONTEXT AND PROBLEM STATEMENT

Our approach is to derive and express the data flow relationships in terms of the control flow graph [1,2] of the program. For the purposes of this paper the control flow graph, G, of a program is a connected, directed graph having a single entry node. G consists of a set of nodes, $N = \{n_1, n_2, \ldots n_\ell\}$, representing sequences of program instructions and a set of edges, E, of ordered pairs of nodes representing the flow of control in the usual way [1]. Exactly what a node represents is intentionally left vague.

The graph depicted in figure 1 has

N = {1,2,3,...7}, (the numbering is arbitrary) and

E = {(1,2), (2,3), (2,7), (3,4),...}

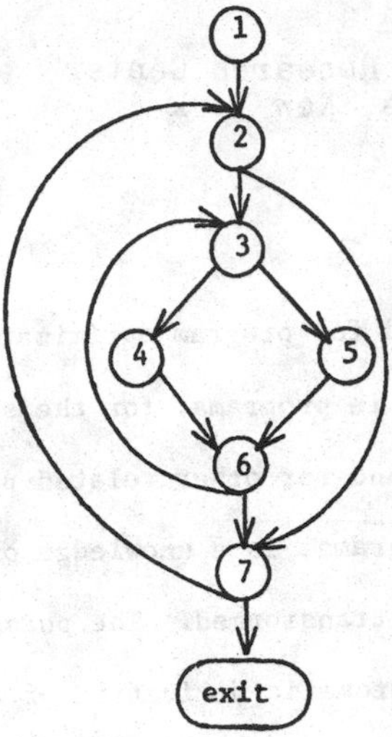

Figure 1

Standard graph theoretic terms such as path, immediate predecessor, etc. are used here without definition.

We can now more precisely describe the data flow problems we are interested in. There are two, the second being a refinement of the first. In the description which follows, the terms "definition" and "use" of "items" are not defined; they can be thought of as referring to the "storing into" and the "accessing or referencing of" "variables".

1. Definition - Use relationships. Given an item X used in a node n_i determine all definitions of X in other nodes of the graph

which can affect the particular use. Inversely, given an item X defined in node n_i determine all the uses of X in other nodes of the graph which can be affected by the given definition. Since the latter problem can be solved from the results obtained from the solution of the first problem we will not address it directly. As an example consider Figure 2 in which definitions of X (denoted by X^d) are assumed to exist in nodes 5 and 7 and uses (X^u) in nodes 2 and 4.

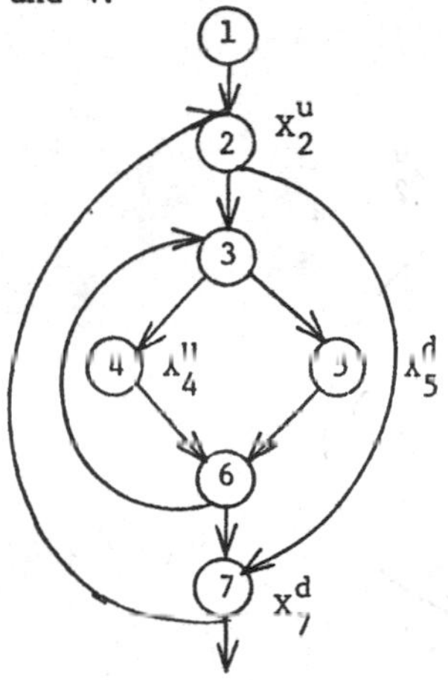

Figure 2

X_7^d can affect X_2^u and X_4^u but X_5^d can only affect X_4^u. We say that a def-use relationship exists between X_7^d and X_2^u (X_7^d - X_2^u), between X_7^d and X_4^u, etc.

Another concept which is useful is that of a definition "reaching" a node. A definition X_i^d is said to <u>reach</u> a node n_j if there is a path

$P = (n_i, \ldots n_j)$ such that there does not exist a node n_k on P which also contains a definition of the item X.

2. Live Paths. Given a definition X_i^d which affects uses $X_j^u, X_{j'}^u, \ldots$ determine all paths $P = \{(n_i \ldots n_j), (n_i \ldots n_{j'}), \ldots\}$ in which X_i^d reaches all nodes. A definition is said to be <u>live</u> in all nodes in all paths in P. The shaded nodes in Figure 3 show the nodes in which X_5^d is live.

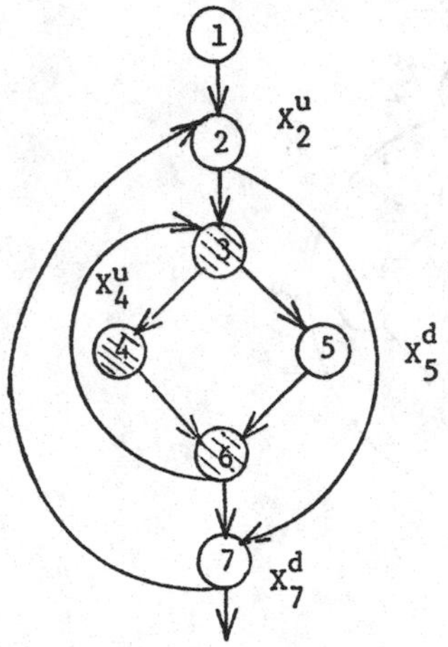

<u>Figure 3</u>

It should be noted that we have formulated the problems as determining the relationships between different nodes and further that the contents of a node is essentially unrestricted. Thus a node could represent an entire procedure.

The outline of the solution to the first problem is now given; the second problem is solved in a similar way but requires additional steps.

SOLUTION TO PROBLEM 1 (in outline form)

1. For each node, n_i, in the graph determine three sets U_i, D_i and P_i:

   U_i is the set of all uses X_i^u in n_i which can be affected by definitions outside n_i.

   D_i is the set of all definitions X_i^d in n_i which can affect uses outside n_i.

   P_i is the set of all definitions X_j^d $(j \neq i)$ which are not affected by definitions in n_i - i.e. the set of items not reset in n_i.

2. Determine the effects of each node on increasingly more global areas of the program. There are two cases

   2.1 G is acyclic. Establish a partial order on the nodes of G: $(n_1, n_2 \ldots n_\ell)$ such that $n_i < n_j$ if there is a path $(n_i \ldots n_j)$. An order satisfying the partial order for the nodes in the graph in Figure 4 is (1,3,2,5,4,6).

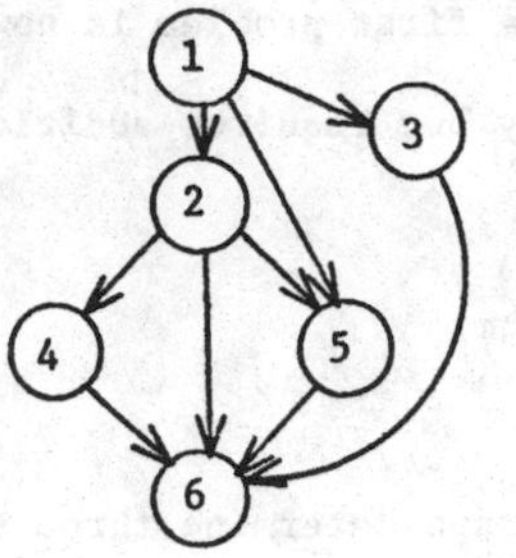

Figure 4

The partial order gives the order for determining the solution. At each node n_i the following 2 sets are created:

(1) R_i - the set of all definitions which reach n_i

(2) A_i - the set of all definitions available on exit from n_i.

Using D_i, the set of definitions which exist in each node, and P_i the R_i and A_i sets are created as follows:

(1) $R_1 = \phi$ (the empty set or any set of definitions known to be available)

(2) $A_i = D_i \cup (R_i \cap P_i)$ thus A_i is the set of definitions available from n_i either as a result of definitions (D_i) in n_i or as a result of definitions (R_i) which reached n_i and were not reset in n_i.

(3) $R_i = \bigcup_j A_j$ for all j which are immediate predecessors of n_i in the graph ($i > 1$).

Assuming we have expressed the elements of the sets so as to permit a definition of an item to be identified with a use of that item we can now immediately determine the def-use relationships by the following: $R_i \cap U_i$ gives the set of definitions in the program which affect uses in n_i.

2.2 G is a cyclic graph. In this case we cannot immediately determine a partial order which establishes an order for problem solution. The interval construct [1,2] of graphs is used to isolate subgraphs which can be partially ordered according to our criteria. (An interval is a maximal, single entry subgraph for which all closed paths contain the entry node.) Each interval can be expressed as a node, a new graph derived and another set of such intervals isolated. Proceeding in this way a problem solution order is established. Consider the graph in Figure 1. Figure 5 shows the graph G of Figure 1 and its sequence of derived graphs: (G^2, G^3, G^4).

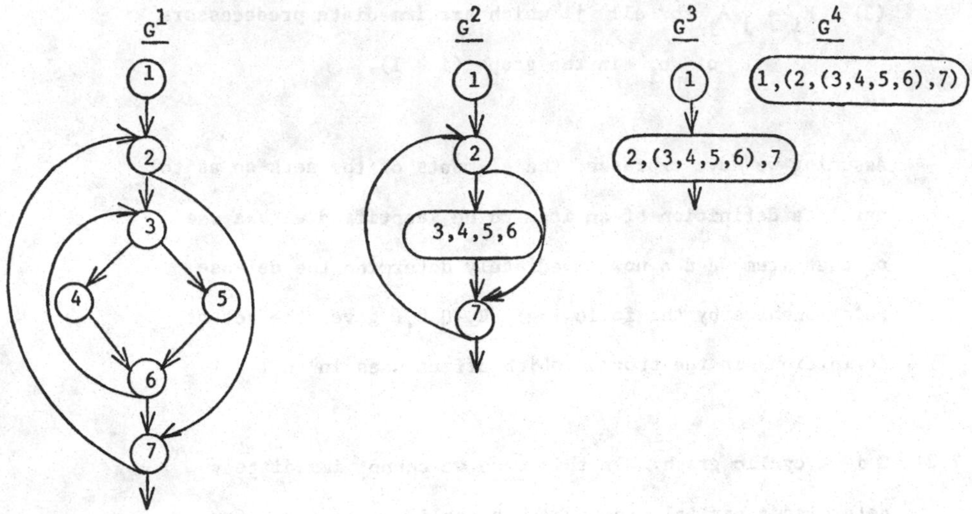

Figure 5

Assuming we have U_i, D_i and P_i for each n_i in G', the problem is to again determine the definitions R_i which can reach each n_i. Consider an interval (such as (3-4-5-6) in G^1). If the definitions which reach the first node in the interval, either from inside the interval or from outside the interval, are known then the solution given for the acyclic graph can be used to determine R_i for each node in the interval. The definitions R_h which reach the first node n_h in the interval from inside the interval are those available from all interval nodes which are immediate predecessors of the first node. For each interval then we obtain R_h by the following:

1) treat the interval as an acyclic graph with a partial ordering on the nodes established as before.

2) $R_1 = \phi$

3) Derive A_i and R_i as in 2.1

4) form $R_h = \bigcup_j A_j$ for all n_j which are in the interval and are immediate predecessors of the first node in the interval.

The remaining problem is to determine the definitions which reach the interval from outside the interval. In terms of the set of derived graphs, the definitions we are interested in are those which reached the node representing the interval in the higher order derived graph. If D_i and P_i were known for each node in each graph, then R_i could be determined for each node by first establishing the R_i for G^ℓ and then determining R_i for each $n_i \in G^{\ell-1}$. Assuming that D_i and P_i are known for each node in G^k we determine D_i and P_i for each node in G^{k+1}. D_i for $n_i \in G^{k+1}$ is simply the union of all definitions which can reach the exit nodes in the interval in G^k which n_i represents. P_i for the interval can be determined by a method analogous to that for D_i. The overall approach can now be given:

(1) For each graph (G^1, $G^2 \ldots G^\ell$) determine

a) R_h for each interval and

b) D_i and P_i for each node (for G^1 these are assumed given)

(2) For each graph ($G^\ell, G^{\ell-1}, \ldots G^1$) determine R_i for each node in each interval by first determining the definitions available on entry and then applying the constructions given in 2.1. The

information available on entry is $R_h \cup R_k$ where n_k is the node representing the interval in the next higher order graph.

Having the R_i we can again form the def-use information from the U_i. An interesting variant in the method outlined above is to collect sets of U_i for nodes in higher order graphs. This allows us to obtain def-use relationships in increasingly more global contexts.

REFERENCES

[1] Allen, F.E. and J. Cocke, "Graph Theoretic Constructs for Program Control Flow Analysis", IBM Research Report RC 3923, July, 1972.

[2] Allen, F. E., "A Basis for Program Optimization", Proceedings of the IFIPS Congress 71, North Holland Publishing Co., Amsterdam, Holland.

TOWARDS AUTOMATICAL CONSTRUCTION OF PARALLEL PROGRAMS

V.E. KOTOV

I.

Automatical construction of parallel programs (desequention or parallelisation) is a main problem in parallel programming and the success of multiprocessor system implementation depends on the solution of this problem. The problem is that it is difficult for the programmer to take advantage of the opportunities given by the proposed methods and languages for parallel programming which allow him to write the problem directly in a parallel form, especially in the case of high-parallel programming. The main reasons for this are as follows:

1.) The aim of parallel computations is the solution of so-called "large problems". The analysis and registration of large amounts of complicated information are necessary to write high-parallel programs for these problems.

2.) It is easier for man to conceive and control the course of the problem solution written in the form of the sequential algorithm because of man's habit and way of thinking.

3.) The rich stock of sequential programs and algorithms is stored and it is not possible and reasonable not to use this stock immediately after the implementation of multi-processor systems.

4.) The "desired" parallelism brought by a programmer to a program is not correlated, generally speaking, with the "real" parallelism of the execution which depends on situations in the system. Whatever instructions about parallel execution were in a program, the last decision on what to do in parallel is taken by the system. These instructions may only facilitate the system without inhibiting the increase of execution parallelism (this increase of parallelism we call desequention).

2 - In theoretical consideration of the desequention a number of interdependent problems arise:

1.) The choice of formal program models (schemata). The desequention can be studied in the framework of one model as, for example, in [7]. The initial program is parallel in this case and after desequention a "more parallel" program is obtained. More often two models are used: the first model represents a sequential program, the second one represents a parallel program. It is desirable to have such sequential models which represent the class of real programs as far as possible and such parallel models which allow the natural parallelism of the problem to be conveyed to a maximum degree (not every method of parallel programming gives such an opportunity). Most sequential models used till now for desequention are simple enough - usually they correspond to programs without cycles or with strong restrictions on the cycles' structure. The most general classes of parallelised programs were studied in [3], [4], [7].

2.) The choice of definitions of the program determinacy and equivalency. It is known that for the same initial data but for different executions the parallel programs could generate different computations, i.e. different histories, time schedules of the executions of elementary program fragments (operators). In other words a parallel program P puts into correspondence with every initial data set V_o, the set $P(V_o)$ of different computations. If or any V_o all computations of $P(V_o)$ are equivalent, the program P is called determinate. It is natural that just determinate parallel programs must be obtained after desequention and, besides, they must be equivalent to the initial sequential programs. The selection of the proper definition of the computation equivalency both for determinacy and for program equivalency determines to a considerable extent the success in desequention.

3.) Formal definition of the parallelism (asynchronity) degree. The equivalent parallel programs could differ by the degree of parallelism. This notion is rather ambiguous and the two methods to give more precise definitions are known.

The first method to compare the programs with the help of the "computation width", i.e. maximal number of parallel executed operators. This method of parallelism comparison is not good for describing a most important property of parallel programs their efficiency of "filling" the multiprocessor system.

The second method is comparison of parallel programs by asynchronity, i.e. by a variety of the computations set generated by the program for the same initial data. We say that program P_1 is more (or less, or as) asynchronous than (as) program P_2 if for any V_o the set $P_1(V_o)$ is more (or less, or as) "rich" as the set $P_2(V_o)$. In particular the inclusion of sets is used for comparison of the $P_1(V_o)$ and $P_2(V_o)$ sets in [7], comparison of the ones is done more subly in [5]. Asynchronity of the parallel program is a more interesting characteristic than parallelism. Firstly, for the known definitions of asynchronity comparison [5], [7] from the fact that program P_1 is not less asynchronous than program P_2 follows that P_1 is not less parallel than P_2. Secondly, asynchronity well characterizes the property of the program to "fill" the multiprocessor system. Therefore, below we shall deal with asynchronity of programs but not with their parallelism.

4.) Maximally asynchronous parallel programs.

After introducing methods of asynchronity comparison it is natural to demand from algorithms of desequention that they should obtain more asynchronous programs as far as possible.

If $\mathcal{P}$ is a class of equivalent programs, then partially ordering programs according to asynchronity, it is possible to single out maximally asynchronous programs in this class. There arises a problem: Does an algorithm exist which allows any program from $\mathcal{P}$ to obtain the maximally asynchronous program in this class?

In [7] this problem is solved for some classes of parallel programs.

One may formulate the problem differently if two distinct classes of models are used for desequention: $\mathcal{P}$ - for sequential programs and $\mathcal{P}'$- for parallel ones.

Does an algorithm exist which allows any sequential program P from $\mathcal{P}$ to obtain a parallel P' maximally asynchronous in class $\mathcal{P}'' \subset \hat{\mathcal{P}}'$ of programs equivalent to program P ?

In such a formulation the problem was solved in [3], [4]. From the maximally asynchronous program definition it is seen that it is closely connected with definitions of program determinacy and equivalency (this fact is of great importance from the methodological side).

5.) Analysis of potential parallelism (asynchronity) of sequential programs and algorithms.

After selecting models of sequential and parallel programs, formal definitions of determinacy, equivalency and maximal asynchronity of programs, the desequention problem is two-fold:

a) analysis of intrinsic potential parallelism (asynchronity) of sequential programs;

b) construction of the parallel program on the basis of this analysis.

Generally speaking, the first problem is not connected with the method of parallel programs organization, and it can be solved in the framework of sequential models. The solution of the second problem to a greater extent depends on the chosen method of parallel programming.

Analysis of intrinsic parallelism or asynchronity of sequential programs makes the relationship between some relations on the set of certain program elements and the possibility of operator parallel execution. This relationship may be simple for certain cases (see, for example, conditions of parallelism of operators following each other which are suggested in [2]), though in the general case it is difficult and even impossible to establish an explicit relationship.

Below we shall describe models and some results obtained in connection with a research of the desequention problem at the Computer Centre of the Siberian Branch of the USSR Academy of Sciences.

II.

1 - Sequential and parallel program models.

1.1. Program models are constructed with the use of the following basic indeterminable notions:

a) values;

b) variables;

c) operations;

d) inputs and outputs.

An <u>Array</u> with dimension ℓ and bounds $k_1, k_2, \ldots, k_\ell$ is a function d which puts variable $d(n_1, n_2, \ldots, n_\ell)$ into correspondence with a finite ordered set of natural numbers $n_1, n_2, \ldots, n_\ell$ such that $1 \le n_i \le k_i$ for all $1 \le i \le \ell$.

The <u>Memory</u> is a set of variables and arrays.

The <u>Interpreted</u> memory is a memory, each variable m of which is brought into correspondence with some set of values V(m).

With every operation f the following are associated:

a) two finite ordered sets - a set of inputs I_f and a set of outputs O_f, each input and output being correspondent to only one operation;

b) a finite set of consecutive natural numbers $1,2,\ldots,k_f$ called <u>alternatives</u>.

A <u>simple operator</u> a on a memory M is a pair (f_a, R_a), where f_a is an operation and R_a is a function bringing a variable of M into correspondence with each input of I_{f_a} and output O_{f_a}.

The set $I_a = R_a(I_{f_a})$ is the set of input variables of operator a, and the set $O_a = R_a(O_{f_a})$ is that of output variables.

The function R_a is always such that if $i_1 \neq i_2$ then $R_a(i_1) \neq R_a(i_2)$ and if $O_1 \neq O_2$ then $R_a(O_1) \neq R_a(O_2)$ where i_1, i_2 are inputs, and O_1, O_2 are outputs of operation f_a.

<u>Interpretation</u> of a simple operator a (on an interpreted memory M) is a pair of functions corresponding to its operation f_a:

a) $$h_a : \underset{m\varepsilon I_a}{X} V(m) \rightarrow \underset{m\varepsilon O_a}{X} V(m) ;$$

b) $$g_a : \underset{m\varepsilon I_a}{X} V(m) \rightarrow \{1,2,\ldots,k_a\} \text{ where } k_a = k_{f_a} .$$

If $k_a=1$, we shall not include the function g_a in interpretation; if $O_a=\emptyset$, we shall not include the function h_a either.

An interpreted simple operator is a simple operator together with some of its interpretation.

The (interpreted) <u>operator</u> differs from a simple (interpreted) one in that the function R_a may put arrays into correspondence with inputs and outputs. If an array with dimension ℓ corresponds to the input (output), then ℓ variables, called <u>indices</u> of the array, also correspond to that input (output). The index values when interpreting are always natural numbers. Setting indices values of all operator arrays, we obtain a simple operator which we call an operator <u>exposure</u>.

By <u>execution</u> of the interpreted operator a an memory M we mean the following sequence of actions taking place in discrete time:

a) some current value of memory $V_t(M) \in \underset{m \in M}{X} V(m)$ is supposed to correspond with every moment of time t.

b) Two moments of time $\bar{t}$ (initiation) and $\bar{\bar{t}}$ (termination) are associated with execution. At moment t the operator fetches the current value of the indices, and by these values it determinates concrete variables corresponding to the inputs and outputs. Thus, the simple operator a' is formed at moment $\bar{t}$. At the same moment of the variables corresponding to the inputs.

c) According to these values, the values of the output variables and an alternative are calculated with the help of functions $h_{a'}$ and $g_{a'}$: at moment $\bar{\bar{t}}$, the output variables in memory assume the calculated values. It is possible that $\bar{t} = \bar{\bar{t}}$.

Considered below are program schemata which represent quadruples $P=(M_i,M_c,B,C)$ where

M_i - data memory;

M_c - interpreted memory called a <u>control</u> memory, the value of its variables - natural numbers - its initial value $V_o^c \in \underset{m \in M_c}{X} V(m)$ being given;

B - base (see below);

C - control (see below).

Module b on memories M_1 and M_c where $M_1 \cap M_c \neq \emptyset$ includes:

a) an operator a_b on memory M_1 (data operator);

b) $\ell+1$ interpreted operators $u_o, u_1, \ldots, u_{k_a}$ are (control operators) on memory M_c where k_a is the alternative number of operator a.

It is also assumed that:

a) all control operators have just one alternative (no function g);

b) indices of all arrays of all module operators belong to M_c.

A module is shown schematically in the figure below. If memory and data operators are interpreted, then the module is also interpreted.

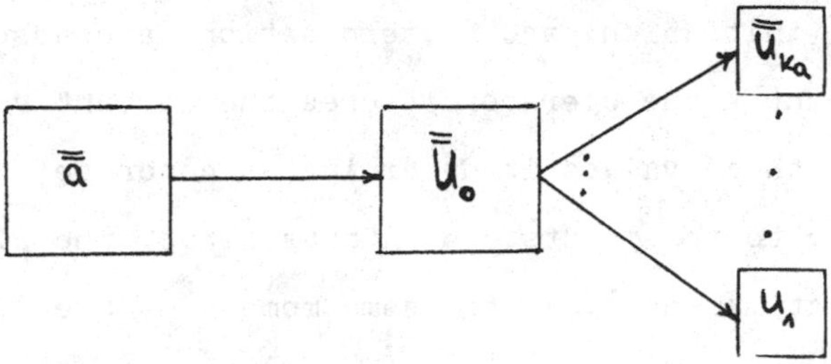

The interpreted module execution consists of the following sequence of actions:

a) with the module execution are associated two moments of time $\underline{t}$ (initiation) and $\bar{t}$ (termination) which are simultaneously initiation $\underline{t}_a$ and termination $\bar{t}_a$ of the execution of data operator a of this module;

b) if the module contains control operator u_o, then $\underline{t}_{u_o} = \bar{t}_{u_o} = \bar{t}_a$;

c) if the module involves control operator u_ℓ, where $1 \le \ell \le k_a$, then this operator is executed only in the case when operator a execution is completed by alternative ℓ; besides, $\bar{t}_{u_\ell} = \bar{\bar{t}}_{u_\ell} = \bar{\bar{t}}_a$.

The interpreted base on memories M_i and M_c is a set of interpreted modules on these memories (the same functions h and g are associated with the identical operations).

Below described schemata of sequential and asynchronous programs are only distinguished by control. Interpretation J of scheme P is the pair (J_B, V_o^i), where J_B is the base interpretation, V_o^i the initial value of memory M_i.

1.2. As a sequential program scheme we use a flow-chart $T = (M_i, M_c, B, G)$, where $G = (B, \Gamma)$ is a directed finite graph with one initial vertex (arcs do not enter it) and with one terminal vertex (arcs do not start from it). The graph vertices set is a base B on M_i and M_c. Arcs the number of which equal to the number of alternatives of data operator of module b start from vertex b; these arcs are denoted by alternatives. From any vertex there is a path to a terminal vertex.

Connected with the interpreted program scheme is the system executing this scheme. Rules of the flow-chart execution with interpretation $J = (J_B, V_o^i)$ by the sequential system are as follows:

a) $V_{t=o}(M_i) = V_o^i$, $V_{t=o}(M_c) = V_o^c$.

b) At the moment of time t=0 the execution of the initial module begins; this execution is completed at the arbitrary moment of time $\bar{\bar{t}}_{in}$.

c) If at a moment of time $\bar{t}_b$ the execution of the module b has terminated and the calculated alternative of this module's data operator is ℓ, then at an arbitrary moment of time $\bar{t}_{b'} > \bar{t}_b$ the execution begins of the module b'^{b} into which the arc with number ℓ from b leads.

d) the whole scheme execution is completed by that of the terminal module.

The problem of desequention was studied for simple flow-charts in which:

a) $M_c = \emptyset$;

b) each module is a simple operator.

Simple schemata are the type of schemata most commonly used in theoretical programming.

However, in the process of simple flow-charts desequention one must use flow-charts of the more common type.

1.3. As a parallel program scheme we use the <u>asynchronous scheme</u> (<u>A - scheme</u>) $X = (M_1, M_c, B, Y)$, where Y is a set of <u>trigger functions</u>. The trigger function is an interpreted operator on memory M_c, function h not entering interpretation and alternatives being two. In other words, the trigger function is a two-valued predicate on memory M_c (let its values - "true" and "false" - correspond to alternatives 1 and 2). Set Y is such that each module b from B is in one-to-one correspondence with trigger function y of Y.

Pair x = (y,b) we call a <u>block</u>.

We have not demanded these sets B and Y be finite as this would lead to the undesirable narrowing of the A-schemata class. However, in order not to deal with infinite schemata let us introduce "dynamism" into the A-schemata as follows. The <u>array of blocks</u> x $(m_1,\dots,m_n)$ is a block together with some singled out indices $m_1, m_2,\dots,m_n$ of arrays entering this block. These indices we call <u>parameters</u> of the blocks array. The array of blocks x $(m_1,\dots,m_n)$ is a function which associates with every parameters value $v_1,\dots,v_n$ a set of blocks $\{x\ (1,\dots,1),\dots,\ x\ (v_1,\dots,v_n)\}$ being obtained by substitution in the trigger function and module of all possible combinations of indices - paramters which do not exceed $v_1,\dots,v_n$ correspondingly.

Evidently one can define the interpreted A-scheme . Rules of execution by <u>asynchronous</u> system of the interpreted A-scheme with interpretation $J = (J_B, V_o^i)$ are as follows:

a) $V_{t=o}\ (M_i) = V_o^i,\ V_{t=o}\ (M_c) - M_o^c$.

b) At each of the arbitrary moments of discrete time $t_1<t_2<\dots<t_k<\dots$ checkings of the values of trigger functions occur (with values of input variables by a unit of time earlier) at all those blocks whose modules are not executed at the moment. In this case each array of blocks generates some set of blocks according to current values of its parameters, and trigger functions of these blocks are checked on a par with others.

c) An arbitrary subset is selected from blocks, the trigger functions values of which turned out to be equal to "true", and modules executions of these blocks are initiated. Each block terminations occur independently throughout arbitrary time irrespective of other blocks terminations.

d) The A-scheme execution is completed then and only then, when none of the modules is executed while checking trigger functions, the values all of the latter being equal to "false".

2 - Determinacy and asynchronity of the program schemata.

2.1. For formulization of program schemata determinacy and equivalency let us introduce the formal notions of computation and computations equivalency.

A computation N on memory M is a set of triples $(a, t_a^j, \bar{t}_a^j)$ where a is a simple operator on memory M, t_a^j and $\bar{t}_a^j$ are time moments, and j is a natural member. In addition,

a) $\forall_a \forall_j (t_a^j < \bar{t}_a^j < t_a^{j+1})$;

b) $\forall_a \forall_j ((a, t_a^j, \bar{t}_a^j) \in N \rightarrow (\forall_{j'} | j' < j)((a, t_a^{j'}, \bar{t}_a^{j'}) \in N)))$.

The computation process may be represented as some time schedule of repeated executions of simple operators where t_a^j is the initiation of the j-th execution of the simple operator a (j-th entry of a in N) and $\bar{t}_a^j$ is the termination of its j-th execution. From the above program schemata execution it is seen that the sequential system S_S associates with every interpreted flow-chart T a set of computations $\mathcal{N} = S_A(T^J)$ on the memory M_1, and the asynchronous system S_A associates with every interpreted A-scheme X a set of computations $\mathcal{N} = S_A(X^J)$ on the memory M_1. These computations are formed by entries of simple operators-exposures of data operators of modules.

The data-flow graph $G_N = (\mathcal{D}, \Gamma_N)$ of computation N is a directed multigraph between vertices of which and operator entries in N there exists the following one-to-one correspondence H:

1) Each vertex $d = H((a, t_a^j, \bar{t}_a^j))$ is marked by the operation of the operator a.

2) From vertex $d_1 = H((a_1, t_{a_1}^j, \bar{t}_{a_1}^j))$
   to vertex $d_2 = H((a_2, t_{a_2}^p, \bar{t}_{a_2}^p))$ an arc marked by a pair of numbers (m, n) exists if :

   a) $R_{a_1}(O_m) = R_{a_2}(i_n)$ where O_m - the m-th output of the operator a_1 operation, i_n - the n-th input of the operator a_2 operation;

b) $\bar{t}^{j}_{a_1} < \bar{t}^{p}_{a_2}$;

c) there is not an entry $(a_3, \bar{t}^{q}_{a_3}, \bar{t}^{q}_{a_3})$ in N such that

$\bar{t}^{j}_{a_1} \leq \bar{t}^{q}_{a_3} < \bar{t}^{q}_{a_2}$ and $R_{a_1}(O_m) \in O_{a_3}$.

3) From vertex $d = H((a, \bar{t}^{j}_{a}, \bar{t}^{j}_{a}))$ there exists an arc marked by one number m which does not lead to any of the graph vertices, if in N there is no entry $(a', \bar{t}^{p}_{a'}, \bar{t}^{p}_{a'})$ such that $\bar{t}^{j}_{a} < \bar{t}^{p}_{a'}$, and $R_a(O_m) \in I_{a'}$ or $\bar{t}^{j}_{a} < \bar{t}^{p}_{a'}$ and $R_a(O_m) \in O_{a'}$.

Two computations are <u>equivalent</u> if their data-flow graphs are identical.

2.2. Scheme P is <u>determinate</u> (for system S) if for any interpretation J all computations of set $S(P^J)$ are equivalent.

Any flow-chart is determinate for a sequential system. The A-scheme may be indeterminate, in [5] a determinacy problem of the A-schemata is studied.

Two schemata P_1 and P_2 for system S_1 and, correspondingly, S_2 are given. The pair of interpretations of these schemata $J_1 = (J_{B_1}, V_o^{i_1})$ and, accordingly, $J_2 = (J_{B_2}, V_o^{i_2})$ are <u>co-ordinated</u> if interpretations of operators with the identical operations coincide for both schemes, and between variables of the memories M_{i_1}, and M_{i_2} a correspondence exists such that the values related by this relation of variables in $V_o^{i_1}$ and $V_o^{i_2}$ are identical. Then, determinate schemata P_1 and P_2 are <u>equivalent</u> if for any pair of coordinated interpretations J_1 and J_2, any computation of set $S_1(P_1^{J_1})$ is equivalent to that of set $S_2(P_2^{J_2})$. (One could say "if a computation" as schemata are determinate.)

3 - Maximally asynchronous A-schemata .

3.1. Computations N_1 and N_2 are <u>similar</u> if for any entry $(a, \xi^j_a, \bar{\xi}^j_a)$ of N_1 entry $(a', \xi^p_{a'}, \bar{\xi}^p_{a'})$ is found in N_2 such that $f_a = f_{a'}$, $\xi^j_a = \xi^p_{a'}$, $\bar{\xi}^j_a = \bar{\xi}^p_{a'}$, and vice versa.

Let $\mathcal{P}$ be a class of equivalent schemata for system S. We shall say that scheme P is maximally <u>asynchronous</u> in class $\mathcal{P}$ if for any scheme $P' \in \mathcal{P}$ and for any pair of <u>co-ordinated</u> interpretations J and J', for any computation in set $S(P'^{J'})$ there exists similar computation in set $S(P^J)$.

If X_T is a class of all A- schemata equivalent to flow chart T then we refer to A-scheme , maximally asynchronous in class X_T, as maximally asynchronous with respect to T.

In [4] the following theorem was proved:

<u>Theorem 1</u>. There exists an algorithm which for any simple flow-chart constructs an equivalent maximally asynchronous A-scheme .

(There is the following restriction: all <u>chains</u> of the flow-chart (paths in graph G out of the initial vertex to the terminal one) are <u>possible</u>, i.e. there exists an interpretation J such that in set S_S, (T^J) is a computation in which operator entries follow in the same order as in a chain.)

But in [4] the definition of A-scheme, maximally asynchronous with respect to a flow-chart differs from the above one. The definition in [4] considers information on schemata which one can not receive from computations. It has been done for the direct substantiation of the algorithm of desequention. It is necessary to show that both old and new definitions of maximal asynchronity are equivalent.

3.2. The definition of A-scheme which is maximally asynchronous with respect to the flow-chart in [4] uses the property of the flow-chart to include the whole information on these connections between modules which restrict the possible parallel execution of these modules. At the level of computations data connections are fixed; hence, one cannot judge the possible asynchronity of the constructed A-scheme on the basis of data-flow graphs of the given flow-chart computations. As a characteristic of the flow-chart potential asynchronity (which will be realized in A-schemata), the notion of the connections graph of a computation in which the above connections are reflected, is introduced in paper [4]. Logical connections fix the presence of control information forming computations; commutational connections fix relations between the modules changing the indices value and the modules whose arrays use those indices.

So, the connections graph of computations N is a directed graph $\bar{G}_N = (\mathcal{D}, \bar{\Gamma}_N)$ between vertices and operators entries in N there exists one-to-one correspondence E such that:

a) An arc leads from vertex $d_1 = E(n_1)$ to vertex $d_2 = E(n_2)$ if between n_1 and n_2 there is a data connection (i.e. in data-flow graph G_N an arc leads from $H(n_1)$ to $H(n_2)$).

b) An arc leads from $d_1 = E(n_1)$ to $d_2 = E(n_2)$ if n_1 is essential for n_2 (see below).

c) An arc leads from $d_1 = E(n_1)$ to $d_2 = E(n_2)$ if n_1 commutes n_2 (see below).

The relation "commute" has no place for operator entries in computations of simple flow-charts as the latter include only simple operators. In A-schemata computations obtained by the desequention algorithm of [4] always imply the first two. Therefore, we shall not take it into account in the future.

The relation "is essential" is to be differently defined for computations of flow-charts and A-schemata.

For flow-charts:

Arc (a_k, a_ℓ) and operator a_k are <u>strictly essential</u> for operator a_i in the flow-chart if:

a) any path in graph G from a_ℓ to a terminal vertex lies through a_i;

b) there exists a path in graph G from a_k to the terminal vertex passing through a_i.

In the graph below operator a_1 is strictly essential for operator a_2, operator a_3 - for a_1 and for itself. The variable m <u>route</u> beginning in vertex a_k of the flow-chart and terminating in vertex a_n is a path $(a_k, \dots, a_n)$ in G such that $m \in O_{a_k}$ and $m \in I_{a_n}$, and m is not an output variable of any way-operator en route.

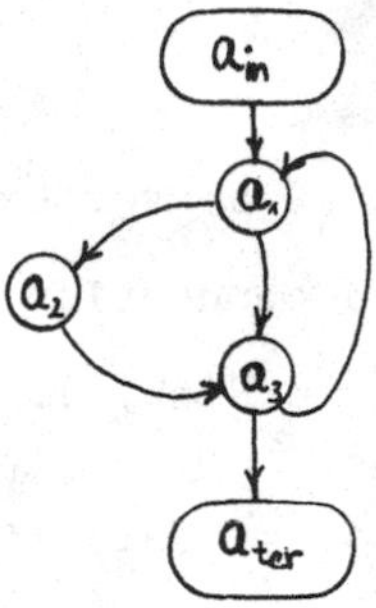

<u>Operator</u> a_k is essential for operator a_i in a flow-chart if a_k is strictly essential for a_i or for some operator which is the beginning of the route terminating in a_i.

Finally, entry n_k^j of operator a_k in computation N of simple flow-chart T is essential for entry n_i^p of operator a_i in N if the operator a_k is essential for the a_i in T.

For A-schemata:

Entry n_k^j of operator a_k in computation N of A-scheme X will be considered to be essential for entry n_i^p of operator a_i in the case when the results of the entry n_k^j execution directly influence the trigger-function value of the block-having operator a_i. Strict definition of this relation is given in [4].

We shall say that entry n_2 depends on entry n_1 in N if in the connections graph $\bar{G}_N$ there is a path from n_1 to n_2.

We shall say that potential asynchronities of equivalent program schemata P_1 and P_2 are equal if for any pair of coordinated interpretations J_1 and J_2, for any pair of computations N_1 and N_2 such that $N_1 \in S_1(P_1^{J_1})$ and $N_2 \in S_2(P_2^{J_2})$, and for two pairs of entries (n_1, n_2) in N_1 and (n_1', n_2') in N_2 corresponding to each other in virtue of N_1 and N_2 equivalency, the following is true: n_2 depends on n_1 in N_1 if and only if n_2' depends on n_1' in N_2.

The A-scheme is maximally asynchronous with respect to the equivalent flow-chart if their potential asynchronities are equal. This is the definition of maximal asynchronity from [4].

Theorem 2. The A-scheme is maximally asynchronous in the sense of [4] with respect to the equivalent flow-chart T if and only if it is maximally asynchronous in the class of all A-schemata equivalent to T.

We do not produce here the whole proof of the theorem but give some explanation. Let the A-scheme X be maximally asynchronous with respect to the flow-chart T in the sense of [4]. We must show that it is maximally asynchronous in the class $\mathcal{X}_T$. Suppose that is not so, then there exists an A-scheme X in $\mathcal{X}_T$, a pair of coordinated interpretations (J, J') and computation N' in $S_A(X'^{J'})$ for which there is no similar computation in $S_A(X^J)$. It is possible only in the case if in N' there exists a pair of entries n_1 and n_2 possessing the following properties:

a) in data-flow graph G_N where $N \in S_A(X'^{J'})$ or $N \in S_A(X^J)$ these entries are mutually independent, i.e. there is no path in G_N from n_1 to n_2, and from n_2 to n_1 (one should say of entries pairs corresponding to each other in virtue of computations equivalency, but for simplicity we shall consider them as of the same pair).

b) in computations of $S_A(X^J)$, entry n_1 is essential for n_2;

c) in computation N', entry n_1 is not essential for n_2.

Then in all computations from $S_A(X^J)$ initiation n_2 occurs only after termination n_1, but in computations $S_A(X'^{J'})$ there can be initiation n_2 before termination n_1 (for example, in N').

From a) and b) it follows that there exists interpretation $\bar{J}$ of scheme X and computation $\bar{N}$ in $S_A(X^J)$ coinciding up to termination n_1 with some computation $N \in S_A(X^J)$ but not including entry n_2 unlike the computation N

From b) it follows, however, that for interpretation J' of the A-scheme coordinated with X' computations from $S_A(X'^{J'})$ include entry n_2. But that contradicts the equivalency of schemata X and X':

From maximal asynchronity of the A-scheme in class $\mathcal{X}_T$ it follows that it is maximally asynchronous with respect to T in the sense of [4], in virtue of the A-schemata and asynchronous systems properties.

3.3. And one more detail to theorem 1:

The notion of schemata equivalency from paper [4] does not coincide with the above one in p. 2.2. Namely, data-control graphs have been used in [4] instead of data graphs of computations. These graphs represent data-flow with added control arcs marking the fact that one of the entries is essential for the other. However, it may be shown here, as well as in the case of maximal asynchronity that the two definitions of equivalency are identical.

4 - Algorithm of desequention

Algorithm of desequention of simple flow-charts suggested in [4] enables to obtain the maximally asynchronous A-schemata. This algorithm is constructed in such a way that it would be possible to develop practical algorithms of desequention. Moreover, in detail it demands substantial completing, as yet. In particular, algorithm complexity greatly increases for flow-charts with a complicated structure of cycles. That is why in practical algorithms of desequention in these cases it will be necessary to use compromised decisions to refuse attaining maximal asynchronity in favour of simple and fast algorithms. It should be noted that in [4] when analysing some relations on the set of schemata elements, only evaluation of complexity of this analysis is obtained but practically suitable algorithms of analysis are not proposed.

The desequention algorithm from [4] involves two stages. At the first stage, simple flow-charts are transformed into equivalent <u>adapted</u> flow-charts (not simple already in the general case).

Scheme P is adapted if for any interpretation, for any $N \in S(P^J)$, and for any pair of entries n and n' the following condition holds: if set $O_a \cap O_{a'} \cup I_a \cap O_{a'} \cup O_a \cap I_a$ is not empty (where a is an operator of entry n, a' is that of entry n') then, either n depends on n' or n' depends on n in N.

The adapted scheme does not include restrictions for possible changing of the order of operator execution arising due to memory allocation. In connection with this there can be module-to-module transformation of the adapted flow-chart. In this case its modules without a change enter the A-scheme setting up a "frame" of trigger functions and control operators.

The adapted flow-charts obtained by the algorithm from [4] have the same potential asynchronity as the initial flow-chart. As such transformation requires, in general, the increase of memory volume, saving memory economy is provided for.

At the second stage of desequention adapted flow-charts are transformed into the equivalent maximally asynchronous A-schemata.

As an illustration we describe the particular case: desequention of simple adapted flow-chart T without cycles.

Denote by A_{jk} the set of all operators of T which are beginnings of those routes of a variable corresponding to the k-th input of operator a_j, which terminate in operator a_j.

We shall call arc (a_k, a_ℓ) in graph G <u>supplemental</u> for vertex a_i relative to vertex a_j if any path $(a_\ell, \ldots, a_j)$ in G does not include a_i, but there exists path $(a_k, \ldots, a_j)$, involving a_i.

For graph arcs we introduce one more designation: (a_s, t) is an arc with the ordinal number t, starting from operator a_s.

We organize control memory M_c bringing control variable α_j with values 0 and 1 into correspondence with each operator a_j of the flow-chart T and also, control variable β_{jt} with values 0 and 1 into correspondence with every arc (a_j, t) if from operator a_j more then one arc begins. Control variable α_o will correspond to a fictitious "initial-operator".

The interpreted control operator u_o for operator a_j will be: $\alpha_j := 1$.

If from operator a_j $n > 1$ arcs start, then n control operators u_ℓ are put into correspondence with it where $1 \leq \ell \leq n$. Operator u_ℓ is: $\beta_{j\ell} := 1$.

Let the input set of variables from I_{a_j} have the length n.

The trigger function y_i representing conjunction of n+1 predicates corresponds to operator a_j:

$$y_i = P_o \,\&\, P_1 \,\&\, P_2 \,\&\, \dots \,\&\, P_n .$$

Predicate P_o is $\alpha_j < \sum_{(a_s,t)\in U} \beta_{st}$ where U is a set of all arcs strictly essential for operator a_j in G (see 3.2.).

Predicate P_r $(1 \leq r \leq n)$ corresponds to the r-th variable of the set I_{a_j} and also is a conjunction of predicates:

$$P_r = p_{r1} \,\&\, p_{r2} \,\&\dots\&\, p_{rm} ,$$

where p_{ri} $(1 \leq i \leq m)$ corresponds to operator a_i of the set A_{jr}.

Predicate p_{ri} is $d_i < \sum_{(a_s,t)\in U'} \beta_{st} + \alpha_i$, where U is a set of arcs supplemental for a_i relative to a_j. Initial values of all control variables, except α_o are supposed to be equal to 0. The initial value α_o is equal to 1.

The obtained set of block forms the maximally asynchronous A-scheme equivalent to the flow-chart T.

The adapted flow-charts desequention in the general case occurs similarly to the above transforming, but predicates p_{ri} and control operators are much more complicated.

5 - Immediate problems in desequention from the point of view of parallel programming practice

a) Developing practical algorithms of analysis of data and control dependencies in simple flow-charts: described algorithms are either applicable to particular cases of flow-charts [2], or unsuitable for practice because they take too much time [4]. Compromised decisions with rough analysis and usage of heuristic methods are necessary.

b) Flow-charts desequention, data operators of which are not simple: In the general approach it is difficult to expect simple and quick solutions here. Investigations of particular cases due to standartisation of control operators give a greater perspective.

c) Introduction into flow-charts of formal equivalents of such notions as procedures and references.

d) "Computer experiments" including the polishing of details of desequention algorithms with the use of computers, collection of statistical information on those properties of real sequential programs which are interesting from the desequention point of view, simulation and a comparative statistical evaluation of parallel computations performed by programs which are obtained after desequention, a creation of experimental algorithms of desequention oriented on existing sequential programming languages.

REFERENCES

[1] KOTOV, V.E., NARINYANI, A.S. "Asynchronous Computational Processes on Memory", Kibernetika, No. 3, pp. 64-71, Kiev, 1966.

[2] BERNSTEIN, A.J. "Analysis of Programs for Parallel Processing", IEEE Transactions on Electronic Computers, vol. EC-15, No. 5, pp. 757-763, Oct. 1966.

[3] KOTOV, V.E., NARINYANI, A.S. "On Transformation of Sequential Programs into Asynchronous Parallel Programs", Proceedings of IFIP Congress 68, North-Holland-Co., Amsterdam, 1969, pp.351-357.

[4] KOTOV, V.E., "Transformation of Flow-Charts into Asynchronous Programs", Cand. of Sci. Thesis, Novosibirsk, 1970.

[5] NARINYANI, A.S., "Asynchronous Computational Processes on Memory", Cand. of Sci. Thesis, Novosibirsk, 1970.

[6] VOLANSKY, S.A. "Graph Model Analysis and Implementation of Computational Sequences", Ph. D. Thesis, School of Engineering and Applied Sciences, University of California, Los Angeles, June 1970.

[7] KELLER, R.M. "On Maximally Parallel Schemata", IEEE Conference Record of the 11th Annual Symposium on Switching and Automata Theory, Oct. 1970, pp.32-50.

A Calculus for the Mathematical Theory of Computation

by Robin Milner

Introduction

The purpose of this paper is to describe a calculus in which many of the important concepts in the Mathematical Theory of Computation may be formally expressed, and in which formal proofs of assertions concerning these concepts may be carried out. There are two distinct reasons for constructing such a calculus. First, it provides a framework in which such assertions may be represented both precisely and elegantly. Second, it enables the proofs of such assertions to be checked by machine. Thus, we aim to achieve a goal formulated by McCarthy [8].

To indicate the particular calculus which we present, consider some assertions in the Theory of Computation which demand formal proof. The most obvious is the assertion that a program is correct. By this we may mean either (1) that the program computes a function for which we have an independent definition, or (2) that its input and output satisfy some given relation. Furthermore, we should like to be able to assert this for programs in an arbitrary programming language.

An important special case of program correctness, which falls into category (2) above, is the correctness of a compiler. Here the input-output relation to be satisfied is that the input (source) program computes the same function as the output (target) program - at least up to some specified encoding and decoding operations. One may describe this relation as the simulation of source program by target program.

A third type of assertion is that certain operations on a program, for example, optimizing transformations, preserve the meaning of the program or more generally, preserve certain properties of its meaning; this qualification includes the case where the transformations preserve only what is computed in some of the program variables.

From these examples one can list several entities which must find expression in the calculus. First, the data objects (integers, lists, arrays, truthvalues, etc.) habitually handled by programs. Second, partial computable functions over these objects. Third, programs themselves as syntactic objects - indeed, these are just a special case of data objects manipulated by programs. Fourth, machine states, since we regard the meaning of program instructions and whole programs as transformations over these states. Fifth, these meanings themselves, as functions over states. Sixth, the semantic function for an arbitrary programming language, which assigns to each program its meaning (in this approach to semantics we follow Scott and Strachey [14]).

From this list it appears that the calculus must be able to discuss an arbitrary rich domain of individuals; partial (and usually computable) functions over these individuals, and also functions of higher type (witness the semantic function mentioned above). Predicate Calculus is at least a priori unsatisfactory, since it not only restricts its attention to toal functions (though one can represent partial functions by the device of introducing an "undefined" individual, as indeed we do in our calculus) but also is not oriented in any way towards computable functions. It also has a rich quantifier structure, which we can show is unnecessary for the expression of many assertions of the type mentioned above. Though this is clearly not a disadvantage for the formulation of these assertions, it is revealing to see them formulated in a calculus with simpler logical structure, and such a calculus may be an advantage for the purpose of automatic proof-finding, due to the smaller search space for proofs.

Before describing the calculus, it is well to contrast it with other approaches to formalizing proofs about programs. First, exemplified by Igarashi [4], is the approach in which the terms of the formal system are the programs of some fixed language (in his case, a version of ALGOL) and the sentences are equivalences between such terms. Similarly for Kaplan [6] the fixed language is that of flowchart programs. The second contrasting approach, currently very popular, is again based on some fixed programming language, but the assertions about programs are formulated in some conventional calculus - for example, predicate calculus; the proofs then employ the techniques of Floyd [1], Manna [9] and Hoare [3]. This approach is exemplified by Good and Ragland [2], Igarashi, London and Luckham [5], and others.

It is likely that, because of their specialization to a particular language, these systems will be initially more convenient for obtaining machine-checked proofs of those assertions which they can formulate.

Our aim, however, is to be able to formulate a wider class of assertions (for example involving more than one programming language), and we hope later to specialize our calculus - by a combination of definitions and derived inference rules - towards particular programming languages so as to yield short proofs. At present, however, we have not examined such specialization in any detail.

<u>Description of the Calculus</u>

The calculus is based on an unpublished proposal of Dana Scott in 1969. It is presented in detail in [10], and we shall give here only a brief description.

The <u>terms</u> of the calculus are those of a typed λ-calculus with the addition of certain constants. The <u>types</u> are as follows: <u>ind</u> and <u>Tr</u> are base types (standing for individuals and truthvalues), and if α and β are types then $(\alpha\to\beta)$ is a type. The type of each term is unambiguously determined by its structure and the types of the constants and variables occuring within it. The intended interpretation of terms is that a term of type α denotes an object in the <u>domain</u> D_2. The latter is a partially ordered set (with ordering relation $\leq$) satisfying two extra conditions:

(1) it has a minimum element uu_α denoted by the constant UU_α, and

(2) every ascending chain has a least upper bound (lut) in D_α.

Furthermore, $D_{\underline{tr}}$ is fixed; it consists of the three truthvalues tt, ff, and uu, denoted by the constants $TT_{\underline{tr}}$, $FF_{\underline{tr}}$ and $UU_{\underline{tr}}$ with ordering given by the diagram

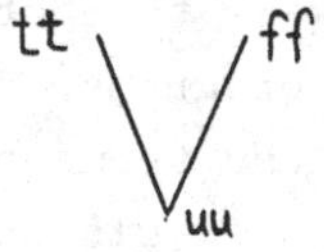

$D_{\underline{ind}}$ is an arbitrary domain; it will typically be constrained by the addition of some non-logical axioms to the calculus. $D_{(\alpha\to\beta)}$ is the domain of <u>continuous</u> functions from D_α to D_β - that is, just those functions which preserve lubs of ascending chains. With the ordering on $D_{(\alpha\to\beta)}$ given by $f\leq g \Leftrightarrow \forall x.f(x)\leq g(x)$ it can be shown that $D_{(\alpha\to\beta)}$ inherits the domain conditions (1) and (2) from D_α and D_β.

Apart from the constants $TT_{\underline{tr}}$, $FF_{\underline{tr}}$ and UU_α already mentioned the only additional constants in the calculus are the conditional combinators $C_{(\underline{tr}\to(\alpha\to(\alpha\to\alpha)))}$ and $Y_{((\alpha\to\alpha)\to\alpha)}$. For terms s, t, u of appropriate type, $C_{(tr\to(\alpha\to(\alpha\to\alpha)))}(s)(t)(u)$ is written $(s\to t,\ u)$. Suppose in a given interpretation (determined by a choice of $D_{\underline{ind}}$) we have a valuation function V : variables $\rightarrow U_\alpha D_\alpha$, which assigns to each variable of type α a member of D_α , and to each constant $TT_{\underline{tr}}$, $FF_{\underline{tr}}$, UU_α the object already specified. To extend V to a valuation function for terms, V : terms $\rightarrow U_\alpha D_\alpha$, we proceed by induction on the structure of terms. Application and λ-abstraction are dealt with in the usual way, and we need only specify further that $V((s_{\underline{tr}} \rightarrow t_\alpha, u_\alpha)) = uu_\alpha$ or $V(t_\alpha)$ or $V(u_\alpha)$ according as $V(s_{\underline{tr}})$ = uu or tt or ff and

$V(Y_{((\alpha \rightarrow \alpha) \rightarrow \alpha)}(S_{(\alpha \rightarrow \alpha)}))$ = the least element x of D_α such that

$V(s_{(\alpha \rightarrow \alpha)})(x) = x$, i.e. the least fixed point of the function

$V(s_{(\alpha \rightarrow \alpha)}) \in D_{(\alpha \rightarrow \alpha)}$.

The latter is justified by the theorem that every member of $D_{(\alpha \rightarrow \alpha)}$ has a least fixed point in D_α.

In general we omit the type subscripts on terms, relying on context to supply them. As an example of a term and its interpretation,

$$V(\lambda f.\lambda x.(p(x) \rightarrow a, f(h(x))))$$

denotes that function g which we might conventionally define recursively by

$$g(x) \Leftarrow \underline{\text{if}}\ p(x)\ \underline{\text{then}}\ a\ \underline{\text{else}}\ g(h(x))$$

with the difference that at an argument where g fails to terminate our function will give as result the "undefined" element uu of the appropriate domain. By this means all our functions are total, and all our terms denote something.

Having dealt with terms the rest of the calculus is easy to describe. An atomic well-formed formula (awff) has the form $s \subset t$ where s and t are terms of the same type. We extend the valuation function V to awffs thus:

$$V(s \subset t) = \begin{cases} \text{TRUE if } V(s) \leq V(t) \\ \text{FALSE otherwise} \end{cases}$$

Note that, outside terms, we are in a two-valued propositional logic.

A well-formed formula (wff) is just a set of awffs, written with commas and interpreted as a conjunction. We abbreviate the wff $s \subset t$, $t \subset s$ by $s \equiv t$. Finally a sentence is an implication ($\vdash$) between wffs. Extension of the valuation function V to wffs and sentences is routine, as is also the definition of the concepts of truth (in an interpretation) and validity of sentences.

Thus outside the terms the calculus has an extremely restrained logical structure - just implication between conjunctions of awffs. The implication may not be iterated. By contrast, the terms are extremely rich in expression; they can represent any function (of arbitrarily high type) which is partially computable with respect to certain primitives. For example, in terms of zero, successor, predecessor and test-for-zero we can represent all partial recursive functions over the natural numbers. The success which we have had in formulating within the calculus assertions in the theory of computation is due to the fact that many of them are indeed logically simple assertions about algorithmically complex entities.

We omit here the details of the rules of inference. They fall naturally into five groups: logical rules, ordering rules, rules concerning truth values and conditionals, λ-conversion and extensionality rules, and finally rules concerning fixed-points. In the last group falls the very powerful rule of induction due to Dana Scott which besides enabling proofs of equivalence of recursively defined functions, also allows one to derive rules of structural induction for recursively defined sets of individuals such as the natural numbers, the finite list structures, and programming languages.

APPLICATIONS OF THE CALCULUS

We now show how to formulate in the calculus three assertions of the types described at the beginning of the introduction. Typically the assertions will take the form A + B, where A is a large wff which characterizes or constrains the domain of individuals, axiomatizes certain primitive functions and defines others. Thus A includes the non-logical "axioms" promised in the previous section (they are not strictly axioms, but wffs). B will often be a single awff.

Our three examples all deal with a particular programming language S built from assignment statements by the formation of compound, conditiona and while statements. A will contain awffs describing the abstract syntax and semantics of S. For the syntax, we represent the Landin-style[7] statement " a wfs (well-formed source program) is <u>either</u> an assignment and has a ehs of which is a name and a rhs of which is a wfse (well-formed source expression), <u>or</u> is a conditional and has an if of which is a wfse and a then of which is a wfs, <u>or</u> is a ....." by the following awff in A, which defines a predicate iswfs:

$$\text{iswfs} = Y(\lambda f.\lambda p.$$
$$\text{isassn}(p) \rightarrow (\text{isname}(\text{ensof}(p) \wedge \text{iswfse}(\text{rhsof}(p))),$$

```
iscond(p) → (iswfse(ifof(p)) ∧ f(thenof(p))
                                f(elseof(p)))
iswhile(p) → ------,
iscmpnd(p) → ------,
UU)
```

There will be a similar definition of iswfse ("is" well-formed source expression).

In addition, A will contain awffs axiomatizing the binary predicate $\wedge$, and also awffs exhibiting the desired relation between the syntactic constructors, selectors, and discriminating predicates, such as

$$\forall n\ e.\quad ehsof(mkassn(n,e)) \equiv n,$$
$$\forall n\ e.\quad rhsof(mkassn(n,e)) \equiv e,$$
$$\forall n\ e.\quad isassn(mkassn(n,e)) \equiv TT$$

where $\forall x{-}{-}{-}.s \equiv t$ just abbreviates $(\lambda x{-}{-}{-}.s) \equiv (\lambda x{-}{-}{-}.t)$, and mkassn(n)(e) - that is, we use a familiar device for representing polyadic functions by monadic functions of higher type

For the semantics of S, we define in A the semantic function MS which takes programs onto state functions, i.e. functions from states to states, where a state is itself a function from names to values - or rather a function in $D_{(\underline{ind} \to \underline{ind})}$ for which we are only interested in its value on those individuals which are names. MS is defined inductively on the structure of S; note that its type is

$$(\underline{ind} \to ((\underline{ind} \to \underline{ind}) \to (\underline{ind} \to \underline{ind})))$$

```
MS ≡ Y(λM.λp.
        isassn(p) → (λs.λm.(m=efsof(p)) → MSE(rhsof(p))(s),s(m))
        iscond(p) → ----,
        iswhile(p) → ----,
        iscmpnd(p) → (λs. M(second of(p))(M(first(p))(s))),
        UU)
```

We have omitted most of this definition - details are in [12] - but note that the meaning of an assignment statement is a state function which alters a given state only at the name which is the left-hand side of the statement by evaluating (using MSE, the semantic function for expressions) its night-hand side in the given state. A will also contain awffs axiomatizing the equality relation $=_{(\underline{ind} \to (\underline{ind} \to (\underline{r}))}$, and a similar definition of MSE.

Example 1. Program Optimization

Suppose that a program p' contains occurences of an expression e, and that no name occuring in e appears on the left hand side of an assignment statement in p'. Then intuitively each evaluation of e during progra execution will yield the same value. So by replacing some or all occurences of e by a new name n, and starting off with the assignment n := e, we shall get the same result (except at the new name n).
More exactly, if p is a program containing n, and p' is the result of substituting e for n throughout p, then subject to the constraints on p' we wish to assert that the programs n := e; p and p'; n := e are equivalent. If we add the constraints to A, together with a definition of the substitution function subst such that subst(e,n,p) = p'
the assertion may be formulated as

$$A \vdash MS(mkcmpnd(mkassn(n,e),p)) \equiv MS(mkcmpnd(subst(e,n,p), mkassn(n,e))).$$

Example 2. Program Correctness

Suppose we add to A a definition - in terms of the constructors mkassn, mkcmpnd, etc. - of a particular program p which, given a natural number as the value of the name n1, will compute its factorial and leave the result at name n2. We wish to assert that p correctly computes the factorial function. We therefore need to add to A some axioms for arithmetic, together with a definition of multiplication (*) and the definition of the factorial function

$$FACT \equiv Y(\lambda f.\lambda x.(x=0) \rightarrow 1,\ x * f(x-1)) .$$

Now it is not correct to assert

$$A \vdash MS(p) \equiv FACT ,$$

since MS(p) denotes a statefunction. So we define in A the initial and terminal functions INPUT : (names → (values → states)) and OUTPUT : (names → (states → values)) by

$$INPUT \equiv \lambda n.\lambda i.\lambda m.(m=n) \rightarrow i,\ UU$$

$$OUTPUT \equiv \lambda n.\lambda s.\ s(n) ,$$

and the composition function o by

$$o \equiv \lambda f.\lambda g.\lambda x.\ f(g(x))\ .$$

We then formulate the assertion of correctness as follows:

$$A \vdash \mathrm{OUTPUT}(n2) \circ \mathrm{MS}(\beta) \circ \mathrm{INPUT}(n1) \equiv \mathrm{FACT}\ .$$

Example 3. Compiler Correctness

Here we are involved not only with the source language S but also with a target language T whose syntax and semantics must also be axiomatized and defined in A. In general the states over which T computes will be different from those for S; they may for example include a pushdown store as a component. Let us talk of S-states and T-states. We may even be concerned with a third programming language C - that in which the compiler is written - but let us suppose that a translating function $\mathrm{comp}_{(\underline{ind} \to \underline{ind})}$ is defined in A, either directly or by axiomatizing the language C, defining its semantic function, exhibiting the compiling program and defining comp as the meaning of that program. Suppose then that by compiler correctness we mean that the S-state function computed by a program p ∈ S may also be computed by first encoding the initial S-state into a T-state, then applying the T-state function computed by comp(p), and finally decoding the resulting T-state into an S-state. This amounts to a mapping

$$\mathrm{SIMUL} \equiv \lambda g.\mathrm{decode} \circ g \circ \mathrm{encode}$$

from T-state functions to S-state functions. So we aim to show that the following diagram commutes:

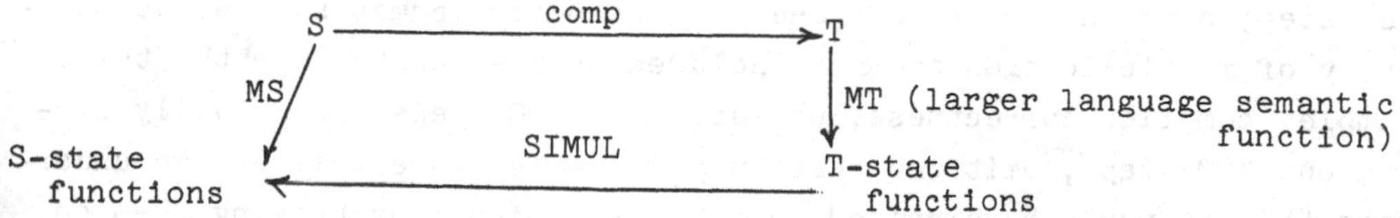

We then formulate the assertion of correctness as follows:

$$A, \mathrm{iswfs}(p) \equiv TT \vdash \mathrm{MS}(p) \equiv \mathrm{SIMUL}(\mathrm{MT}(\mathrm{comp}(p))).$$

MACHINE-CHECKED PROOFS

We have a program, LCF, for interactively generating proofs in the calculus. The program and details of its use are given in Milner [10]. Although the program is in some respects still rudimentary, it has some features which make the proof process tolerable in cases where a program for simply checking proofs in the basic calculus would be intolerable to use. First, since the antecedent wff of each sentence in a proof typically consists of an often large subset of the antecedent A of the desired theorem, together with certain assumptions to be later discharged it is arranged that all of these after their first mention are never explicitly typed by the user or displayed by the machine, but merely referenced by a line number. Second there is a facility for generating subgoals which has the effect of further significantly reducing the amount of typing required from the user. Third, the user may prove intermediate theorems, file them away, and later recall them and instantiate them as required. Fourth, a powerful simplification mechanism, which employs a set of simplification rules specified and varied by the user, carries out a large proportion of the primitive steps of the proof automatically.

It is probably true to say that the absence of any one of these features would have made our longer proofs impracticable. The three examples given in the previous section have been proved on the machine (except certain parts of the third example), and are reported in greater detail in [11, 15, 12]. The first example took about 850 steps - though after our subsequent experience we believe that this figure could be substantially reduced. The correctness of the factorial program took only 40 steps; this small figure is due to the extensive use of simplification. (In these figures we are counting each simplification as a single inference step; also the proofs of general arithmetic lemmas such as associativity of multiplication are not included in the count). For the third example, compiler correctness, we estimate 1000 steps; we actually carried out 700 steps, omitting certain parts which were well enough understood that we would have gained no extra experience by proving them on the machine.

What have we learnt from this endeavour? First, we have some support for the thesis that many valid assertions expressible in the calculus can indeed be proved therein. Because of the inherent incompleteness of the calculus (we can for example express the equivalence of any pair of primitive recursive functions) this <u>is</u> only a thesis, and it follows hat experimental evidence is appropriate. Second, we have gained some dea of the magnitude of the task of, for example, proving compiler orrectness. It is not impossibly large for a simple source language, ven with our somewhat unsophisticated program. Third, we have evidence hat with the addition of some simple sophistications we can perhaps alve the number of inference steps required, and we have some ideas for lerived (macro) inference rules which will reduce the number even further. 'ourth, in the compiler proof we learnt that some method of structuring he proof was essential. In this case we were able to use simple algebraic echniques; by proving that each mapping in our square diagram is a omomorphism between appropriately defined algebras we had only to prove hat the diagram commutes on the generators of the word algebra S of ource programs, since the commutativity for the whole of S follows by unique extension theorem for homomorphisms. We would like similar echniques to apply also to more complex source languages and compilers; ndeed, the possibility of structured proof of compiler correctness hould be an influencing factor in the design of high-level programming anguages.

'LANS FOR FURTHER WORK

'here are many directions in which this research should be and is being ontinued. First, the specialization of the calculus towards correctness roofs for particular programming languages. Second, the introduction f a facility for deriving inference rules with the aim of shortening ll proofs. Third, the design of some proof-finding heuristics, though e believe that we should not carry this effort too far initially, in iew of its great difficulty. Rather we would prefer to concentrate- 'ourth-on the discovery of further techniques for structuring proofs in particular area, such as compiler correctness. Fifth, the work of Scott [13] pares the way for the use of a type-free calculus, which is sometimes more convenient and sometimeseven necessary for expressing he semantics of certain programming languages.

ACKNOWLEDGMENTS

The success of this work was largely implicit in the insight of Dana Scott's original proposal of the calculus. I am grateful to John McCarthy 'or his influence in the choice of applications; to Richard Weyhrauch 'or his collaboration in carrying out the case-studies, and for his 'aluable suggestions for improvement of the machine program; and to Malcolm Newey for his expert assistance in enhancing and maintaining he implementation.

REFERENCES

[1] Floyd, R.W., Assigning Meanings to Programs. Proceedings of a Symposium in Applied Mathematics, Vol. 19, pp. 19-32 (ed. Schwartz, J.T.) Providence, R.I., Amer. Math. Soc. 1967.

[2] Good, D.I. and Ragland, L.C., NUCLEUS - A Language for Provable Programs, Proceedings of SIGPLAN Symposium on Computer Program Test Methods, Prentice Hall, 1972 (to appear)

[3] Hoare, C.A.R., An Axiomatic Basis for Computer Programming. Comm. ACM, Vol. 12, No. 10, October 1969, pp. 576-580, 583.

[4] Igarashi, S., Semantics of ALGOL-like Statements. AI Memo No. 129, Stanford University, 1970.

[5] Igarashi, S,, London, R.L. and Luckham, D.C., Interactive Program Verification: A Logical System and its Implementation. AI Memo, Stanford University, 1972 (to appear)

[6] Kaplan, D.M., A Formal Theory Concerning the Equivalence of Algorithms. AI Memo No. 59, Stanford University, 1968.

[7] Landin, P.J., The Next 700 Programming Languages. Comm. ACM, Vol. 9, No. 3, March 1966, pp. 157-166.

[8] McCarthy, J., A Basis for the Mathematical Theory of Computation. Computer Programming and Formal Systems, pp.33-70, (eds. Braffort, P. and Hirschberg, D.) Amsterdam, North-Holland, 1963.

[9] Manna, Z., The Correctness of Programs. JCSS Vol. 3, pp. 119-127, 1969.

[10] Milner, R., Logic for Computable Functions; Description of a Machine Implementation. AI Memo No. 169, Stanford University, 1972.

[11] Milner, R., Implementation and Applications of Scott's Logic for Computable Functions. Proc. ACM Conference on Proving Assertions about Programs, New Mexico, State University, pp.1- 1972.

[12] Milner, R. and Weyrauch, R.W., Proving Compiler Correctness in a Mechanized Logic. Machine Intelligence 7, Edinburgh University Press, 1972 (to appear)

[13] Scott, D.S., Continuous Lattices, Proc. 1971 Dalhousie Conference, Lecture Notes in Mathematics, Springer-Verlag, Heidelberg.

[14] Scott, D.S. and Strachey, C., Towards a Mathematical Semantics for Computer Languages. Proc. Symposium on Computers and Automata, Microware Research Institute, Symposia Series, Vol. 21, Polytechnic Institute of Brooklyn, 1971.

[15] Weyrauch, R.W. and Milner, R., Program Semantics and Correctness in a Mechanized Logic. Proc. USA-Japan Computer Conference, Tokyo, October 1972 (to appear)

ADMISSIBILITY OF FIXED-POINT INDUCTION IN FIRST-ORDER LOGIC OF TYPED THEORIES

Shigeru Igarashi (Kyoto University)

1. INTRODUCTION

D. Scott postulated a logic of typed functions combined with fixed-point induction [10]. R. Milner modified this logic into a formal system called LCF so as to handle λ-expressions conveniently, and implemented it in an interactive proof checker [6]. Since an early period of this implementation it has been thought that some predicate calculus-like facility may be needed for some or other reasons, so that in the machine version of LCF are included a kind of universal quantifier and implication, the latter being one level lower than the implication included in the original logic. These operators, however, can be used in quite a restricted manner, for they are only abbreviations of legitimate formulas in LCF. Especially implication cannot be nested.

The writer devised a formal means to carry out derivations of a predicate calculus whose objects were typed λ-expressions within LCF, which calculus included in universal quantifier as well as usual propositional operators but not the existential quantifier, which could not be replaced by negation and universal quantification since Gentzen's intuitionistic system was used as the basis. J. McCarthy [4] proposed to use the full classical predicate calculus as a super-structure of LCF, quantifiers ranging over LCF objects. He suggested also some generalization of such a system. The formal system discussed in the present paper is in the essentials along the last line. The main purpose of the present paper is to allow Scott-type fixed-point induction as much as possible in the intended logic.

This point will be explained more concretely. Suppose f and g are continuous partial functions. The predicate f=g, where the equality means the "strong equality", i.e. if one side is undefined so is the other, is not continuous. But as in Scott's logic we can use fixed-point induction in order to prove this equality. Then what will happen to the following formula which we are going to allow in the intended logic?

$$\forall x(f(x)=a \rightarrow g(x)=h(x)) ,$$

with the axiom $\quad f=\mathrm{Min}\ \lambda f \lambda x J(f,x)$,

→ being implication in the classical sense, Min the minimal fixed-point of the function to which it is prefixed, and J(f,x) a term in LCF. It

are continuous, which condition is rather natural in order to consider its fixed-point, and the range of f is discrete, like a boolean function, then we can apply fixed-point induction without incurring inconsistency, even if g and h are non-continuous functions. In fact the continuity of g and h does not matter in this case, for fixed-point induction is not sound unless the above conditions are satisfied.

We shall give a syntactic characterization of the formulas for which fixed-point induction is sound, so that machines can check automatically whether or not a given formula admits application of the inference rule corresponding to fixed-point induction.

2. FIRST-ORDER LOGIC OF TYPED THEORIES

We consider a kind of infinitely many-sorted first-order logic in the classical sense [12]. The objects are individuals in the usual sense together with functions of individuals or previously defined functions. Each type can be regarded as a sort. Only objects are typed, and we do not consider predicate variables. The intended formal system will be abbreviated as FLT. We shall partially follow Shoenfield's style [11].

2.1 Language

Types

A1 - We presuppose that there are a number of types called the "base types". Some of the base types can be "ordered types". Types are denoted by α, β, etc. and the ordered types are postfixed by the letter "o", like αo. No relationships between α and αo are assumed if both α and αo happen to be base types. Types other than the base types are called the "function types".

A2 - If α and β are types, so is $\alpha \to \beta$. Both $\alpha 1 \to \alpha 2 \to \ldots \to \alpha n \to \beta$ and $\alpha 1, \alpha 2, \ldots, \alpha n \to \beta$ are used as the abbreviations of $\alpha 1 \to (\alpha 2 \to (\ldots \to (\alpha n \to \beta) \ldots))$.

A3 - If o and o are types, which must be ordered types, so is $(\alpha o \to \beta o)o$.

Because of this construction we can consistently abbreviate "o"s except the outmost one. For instance, $(\alpha o \to (\beta o \to (\beta o \to \beta o)o)o)o$ is abbreviated by $(\alpha \to \beta \to \beta \to \beta)o$.

Alphabet

The alphabet of the intended formal system consists of α-constants and α-variables for each type α, (α1, ... , αn)-predicates, i.e. predicate constants, for each n-tuple (α1, ... , αn) of types (n $\geq$ 0), and the following logical symbols,

$$= \; (\; , \;) \; \neg \; \vee \; \exists \; \text{Min} \quad .$$

If α is a base type, an α-constant of variable can be called an individual constant or variable. Otherwise, an α-constant or variable can be called a function constant or variable. It must be noted that functions of arbitrary finite order appear. An (α1, ... , αn)-predicate is an n argument predicate in the usual sense, the i-th argument being of type αi for each i (1 $\leq$ i $\leq$ n).

We shall use several defined symbols which are standard in logic as follows

$$\& \; \rightarrow \; \forall \; \leftrightarrow$$

The symbol → stands for implication, and ↔for logical equivalence. Thus → means function in the text and implication in formulas.

Terms

B1 - If a is an α-constant, then a is an α-term. If x is an α-variable, then x is an α-term.

B2 - If t is an α→β-term and u is an α-term, then t(u) is a β-term. t(u) can be also written as (t,u), and (t(u))(v) as t(u,v).

B3 - If t is an (αo → αo)o-term, then Min t is an αo-term.

B4 - If t is an αo-term and αo is a function type, then t is an α-$_{t}s_{r}{}^{m}$.

Formulas

C1 - If t and u are α-terms, then t=u is a formula.

C2 - If p is an (α1,...,αn)-predicate that is different from =, and ti is an αi-term for each i (1 $\leq$ i $\leq$ n), then p(ti,...,tn) is a formula.

C3 - If A is a formula, then ¬A is a formula.

C4 - If A and B are formulas, then A∨B, A&B, and A→B are formulas.

C5 - If A is a formula and x is an α-variable, then xA and xA are formulas.

2.2 INTERPRETATION

We choose a non-empty set $D|\alpha|$, or $D\alpha$, for each base type α as the domain of individuals of type α. If α is an ordered base type, we assume further that D^{α} is an ordered set $(L,\leq)$ satisfying the following conditions.

(i) $(L,\leq)$ is an $\aleph_0$-inductively ordered set in that L is non-empty and every non-empty countable set X such that $X\subset L$ and X is linearly ordered has sup X in L.

(ii) $(L,\leq)$ has the least element, i.e. inf L, which shall be denoted by 0.

Suppose $D\alpha$ and $D\beta$ have been defined. We let $D[\alpha\to\beta]$ be the set of all the functions of $D\alpha$ into $D\beta$. If α and β are ordered type, we let $D[(\alpha\to\beta)o]$ be the set of all the $\aleph_0$-continuous functions belonging to $D[\alpha\to\beta]$ together with the order relation $\leq$ defined by

$$f\leq g \text{ iff } f(x)\leq g(x) \quad \text{for any } x\in D\alpha ,$$

where the $\aleph_0$-continuity is defined as follows.

<u>Definition</u>. A "sequence" X in a set L is a function of the set of the positive integers into L. Xn denoting the n-th term X(n). X is written as (Xn) sometimes. A "monotone increasing" sequence X in $(L,\leq)$ is a sequence in $(L,\leq)$ such that

$$X1 \leq X2 \leq \ldots \leq Xn \leq \ldots ,$$

f is "$\aleph_0$-continuous" iff

$$f(\sup X) = \sup f(X),$$

for any monotone increasing sequence X in $(L,\leq)$, where f(X) denotes the set $\{f(x)|x\in X\}$,

<u>Remark</u>. f is $\aleph_0$-continuous in this sense iff f(sup X) = sup f(X) for any countable directed set $X\subset L$. (See section 3). This property will be called the $\aleph_0$-continuity, while a stronger definition of continuity is

that f(sup X) = sup f(X) for any directed set $X \subset L$. f is said to be "monotone" iff $f(x) \leq f(y)$ whenever $x \leq y$. The $\aleph_0$-continuity implies the monotonicity, which can be shown as follows [10].

Suppose $x \leq y$. Let X1 be x and Xn be y for any $n \geq 2$, so that X is a monotone increasing sequence. By $\aleph_0$-continuity, f(sup X) = sup f(X). But sup X = y and $f(x) \leq$ sup f(X). Therefore $f(x) \leq f(y)$.

By this construction Dαo can be shown to satisfy the conditions (i) and (ii), so that the inductive definition works. In fact, the function g: Dαo→Dβo such that

$$g(x) = 0 \quad \text{for any } x \in D\alpha o$$

is the least element of D[(αo→βo)o], and, for each ascending chain {fn} in D[(αo→βo)o], the function h; $D^{\alpha}o \rightarrow D^{\beta}o$ that maps each element x of $D^{\alpha}o$ onto sup{fn(x)} is sup {fn}.

With each α-constant a in FLT is associated an element a* of D_{α}. With each (α1,...,αn)-predicate p in FLT is associated an n-ary relation p* in Dα1x...xDαn. Such a collection of Dα's will be denoted by D, and FLT(D) will denote the language obtained from FLT by adding a new α-constant, called a "name", for each element of Dα, for each α.

A term is "closed" if no variables occur free in it. Especially, a variable-free term is closed in this sense. We use this terminology because we shall extend the syntax of terms later in order to axiomatize LCF, in which λxx is a closed term, though it is not variable-free. We define an α-individual πt for each closed α-term t by induction on terms.

D1 - If t is an individual symbol, then t must be an α-constant since t is closed. We let πt be a*∈Dα.

D2 - If t is u(v), then u must be a closed α→β-term and v a closed α-term so that πu∈D[α→β] and πv∈Dα. We let π(u(v)) be πu(πv).

D3 - If t is Min u, then u must be a closed (αo→αo)o-term, so that πu is an $\aleph_0$-continuous function of type αo→αo. Let f denote πu. We let πt be inf{x|f(x)=x} (with respect to the ordering of αo), namely the least fixed point of f, which is shown to exist as follows [10].

Let f,n,x denote

$$f(f(\ \dots \ f(x) \ \dots \ )) \quad \text{(f occurs n times)},$$

for each $n \geq \emptyset$. Especially, f, $\emptyset$, x is x. Then sup{f,n,0}, or sup{f,n,0|$\emptyset \leq n < \omega$} strictly, is in fact inf{x|f(x)=x}. By $\aleph_0$-continuity,

$$\begin{aligned} f(\sup\{f,n,0\}) &= \sup\{f(f,n,0)\} \\ &= \sup\{f,(n+1),0\} \\ &= \sup\{f,n,0 \mid 1 \leq n < \infty\} \\ &\leq \sup\{f,n,0\}. \end{aligned}$$

By monotonicity (see the above remark),

$$\sup\{f,n,0\} \leq f(\sup\{f,n,0\}).$$

Thus

$$f(\sup\{f,n,0\}) = \sup\{f,n,0\}.$$

Namely sup{f,n,0} is a fixed point of f. Let a be an element of $D_{\alpha o}$ such that f(a)=a. Since $0 \leq a$, $f(0) \leq f(a) = a$, by monotonicity. Then, by mathematical induction, $f,n,0 \leq a$ for any n, so that $\sup\{f,n,0\} \leq a$. Thus sup{f,n,0}=inf{x|f(x)=x}.

D4 - If t is a closed αo-term and αo is not a base type, then $\pi t \in D_{\alpha o}$ and $D_{\alpha o} \subset D_\alpha$, so that $\pi t \in D_\alpha$.

A truth value is either T or F. T means "true" and F "false".

A formula is "closed" if no variable occur free in it. We define a truth value πA for each closed formula A in FLT(D) by induction on formulas. A [ ], or t [ ], denotes a formula, or a term with voids, and A[x], or t[x], results of replacing them by x.

E1 - If A is t=u, then t and u must be closed α-terms for a certain α, since A is closed. We let

$$\pi A = T \text{ iff } \pi t = \pi u.$$

E2 - If A is $p(t_1,\ldots,t_n)$ where p is different from =, we let

$$\pi A = T \text{ iff } p^*(t_1,\ldots,t_n).$$

E3 - If A is $\neg B$, then we let

$$\pi A = T \text{ iff } \pi B = F.$$

E4 - If A is BvC, then we let

$$\pi A = T \text{ iff } \pi B = T \text{ or } \pi C = T.$$

E5 - If A is $\exists xB[x]$ and x is an α-variable, then B[a] is closed for each α-name a. We let

$$\pi A = T \text{ iff } \pi(B[a]) = T \text{ for some } \alpha\text{-name a.}$$

A "D-instance" of a formula $A[x_1,\ldots,x_n]$ of FLT is a closed formula of the form $A[a_1,\ldots,a_n]$ in FLT(D), where a_i is an α_i-name if x_i is an α_i-variable ($1 \leq i \leq n$). A formula A of FLT is "valid" in D if $\pi A' = T$ for every D-instance A' of A. In particular, a closed formula A of FLT is valid iff $\pi A = T$.

2.3 TRUTH FUNCTIONS ASSOCIATED WITH FORMULAS

To study the properties of formulas we shall consider truth functions, namely functions whose values are the truth values T and F, associated with formulas in the natural manner. For the convenience of the later description we use the following terminologies.

Let x be an α-variable, and A[x] a formula in which at most x occurs free. Since A[a] is a closed formula for each α-name a, we can define a function f: $D_\alpha \to (T,F)$ that sends each a* onto the truth value $\pi A[a]$. f is called "the truth function determined by A and x in D", or, if there is no ambiguity, "the truth function determined by A".

Let $A[x_1,\ldots,x_n]$ be a formula in which at most variables $x_1,\ldots,x_n$, respectively of type $\alpha_1,\ldots,\alpha_n$, occur free. A "(D,x_i)-instance" of $A[x_1,\ldots,x_n]$ in FLT is a formula in FLT(D) of the form $A[a_1,\ldots,a_{(i-1)}, x_i, a_{(i+1)},\ldots,a_n]$ where $a_1,\ldots,a_n$ are names of type $\alpha_1,\ldots,\alpha_n$. Thus at most x_i occurs free in formulas those are (D,x_i)-instances of a formula ($1 \leq i \leq n$). Therefore each (D,x_i)-instance determines a truth function.

$A[x_1,\ldots,x_n]$ also "determines" an n-ary truth function f: $D[\alpha_1]x \ldots xD[\alpha_n] \to (T,F)$ that sends each n-tuple $(a_1*,\ldots,a_n*)$ onto $\pi A[a_1,\ldots,a_n]$.

2.4 LOGICAL AXIOMS AND RULES

We shall accept the following axioms and rules for FLT.

Rule of substitution. In the below schemata of axioms or rules, arbitrary variables can be substituted in place of a, x, y, z, x_1, y_1, $z_1,\ldots,x_n$, y_n, z_n, and w, arbitrary terms in place of t, u, v, and s, an arbitrary n-ary predicate in place of p for each n, and an arbitrary formula in place of A, B, and C, subject to the restrictions that the results of substitutions should be well-formed formulas and that any free occurrence of variables should be kept free. On the induction axiom are imposed the additional restriction that only those formulas of the form A[ ] that "admit induction syntactically" are substituted in place of A[ ]. The effective definition of formulas that admit induction syntactically is given in section 6.1.

Logical Axioms

propositional axiom - $\neg A \vee A$

identity axiom - $x = x$

equality axiom - $x = y \quad \text{Min } x = \text{Min } y$

$x = y \quad z(x) = z(y)$

$x_1 = y_1 \rightarrow \ldots \rightarrow x_n = y_n \rightarrow p(x_1,\ldots,x_n) \rightarrow p(y_1,\ldots,y_n)$

extensionality axiom - $x = y \leftrightarrow \forall z(x(z) = y(z))$

stationariness axiom - $x(\text{Min } x) = \text{Min } x$

induction axiom - $A[0] \rightarrow \forall y(A[y] \rightarrow A[x(y)]) \rightarrow A[\text{Min } x]$

Rules of inference. We shall accept all the rules in Gentzen's system of Natural Deduction [1], or NJ, with the following modification of the quantifier-introduction and elimination rules (a designates a variable in this section).

$\forall$-introduction rule.

$$\frac{A[a]}{\forall x A[x]} \langle a \rangle$$

$\forall$-elimination rule.

$$\frac{\forall x A[x]}{A[t]}$$

$\exists$-introduction rule.

$$\frac{A[t]}{\exists x A[x]}$$

$\exists$-elimination rule.

$$\frac{\exists x A[x] \quad \begin{matrix}\{A[a]\} \\ C\end{matrix}}{C} \langle a \rangle$$

Restriction: In the $\forall$-elimination rule and the $\exists$-introduction rule, the eliminated or introduced bound variable, replacing t, must be of the same type as the corresponding term, replacing t. In the

∀-introduction rule and the ∃-elimination rule, the introduced or eliminated bound variable, replacing a, must be of the same type as the corresponding free variable (eigenvariable), replacing a.

<a> indicates the restriction, in the original NJ, that the free variable substituted in place of a occurs only in the places explicitly designated by a. Thus, for instance, in the ∀-introduction rule the free variable replacing a must not occur in the formula designated by $\forall x A[x]$, nor in any assumption formula of that formula.

As appears in the above rule we use { }, instead of [ ] in the original notation, to indicate the assumption formula which is not carried beyond the bar. Besides, we shall use $A \dashrightarrow B$ sometimes, as well as { }, to denote that A is an assumption formula of B, and $A_1,\ldots,A_m \dashrightarrow B_1,\ldots,B_n$ to denote a "sequent", in the sense of Gentzen's LK. For instance, the ∨-elimination rule can be expressed in the following ways, and we shall use all of them in the sequel for the convenience of description.

∨-elimination rule.

$$\frac{A\vee B \qquad \begin{matrix}\{A\}\\ C\end{matrix} \qquad \begin{matrix}\{B\}\\ C\end{matrix}}{C}$$

Infer C from $A\vee B$, $A \dashrightarrow C$, and $B \dashrightarrow C$.

Infer $P \dashrightarrow C$ from $P \dashrightarrow A\vee B$, $A,P \dashrightarrow C$, and $B,P \dashrightarrow C$.

An inference rule of the last form, i.e. a rule to infer a sequent from other sequents is called a "relativized" inference rule. A sequent of the form $A_1,\ldots,A_m \dashrightarrow B_1,\ldots,B_n$ is "valid in D" iff the formula $A_1 \& \ldots \& A_m \rightarrow B_1 \ldots B_n$ is valid in D. A relativized inference rule is "sound" iff the consequence of the rule is valid in D (as sequent) whenever all of its premises are valid in D, for any D.

We can treat the logical axioms in the form of inference rules. We list them in the generalized forms for the practical derivation. These rules are derived rules actually.

propositional rule.

$$\frac{}{\neg A\vee A}$$

identity rule.

$$\frac{}{t=t}$$

equality rule.

$$\frac{t=u \quad A[t]}{A[u]}$$

stationariness rule.

$$\frac{}{t(\mathrm{Min}\ t)=\mathrm{Min}\ t}$$

induction rule.

$$\frac{A[0] \quad A[a]\to A[t(a)]}{A[\mathrm{Min}\ t]} \ \langle a\rangle$$

<a> indicates the same restriction as described above. Thus the variable substituted in place of a must not occur free in A[Min t], nor in A[0], nor in any assumption formula of A[Min t].

Apparently the induction axiom, or rule, is not acceptable unless some adequate restriction, like the one indicated in the rule of substitution, is imposed on it. First, in order to instantiate this axiom by a name b, substituting b in place of x, πb must be $\aleph_0$-continuous so that Scott-type fixed point induction makes sense, which restriction is satisfied in the present formalism, for Min b is not a well-formed term otherwise. Second, even if Min b represents an $\aleph_0$-continuous function of an appropriate type, there exist many formulas which make this axiom not valid. The main purpose of this paper is to characterize those formulas for which the induction axiom is valid, so that they admit the application of this rule.

Remark. The first equality axiom can be omitted if we treat Min as an $((\alpha_0 \to \alpha_0)0 \to \alpha_0)0$-constant.

3. WEAKLY CONTINUOUS FUNCTIONS

The validity of the induction axiom reflects the properties of truth functions associated with formulas of FLT. The first such property will be called the weak continuity. It must be noted that most of the truth functions determined by formulas of FLT are not continuous, and we are going to establish some criteria for such non-continuous predicates to make the induction axiom valid. The weak continuity can be defined for functions, so that we discuss this property in general.

Through out this section, L denotes an $\aleph_0$-inductively ordered set with the least element O (see the section 2.2), and L' a complete lattice. Namely, L' is an ordered set such that inf X and sup X exist for any subset X of L'. O and I shall denote the least element of L', or inf L', and the greatest element of L', or sup L', respectively.

Let X be a sequence in L'. We consider the monotone increasing sequence Y defined by $Y_n = \inf\{X_m | m > n\}$, and the monotone decreasing sequence Z defined by $Z_n = \sup\{X_m | m > n\}$, which are well-defined by completeness. Then, by completeness again, sup Y and inf Z exist, which are called "liminf X" and "limsup X" respectively.

3.1 Definition. A sequence X in a complete lattice L' is "convergent iff

$$\liminf X = \limsup X.$$

In such a case we define lim X by

$$\lim X = \liminf X$$
$$= \limsup X.$$

A sequence X in an ordered set is a "quasi-ascending chain" iff it is an ascending chain or there exists a number M s.t.

$$x_1 < x_2 < \dots < x_M = x_{(M+1)} = \dots = x_{(M+n)} = \dots \quad .$$

In the latter case X is said to be "semi-finite".

3.2 Proposition. Let f be a function s.t. f: L → L'. f(X), i.e. the sequence $\{f(X_n)\}$, is convergent for any semi-finite X, and

$$\lim f(X) = f(\sup X).$$

Proof. Apparently

$$\lim f(X) = f(X_M) \text{ and } X_M = \sup X,$$

where M satisfies the condition of definition 3.1.

3.3 Proposition. Let f be a function s.t. f: L → L'. f is $\aleph_0$-continuous iff

$$f(\sup X) = \sup f(X),$$

for any countable directed set X s.t. $X \subset L$.

Proof. The sufficiency is trivial. We prove the necessity. Let X be a countable directed set s.t. $X \subset L$. Then we can choose a quasi-ascending chain Y s.t. $Y \subset X$ and Y is cofinal in X so that

$$\sup Y = \sup X.$$

Suppose f is $\mathcal{X}_0$-continuous. Then, by $\mathcal{X}_0$-continuity,

$$f(\sup Y) = \sup f(Y).$$

But

$$\sup f(Y) \leq \sup f(X),$$

since $Y \subset X$.

Thus

$$\begin{aligned} f(\sup X) &= f(\sup Y) \\ &= \sup f(Y) \\ &\leq \sup f(X). \end{aligned}$$

By monotonicity (see the remark in section 2.2),

$$f(x) \leq f(\sup X) \qquad \text{for any } x \in X,$$

since

$$x \leq \sup X,$$

so that

$$\sup f(X) \leq f(\sup X).$$

Therefore

$$f(\sup X) = \sup f(X).$$

3.4 Definition. Let L be an $\mathcal{X}_0$-inductively ordered set, and L' a complete lattice. $f: L \to L'$ is "weakly continuous" iff

$$f(\sup X) = \lim f(X),$$

for every ascending chain X in L. (This relationship implies that lim f(X) exists, for the left hand side always exists.)

3.5 Proposition. f is weakly continuous iff

$$f(\sup X) = \lim f(X)$$

for any quasi-ascending chain X.

Proof. Apparent from proposition 3.2.

3.6. Theorem. f is $\mathcal{X}_0$-continuous iff f is weakly continuous and monotone.

Proof. necessity: Suppose f is $\mathcal{X}_0$-continuous, so f is monotone and for any chain X is $f(X_1) \leq f(X_2) \leq \dots$.

Therefore

$$\sup f(X) = \lim f(X).$$

By $\mathcal{X}_0$-continuity,

$$f(\sup X) = \sup f(X),$$

so that

$$f(\sup X) = \lim f(X),$$

sufficiency: Let X be an quasi-ascending chain. We have to show

$$f(\sup X) = \sup f(X).$$

By weak continuity,

$$f(\sup X) = \lim f(X),$$

and, by monotonicity,

$$\lim f(X) = \sup f(X),$$

so that

$$f(\sup X) = \sup f(X).$$

3.7. Theorem. f is weakly continuous iff for any $\mathcal{X}_0$-continuous function $g: L \to L'$ the following relationship holds:

$$f(\text{Min } g) = \lim f(g,n,0),$$

where Min g denotes the least fixed point of g, i.e. $\inf\{x \mid g(x) = x\}$, which can be expressed as $\sup\{g,n,0\}$ (see section 2.2).

We need the following lemma in order to prove this theorem.

3.8. Lemma. Let X be a quasi-ascending chain in L. Then there exists an $\mathcal{X}_0$-continuous function $f: L \to L$ s.t.

$$f,n,0 = X_n \qquad \text{for any } n.$$

Proof of lemma. The following construction suffices.

$$f(x) = \begin{cases} X_1, & x = 0; \\ X_{(n+1)}, & x \neq \emptyset \text{ and } x \leq X_i \text{ does not hold for any } i \text{ s.t. } i \leq n-1, \text{ and } x \leq X_n \text{ holds } (n \geq 1); \\ \sup X, & x \leq X_n \text{ does not hold for any } n. \end{cases}$$

(This construction was given by R.Milner).

Proof of theorem 3.7. necessity: Suppose g is $\mathcal{X}_0$-continuous, then

$$\text{Min } g = \sup\{g,n,0\}.$$

$\{g,n,0\}$ is a quasi-ascending chain, so that by weak continuity

$$f(\text{Min } g) = \lim f(g,n,0),$$

sufficiency: Let X be a quasi-ascending chain in L. Then by lemma 3.8 there exists an $\mathcal{X}_0$-continuous function g s.t.

$$g,n,0 = X_n.$$

Assume

$$f(\text{Min } g) = \lim f(g,n,0).$$

We note that

$$\text{Min } g = \sup X$$

and

$$\lim f(g,n,0) = \lim f(X).$$

Therefore

$$f(\sup X) = \lim f(X).$$

3.9. Theorem. f is weakly continuous iff

$$\limsup f(X) = f(\sup X)$$

for every ascending chain X in L.

Proof. The necessity is trivial, so that we prove the sufficiency. Let X be an ascending chain in L. We prove that

$$\liminf f(X) = \limsup f(X)$$

follows the latter condition of the theorem. Let a and b denote liminf f(X) and limsup f(X), respectively. We prove a = b. We can choose a subsequence Y of X s.t.

$$\lim f(Y) = a,$$

since a is liminf f(X). Then, by definition,

$$\limsup f(Y) = a.$$

We note that Y is also an ascending chain in L, so that

$$\limsup f(Y) = f(\sup Y)$$

by the supposition of the theorem. Since Y is cofinal in X,

$$\sup Y = \sup X,$$

so that

$$f(\sup Y) = f(\sup X).$$

But

$$f(\sup X) = b$$

again by the supposition of the theorem. Thus

$$\limsup f(Y) = b.$$

Namely,

$$a = b.$$

4. Admissibility of Fixed-Point Induction

We shall discuss properties of predicates. For the convenience of mathematical description we introduce the ordering of truth values such as

$$F \leq T.$$

This ordering is outside our logic, and it must be noted that the concept of weak continuity of predicates as well as that of admissibility of induction introduced below can be stated without referring to this ordering (see 4.6 below), though it makes some arguments more understandable.

Since we considered total predicates when we interpreted formulas, the concept of monotonicity or $\aleph_0$-continuity has little importance as long as we assume T and F are not comparable with each other. For, then, the only monotone or continuous predicates are the identically true predicate and the identically false one. We shall use, however, the concepts of monotonicity and continuity of predicates with respect to the above ordering. These concepts mainly related to the existential quantifier.

4.1 Definition. Let T_0 denote the complete two element lattice. Namely T_0 consists of O and I, while $O \leq I$. (T_0 can be regarded as a $T_\emptyset$-space whose open sets are $\emptyset = \{\ \}$, $\{I\}$, and $\{O,I\}$, which is also a continuous lattice, as discussed by D. Scott). We shall use this lattice to represent the truth values, O and I corresponding to F, i.e. false, and T, i.e. true, respectively, so that

$$F \leq T.$$

4.2 Definition. A "truth function" on L is a function s.t.

$$L \to T_0.$$

a) A truth function f "admits induction weakly" iff

$$f(g,n,O) = T \text{ for every } n\ (n \geq \emptyset) \text{ implies } f(\mathrm{Min}\ g) = T\ .$$

Especially, f(x) admits induction weakly if f(O) = F.

b) A truth function f on L "admits induction strongly" iff

$$\lim f(g,n,O) = T \text{ implies } f(\mathrm{Min}\ g) = T\ .$$

4.3 Proposition. Let X denote an ascending chain in L, and f a truth function on L.

a) f admits induction weakly iff

$$f(0) = T \text{ and } f(X_n) = T \text{ for every } n \ (1 \leq n) \text{ imply } f(\sup X) = T,$$

for any X.

b) f admits induction strongly if f admits induction weakly and f(0) = T.

c) The following conditions are equivalent to each other:

(i) f admits induction strongly.

(ii) $\lim f(X) \leq f(\sup X)$ for any ascending chain X for which $\lim f(X)$ exists.

(iii) $\limsup f(X) \leq f(\sup X)$ for any ascending chain X.

Proof. a) similar to the proof of theorem 3.7 using lemma 3.8.

b) Suppose

$$\lim f(X) = T.$$

Then

$$f(X_n) = T \text{ for almost every } n, \text{ (see 4.6)}$$

so that we can choose a quasi-ascending subchain Y_m of X s.t.

$$Y_1 = 0 \text{ and } f(Y_m) = T \text{ for every } m.$$

By weak admissibility,

$$f(\sup Y) = T.$$

By cofinality,

$$f(\sup X) = T.$$

c) We prove that (i) implies (iii), the rest being left to the reader. Suppose

$$\limsup f(X) \leq f(\sup X).$$

If $\limsup f(X) = F$, then $\lim f(X) = F$, so that

$$\lim f(X) \leq f(\sup X).$$

Suppose

$$\limsup f(X) = T.$$

Then we can choose an ascending subchain Y of X s.t.

$$\lim f(Y) = T .$$

By cofinality of Y in X,

$$\sup Y = \sup X,$$

and, by strong admissibility,

$$f(\sup Y) = T.$$

Thus

$$\limsup f(X) = f(\sup X).$$

4.5 Theorem. Of the following conditions the upper ones are implied by the lower ones,

(i) f admits induction weakly,

(ii) f admits induction strongly,

(iii) f is weakly continuous,

(iv) f is $\aleph_0$-continuous.

Proof. We shall see that (iii) implies (ii), the rest having been proved. Suppose f is weakly continuous, and lim f(X) exists. Then

$$\lim f(X) = f(\sup X),$$

by weak continuity.

4.6 Remark. As noted in the beginning, the concepts of admissibility of induction and weak continuity of truth functions are independent of the ordering of truth values, for we can regard the relationship

$$\lim f(g,n,0) = T$$

simply as stating

$$f(g,n,0) = T \quad \text{for almost every } n,$$

because of the finiteness (thence discreteness, see 5.4) of T_0. Thus these conditions can be restated as follows.

a) A truth function f admits induction weakly iff

$$f(g,n,0) = T \ \text{ for every } n \ (n \geq \emptyset) \ \text{ implies } f(\text{Min } g) = T.$$

b) f admits induction strongly iff

$$f(g,n,0) = T \text{ almost every } n \text{ implies } f(\text{Min } g) = T.$$

c) f is weakly continuous iff

$$f(g,n,0) = f(\text{Min } g) \text{ almost every } n.$$

4.7 Definition. Let x be an α_0-variable, and A a formula in which at most x occurs free, A "admits induction weakly w.r.t. x in D" if the truth function determined by A and x in D admits induction weakly. If A is an arbitrary formula, A admits induction weakly w.r.t. x in D iff every (D,x)-instance of A admits induction weakly.

A"admits induction weakly w.r.t. x" iff A admits induction weakly in any D.

We define the concepts that A "admits induction strongly w.r.t. x (in D)" and that A is"weakly continuous in x (in D)" similarly.

4.8 Theorem. The induction axiom $A[0] \to \forall y(A[y] \to A[a(y)]) \to A[\text{Min } a]$ is valid iff A admits induction weakly w.r.t. x.

Proof. We prove the sufficiency first. sufficiency: Let D be any collection of D_α's. $B[0] \to \forall y(B[y] \to B[a(y)]) \to B[\text{Min } a]$ be a D-istance of the induction axiom, so that at most y occurs free in $B[y]$. Let F(x) denote the truth function determined by $B[x]$, and f(x) the function determined by a(x), i.e., πa. $B[x]$ admits induction weakly in D because of the assumption that $A[x]$ does. Thus

$$F(f,n,0) \text{ for any } n \geq \emptyset \text{ implies } F(\text{Min } f),$$

while Min f is $\pi(\text{Min } a)$. Assume the truth values of $B[0]$ and $\forall y(B[y] \to B[a(y)])$ are both T. Then

$$F(0) = T,$$

and

$$F(b) = T \text{ implies } F(f(b)) = T \text{ for any } b.$$

Therefore we have

$$F(f,n,0) = T \quad \text{every } n \geq \emptyset,$$

so that, by weak admissibility of F(x),

$$F(\text{Min } f) = T.$$

Therefore the truth value of $B[\text{Min } a]$ is T. Thus $B[0] \to \forall y(B[y] \to B[a(y)]) \to B[\text{Min } a]$ is valid in D. Hence the induction axiom is valid in D.

necessity: We use the same notations as above. By definition of validity any D-instance of the axiom must be valid. Therefore if the truth values of B[0] and $\forall y(B[y] \to B[a(y)])$ are both T, i.e., F(f,n,0) = T every $n \geq 0$, the truth value of B[Min a] is T. Namely F(Min f) = T.

4.9 Definition. A[x] "admits relativized induction w.r.t. x" iff A[x] makes the induction rule sound. Namely, the rule obtained from the schema of induction rule by substituting A[x] in place of the meta-variable A is sound.

4.10 Theorem. A[x] admits relativized induction if A x admits induction weakly.

Proof. We have to prove the soundness of the following rule.

$$\frac{P \dashrightarrow A[0] \qquad\qquad A[a],\ P \dashrightarrow A[t(a)]}{P \dashrightarrow A[\mathrm{Min}\ t]} \ \langle a \rangle$$

Let C denote C_1 & ... & C_m where P is $C_1, \ldots, C_m$. The rule is sound iff $(C \to A[0]) \to (C \to \forall y(A[y] \to A[t(y)])) \to (C \to A[\mathrm{Min}\ t])$ is valid by definition. Therefore we shall prove for any D, every D-instance of this formula, say $(E \to B[0]) \to (E \to \forall y(B[y] \to B[b(y)])) \to (E \to B[\mathrm{Min}\ b])$, is valid, where b is an arbitrary variable-free term of the same type as t, i.e. $(\alpha_0 \to \alpha_0)_0$ for some α_0. Obviously we have only to prove for the case that b is a name. For, if b is not a name, there is some name b' s.t. $\pi b = \pi b'$, and the validity can be established easily using this fact and the case that b is a name. Let F(x) be the truth function determined by B[x], and f be πb. Then the following condition is sufficient:

If πE = T, F(0) = T, and, πE = T and F(c) = T imply F(f(c)) = T for any $c \in D\alpha_0$, then F(Min f) = T.

Min f is π(Min b) by definition. Assume the premise of the above condition. Then by induction,

$$F(f,n,0) = T \qquad \text{every } n \geq 0.$$

By the assumption that A[x] admits induction weakly, so does B[x], so that F(x) admits induction weakly. Therefore

$$F(\mathrm{Min}\ f) = T.$$

4.11 Theorem. A[x] admits LCF induction if A[x] admits relativized induction, where by LCF induction is meant the relativized rule in LCF to infer A[y] from y = Min x, A[0], and A[a] $\dashrightarrow$ A[x(a)].

Proof. We see that LCF induction rule is a derived rule.

```
y = Min x, P --> A[O]    A[a], y = Min x, P --> A[x(a)]
------------------------------------------------------ <a> induction
          y = Min x, P --> A[Min x]
------------------------------------------------------     equality
          y = Min x, P --> A[y]
```

4.12 Corollary. A x admits LCF induction if A[x] admits induction weakly.

5. Characterization of Predicates that admit Fixed-Point Induction.

We study what kind of formulas admit induction. For the readability of proofs we shall discuss them in terms of truth functions that have one argument designated by x. The theorems below can be so applied to every instance of formula that the result will be regarded as statements about formulas in general by definition (see 4.7). For this purpose logical combinators below should be understood as functions or functionals whose values are T or F. For instance $\forall y F(x,y)$ denotes the truth function determined by $\forall y A[x,y]$ where F(x,y) is the truth function determined by A[x,y] in D. The relation $\leq$ is not a logical symbol of FLT, but it will be used as a predicate later on in connection with LCF.

5.1 Theorem. The relationship $f(x) \leq g(x)$ admits induction strongly if f(x) and g(x) are $\aleph_0$-continuous.

Proof. Let F(x) denote the corresponding truth function, i.e.,

$$F(x) = \begin{cases} T & f(x) \leq g(x); \\ F & \text{otherwise.} \end{cases}$$

Let X be an ascending chain in L. Suppose

$$\lim F(X) = T,$$

so that

$$f(X_n) \leq g(X_n) \quad \text{for almost every } n.$$

Then, by monotonicity of g,

$$f(X_n) \leq g(\sup X) \quad \text{for almost every } n.$$

Therefore we can choose an ascending subchain Y of X s.t.

$$f(Y_m) \leq g(\sup X) \qquad \text{for every } m.$$

Thus

$$\sup f(Y) \leq g(\sup X).$$

But, by $\aleph_0$-continuity of f,

$$f(\sup Y) = \sup f(Y),$$

so that

$$f(\sup Y) \leq g(\sup X).$$

By cofinallity of Y in X,

$$\sup Y = \sup X.$$

Thus

$$f(\sup X) \leq g(\sup X),$$

i.e.,

$$F(\sup X) = T.$$

5.2 Remark. $f(x) \leq g(x)$, f and g being continuous, is not always weakly continuous, (the fact that it is not $\aleph_0$-continuous being well-known). Let N' be the natural numbers with the infinity ω ordered in the usual sense. Define f, g: $N' \to N'$ by

$$f(x) = x + 1$$
$$g(x) = x.$$

Let X be s.t.

$$X_n = n \quad \text{each } n \text{ s.t. } 1 \leq n \leq \omega.$$

Then

$$F(X_n) = F \quad \text{each } n,$$

but

$$F(\sup X) = T.$$

5.3 Theorem. Let f be an $\aleph_0$-continuous function into a discrete lattice L', c an element of L'. Then the relationship

$$f(x) = c$$

is weakly continuous.

Proof. Let X be an ascending chain in the domain of f. By theorem 5.1 $f(X_n) = c$ almost every n implies $f(\sup X) = c$. Suppose

$$f(X_n) \neq c \qquad \text{almost every } n.$$

We have to prove

$$f(\sup X) \neq c.$$

Let Y_n denote $f(X_n)$ for each n. By monotonicity of f,

$$a = Y_1 \leq \dots Y_n \leq Y_{(n+1)} \leq \dots \leq b,$$

where b denotes sup Y. Y must have at least an accumulating point, for, otherwise, we could choose an ascending chain Z that is a subset of Y s.t.

$$a < Z_1 < \dots < Z_n < Z_{(n+1)} < \dots < b,$$

which contradicts the discreteness of L'. By monotonicity such an accumulating point is unique and will be denoted by d.
Thus

$$Y_n = d \qquad \text{almost every } n.$$

By the supposition

$$c \neq d.$$

By monotonicity again, d is the greatest element of Y, so that

$$d = \sup f(X).$$

By $\mathcal{X}_0$-continuity,

$$\begin{aligned} f(\sup X) &= \sup f(X) \\ &= d \\ &\neq c. \end{aligned}$$

Thus

$$f(\sup X) \neq c.$$

5.4 Remark. In the above proof we used "discreteness" to mean there is no ascending chain X s.t.

$$a < X_1 < X_2 < \dots < X_n < \dots < b,$$

for any a and b.

5.5 Theorem. a) F(x)vG(x) admits induction strongly if F(x) and G(x) do.

b) F(x)vG(x) is weakly continuous if F(x) and G(x) are.

Proof. a) Suppose

$$\text{limsup } F(X) \vee G(X) = T. \qquad \text{(Cf. 4.3.c(iii))}$$

Then either

$$\text{limsup } F(X) = T$$

or

$$\text{limsup } G(X) = T,$$

so that either

$$F(\sup X) = T$$

or

$$G(\sup X) = T$$

by strong admissibility. Thus

$$F(\sup X) \vee G(\sup X) = T.$$

b) By weak continuity,

$$F(\sup X) = F(X_n) = a \qquad \text{for almost every } n$$

and

$$G(\sup X) = G(X_n) = b \qquad \text{for almost every } n,$$

for some a and b. Therefore

$$F(X_n) \vee G(X_n) = a \vee b \qquad \text{for almost every } n.$$

At the same time,

$$F(\sup X) \vee G(\sup X) = a \vee b.$$

5.6 Remark. a) $F(x) \vee G(x)$ does not necessarily admit induction weakly even if $F(x)$ and $G(x)$ do. We consider N' (see remark 5.2) again. Let

$$F(x) = \begin{cases} T & x = \emptyset; \\ F & \emptyset < x \leq \omega; \end{cases}$$

and

$$G(x) = \begin{cases} T & \emptyset < x < \omega; \\ F & x = \emptyset \text{ or } x = \omega. \end{cases}$$

Then F and G admit induction weakly, and

$$F(n) \vee G(n) = T \qquad \text{for every } n \geq \emptyset.$$

But

$$F(\omega) \vee G(\omega) = F.$$

b) $F(x) \vee G(x)$ does not necessarily admit induction weakly even if one of $F(x)$ and $G(x)$ is weakly continuous and the other admits induction weakly. For, in fact, $F(x)$ in the above example is weakly continuous.

5.7 Theorem. a) $F(x) \& G(x)$ admits induction weakly if $F(x)$ and $G(x)$ do.
b) $F(x) \& G(x)$ admits induction strongly if $F(x)$ and $G(x)$ do
c) $F(x) \& G(x)$ is weakly continuous if $G(x)$ and $F(x)$ are.

Proof: left to the reader.

5.8 Theorem. $\neg F(x)$ is weakly continuous if $F(x)$ is.

Proof. Let a denote the truth value $F(\sup X)$. By weak continuity,

$$F(X_n) = a \qquad \text{for almost every } n.$$

Let b denote the truth value $\neg a$. Then

$$\neg F(X_n) = b \qquad \text{for almost every } n.$$

Besides,

$$\neg F(\sup X) = b.$$

5.9 Remark. a) $\neg F(x)$ does not necessarily admit induction weakly even if $F(x)$ admits induction strongly. Let $F(x)$ be the truth function determined by $x \leq \omega$ & $\omega \leq x$, which is equivalent to $x = \omega$, in N'. Then $F(x)$ admits induction strongly because of theorems 5.1 and 5.7(b).

Let X_n be the n-th natural number for each n. Then

$$\neg F(X_n) = T \qquad \text{for } n \geq 0.$$

But

$$\neg F(\sup X) = \neg F(\omega) = F.$$

Thus $\neg F(x)$ does not admit induction weakly.

b) By the above argument, the negation of a formula of LCF does not admit induction weakly in general.

5.10 Theorem. If $F(x)$ and $\neg F(x)$ both admit induction strongly then $F(x)$ is weakly continuous.

Proof. We prove that $F(X)$ is convergent for any ascending chain X. The case that

$$\text{limsup } F(X) = F$$

is trivial. Suppose

$$\text{limsup } F(X) = T.$$

We prove

$$\text{liminf } F(X) = T$$

by contradiction. Assume

$$\text{liminf } F(X) = F,$$

so that

$$\text{limsup } \neg F(X) = T.$$

By strong admissibility,

$$\neg F(\sup X) = T,$$

i.e.

$$F(\sup X) = F.$$

Thus $F(x)$ does not admit induction strongly, which is a contradiction.

5.11 Theorem. a) $F(x) \rightarrow G(x)$ admits induction strongly if $F(x)$ is weakly continuous and $G(x)$ aemits induction strongly.

b) $F(x) \rightarrow G(x)$ is weakly continuous if $F(x)$ and $G(x)$ are.

Proof. $F(x) \to G(x)$ is a tautology of $\neg F(x) \vee G(x)$, so that theorems 5.8 and 5.5 suffice.

5.12 Remark. $F(x) \to G(x)$ does not necessarily admit induction weakly even if $F(x)$ admits induction strongly and $G(x)$ is $\aleph_0$-continuous. Let $G(x)$ be F, i.e., the identically false truth function. Then $F(x) \to G(x)$ is a tautology of $\neg F(x)$. Consider the example of remark 5.9.

Hereafter y is used to indicate the argument instead of x.

5.13 Theorem. a) $\forall x F(x,y)$ admits induction weakly w.r.t. y if $F(x,y)$ does.

b) $\forall x F(x,y)$ admits induction strongly w.r.t. y if $F(x,y)$ does.

Proof. a) Suppose

$$\forall x F(x,0) = T$$

and

$$\forall x F(x,Y_n) = T \qquad \text{for every } n.$$

Then

$$F(a,0) = T$$

and

$$F(a,Y_n) = T \qquad \text{for every } n,$$

for any a. Therefore, by weak admissibility,

$$F(a,\sup Y) = T \qquad \text{for any } a.$$

Thus

$$\forall x F(x,\sup Y) = T.$$

b) Suppose

$$\limsup \forall x F(x,y) = T.$$

Then

$$\limsup F(a,Y_n) = T \qquad \text{each } a.$$

By strong admissibility,

$$F(a,\sup Y) = T \qquad \text{each } a.$$

Thus

$$\forall x F(x,\sup Y) = T.$$

5.14 Remark. a) $\forall x F(x,y)$ is not necessarily weakly continuous even if $F(x,y)$ is. Let f be s.t.

$$F(x,y) = \begin{cases} T & x < \omega \text{ and } x < y, \text{ or } x = \omega; \\ F & \text{otherwise.} \end{cases}$$

Then F is weakly continuous in y, for

$$\lim F(a,Y_n) = F(a,\omega) = T \qquad \text{each } a < \omega,$$

and

$$F(\omega,Y_n) = F(\omega,\omega) = T \qquad \text{for every } n,$$

for any ascending chain Y_n in N'. Moreover,

$$\forall x F(x,Y_n) = F \qquad \text{for every } n,$$

so that

$$\lim \forall x F(x,Y) = F.$$

But

$$\forall x F(x,\sup Y) = \forall x F(x,\omega) = T.$$

b) $\forall x F(x,y)$ is not necessarily weakly continuous even if $F(x,y)$ is $\aleph_0$-continuous in y. For $F(x,y)$ defined above is $\aleph_0$-continuous in y, because it is not only weakly continuous but also monotone (cf. theorem 3.6).

3.15 Theorem. a) $\exists x F(x,y)$ admits induction strongly if $F(x,y)$ is monotone in y,

b) $\exists x F(x,y)$ is monotone and weakly continuous (and therefore $\aleph_0$-continuous. See theorem 3.6) if $F(x,y)$ is.

Proof. a) Suppose

$$\lim \exists x F(x,y) = T,$$

so that for some a and M

$$F(a,YM) = T.$$

By monotinicity,

$$F(a,\sup Y) = T.$$

Thus

$$\exists x F(x,\sup Y) = T.$$

b) We prove

$$\exists x F(x,\sup Y) = \liminf \exists x F(x,y) = \limsup \exists x F(x,y)$$

for each ascending chain Y by case analysis. (i) Suppose

$$\limsup \exists x F(x,y) = T,$$

so that

$$F(a,YM) = T \qquad \text{for some a and M.}$$

By monotonicity,

$$F(a,Y_n) = T \qquad M \leq n,$$

i.e.,

$$\lim \exists x F(x,y) = T.$$

Also by monotonicity, $F(a,YM) = T$ implies

$$F(a,\sup Y) = T,$$

so that

$$\exists x F(x,\sup Y) = T.$$

(ii) Suppose

$$\limsup \exists x F(x,Y) = F,$$

i.e.,

$$\lim \exists x F(x,Y) = F.$$

Then there exists $M(a)$ for each a, s.t.

$$F(a,YM(a)),$$

so that , by monotonicity,

$$F(a,Y_n) = F \qquad \text{for any } a \text{ and } n,$$

(otherwise $F(b,Y_m) = T$, $M \leq m$ for some b and M, which implies

$$\lim \exists x F(x,Y) = T.)$$

Thus

$$\lim F(a,Y) = F \qquad \text{for any } a,$$

so that by weak continuity,

$$F(a,\sup Y) = F \qquad \text{for any } a.$$

Therefore

$$\exists x F(x,\sup Y) = F.$$

5.16 Remark. a) $\exists x F(x,y)$ is not necessarily weakly continuous even if $F(x,y)$ is monotone (and therefore admits induction strongly by theorem 5.15) in y. Let $F(x,y)$ be

$$\forall z(z < \omega \rightarrow z < y).$$

Then $F(x,y)$ is monotone in y, and

$$F(x,n) = F \qquad \text{for every } n \text{ and any } x,$$

so that $\exists x F(x,n) = F$ for every n.

But

$$\exists x F(x,\omega) = T,$$

because

$$F(x,\omega) = T.$$

b) $\exists x F(x,y)$ is not necessarily weakly continuous even if $F(x,y)$ is monotone and admit induction strongly. Let

$$G(x,y) = \begin{cases} T & y \leq x\ \omega\ ; \\ F & \text{otherwise.} \end{cases}$$

Namely,

$$G(x,y) = \neg F(x,y).$$

$F(x,y)$ being the truth function described in remark 5.14 so that $G(x,y)$ is weakly continuous in y by theorem 5.8. But

$$\exists x G(x,n) = T \qquad \text{every } n,$$

and

$$\exists x G(x,\omega) = F.$$

6. Syntax of Formulas that admit Induction.

6.1 Tables of Inheritance of Admissibility.

We summarize the inheritance of admissibility of induction in the tables so that they can be checked by machines easily.

These tables shall be regarded as a part of the postulates of FLT for technical (logical) reasons. Since the weak admissibility of induction is an informal concept that is not effective, we cannot accept a formal system described in terms of that concept, although we would like to use the induction axiom, or rule, for every formula that admits induction weakly. Instead we regard these tables as an inductive definition, and hence an effective definition of formulas that "admit induction syntactically". Namely we call a formula A[ ] to admit induction syntactically iff A[x] is concluded to admit induction weakly w.r.t. x using only these tables, the primitive cases listed in I1 serving as the base step of inductive definition.

We add the following definition for practical purposes.

Definition. A formula A is said to be "constant w.r.t. x" iff A does not depend on x. A term t is an "LCF term" iff all the constants and variables occuring in t are of continuous types. A formula of the form $t \leq u$ where t and u are LCF terms is called an "LCF awff".

Obviously a sufficient condition for A to be constant w.r.t. x is that x does not occur free in A. Proofs concerning the inheritance of admissibility related to this condition are left to the reader.

11. The following conditions are hierarchical in the sense that the lower are the stronger conditions.

(primitive cases)

A admits induction weakly.	
A admits induction strongly.	$t \leq u$ (t and u are LCF terms)
A is weakly continuous.	t=0, t=TRUE, t=FALSE (t is an LCF term)
A is constant.	x does not occur free in A

(i) A admits relativized induction and LCF induction w.r.t. x if A admits induction weakly w.r.t. x.

(ii) A is $\aleph_0$-continuous iff A is weakly continuous and monotone.

(iii) A admits induction weakly w.r.t. x if A is monotone w.r.t. x.

12. Table for &, v, and →.
If A and B satisfy the conditions stated in the first column and the first row, respectively, then A&B, AvB, and A→B satisfy the conditions shown in the corresponding places.

A	B op	adm, weak,	adm, str,	weak, cont,	const,
adm, weak,	&	adm, weak,	adm, weak,	adm, weak,	adm, weak,
	v	x	x	x	adm, weak,
	→	x	x	x	adm, weak,
adm, str,	&	adm, weak,	adm, str,	adm, str,	adm, str,
	v	x	adm, str,	adm, str,	adm, str,
	→	x	x	x	adm, str,
weak, cont,	&	adm, weak,	adm, str,	weak, cont,	weak, cont,
	v	x	adm, str,	weak, cont,	weak, cont,
	→	x	adm, str,	weak, cont,	weak, cont,
const,	&	adm, weak,	adm, str,	weak, cont,	const,
	v	adm, weak,	adm, str,	weak, cont,	const,
	→	adm, weak,	adm, str,	weak, cont,	const,

13. Table for $\neg$, $\forall$, and $\exists$.

All the conditions are w.r.t. x.
If x and y are identical then $\forall yA$ and $\exists yA$ are constant w.r.t. x.

A	$\neg$ A	$\forall$yA	$\exists$yA in general	$\exists$yA A: monotone
adm, weak,	x	adm, weak,	x	adm, str,
adm, str,	x	adm, str,	x	adm, str,
weak, cont,	weak, cont,	adm, str,	x	weak, cont,
const,	const,	const,	const,	const,

6.2 Example of formula that admits induction

$\forall xF(x,y)$ is weakly continuous if $F(x,y)$ is anti-monotone and admits induction strongly w.r.t. y.

For, $\forall xF(x,y)$ is a tautology of $\neg\exists x\neg F(x,y)$. Suppose $F(x,y)$ is anti-monotone and admits induction strongly w.r.t. y. $\neg F(x,y)$ is monotone, so that $\neg F(x,y)$ admits induction strongly, for a monotone predicate admits induction strongly trivially. Then $\neg F(x,y)$ is weakly continuous by theorem 5.10, so that $\exists x \neg F(x,y)$ is weakly continuous by theorem 5.15b. Thus $\neg\exists x\neg F(x,y)$ is weakly continuous by theorem 5.8 (see tables of 6.1).

We can check this result by a direct proof as follows.

Proof. Case i) Suppose

$$\limsup \forall xF(x,Y) = F, \text{ i.e., } \lim \forall xF(x,Y) = F .$$

Then there exists M s.t.

$$\forall xF(x,YM) = F,$$

so that there is some a s.t.

$$F(a,YM) = F.$$

By anti-monotonicity,

$$F(a, \sup Y) = F,$$

so that

$$\forall xF(x, \sup Y) = F.$$

Case ii) Suppose

$$\limsup \forall x F(x,Y) = T.$$

Then,

$$\limsup F(a,Y) = T \quad \text{each } a,$$

so that

$$F(a,Y_n) = T \quad \text{for every } n, \text{ each } a,$$

i.e.,

$$\lim F(a,Y) = T.$$

(Otherwise $\limsup F(a,Y) = F$ by anti-monotonicity.) By strong admissibility,

$$F(a, \sup Y) = T \quad \text{each } a,$$

so that

$$\forall x F(x, \sup Y) = T.$$

7. Translation of LCF into First-Order Logic of Typed Theories

7.1 Axiomatization

In order to axiomatize LCF, first we need to extend the syntax of terms so as to include λ-expressions as follows.

B5. If t is an α_o-term in which only constants and variables of ordered types occur, and x is a β_o-variable, then λxt is $(\beta_o \to \alpha_o)_o$-term. Any occurrence of x in λxt is not free.

The corresponding interpretation is as follows.

D5. If t is $\lambda x u[x]$ and x is a β_o-variable, u[a] must be a closed α_o-term for each β_o-name a so that $\pi(u[a]) \in D_{\alpha o}$, for some α_o. We let πt be the function which sends each $\pi a \in D_{\beta o}$ onto $\pi(u[a])$. Such a function is known to be continuous [10, 7].

Remark. The proof of continuity of the functions represented by λ-expressions, namely the terms involving the operator λ, requires induction on the structure of terms. The case that sup D_α's do not exist in general has been treated by R. Milner.

We introduce an ordered base type denoted by B_o, three B_o-constants O, TRUE, and FALSE, and, a $(B_o \to \alpha_o \to \alpha_o \to \alpha_o)_o$-constant ⊃ and an (α,α)-predicate $\leq$ for each α.

$D[B_o]$ consists of three elements, $TRUE^*$ and $FALSE^*$ being incomparable. Hereafter, we use the same symbol to denote a B_o-constant and the truth value represented by it.

$\supset(t,u,v)$, namely $((\supset(t))(u))(v)$ reads "if t then u else v" and is written as $t\supset u,v$ usually. We let $a\supset b,c$ be 0, b, and c. If a is 0, TRUE, and FALSE, respectively, for each $a\in B_o$, $b\in D_{\alpha o}$, and $0\in D_{\alpha o}$. This function is continuous [10].

$x\leq y$ represents the order relation discussed in the previous sections, mathematically. Intuitively, however, $x\leq y$ means that y is "defined" more than or as much as x, x=0 read "x is undefined". If x and y are functions, this means y is an extension of x as function.

We give the following non-logical axioms. An arbitrary term with voids can be substituted in place of t[ ], provided that the variable designated by x does not occur free in that term. t[x] and t[y] denote the terms obtained from it by substituting arbitrary variables designated by x and y, respectively, in place of its voids.

Nonlogical Axioms

reflexivity,	$x\leq x$,	
antisymmetry,	$x=y\leftrightarrow x\leq y \;\&\; y\leq x$.	
transitivity,	$x\leq y \;\&\; y\leq z \rightarrow x\leq z$.	
extensionality,	$x\leq y\leftrightarrow\forall z(x(z)\leq y(z))$.	
monotonicity,	$x\leq y \rightarrow z(x)\leq z(y)$	z must be an α_o-variable.
minimal elements,		
	$0\leq x$	
	$0(x)\leq 0$	
truth values,	$x=0 \vee x=TRUE \vee x=FALSE$	x must be a B_o-variable.
	$\neg 0=TRUE$,	
	$\neg 0=FALSE$,	
	$\neg TRUE=FALSE$,	

conditionals, $0 \supset x,y = 0$,

$TRUE \supset x,y = x$,

$FALSE \supset x,y = y$,

λ-conversion, $(\lambda x t[x])(y) = t[y]$.

Remark. To add λ-expressions is just introducing denotations for continuous objects. If we do not intend to prove the facts about λ-expressions the λ-conversion axiom can be replaced by the following weaker axiom.

$$\exists x \forall y (x(y) = t[y]).$$ x must not occur free in t.

In the ε-logic $\varepsilon x \forall y (x(y) = t[y])$ designates the same object as $\lambda x t[x]$, while the uniqueness comes from the extensionality axiom.

7.2 Adequacy

We need to see that all the inference rules in LCF can be adequately expressed in the present calculus in the form of theorems or derived rules, which means that we do not lose anything by changing the logic. In other words, we are dealing with an extension of LCF in that we can prove a theorem A in the new calculus if A is a theorem in LCF, and, moreover, we can use any rule of LCF in the present calculus. We have only to examine those rules that are neither of the nature of propositional calculus nor expressed as one of the logical or nonlogical axioms.

J1. Abstraction rule (LCF)

$$\frac{t[a] \leq u[a]}{\lambda x t[x] \leq \lambda x u[x]} \quad \langle a \rangle$$

Derivation

$$\frac{t[a] \leq u[a]}{\lambda x t[x](a) \leq \lambda x u[x](a)}$$ λ-conversion (and equality)

$$\frac{\lambda x t[x](a) \leq \lambda x u[x](a)}{\forall y((\lambda x t[x])(y) \leq (\lambda x u[x])(y))} \quad \langle a \rangle$$ ∀-introduction

$$\frac{\forall y((\lambda x t[x])(y) \leq (\lambda x u[x])(y))}{\lambda x t[x] \leq \lambda x u[x]}$$ extensionality

J2. Function rule (LCF)

$$\frac{}{\lambda x y(x) = y}$$

Derivation

$$\cfrac{\cfrac{(\lambda xy(x))(z) = y(z)}{\forall z((\lambda xy(x))(z) = y(z))}\ \langle z\rangle}{\lambda xy(x) = y}$$

λ-conversion
∀-introduction
extensionality

J3. Cases rule (LCF)

$$\frac{\begin{matrix}\{t=0\} & \{t=\mathrm{TRUE}\} & \{t=\mathrm{FALSE}\} \\ A & A & A\end{matrix}}{A}$$

Derivation

$$\frac{t=0 \lor t=\mathrm{TRUE} \lor t=\mathrm{FALSE} \quad \begin{matrix}\{t=0\} & \{t=\mathrm{TRUE}\} & \{t=\mathrm{FALSE}\} \\ A & A & A\end{matrix}}{A}\ \lor\text{-elimination (twice)}$$

J4. Induction rule (LCF). It suffices to show that any conjunction of LCF awffs admits induction syntactically in the sense of section 6.1, for LCF is a formal system that carries out relativized deduction for these sentences. Each LCF awff admits induction strongly w.r.t. any variable (table 11, 6.1) subject to the type conformity. So does any conjunction of them (table 12, 6.1).

7.3 Example taken from Proof of Compiler Correctness

The following example is taken from an FLT-like proof of McCarthy-Painter's theorem [5]. The proof of this theorem in LCF is discussed in [8] and [13].

We presuppose there are three types called language 1, language 2, and the meaning space. These need not be base types. In particular the meaning space can be the type (states)→(states). Namely the meaning space is the set of partial functions of (states) into itself. A conceptual compiler carries out a translation of language 1 into language 2, an expression x in language 1 being mapped onto obj(x). We need not assume continuity of the meaning space and function obj for the present argument, which is, however, not an important point. We use the following constants, each of them being either an individual constant or a function in the usual sense. The asterisked constants are assumed to have been given appropriate axioms.

constant		type	comment
isconst	*	(language1→Bo)o	isconst(8) = TRUE.
isvar	*	(language1→Bo)o	isvar(a) = TRUE,
isexp		(language1→Bo)o	isexp((8+a)+(9+b))=TRUE
arg1	*	(language1→language1)o	arg1((8+a)+(9+b))=8+a,
arg2	*	(language1→language1)o	arg2(8+a) = a.
obj	*	language1→language2	
mean1	*	language1→meaning space	
mean2	*	language2→meaning space	

We use a (language1,language2)-predicate Correct(x,y) to mean y is a correct object program for expression x. Correct(x,y) is not continuous in general, because it is usually defined by an axiom like

(ax,1) $\forall x \forall y(\text{Correct}(x,y) \leftrightarrow \text{mean1}(x) = \text{mean2}(y))$, (+)

The function isexp is defined by the following axiom,

(Ax,2) $\text{isexp} = \text{Min}\, \lambda f\, \lambda x(\text{isconst}(x) \supset \text{TRUE}, (\text{isvar}(x) \supset \text{TRUE}, (f(\text{arg1}(x)) \supset (f(\text{arg2}(x) \supset \text{TRUE},\text{FALSE}),\text{FALSE})))$.

The theorem we want to prove is

(1) $\forall x(\text{isexp}(x) = \text{TRUE} \rightarrow \text{Correct}(x,\text{obj}(x)))$.

Correct(x,obj(x)) is, however, not sufficient as an induction hypothesis in general, so that we prove first a formula of the form

(2) $\forall x(\text{isexp}(x) = \text{TRUE} \rightarrow A)$,

usually, where A is the conjunction of a certain generalization of Correct(x,obj(x)) and additional conditions peculiar to each compiling algorithm. More concretely, we shall consider a compiler which works with a counter, n, indicating that the addresses whose mnemonic names are TS(1), ... , TS(n) are occupied as temporary storages. We define the following constants, the last three related to the loading or allocation. The set of integers, or addresses, is a base type, varsno(x) is the number of distinct variables occuring in x, varno(z,x) denotes some numbering of such variables.

constant		type	comment
compl	*	(language1,integers) → language2	
TS		integers → integers	
varno	*	(language1,language1) → integers	varno(a,(8+a)+(9+b)) = 1.
varsno	*	language1 → integers	varsno((8+a)+(9+b)) = 2.
loc		(language1,language1) → integers	

In this case, obj(x) is defined by the following axiom,

(Ax.3) $\forall x(\text{obj}(x) = \text{compl}(x,\emptyset))$.

A typical form of A is

(3) $\forall n(n \geq \emptyset \rightarrow \text{Correct}(x,\text{compl}(x,n))\ \&\ \text{Unaffected}(x,n,\text{compl}(x,n)))$,

where Unaffected is a (language1, integers, language2)-predicate s.t. Unaffected(x,n,y) means the object program y does not destroy the contents of the storages corresponding to the program variables occuring in the source program x or any of TS(1), ... , TS(n).

If we make the addresses absolute by the below axiom, which corresponds to a particular loading obvously, the object program becomes as fig. 1 below. Occur(z,x) reads z occurs in x.

(Ax.4) $\forall z \forall x(\text{isvar}(z) = \text{TRUE} \rightarrow \text{Occur}(z,x) \rightarrow \text{loc}(z,x) = \text{varno}(z,x))$,
$\forall x \forall n(\text{loc}(\text{TS}(n)) = \text{varsno}(x)+n)$.

compl((8+a)+(9+b),n)

(instruction)		(mnemonics)
LI	8	
ADD	1	a
STO	n+3	TS(n+1)
LI	9	
ADD	2	b
STO	n+4	TS(n+2)

memory map

∅	accumulator
1	a
2	b
3	TS(1)
	....

(instruction) (mnemonics)

LI n+3 TS(n+1)
ADD n+4 TS(n+2)

Let n = Ø to get obj((8+a)+(9+b)).

n+2	TS(n)
n+3	TS(n+1)
n+4	TS(n+2)

fig.1 Example of object program and memory map

Let A[x] denote (3) hereafter. We note that neither isexp nor n occurs free in A[x]. Then, the formula (2) admits LCF induction w.r.t. "isexp" as follows,

isexp(x) = TRUE	weak, cont. w.r.t. isexp;
A(x)	const, w.r.t. isexp;
isexp(x) = TRUE → A[x]	weak, cont. w.r.t. isexp;
x(isexp(x) = TRUE → A[x])	adm. str. w.r.t. isexp.
	(See tables in section 6.1.)

Thus we can infer (2) from (4) and (5) below.

(4) ∀x(O(x) = TRUE → A[x]).

(5) ∀x(f(x) = TRUE → A[x]) →
∀x((isconst(x) ⊃ TRUE,(isvar(x) ⊃ TRUE,
(f(arg1(x)) ⊃ (f(arg2(x)) ⊃ TRUE,
FALSE),FALSE))) = TRUE → A[x]).

We can improve the readability by the following consideration. Let p be ar (α→ Bo)-term. Then we let $\tilde{p}$ and p stand for the formulas p = TRUE and p = FALSE, respectively. This causes no confusion because of the syntax we employed. Obviously

$$p \vee \tilde{p}$$

is not valid, while p∨ ¬p is. We notice the relationship

$$(p \supset q,r) \leftrightarrow p\&q \vee \tilde{p}\&r, \qquad (*)$$

Which is provable in FLT, since this formula is an abbreviation of

$$(p \supset q,r) = TRUE \leftrightarrow p = TRUE \ \& \ q = TRUE \vee p = FALSE \ \& \ r = TRUE.$$

(*) It is a little interesting, and also useful, that this old relationship still holds in a calculus that includes the undefined truth value. See, e.g., [2].

Thus we can rewrite (4) and (5) as follows,

(4') $\forall x(O(x) \twoheadrightarrow A[x])$.

(5') $\forall x(f(x) \twoheadrightarrow A[x])$

$\forall x(isconst(x) \vee isvar(x) \vee \sim isconst(x) \& \sim isvar(x)$
$\& f(arg1(x)) \& f(arg2(x)) \twoheadrightarrow A[x])$.

It must be noted that there are some substitutes in LCF for formulas like (1) - (4), though these formulas are not allowed as legitimate formulas in it and the interpretation becomes different. By the deduction theorem in first-order logic we can also express the sentence (5') by a formula of FLT, replacing $\twoheadrightarrow$ by $\rightarrow$ and binding f by universal quantifier, obtaining

(5'') $\forall f(\forall x(f(x) \twoheadrightarrow A[x])$
$\forall x(isconst(x) \vee isvar(x) \vee \sim isconst(x) \& \sim$
$isvar(x) \& f(arg1(x)) \& f(arg2(x)) \twoheadrightarrow A[x]))$.

For such a formula there seem to be no natural substitutes in the form of LCF formulas.

Discussions

The writer has been motivated toward the study described in this paper through an attempt to translate his formal system representing the equivalence of Algol-like statement 2,3 into LCF. For that purpose having some predicate calculus-like facility seems to be essential, for we need to express implication between strong equivalence in the form of formula.

From the writer's point of view, the following are among the possible advantages of having some predicate calculus-like things within logic for computable functions.

1. (human engineering) In not a few cases, the conventional logical operators make the writing and understanding of descriptions easier. Besides, many people are familiar with expressions and derivation in predicate calculus, especially, of first-order.

2. (underlying theories) In the practical field of application of such a logic, for instance proving correctness of compilers, we have to handle

underlying theories whose representations in predicate calculus seem to be natural, like elementary set theory. We do not care if some of the sets involved in our proof are not computable or continuous, even if they might be in fact computable. There are also theories of equivalence and correctness of programs which are related to predicate calculus.

3. (meta-theorems) There will be many facts about the objects of LCF that can be stated only in the form of meta-theorems of LCF, while significant portion of them could be stated as theorems in an extended logic. Then handling derived rules and applying already proved theorems will become more convenient.

Obviously these desirable properties will not be obtained before considerable experiments. Moreover there must be some compromise. For instance, if we use entire classical predicate calculus as in the present paper, we are out of the LCF-like world that consists of solely continuous functions, losing some neetness of the formalism and relative simplicity of implementation. Employing second or higher order predicate calculus might give us more complexity as well as power.

It must be noted that J. McCarthy [4] suggested that in some generalization of Scott's logic using predicate calculus we should be able to prove the continuity of functions. It seems that FLT is capable of doing that in spite of the limitation that no predicate variables are allowed, for we have quantifiers ranging over typed sets in effect. A fixed-point induction based mainly on monotonicity within second-order predicate calculus has been discussed by D.Park [9].

Acknowledgements

The writer acknowledges J.McCarthy, R.Milner, R.Weyhrauch, R.London, and D.Luckham for stimulating discussions, valuable suggestions, and helpful comments on an earlier draft.

References

[1]Gentzen, G., Untersuchungen über das logische Schließen, Mathematische Zeitschrift, 39 (1934-5).

[2] Igarashi, S., An axiomatic approach to the equivalence problems of algorithms with applications, Reports of Computer Centre, University of Tokyo, 1, No. 1 (1968).

[3] Igarashi, S., Semantic of Algol-like statements, Symposium on Semantics of Algorithmic Languages, Engeler, E. (ed.), Lecture Notes in Mathematics, 188, Springer-Verlag (1971).

[4] McCarthy, J., On adding quantifiers to LCF, private communication, Stanford (1972).

[5] McCarthy, J., & Painter, J., Correctness of a compiler for arithmetic expressions, Proceedings of a Symposium in Applied Mathematics, 19, Schwartz, J.T. (ed.), American Mathematical Society, (1967).

[6] Milner, R., Implementation and applications of Scott's logic for computable functions, Proceedings of a Conference on Proving Assertions about Programs, New Mexico State University, SIGPLAN Notices 7 (1972).

[7] Milner, R., Private Communication, Stanford (1972).

[8] Milner, R. and Weyhrauch, R., Proving compiler correctness in a mechanized logic, Machine Intelligence 7, Michie, D. (ed.) Edinburgh University Press (1972, to appear).

[9] Park, D., Fixpoint induction and proofs of program properties, Machine Intelligence 5, Meltzer, B. and Michie, D. (eds.), Edinburgh University Press (1970).

[10] Scott, D., Private Communication, Oxford (1969).

[11] Shoenfield, J.R., Mathematical Logic, Addison-Wesley Publ. Co. (1967).

[12] Wang, H., Logic of many-sorted theories, Journal of Symbolic Logic, 17, No. 2 (1952).

[13] Weyhrauch, R. and Milner, R., Program semantics and correctness in a mechanized logic, Proceedings of USA-Japan Computer Conference, Tokyo, (1972, to appear).

A Formal Approximation Theory of Semantic Data Types

Takayasu ITO

Central Research Laboratory
Mitsubishi Electric Corporation
Amagasaki, Japan

INTRODUCTION

Dana Scott introduced the notions of data type and the approximation between data types in a formal manner. He proposed a number of computational models of data types as a basis of mathematical semantics, introducing a new partial ordering $\sqsubseteq$ and restricting the class of permissible functions as monotone continuous functions defined complete lattices of data types.

Furthermore the axioms of extensionality and comprehension are introduced to allow the effective function operation and the class of self-applicative functions.

One of the basic facts in Scott's theory is that monotone functions on complete lattices have (minimal) fixed points. In order to construct complete lattices of data types, Scott introduces the two ficticious elements $\perp$ (the bottom element) and $\top$ (the top element).

The correspondence of $\perp$ and $\top$ depends on given problems; for examples,

(a) $\perp$ may be the empty set and $\top$ the set of all programs

(b) $\perp$ may be the function undefined everywhere and $\top$ the function contradictory everywhere.

The former may correspond to the model of regular program schemata (Ito,1968), and the latter corresponds to the model of recursive microprograms (Ito,1971).

But if the semantics of a program is defined by its effect on the state, we may have some ontological difficulty of accepting these ficticious entities.

Especially this difficulty may occur when we relate the mathetical semantics into an operational semantics.

This problem occurred when the author intoduced the notion of regular program schemata and gave a correspondence between the undefined program ϕ and and the empty set in 1967, although, of course, these enabled us to have a concise mathematical theory.

In this paper we try to avoid Scott's ficticious entities, hoping to have a natural theory of mathematical semantics.

From a semantic standpoint we regard programming languages as a collection of semantic transformations on a certain universe. We try to provide a universe in terms of $\sqsubseteq$-ordering relation. In order to explain some mathematical meanings of our theory, we discuss how a model of set-theory can be imbedded in a model of our universe of $\sqsubseteq$-relational system, which is also the universe of a programming language.

One of our undorlying assumptions is that any programming language has a finite computable character, hence we assume that any programming language has a finite number of semantic categories (of course, each semantic category may contain infinite objects).

AXIOMATIC THEORY OF APPROXIMATION OF SEMANTIC DATA TYPES

Semantic data types are a set of objects of a certain type, which may be called a domain. The object of semantic data types may not possess a finite representation, but it may be thought to be an approximation to be an object which has such a representation. This suggests the importance of a relationship of approximation over the data types.

We introduce a predicate $x \sqsubseteq y$ to idicate that x is an approximation to y.

This paper discusses an axiomatic theory of approximation on data types, using this predicate $\sqsubseteq$.

The axiomatic theory of approximation consists of three axioms and one axiom scheme as follows:

Axiom 1 (Transitivity)

$$\forall x \forall y [x \sqsubseteq y \Leftrightarrow \exists z (x \sqsubseteq z) \wedge \forall w (w \sqsubseteq x \Rightarrow w \sqsubseteq y)]$$

Axiom 2 (Extensionality)

$$\forall x \forall y [x = y \Leftrightarrow \forall z (z \sqsubseteq x \Leftrightarrow z \sqsubseteq y)$$

Axiom 3 (Distinguishability)

$$\forall x \forall y [\neg (x \sqsubseteq y) \wedge \exists z (x \sqsubseteq z) \Rightarrow \exists w (w \sqsubseteq x \wedge \forall v \neg (v \sqsubseteq w \wedge v \sqsubseteq y))]$$

Axiom 1 means that x is an approximation of y if and only if x is an approximation to something and every approximation of x is an approximation to y. Axiom 2 says that x is the same data type if and only if they share all their approximations in common. This axiom defines the equality in approximation theory.

Axiom 3 says that if x is not an approximation to y and x is an approximation to something, then there is an approximation of x which is not an approximation to y.

Next we introduce the notion of O-domain in the following way.

Definition: Let $\varphi[x]$ be a formula of predicate calculus with $\sqsubseteq$.

Then we define $\Phi(x;\varphi[x])$ the set of all data types which satisfy $\varphi[x]$ as follows:

$z \sqsubseteq \Phi(x;\varphi[x])$ if and only if

$$\forall w[w \sqsubseteq z \Rightarrow \exists x \exists v[\varphi[x] \wedge v \sqsubseteq x \wedge v \sqsubseteq w]] \wedge \exists u(z \sqsubseteq u)$$

$\Phi(x;\varphi[x])$ is called Φ-domain.

This definition says that z is an approximation of the set of all data types denoted by $\Phi(x;\varphi[x])$ if every approximation of z is some x satsfying $\varphi[x]$.

Axiom Scheme (Comprehension Axiom Scheme)

$$\exists y \forall z[z \sqsubseteq y \Leftrightarrow z \sqsubseteq \Phi(x;\varphi[x])$$

This axiom scheme says that each Φ-domain exists and is the least upper bound to the set of x satisfying $\varphi[x]$.

BASIC THEOREMS IN APPROXIMATION THEORY

Within the framework of the axiomatic theory of approximation, we can prove the following theorems:

Theorem 1

(i) Reflexivity

$$\forall x[\exists y(x \sqsubseteq y) \Rightarrow (x \sqsubseteq x)]$$

(ii) Antisymmetricity

$$\forall x \forall y [x \sqsubseteq y \wedge y \sqsubseteq x \Rightarrow x = y]$$

(iii) Transitivity

$$\forall x \forall y \forall z [x \sqsubseteq y \wedge y \sqsubseteq z \Rightarrow x \sqsubseteq z]$$

Theorem 2

(i) The least upper bound is unique with respect to the partial ordering $\sqsubseteq$. The least upper bound coincides with Φ-domain.

$$\exists ! y \forall z [z \sqsubseteq y \Leftrightarrow z \sqsubseteq \Phi(x; \varphi[x])]$$

($\exists ! x P(x)$ means that there exists a unique x such that P(x))

(ii) $\forall x \forall y [x \sqsubseteq y \Leftrightarrow \forall z (z \sqsubseteq x \Rightarrow \exists w [w \sqsubseteq z \wedge w \sqsubseteq y]) \wedge \exists u (x \sqsubseteq u)$

x is an approximation to y if and only if every approximation of x has an approximation in common with y and x is an approximation to something.

(iii) $\forall y [y = \Phi(x; x \sqsubseteq y)]$

This says that y is the least upper bound of its approximation.

BOOLEAN ALGEBRA AS A MODEL OF APPROXIMATION THEORY

In this paragraph we develop the theory to show that a Boolean algebra can be a model of approximation theory.

Definition:

(i) $\mathbb{1} = \Phi(x; x = x)$

(ii) $\mathbb{O} = \Phi(x; x \neq x)$

$\mathbb{1}$ is the universe of approximation theory, but $\mathbb{O}$ is not any data type and has no approximation to it. Thus $\mathbb{O}$ is the only object without any approximation property. Thus there is a clear distinction between $\mathbb{O}$ and Scott's $\perp\!\!\!\perp$.

Theorem 3

(i) $\forall x[x\sqsubseteq\mathbb{1}\Leftrightarrow\exists y(x\sqsubseteq y)$

(ii) $\neg(\mathbb{O}\sqsubseteq\mathbb{1})$

(iii) $\forall x[(\forall y\ \neg(y\sqsubseteq x))\Leftrightarrow x=\mathbb{O}]$

Every data type is an approximation to the universe $\mathbb{1}$. $\mathbb{O}$ is not an approximation of the universe. $\mathbb{O}$ has no approximation.

Definition:

(i) $y\oplus z=\overline{\Phi}(x;x\sqsubseteq y\vee x\sqsubseteq z)$

(ii) $y\circ z=\overline{\Phi}(x;x\sqsubseteq y\wedge x\sqsubseteq z)$

These define the union and intersection of two approximations.

Theorem 4

(i) $y\oplus z=\overline{\Phi}(x;x=y\vee x=z)$

(ii) $\forall x\forall y\forall z[x\sqsubseteq y\vee x\sqsubseteq z\Rightarrow x\sqsubseteq y\oplus z]$

(iii) $\forall x\forall y\forall z[x\sqsubseteq y\wedge x\sqsubseteq z\Rightarrow x\sqsubseteq y\circ z]$

(iv) $\forall y\forall z[y\circ z\sqsubseteq\mathbb{1}\Rightarrow y\circ z\sqsubseteq z\wedge y\circ z\sqsubseteq y]$

(v) $\forall y\forall z[\neg\exists x(x\sqsubseteq y\wedge x\sqsubseteq z)\Leftrightarrow y\circ z=\mathbb{O}]$

(vi) $\forall y\forall z\forall w[(\forall x[x\sqsubseteq y\vee x\sqsubseteq z\Rightarrow x\sqsubseteq w]\wedge[y\oplus z\sqsubseteq\mathbb{1}])\Rightarrow y\oplus z\sqsubseteq w]$

(vii) $\exists y\exists z[y\sqsubseteq\mathbb{1}\wedge z\sqsubseteq\mathbb{1}\wedge y\neq z]\Rightarrow\neg\forall y\forall z[y\sqsubseteq\mathbb{1}\wedge z\sqsubseteq\mathbb{1}\Rightarrow y\circ z\sqsubseteq\mathbb{1}]$

(viii) $\forall y[y\oplus\mathbb{O}=y]$

(ix) $\forall y[y\circ\mathbb{O}=\mathbb{O}]$

(x) $\forall x[x\sqsubseteq y\circ z\Rightarrow x\sqsubseteq y\wedge x\sqsubseteq z]$

$y\oplus z$ is the least upper bound of y and z.

$y\circ z$ is the greatest lower bound of y and z.

Definition:

$$y^* = \Phi(x;\ \forall z(z \sqsubseteq x \Rightarrow \neg z \sqsubseteq y))$$

Theorem 5

(i) $\mathbb{O}^* = \mathbb{1} \wedge \mathbb{1}^* = \mathbb{O}$

(ii) $\forall x \forall y \neg[x \sqsubseteq y \wedge x \sqsubseteq y^*]$

(iii) $\forall x[x \oplus x^* = \mathbb{1}]$

These result indicate that a model of approximation theory is a model of Boolean algebra. For example, if $x \sqsubseteq y$ correspond to $(x \leqslant y \wedge x \neq 0)$, we can prove the axioms of approximation theory as the theorems of Boolean algebra.

SET THEORY AND APPROXIMATION THEORY OF DATA TYPES

It is reasonable to assume that the universe of programming languages can be considered to be a model of set theory. It is not difficult to see that approximation theory of data types can be modeled in set theory. But our approximation theory of data types is weaker than set theory, so that it is not trivial to find an appropriate model of approximation theory of data types which may serve both a set theory and the universe for semantic categories of programming languages.

In this paragraph we explain how a set theory can be imbedded in an appropriate model of approximation theory of data types. First we introduce a function $\theta[x]$ which means the set consisting of x and satisfies the following properties

(i) $\forall x \exists z \forall y(x \neq y \Rightarrow z \sqsubseteq \theta[x] - \theta[y])$

(ii) $\forall x(\theta[x] \sqsubseteq \mathbb{1})$

Then a data type is a set if it satisfies the following equation.

$$x = \Phi(z;\ z \sqsubseteq x \wedge \exists y(\theta[y] = z))$$

Let us denote this equation $\mathcal{S}(x)$. Then the membership relation can be defined as follows:

$$x \in y \Leftrightarrow \mathcal{S}(y) \wedge \theta[x] \sqsubseteq y$$

We have the following properties.

(i) $\forall x[\mathcal{S}(\theta[x])$

(ii) $\forall x[\exists y(x \sqsubseteq \theta[y] \wedge x \neq \theta[y]) \Rightarrow \neg\mathcal{S}(x)$

Using these relations we can express the axioms of set theory within the framework of approximation theory. For example

(A) Axiom of Extensionality

$$\forall x \forall y [\mathcal{S}(x) \wedge \mathcal{S}(y) \Rightarrow (\forall z [\theta[z] \sqsubseteq x \Leftrightarrow \theta[z] \sqsubseteq y] \Rightarrow x = y)$$

(B) Null set

$$\exists x [\mathcal{S}(x) \wedge \forall y(\neg\, \theta[y] \sqsubseteq x)$$

In this manner we can translate all of the axioms of Zermelo-Fraenkel axiom system into approximation theory of data types.

REMARKS

In this paper we established an axiomatic theory of approximation of data types, which consists of only three axioms and one axiom scheme.

Our theory is similar to Dana Scott's lattice-theoretic approach on data types, but it does not assume the existence of Scott's ficticious element $\perp$ and $\top$, whence the lattice theory of data types.

The results of this paper says that

(1) approximation theory of data types is well-formed

(2) three axioms and one axiom scheme are enough to model set theory

(3) a model of set theory is actually imbeddable in approximation theory

(4) approximation theory of data types meet the universe of semantic categories of programming languages.

Since approximation theory of data types are a theory of partially ordered set, there will be some connection of partially ordered set with topology, through the T_0-spaces as mentioned in Birkhoff. Some instance of Comprehension Axiom Scheme may provide an induction scheme. But applications of approximation theory of semantic data types are left for future.

REFERENCES

Birkhoff,G.: Lattice Theory,AMS Colloquim Publication Volume XXV (1961)

Cohen,P.J.: Set Theory and the Continuum Hypothesis, Benjamin(1966)

Ito,T.: Some formal properties of a class of program schemata, IEEE Symposium on Switching and Automata Theory(1968)

Ito,T.: A theory of formal microprograms,NATO Advanced Study Institute on Microprogramming(1971) (This is based on the author's unpublished memo of 1967 entitled "On certain representations of algorithms I,II")

Ito,T.: Mathematical theory of programs and its applications, Journal of IEE in Japan,vol.91,no.8(1971) (in Japanese)

McCarthy,J.: Toward a mathematical science of computation, Proc. IFIP'62(1963)

Scott,D.: Outline of a mathematical theory of computation, Proc. Fourth Annual Princeton Conference on Information Sciences and Systems(1970)

Scott,D.: The lattice of flow diagrams, Symposium on Semantics of Algorithmic Languages, Lecture notes in mathematics,vol.188, Springer-Verlag(1971)

Scott,D. and C. Strachey: Towards a Mathematical Semantics of Computer Languages, Proc. of the Symposium on Computers and Automata, Microwave Research Institute Series Volume 21, Polytechnic Institute of Brooklyn(1972)

SOME FEATURES OF A LANGUAGE FOR A PROOF-CHECKING PROGRAMMING SYSTEM

G.S.Tseytin

One of the things we need in order to use theorem-proving techniques in actual programming (and not only in illustrations) is a language that would enable a programmer to state his reasoning about the program in a convenient form that easily matches his way of thinking. In this paper an approach to creating such a language is suggested and some features of it are discussed. Thus the main attention is given to making statements about programs rather than to proving them.

Later these statements may be translated into the language of some logical system and submitted to some proof-searching procedure. If the statements supplied by the programmer contain sufficient information to cover each minor step of the program execution then proof-searching may amount essentially to proof-checking. Furthermore, it would be desirable to eliminate the need for translation from the programming language into a logical language by constructing a language in which the same text may be both a program and a proof of its correctness. The language outlined in this paper might be a step toward this goal.

When a natural way for making statements about programs is sought one should have in mind that often the programmer s conception of a program and his belief that the program (or a part of it) actually does what it is intended for may be based on reasoning involving not only objects represented in the computer memory, but also other objects (e.g., common mathematical objects) that are not, or even cannot be, so represented. The programmer has also to consider relations between his `problem objects` and `computer objects`. Thus the language should provide facilities for introducing such objects and writing statements about them.

The new language is constructed as an extension of some programming language of conventional type, e.g., ALGOL 68 or some sublanguage of it. In fact, the only features of ALGOL 68 needed for this paper are some of its basic constructions, the system of modes and the terminology of syntax. For simplicity synchronized parallel elaboration is omitted here and collateral elaboration is replaced by serial.

Some external objects (i.e., texts or their parts) in the new language specify objects or actions in the memory of a computer in the conventional way. Other external objects don`t specify anything in the computer at execution time and are relevant at proof-checking time only. The syntax does not distinguish between these two types of external objects. A notion may have terminal productions of both types or of `mixed` type.

Thus the proposed language is a logical language rather than a programming language but its structure is compatible with that of programming languages and a conventional program is just a particular case of what can be written in this language. No guarantee is given however for arbitrary text in this language to have anything to do with programming at all.

Now some particular features will be discussed into which a conventional programming language (in this paper ALGOL 68) should be extended. The representation of the examples in the sequel is only tentative. Some self-explanatory identifiers are used without declarations.

1. Modes. A mode is a designation of a class of objects. New means for introducing classes (in addition to those already existing in ALGOL 68) may be as follows:

1.1. Submodes (the meaning of the examples is obvious):

a) submode nat = int i: i ge 0;

b) submode sub = int k: (k ge i and k le j);

1.2. \`Set\` and \`mapping\` modes:

a) mode a = set nat;

b) mode b = map (nat) real;

Here a designates the class of all subsets of the set of natural numbers (nat being as defined in 1.1.a), and b the class of all sequences of real numbers. Note that no computer representation is provided for objects of such modes.

1.3. Modes without definition. E.g.,

mode employee;

Such modes can come from particular problems; properties of the designated classes of objects may be specified by introducing special axioms.

2. Logic.

2.1. Quantifiers in boolean clauses and lambda notation for mappings:

a) (some real x; any real y; x le y**2);

b) submode ex = int i: i gt 2;

map (ex) bool f = (lambda ex i; some int a,b,c; a*b*c ne 0 and a**i + b**i = c**i);

f(k) and (submode ltk = ex l: l lt k; any ltk l; not f(l));

As the examples show, the values of such clauses need not be immediately computable.

2.2. Recursively defined predicates. A predicate may be defined by means of a procedure or a mapping whose definition may be recursive as well. This method is of essence when handling objects of recursive modes.

Examples.

a) union list = (string, cell);

struct cell = (ref list car, cdr);

The most natural definition of the predicate \`a list

contains an atom (directly or not) is by means of a recursive procedure.

b) **mode** **pp** = **proc** (**pp**, **int**);

int m;

pp p = (**pp** q, **int** n):

(m **plus** 1; **if** n **gt** 0 **then** q(p, n-1) **fi**);

The following property of p is obvious: every call of p with p as the first actual parameter increments the value referred to by m. Can one generalize this to a more general property of p that can be formulated without exactly specifying the first parameter? Simply to drop the restriction on the first parameter would be wrong, while saying that every call of p increments the value referred to by m provided that every call of its first parameter does would be insufficient even for p(p,n) (this difficulty has been pointed out by M.N.Dolitsky).

The solution is to define the required property recursively: a **pp**-object q is said to have the property Z if every call of it increments the value referred to by m provided that the value of the first actual parameter of the call has the property Z. (On formulating properties of procedures see 6.3.)

2.3. Particular objects without definition. Like undefined modes (1.3) they may come from particular problems, e.g.,

proc (**employee**) **employee** superior.

Such objects may be treated as formal parameters (6.2).

2.4. Axioms. Introduction of additional axioms pertaining to some particular problem may become necessary (not only in connection with 1.3 and 2.3) unless we expect the proof-checker to do the job of generations of mathematicians. The axioms may be listed in the beginning of the program; some similar statements are considered in 4.5.1 and 4.5.2.

3. Memory state.

3.1. In order to fit the semantics of ALGOL 68 (which, in its turn, is slightly modified here) a memory state is regarded as consisting of a list of name--value pairs (connected by the relation `to refer to`) and of a stack. An item on the stack may be either a value, possibly with an identifier attached to it, or a label identifier (see 4.1, 4.2).

3.2. The concept of name should be extended for the following reason. As has been already mentioned, a programmer doesn`t think of his program in terms of `computer objects` alone; he thinks of `problem objects` and, moreover, he may think of variable problem objects that change their values while the program is running. It may happen that some computer object is regarded as a representation of such a variable problem object, i.e., a certain relation between the values of the two objects is supposed to be maintained on each step. But even in this case the relation may fail to determine uniquely the current value of the problem object.

It is suggested therefore to think of the value of such a variable problem object as being referred to by a special `ghost` name that doesn`t actually exist in the memory of the computer; at the points where the value is changed a special assignment to this name is added to the program. `Ghost` names are generated by special generators and their scope is the whole program.

Example. An analytic function may be represented by its value and the values of its first and second derivatives at 0 (the rest being irrelevant for the computation). Then one may write:

```
    compl a0, a1, a2; ghost anfunc f; ...
    begin f := (lambda compl z; f(z)*f(z));
a2 := 2*a0*a2 + a1*a1; a1 := 2*a0*a1; a0 := a0*a0 end; ...
    if a0 = 0 then f := (lamda compl z; f(f(z)));
a2 := a2*a1*(a1 + 1); a1 := a1*a1 fi; ...
```

Of course, no object involving a ghost name may be referred to by a real name.

4. Semantics. The semantics of the new language is defined in terms of binary relations between memory states (the states before and after the `elaboration`). A binary relation is defined for each `program` in this language in a recursive manner.

True enough, a programmer seldom thinks in terms of a memory state as a whole, so much the less in terms of sets of memory states. However, this technique is used here as a mathematical language for definitions. Some combinations of notions so defined turn out to represent ideas a programmer can better grasp immediately than in set-theoretic terms. (Note that, in general, simplicity of exact definition of a programming language and its convenience in use are not the same thing.)

4.1. The effect of elaboration of a clause delivering a value (of an identity declaration) is, apart from possible side effects, that the value is put on the stack (with the identifier attached to it). This defines the binary relations corresponding to such phrases.

The binary relation corresponding to a `compound clause` (i.e., one made up by means of the go on symbol) is obviously defined as the composition of the binary relations corresponding to the constituents. The semantics of unitary clauses like X:=Y or P(A,B), etc. (X,Y,P,A,B standing for some clauses) is defined by decomposing them into X;Y;<u>assign</u> or P;A;B;<u>call</u> respectively, the semantics of <u>assign</u>, <u>call</u>, etc. being defined in an obvious (though not simple) way.

Likewise, one can define the semantics of conditional clauses by deriving the corresponding binary relation from those corresponding to their constituents.

4.2. Similar treatment of jumps involves a certain difficulty. To make recursive definitions possible in this case too, the following approach is adopted, based on some ideas of C.A.R.Hoare.

The effect of a jump is that the label identifier is put on the stack. For each label identifier a new procedure is declared whose body is equivalent to the part of the program from that label up to the end of the serial clause to which the label belongs. Then each serial clause is decomposed into compound clauses, conditionals and calls as shown in the following example.

Let L1, L2 be label identifiers, U1, U2, ... unitary phrases, possibly involving jumps to these or to other labels. Let label L (nolabel) be a boolean clause that returns true iff the stack has the label identifier L (no label identifier) on the top; when label L returns true the identifier L is unstacked. Then the serial clause

U1; L1: U2; U3. L2: U4

is transformed in a backward pass as follows (supposing that U1, ... U4 have been already so transformed):

```
    proc P2 = : U4;
    proc P1 = :
(U2; if label L1 then P1 elsf label L2 then P2
elsf nolabel then
U3; if label L1 then P1 elsf label L2 then P2
elsf nolabel then skip fi fi);
    U1; if label L1 then P1 elsf label L2 then P2
elsf nolabel then P1 fi.
```

4.3. New notations are introduced to represent some familiar operations on binary relations.

4.3.1. simult (A, B, ..., K) means set-theoretic intersection of binary relations.

4.3.2. altern (A, B, ..., K) means set-theoretic union.

4.3.3. except A means set-theoretic complement.

4.3.4. for int x simult A(x) and for int x altern A(x) mean `infinite` intersection and union respectively (there may be any other formal parameter instead of int x).

4.3.5. reverse A means the binary relation inverse to

that corresponding to A.

4.3.6. anyway means the relation that holds between any two states.

4.3.7. Note that simult means neither serial nor collateral elaboration. E.g.,

simult (i plus 1, j plus 1)

where i and j possess distinct names means the empty relation since i plus 1 does not change the value referred to by j and vice versa. The collateral elaboration of A and B may be described by

altern ((A; B), (B; A))

supposing the elaborations of A and B are inseparable actions.

4.4. A two-place operation with is introduced, with two versions of semantics (for the choice of the version see 5.1).

Version I. A with B defines the same binary relation as simult(A,B).

Version II. Let wrong exit be a label identifier not declared anywhere in the program. Then the binary relation defined by A with B is

altern (simult (A, B),
(simult (A, except B); go to wrong exit)).

4.5. Some construction derived from these operations may be of particular interest for programmers.

4.5.1. Let A be a boolean unit. Then

now A

stands for

: (A with true).

This may be used in situations like

int i; i:=1; i plus 1; now i=2; i plus 1; now i=3; ...

4.5.2. An important modification of now is perm, used to introduce relations between data that are supposed to hold permanently. Adding

perm A

to the declaration prelude of a serial clause is an abbreviation for inserting <u>now</u> A in the place of <u>perm</u> A and after each of the subsequent unitary phrases of that serial clause. E.g., in the example of 3.2 one can add

<u>perm</u> (f(0) = a0 <u>and</u> derivative(f)(0) = a1
<u>and</u> derivative(derivative(f))(0) = a2);

Note that this would be incorrect if the occurrences of <u>begin</u> and <u>end</u> were removed from that example because in that case one would have to insert <u>now</u> statements also after the semicolons between <u>begin</u> and <u>end</u> where the relationship does not hold.

4.5.3. Let <u>same</u> denote the binary relation that holds between any two memory states containing the same item on the tops of their stacks. Let, further, M and N be any two modes (i.e., declarers) and R a (M,N)<u>bool</u> operation indication. Then the confrontation

X <u>becomes</u> R Y

(X being a firm M tertiary and Y a firm N tertiary) means

(N y = Y; <u>submode</u> <u>m</u> = M x: (x R y);
<u>for</u> <u>m</u> x <u>altern</u> x); <u>same</u>; <u>reverse</u> X.

Examples:

a) (cf. 2.2.b) m <u>becomes</u> <u>gt</u> m;

b) (x:=sqrt(y)) <u>with</u> (x**2 <u>becomes</u> = y);

c) (i <u>plus</u> 1; j <u>plus</u> 1) <u>with</u>
<u>if</u> i <u>isnt</u> j <u>then</u>
<u>simult</u> (i <u>becomes</u> = i+1, j <u>becomes</u> = j+1)
<u>else</u> <u>anyway</u> <u>fi</u>;

d) <u>submode</u> <u>sub</u> = <u>int</u> i: (i <u>gt</u> 0 <u>and</u> i <u>le</u> n);
(<u>for</u> i <u>to</u> n <u>do</u> a[i] <u>plus</u> 1) <u>with</u>
<u>for</u> <u>sub</u> i <u>simult</u> (a[i] <u>becomes</u> = a[i] + 1).

5. Termination.

5.1. A statement to be proved about the program may imply that the program terminates (under some conditions) or only specify some relations for the case when the program terminates. Correspondingly, the proposed language has two interpretations, terminative and non-terminative . In the first interpretation the program is considered all right only when it terminates and version I of 4.4 is used. In the second interpretation version II of 4.4 is taken and all that is wanted for a program is that it should never reach the wrong exit.

5.2. In the terminative interpretation an additional facility is needed for termination proofs. A special rank statement with an integral operand may be attached to any program part responsible for repetition, i.e., a procedure body, a label or a repetitive statement body. The operand is evaluated whenever the corresponding program part is encountered during the elaboration, and the value must be non-negative but smaller than the value of the operand of the 'senior' execution, if any, of the same rank statement. A formal definition for procedures with parameters and result may look as follows.

Let V (A, F) stand respectively for virtual (actual, formal) parameters, D for a virtual declarer, B for a D unit, I for an integral unit and P for a proc(V)D primary. A new mode is declared:

```
    struct proc1(V)D =
(ref int rank, proc(ref int, V)D routine);
```

Then throughout the program the following changes are made:

a) the mode proc(V)D is replaced by proc1(V)D,

b) every proc(V)D routine denotation of the form

```
    (F)D: B rank I
```

is replaced by

```
    proc1(V)D:
(ghost int := -1
comment a negative number stands for omega co,
(ref int rank, F)D:
begin int r = rank; rank := I;
now rank ge 0 and (r lt 0 or rank lt r);
D b = B; rank := r; b end),
```

c) every call of the form P(A) is replaced by (routine <u>of</u> P) (rank <u>of</u> P, A).

The semantics of <u>rank</u> for procedures without parameters or result is defined similarly and the cases of labels and repetitive statements are reduced to the former case by 4.2.

Some operation may also be introduced to access the rank of a routine.

Example:

```
    proc ackermann = (int x, y) int :
if x = 0 then y + 1 else
proc ackx = (int z) int : ackermann (x - 1,
if z = 0 then 1 else ackx (z - 1) fi)
rank z;
ackx(y) fi rank x;
```

If each procedure body, label and repeptitive statement body in a program is fitted with a <u>rank</u> statement then 'non-terminative' correctness of the program (see 6.1) automatically implies its 'terminative' correctness. (Proof: it is sufficient to apply 4.2 and then to prove for each procedure in the program that the elaboration of the program cannot involve a sequence of embedded calls containing infinitely many copies of this procedure; the proof for a procedure whose body is contained in the body of another procedure uses the same fact for the embracing procedure, so the proof must start from the longest procedure.)

This technique is sufficient for recursions of types smaller than omega**omega. A stronger system can be obtained by allowing the rank to be an ordinal from some larger class rather than a natural number or, possibly, by changing the rules for 'seniority' of <u>rank</u> statements.

6. Correctness. The statement to be proved about the program is termed correctness. It is defined recursively with the use of binary relations; however it applies to the program itself rather than to the corresponding binary relation.

6.1. Some cases from the recursive definition of correctness are given below.

If A is a phrase and S a memory state then a state T is said to be an A-predecessor (A-successor) of S if the pair (T,S) (respectively, (S,T)) satisfies the binary relation corresponding to A.

A clause A;B is correct if both A and B are correct and for any memory state that has an A-predecessor one of the following holds, depending on the interpretation chosen:

a) for the terminative interpretation, S has a B-successor,

b) for the non-terminative interpretation, S has no B-successor with the wrong exit label on the top of the stack.

Correctness of conditional clauses is defined in a similar fashion.

A clause A with B is correct whenever A is correct. An altern clause is correct when all of its constituents are. No simult, except or reverse clause is correct.

6.2. Data for the program are treated as formal parameters. Thus a correctness statement applies to a procedure.

Example. The following procedure is correct.

```
     (ref real x) : (now x ge 0;
(x := sqrt(x)) with (x**2 becomes = x);
now x ge 0).
```

6.3. To describe properties of some routine one may use a correctness statement for some procedure involving calls of that routine. Thus, a correct operator is introduced, converting a routine denotation (possibly containing global identifiers) into a boolean clause.

Examples:

```
     a) correct ([1: , 1: ] real matrix) :
(now 1 upb matrix ne 2 upb matrix;
det(matrix); now false;
```

```
dimension error : skip);
```

b) (see 2.2.b)

```
map (pp) bool z =
(lambda pp q; correct (pp q1, int n) :
(now z(q1) and n ge 0;
q(q1, n) with (m becomes gt m))).
```

c) Given a set int n and a proc(proc(int)) p, the following boolean clause has the value true iff p enumerates n without repetitions (the interpretation is terminative):

```
begin ghost set int m; ghost bool repetition;
correct (proc(int) q) :
(now correct (int x) : (skip; q(x) with
if in(x, m) then repetition becomes = true
else m becomes = union(m, set(x)) fi);
m := empty set; repetition := false; p(q);
now not repetition and m = n) end.
```

Now let this condition be satisfied and let a map(set int)int sum satisfy the axioms:

```
    sum(empty set) = 0;
    (any set int m; any int x; in(x, m) or
sum(union(m, set(x))) = sum(m) + x);
```

Then in order to prove the correctness of

```
    begin int s := 0;
proc qq = (int x) : s plus x;
p(qq); now s = sum(n) end
```

one may write

```
    begin int s := 0; proc qq = (int x) : s plus x;
ghost set int m; ghost bool repetition;
proc q = (int x) : (qq(x);
if in(x, m) then repetition := true
else m := union(m, set(x)) fi);
now correct (int x) :
(perm repetition or s = sum(m); q(x) with
if in(x, m) then repetition becomes = true
else m becomes = union(m, set(x)) fi);
m := empty set; repetition := false;
```

perm repetition **or** s = sum(m);
p(q); **now** **not** repetition **and** m = n;
now s = sum(n) **end**.

6.4. For a given procedure the proof-checker must find a proof of its correctness. If it fails it identifies the syntactic step in the construction of the procedure where the proof is not found (either because of an error or for insufficient information).

7. Convertibility. Supposing the correctness of a `program` in this language has been already proved one has still to convert it into a conventional program.

A syntactic property of convertibility can be defined to characterize a class of `programs` that are converted into conventional computer programs simply by dropping all `uncommon` parts.

More generally, one can define the following relationship: a conventional program P incarnates a `generalized` program Q if any memory state S having a Q-successor is transformed by P into a memory state that is the same as some Q-successor of S except possibly for ghost names.

One may look for classes of programs that can be incarnated not by direct conversion but by some heuristic methods (e.g., some parts of a program might contain only logical conditions and no operations on memory); this is the problem of automatic program writing.

Lecture Notes in Economics and Mathematical Systems

Vol. 48: M. Constam, FORTRAN für Anfänger. VI, 148 Seiten. 1973. DM 16,–

Vol. 65: W. Everling, Exercises in Computer Systems Analysis. VIII, 184 pages. 1972. DM 18,–

Vol. 68: J. Loeckx, Computability and Decidability. An Introduction for Students of Computer Science. VI, 76 pages. 1972. DM 16,–

Vol. 75: GI-Gesellschaft für Informatik e. V. Bericht Nr. 3. 1. Fachtagung über Programmiersprachen. München, 9.–11. März 1971. Herausgegeben im Auftrag der Gesellschaft für Informatik von H. Langmaack und M. Paul. VII, 280 Seiten. 1972. DM 24,–

Vol. 78: GI-Gesellschaft für Informatik e. V. 2. Jahrestagung, Karlsruhe, 2.–4. Oktober 1972. Herausgegeben im Auftrag der Gesellschaft für Informatik von P. Deussen. XI, 576 Seiten. 1973. DM 36,–

Vol. 81: Advanced Course on Software Engineering. Edited by F. L. Bauer. XII, 545 pages. 1973. DM 32,–

Vol. 83: NTG/GI-Gesellschaft für Informatik, Nachrichtentechnische Gesellschaft. Fachtagung „Cognitive Verfahren und Systeme", Hamburg, 11.–13. April 1973. Herausgegeben im Auftrag der NTG/GI von Th. Einsele, W. Giloi und H.-H. Nagel. VIII, 373 Seiten. 1973. DM 28,–

This series aims to report new developments in computer science research and teaching – quickly, informally and at a high level. The type of material considered for publication includes:

1. Preliminary drafts of original papers and monographs
2. Lectures on a new field, or presenting a new angle on a classical field
3. Seminar work-outs
4. Reports of meetings, provided they are
   a) of exceptional interest and
   b) devoted to a single topic.

Texts which are out of print but still in demand may also be considered if they fall within these categories.

The timeliness of a manuscript is more important than its form, which may be unfinished or tentative. Thus, in some instances, proofs may be merely outlined and results presented which have been or will later be published elsewhere. If possible, a subject index should be included. Publication of Lecture Notes is intended as a service to the international computer science community, in that a commercial publisher, Springer-Verlag, can offer a wider distribution to documents which would otherwise have a restricted readership. Once published and copyrighted, they can be documented in the scientific literature.

Manuscripts

Manuscripts should comprise not less than 100 pages.
They are reproduced by a photographic process and therefore must be typed with extreme care. Symbols not on the typewriter should be inserted by hand in indelible black ink. Corrections to the typescript should be made by pasting the amended text over the old one, or by obliterating errors with white correcting fluid. Authors receive 75 free copies and are free to use the material in other publications. The typescript is reduced slightly in size during reproduction; best results will not be obtained unless the text on any one page is kept within the overall limit of 18 x 26.5 cm (7 x 10½ inches). The publishers will be pleased to supply on request special stationary with the typing area outlined.
Manuscripts in English, German or French should be sent to Prof. G. Goos, Institut für Informatik, Universität Karlsruhe, 75 Karlsruhe/Germany, Zirkel 2, Prof. J. Hartmanis, Cornell University, Dept. of Computer-Science, Ithaca, NY/USA 14850, or directly to Springer-Verlag Heidelberg.

Springer-Verlag, D-1000 Berlin 33, Heidelberger Platz 3
Springer-Verlag, D-6900 Heidelberg 1, Neuenheimer Landstraße 28–30
Springer-Verlag, 175 Fifth Avenue, New York, NY 10010/USA

ISBN 3-540-06720-5
ISBN 0-387-06720-5